Air War 'Varsity'

Martin W. Bowman

Pen & Sword
AVIATION

First Published in Great Britain in 2017 by
Pen & Sword Aviation
an imprint of
Pen & Sword Books Ltd
47 Church Street, Barnsley, South Yorkshire S70 2AS

A CIP catalogue record for this book is
available from the British Library.

Typeset in 10/12pt Palatino
by GMS Enterprises PE3 8QQ

Printed and bound in England by
TJ International Ltd, Padstow, Cornwall

Pen & Sword Books Ltd incorporates the Imprints of Pen & Sword
Aviation, Pen & Sword Family History, Pen & Sword Maritime, Pen & Sword
Military, Pen & Sword Discovery, Wharncliffe Local History, Wharncliffe
True Crime, Wharncliffe Transport, Pen & Sword Select, Pen & Sword
Military Classics, Leo Cooper, The Praetorian Press, Remember When,
Seaforth Publishing and Frontline Publishing.

For a complete list of Pen & Sword titles please contact
PEN & SWORD BOOKS LIMITED

47 Church Street, Barnsley, South Yorkshire, S70 2AS, England
E-mail: enquiries@pen-and-sword.co.uk
Website: www.pen-and-sword.co.uk

Contents

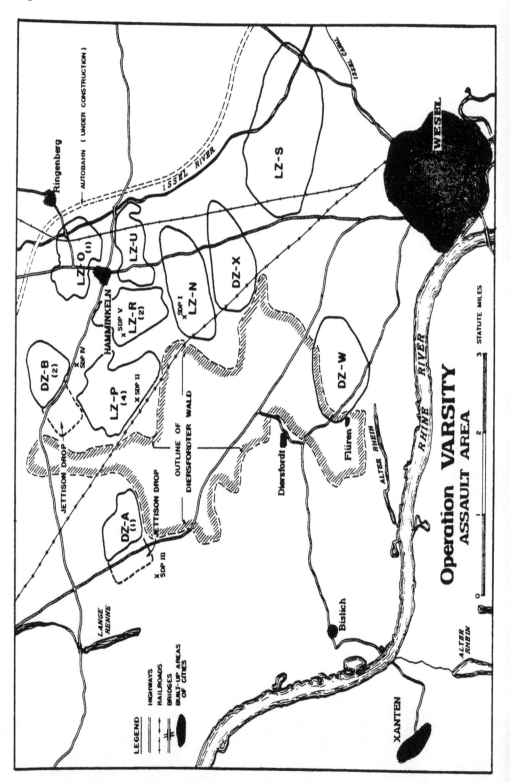

Operation VARSITY
ASSAULT AREA

LEGEND
HIGHWAYS
RAILROADS
BRIDGES
BUILT-UP AREAS OF CITIES

AUTOBAHN (UNDER CONSTRUCTION)

0   1   2   3   STATUTE MILES

Prologue

We were packed in the back of the Horsa like sardines in a tin and as usual the armchair experts who had told us it would be basically an unopposed landing couldn't have got it more wrong. Jerry may have been bombed, rocketed and shelled, but he was far from finished and he was throwing everything at us bar the kitchen sink. The glider was shaking as the flak exploded nearby and bits of shrapnel cut through the outer skin like a knife through butter. The moment we cast off, the pilot dropped the nose down so much I thought we were going to roll on to our back. And he held it there until the very last moment, when he applied the huge wing flaps, lifted the nose and we hit the ground with an almighty bang and skidded along, bouncing and spinning out of control. Except for the flaps, once you're on the ground where you go is pure luck. We hit something big and spun around and there was a great tearing sound as part of the port wing got ripped off. I thought this is it, we're done for, when suddenly we came to an instant jarring halt and the whole fuselage lifted up to a forty-five-degree angle before smashing down onto the ground. Bodies went everywhere and there was pandemonium as the lads picked each other up, swore and cursed the pilot and pulled mates from under the scattered debris. The platoon commander took charge and we all scrambled around for our weapons and kit, slashed open the sides of the Horsa and jumped out.

Miraculously, there were no serious injuries, just shock, cuts, severe bruising and a couple of the lads with broken arms. Everyone thought the crew must have been killed, but they too walked away with only minor cuts and bruising. A miracle had happened right there in the middle of a battlefield. We were lucky as the Jerries weren't bothered with us as they had enough targets to keep them happy already. As we got ready to move off, the senior pilot, a RAF flying officer with the typical handlebar moustache, shouted out in plum-like tones, I say chaps that that was jolly good fun, wasn't it. Anyone want to try it again when all this vulgar violence business is over with?

The Flying Brick by Billy Griffin Quoted in *Paras: Voices of the British Airborne Forces in the Second World War* by Roger Payne OAM (Amberley 2014 and 2016).

Preface

Before embarking on Operation 'Varsity' it is well to consider for a moment, the implications resulting from previous full-scale airborne operations, notably 'D-Day', 6 June 1944 and in particular, Operation 'Market-Garden' in September that same year, both of which greatly influenced the decisions taken during planning for 'Varsity-Plunder'.

The interval of three months between Operations 'Neptune/Overlord'- the successful invasion of Normandy on 6 June 1944 and 'Market-Garden', the next airborne operation in the European Theatre, in mid-September that same year, was marked by important organizational changes and by unprecedented fluctuations in the extent and character of troop carrier utilization. The principal change was the creation of First Allied Airborne Army. Even before 'Neptune' was launched the British, who had set up a command known as Headquarters Airborne Troops for their own airborne in 1943, had recommended the establishment of a headquarters to command all Allied airborne units in the Theatre. This was not necessary in Normandy because British and American airborne operations there were separate. However, future operations involving several airborne divisions of different nationalities might need central control. The British intimated that their existing airborne headquarters might well provide a commander and cadre for the one proposed.

On 20 June 1944 General Dwight D. Eisenhower who had commanded the Allied forces in the Mediterranean theatre ever since their first landings in North Africa and on 5 December 1943 was chosen as the Supreme Commander of the Allied Expeditionary Force (SCAEF)[1], approved the idea of a unified command for the airborne troops, but coupled with his approval a more sweeping proposal for a command which would control troop carriers as well. The British felt strongly that their airborne commander, General Frederick Arthur Montague 'Boy' Browning, should be chosen to head the new command. The Americans thought it proper to name an American, since they were contributing most of the troop carrier forces and a majority of the airborne. On 16 July Eisenhower's final choice fell on 53-year old Major General Lewis Hyde Brereton. American tactical air units in England had been organized into the Ninth Air Force under his command on 16 October 1943. Born in Pittsburgh in 1890 Brereton was a 1911 graduate of the Naval Academy and began his military career as an Army officer in the Coast Artillery Corps prior to World War I and then spent the remainder of his service as a career airman, overcoming a disastrous beginning, restoring his reputation and commanding air forces in a wide variety of combat activities in four theatres of operations. Although junior to Browning by a few months (he was made lieutenant general in April 1944; Browning had held the rank since December 1943), he had a length and variety of service unsurpassed in the AAF, had commanded air forces in the Far East, North Africa and England and as commander of the Ninth Air Force had acquired a working knowledge of IX Troop Carrier Command. On 4 August 1944 he accepted Lieutenant General Browning as his deputy commander.

Airborne Army exercised command of the British airborne troops through Headquarters, Airborne Troops (subsequently re-designated 1st Airborne Corps) under Browning and command of the American airborne through XVIII Airborne Corps, a new headquarters under the command of 50-year old Major General Matthew Bunker Ridgway. Born 3 March 1895 at Fort Monroe, Virginia, he had graduated in 1912 from English High School in Boston and applied to West Point because he thought that would please his father (who was a West Point graduate). Ridgway helped plan the airborne element of the invasion of Sicily in July 1943 and led the 82nd Airborne Division into battle. This was the first major airborne operation in US history, and his men took heavy losses.

As General Patton's men crossed the Seine on 19 August 1944 it was evident that the German armies in France were shattered and could make no effective stand short of the Siegfried Line in the east and the Rhine in the north. General Bradley recommended a drive eastward through the Siegfried Line. General Bernard L. Montgomery, commander of 21st Army Group, favoured a thrust through the Low Countries and across the Rhine onto the plains of northern Germany. This would breach the last possible barrier between the Allies and Berlin and would also help solve the supply problem through capture of the Channel ports and Antwerp. The transportation shortage made it impossible to deliver a major effort in both directions at once. On the evening of 3 September Montgomery asked Airborne Army for an operation by the British 1st Airborne Division and the Polish Parachute Brigade to secure a crossing of the Rhine in the stretch between Arnhem and the thirteenth-century Hanseatic city of Wesel. On the 8th Montgomery's staff selected Arnhem as the crossing point, largely because the flak around Wesel was considered prohibitively thick. On the morning of 10 September General Eisenhower flew to Brussels to confer with Montgomery on the strategy they would use in the coming weeks. In a stormy session aboard Eisenhower's aircraft Montgomery won his superior's approval for Operation 'Market-Garden'. 'Monty' then set 17 September as 'D-Day'. It would involve an airborne 'carpet' comprising not only the First Airborne Division and the Polish airborne but also the American 82nd and 101st Divisions along the road to Arnhem; 'Garden' being the ground component.

Brereton ruled that 'Market' would be flown in daylight. This decision was not unprecedented. During the invasion of southern France, General Williams had sent in paratroop missions at dawn and gliders by daylight with negligible losses. A noteworthy innovation was the massing of serials in three parallel lanes 1½ miles apart. 1,055 planeloads of paratroops and 478 gliders were to be delivered in the initial lift within 65 minutes, the same time it took to bring in 369 sticks of paratroops for the 82nd Division in 'Neptune'. To take and hold one or more of the crossings in Arnhem was the task of the British First Airborne Division using three zones made up of fields, pasture and heath bordered by pine woods; good enough in themselves but they were all over five miles away from the single-span steel road bridge which crossed the Lower Rhine into the city of Arnhem which was the chief objective of the troops. Precious time would be consumed merely in marching to the bridge. The risk of delay by roadblocks was great. In addition, part of the force would have to be left behind to hold zones for use by other missions on 'D+1'. The British airborne staff officers were not unaware of these handicaps but Major General Robert E. Urquhart, Commander of First Airborne Division, preferred good zones at a distance to bad zones near his objectives. Another consideration was fear of anti-aircraft guns, great numbers of which were said to be massed near the bridge. Consequently no 'D-Day' drops or landings or coup-de-main operations were to be made near Arnhem.

Almost without exception the troop carrier units in 'Market' had flown missions before. The Ninth Troop Carrier Command had the same three wings, fourteen groups and pathfinder unit that it had had in 'Neptune' and all wings and all groups but the 315th and 434th had participated in at least one other airborne operation, either in 1943 or during the invasion of southern France. The RAF had in 38 Group the same ten squadrons which they had used in June but had increased 46 Group from five to six squadrons. In most cases the troop carriers were located at good bases, at which they were well established and were teamed with troops which were stationed nearby and had flown with them before from those bases. The IX TCC went into 'Market' with much the same resources it had had for 'Neptune'. Losses of aircraft and crews had been replaced and on 16 September the command had 1,274 operational aircraft and 1,284 assigned and available crews. The British had 321 converted bombers in 38 Group and 164 Dakotas (C-47s) in 46 Group.

The supply of gliders had increased despite the loss of almost all of those used in Normandy. By the end of August IX TCC had 1,629 operational Wacos and by 16 September it had 2,160 of them. Plans called for the employment of about 90 percent of these gliders in 'Market'. The British had 812 Horsas, the Americans only 104 of them. However, the latter had an acquired distaste for the Horsa and did not intend to use it. In addition to its Horsas 38 Group possessed 64 of the huge Hamilcar gliders, which were capable of carrying tanks. About 1,900 American glider pilots were on hand at the end of August, but the arrival of 200 more by air a few days later gave IX TCC a total of 2,060 on the eve of 'Market'. Since General Paul Williams and General Louis Brereton had decided not to use co-pilots on American gliders, they had enough glider pilots for the proposed missions, but they would have virtually no reserves.

As in June, the aircraft of IX TCC were without armour or self-sealing fuel tanks. The long struggle for safer fuel tanks had appeared to be won when, while in England on a tour of inspection in the latter part of June,

Robert A. Lovett, Assistant Secretary of War for Air, promised that IX TCC would get at least enough for its pathfinders. However, the tanks were then very scarce; AAF Headquarters was unwilling to reallocate them; and the troop carriers got none. Some were shipped in September but did not arrive in time for 'Market'.

Only about 400 of the Wacos had nose reinforcements of either the Corey or the Griswold type and only about 900 had parachute arrestors. Large orders for arrestors and protective noses had been sent to the United States long before 'Market', but delivery had been slow. One cause of delay had been disagreement and vacillation in the United States as to which type of nose should be produced.

'Market' is unique as the only large American airborne operation during World War II for which there was no training programme, no rehearsal, almost no exercises and a generally low level of tactical training activity. From 12 August to 17 September there were only five days on which FAAA (First Allied Airborne Army) did not believe that an airborne operation was just around the corner. This belief made training plans seem superfluous and realistic exercises a rash commitment.

On 14 September the troop carrier units were alerted and restricted and American airborne troops began moving into bivouac at the bases. Early in the evening on the 15th wing commanders and key members of their staffs were fully briefed at Eastcote. On their return that night they briefed the wing staffs and the group commanders. About the same time field orders for the operation arrived at the wings from troop carrier headquarters. Early next morning rigid restrictions and security measures were imposed at all bases. During the day group staffs were briefed and wing and group field orders were issued. In the afternoon and evening of 16 September, 'D-1', the groups briefed their combat crews. The briefings were generally regarded as well organized and comprehensive. However, detailed maps were in such short supply that there were hardly enough for the group staffs and as usual there was an acute lack of low-level photographs of the zones and run-in areas. The final briefings, held on the morning of the 17th just before the crews went to their aircraft, were short and were concerned mainly with weather conditions. 'Market' needed three days in a row of good flying weather to give it a reasonable chance of success. Finally, at 1630 on 16 September ('D-1') the experts delivered a favourable report on the coming four-day period. Brereton gave orders at 1900 hours that the airborne carpet would be laid along the road to Arnhem.

Before the carpet could be laid, the ground had to be cleared. This work was begun on the night of 'D-1' when 200 Lancasters and 23 Mosquitoes of 1 and 8 Groups bombed airfields at Leeuwarden, Steenwijk-Havelte, Hopsten and Rheine within fighter range of 'Market' objectives and 54 Lancasters and five Mosquitoes of 3 and 8 Groups attacked formidable flak installations around a bridge at Moerdijk which menaced aircraft flying the northern route. Two Lancasters were lost from the Moerdijk raid. About 1,180 tons of bombs were dropped during the operation and the runways of all airfields were well cratered but there were only near misses at the flak position, although its approach road was cut.

On the morning of 17 September Eighth Air Force dispatched 872 B-17s to attack 117 installations, mostly anti-aircraft batteries, along the troop carrier routes before the troop carriers appeared. All told, the Fortresses dropped 2,888 tons of fragmentation bombs and 29 tons of high explosive. Another operation that morning was an attack by 85 Lancasters and fifteen Mosquitoes of the RAF, escorted by 53 Spitfires of ADGB, against coastal defences on Walcheren Island. It was presumably intended to mislead the Germans into thinking that Walcheren, which lay between the two troop carrier routes, was the objective of the initial troop carrier missions. The last preliminary operation on the morning of the 17th was the dispatch of fifty Mosquitoes, 48 Mitchells and 24 Bostons of 2nd Tactical Air Force against German barracks at Nijmegen, at Arnhem and at Ede ten miles northwest of Arnhem. Six Mosquitoes made low-level attacks on the barracks at Nijmegen with four tons of high explosive. Thirty-four Mosquitoes dropped 27 tons of bombs on Arnhem at a price of three aircraft lost to flak. At Ede thirty Mitchells and thirteen Bostons bombed from medium altitude with 63 tons of high explosive. Because of cloud conditions and other difficulties 23 or more pilots returned without bombing and the remainder hit targets of opportunity. In retrospect it appears that these attacks on barracks did not have much effect on the enemy's power to resist.

An appraisal of 'Market-Garden' may well start with the question of why it did not succeed. First and foremost comes the extraordinary revival of German fighting capacity brought about by General Model. Intelligence reports of over-all enemy strength were quite accurate, but as late as 14 September a Second Army estimate described the enemy as weak, demoralized and likely to collapse entirely if confronted with a large airborne attack. Had that been so, 'Market' would have been a sure thing. No amount of bad luck could have done more than delay its success. Another factor, which enabled the Germans to bring their strength to bear, was in locating General Urquhart's zones between five and eight miles from the objective. This was contrary to all airborne doctrine and he later admitted that it had been an unnecessary and fatal error. It cost the division the advantage of surprise and compelled it to divide its forces in the face of the enemy in order to keep possession of the landing zones for later missions.

Next in order and first in General Montgomery's estimation was the effect of bad weather in delaying the arrival of the Poles from 'D+2' to 'D+4' and that of the 325th Glider Regiment from 'D+2' to 'D+6'. He believed that if the two units had arrived on schedule the Poles could have broken through to the Arnhem Bridge and the 325th might have provided the extra infantry needed to win the Nijmegen Bridge and fight through to Arnhem, presumably before nightfall on the 20th. Such an achievement by those two units could perhaps have made the difference between defeat and victory.

Bomber pilot, Kenneth Frere, who in August 1944 joined 296 Squadron in 38 Group, which was equipped with the unloved Armstrong Whitworth Albemarle at Brize Norton wrote: 'The four Albemarle squadrons played an important role in Operation 'Overlord'. As more 'redundant' Short Stirlings and Handley Page Halifaxes were released by Bomber Command, two of these squadrons converted to Stirlings. Soon after 'D-Day' only 296 and 297 Squadrons still had their Albemarles. I spent August practicing mass glider tows, parachute dropping and navigational exercises with gliders. 38 Group squadrons were based in the southern counties of England where they were well placed for operations into France, including the support for the SAS and for the French Resistance which was another part of 38 Group's tasks. However, when the front line moved into Belgium and beyond it was out of range for Albemarles towing loaded gliders. During October 1944 the two remaining Albemarle squadrons moved to Earls Colne in Essex and conversion to Halifaxes began. Early in November we started flying our Albemarles to Peplow, in Cheshire, that undiscovered country from whose bourn no Albemarle returns (as Hamlet nearly put it). It was the end of the line for an interesting, but essentially unsatisfactory aircraft. It was no good as a bomber, never used as a dive bomber, underpowered as a tug aircraft, awkward for parachute dropping, hopeless as a load carrier and hard work on long flights because 'George' (the automatic pilot) refused to fly it straight and narrow. But it was fun to fly, it looked good and I am sorry that not a single example remains with us today.'

After the successful invasion of Europe the 38 Group Halifaxes were employed on a variety of SOE operations as well as others of a similar clandestine nature involving the SAS and occasionally towing gliders. Both squadrons were also involved in the ill-fated landings during Operation 'Market Garden'.

'From 2 September onwards we spent our time moving Horsa gliders over to Manston, as near to Holland as it was possible to get. On 15 September the Albemarle squadrons were all relocated at Manston in readiness for Operation 'Market'. There were not enough aircraft to fly the entire 'Garden' force into Arnhem on one day. At 1025 on 17 September Stirlings in 38 Group took off to drop pathfinder parachutists to mark the dropping zones and landings zones. The slower glider combinations had begun taking off at 0940, towing 304 Horsas, thirteen Hamilcars and four Hadrians. Albemarles from Manston towed 56 of the Horsas. The weather was unkind and of the 321 gliders which were towed off 26 parted company with their tugs either over England, over the sea or over Holland. The second lift on 18 September was held up for nearly five hours because of fog in England. Albemarles which took off from Manston that day towed 42 of the 275 Horsas: of these 257 reached the landing zones. From the astrodome my navigator could see only a part of the glider train which stretched out behind us and ahead of us. Other 38 Group squadrons towed fifteen Hamilcars, fourteen of which made it to Arnhem in spite of much more flak and small arms fire from the German forces along the route. There was a third lift on 19 September made up of 36 Horsas, plus seven

Horsas and a Hamilcar whose flights had been aborted during the two previous days. Flak was even heavier and two Horsas were shot down, eleven had broken towropes and two returned to base because of engine failures in the tug aircraft. There were no Albemarles in the third lift and, because of the aircraft's poor freight capability, 296 and 297 squadrons played no part in the heroic resupply operations during the rest of the Arnhem battle. Twenty-five members of 38 Group lost their lives during the glider operations and a further 77 during the next four days of the resupply flights.'

The American troop carriers could not have speeded up the operation by using more or larger transport aircraft, since they had put into 'Market' almost every aircraft and crew they had. The C-46 was not yet available to IX TCC and the C-47 units of the 302nd Transport Wing were neither trained nor available for airborne missions. One remedy for this limited capacity would have been to fly two sets of missions in one day as had been done in southern France over a course comparable to that flown in 'Market' but the September days were too short for adequate rest and servicing between the missions. The American glider missions could have been completed on 'D+1' by using Horsa gliders or by flying Wacos in double-tow, but the Americans had acquired an aversion to the Horsa and double-tow, though used later in 'Varsity'. Double-tow from England would also have involved a fuel problem, but this could have been met by the use of extra tanks or by allowing the units involved to land at bases in Belgium. Although it can be argued that some troop carrier and airborne units should have been already deployed in northern France, the logistical situation there would probably have made such a move an excessive strain on available resources. Under the circumstances, the decision to fly all missions from England must be regarded as logical.

Weaknesses in communications, air support, resupply and the combat qualifications of American glider pilots contributed to the failure of 'Market'. Air support for the airborne troops after they landed was the responsibility of the Second Tactical Air Force. 2nd TAF was gravely handicapped by orders not to send support missions over the 'Market' area when airborne missions were in progress. This restriction, intended to reduce congestion and prevent possible clashes between friendly forces was transformed by weather conditions, repeated short postponements of airborne missions and 2nd TAF's remoteness from Brereton's headquarters into something like a prohibition. Over and over again support units would be grounded in the early morning by bad weather and after that by the prospect of an airborne mission, which they would belatedly learn had been postponed a few hours. By the time the actual mission had come and gone the evening mists would be gathering or the clouds rolling in. Had support missions been flown like those of the troop carriers over a specified corridor and had they been under effective ground-air control at destination, the restriction might have been dispensed with, making it possible to send aircraft to the aid of the airborne whenever weather permitted. Instead direct air support during the nine decisive days of

'Market' was decidedly inadequate except in a handful of cases. All in all, it must be said that ground support in 'Market' was a difficult task badly handled and that the support provided was too little and too late.

The British glider pilots, who were organized as ground troops in a special glider pilot regiment, made a much better combat showing in 'Market' than the American glider pilots, who were simply an element within the troop carrier squadrons. Lieutenant General Matthew B. Ridgway, who commanded the airborne, observed that since the primary duty of glider pilots was to fly gliders, they belonged with the troop carriers. On 25 September, as British troops were beginning their withdrawal, Major General James M. Gavin, commanding the 82nd Airborne Division wrote to the commander of 9th Troop Carrier Command saying: 'In looking back... one thing in most urgent need of correction [is] the method of handling our glider pilots. Despite their individual willingness to help, I feel they were definitely a liability to me... They frequently became involved in small unit actions... or simply left to visit nearby towns. Glider pilots without unit assignment... improperly trained, aimlessly wandering about cause confusion and generally get in the way. I believe now that they should be assigned to airborne units, take training with the units and have a certain number of hours allocated periodically for flight training.'[2]

In spite of its failure and in spite of some mistakes 'Market' was from the troop carrier point of view a brilliant success. Cautious critics noted that crushing air superiority had been needed in 'Market' to protect airborne missions in daylight from enemy aircraft and flak. Some 5,200 sorties had been flown to protect the troop carriers from the remnants of the Luftwaffe and to neutralize anti-aircraft batteries.[3] Flak suppression had proven both difficult and dangerous against well-camouflaged opponents who knew when to hold their fire. Nevertheless, the guns had been silenced. As for the Luftwaffe, it was never able to break through the cordon of Allied fighters. Its only successful attacks against the troop carriers were made on one occasion when arrangements for escort and cover had broken down.

'Market Garden' has been described in an official report as 'by far the biggest and most ambitious airborne operation ever carried out by any nation or nations.' Of over 10,200 British airborne troops landed in the Arnhem area, 1,440 were killed or died of their wounds. 3,000 were wounded and taken prisoner and 400 medical personnel and chaplains remained behind with the wounded and about 2,500 uninjured troops also became PoWs. There were also 225 prisoners from the 4th Battalion, the Dorsetshire Regiment. About 450 Dutch civilians were killed. The operation also cost 160 RAF and Dominions aircrew, 27 USAAF aircrew and 79 Royal Army Service Corps despatchers killed and 127 taken prisoner. A total of 55 Albemarle, Stirling, Halifax and Dakota aircraft from Nos. 38 and 46 Groups failed to return and a further 320 damaged by flak and seven by fighters while 105 Allied fighter aircraft were lost.

When all is said it is not the monumental size nor the operational intricacies of 'Market' which linger longest in the memory. It is the heroism of the men who flew burning, disintegrating aircraft over their zones as coolly as if on review and gave their lives to get the last trooper out, the last bundle dropped. It is the stubborn courage of the airborne troops who would not surrender though an army came against them. Troop carrier crews and airborne troops did all that men could do. 'There was', as Gavin said, 'no failure in 'Market''.

Kenneth Frere on 296 Squadron wrote: 'After Arnhem the 38 Group squadrons went back on to individual supply-dropping flights into Northern Europe. At the end of September we began moving gliders into Essex. This took the glider force nearer to Germany as a preparation for what became Operation 'Varsity-Plunder''.

Endnotes Chapter 1

1   Eisenhower's headquarters was commonly known as SHAEF; an abbreviation of its full title. Supreme Headquarters Allied Expeditionary Force.
2   *Silent Wings* by Gerald Devlin (St. Martin's Press 1985).
3   The Eighth and Ninth Air Forces devoted 836 out of 3.352 sorties to flak neutralization.

Chapter 1
'Varsity'

We know you're coming tomorrow and we know where you're coming - at Wesel.
So don't worry about your landing; flak will be so thick you can walk down from
the sky.
Radio Berlin broadcast on Saturday 23 March by 'Axis Sally'; a generic name
for Mildred Gillars, a German-American who broadcast for Germany.

Fifty miles upstream from Arnhem, the Rhine curves south past Wesel, 1,500 feet wide at this point; swift-flowing, with many tricky currents. Fed by the heavy rains of January and February 1945 the river pressed against the two systems of dykes that protected the town from its ravages, flooding the area between them. The last natural obstacle in the crumbling Reich, it was originally supposed that this vital and navigable waterway carrying trade and goods deep inland might be crossed before the end of November and then, after the German Ardennes offensive faltered and a full-scale counteroffensive got under way, thoughts returned to an advance on a broad front to the Rhine, assaults across it north of the Ruhr between Emmerich and Wesel and south of the Ruhr between Mainz and Karlsruhe, culminating in a dual trust into the heart of Germany resulting in decisive and final victory. In early February Montgomery believed that the Rhine crossing might be made by 15 March, but stubborn German resistance caused the target date to be set back to the 25th and then to 31 March. In Britain in March the public read in their newspapers the name and date of an impending massive Allied air and ground operation against Germans defending the Rhine. Even in the backwaters of Essex the operation was one of the worst kept secrets of the war. Mr. E. V. Foreman recalled that even though Rivenhall airfield near his home at Buckhurst Hill 'was sealed off and barbed wire was everywhere' this was the eve of 'Varsity-Plunder', 'which was certainly common knowledge in our local hostelry, 'The White Hart' in Kelvedon.'[1] Mr. Foreman worked on the airfield when it was under construction as an American fighter base, changing these for B-26 Marauder bombers after a few weeks and finally becoming the home for RAF secret operations squadrons. Now, Rivenhall was needed for the Rhine crossing operation which the defenders, anticipating an airborne assault in the Wesel-Emmerich sector, had prepared for it. They appeared to have at least 10,000 men in carefully organized defensive positions in the Diersfordt area.

Finally, on 2 March the US Ninth Army broke through to the Rhine at Neuss. Lieutenant General William Hood Simpson, born on 18 May 1888, at Weatherford, Texas and a 1909 graduate of West Point, New York, seeing little opposition ahead of his forces, proposed to make a surprise crossing at Uerdingen, a weakly-defended town, but Montgomery, who had temporary command of the Ninth Army, turned 'Big Simp' down. On 7 March a spearhead unit of General Courtney Hicks Hodges' First (US) Army reached the west bank of the Rhine in the central sector. A notable 'mustang' officer, rising from private to general, while serving as a lieutenant colonel in the 6th Infantry Regiment, 5th Division in the closing days of World War One, Hodges earned the DSC for heroism while leading an attack across the Marne River. Now, to everyone's astonishment, the Germans still had not blown the Ludendorff Bridge at Remagen just south of Bonn. Furthermore, it appeared poorly guarded. To their still greater amazement, a patrol sent dashing across that bridge reached the other side before the Germans set off the explosives planted there. The exultant American generals near the Rhine rushed reinforcements and tanks across the bridge on their own authority.

Montgomery decided to advance the target date for Varsity', part of Operation 'Plunder', the British amphibious operations by the British Second Army, under Lieutenant General Sir Miles C. Dempsey and the US Ninth Army to 24 March. 'Monty' was, as always, inclined to prefer a 'set piece' to impromptu action and since it was clear that a crossing in the Wesel area would meet substantial opposition, he stuck to his plans for an overwhelming blow requiring a fortnight for deployment, a tactic that found favour with the Supreme Commander, General Eisenhower and the Combined Chiefs of Staff. Troops of General George S. Patton's Third Army managed to force another breakthrough on the evening of 22 March after the construction of a pontoon bridge and he sent his 5th Division over the east bank of the Rhine between Nierstein and Oppenheim. 'Old Blood and Guts' later boasted that he had urinated into the river as he crossed. His superior, General Bradley, released news of this crossing to the press at a *time calculated to take some of the lustre from the news of Montgomery's crossing.* Bradley later remembered that Patton had strongly urged the announcement saying *I want the world to know that Third Army made it before Monty starts across.*

Some German generals considered a parachute drop over the Rhine inevitable and efforts were made to determine the most probable spot, an Allied report had been captured analysing the parachute drop at Arnhem in September 1944 and from this document the Germans learned that Allied views were now against a paratroop landing too far away from the grounds troops destined to contact it. By plotting the areas that were topographically suitable for a parachute drop and not too far from the Rhine, the most likely area seemed to be just east of Wesel. It was therefore expected that the crossing would be made in this neighbourhood. But German Army Group H experts preferred the neighbourhood further north at Emmerich as the British target to capture the line of the River Issel.

The most important lesson taught by 'Market' and airborne operations in 'Neptune' was that airborne assaults on a corps scale could be successfully executed; something which had been seriously doubted after the painful experiences in Sicily. While in Normandy and Holland the lift had to be spread over several days, that for the Rhine crossing would be concentrated into a four-hour period; thirteen hours after the initial crossing by surface forces and after bridgeheads had been firmly established. This would greatly increase the impact of the assault and reduce escort requirements and the risk that bad weather would ground important elements of the force. It also freed the airborne troops from the need to keep a large part of their men guarding drop and landing zones for subsequent missions. So essential did Montgomery consider his airborne cohorts that on 19 February his chief of staff had told Brereton that if the troop carriers were grounded by bad weather 'Plunder' would be postponed until they could go. Airborne Army required visibility of at least three miles, a ceiling above 1,500 feet and winds less than 20 mph and at least two days of good weather immediately before 'D-Day' for preliminary air operations. Later Montgomery agreed that a postponement of up to five days would be acceptable. He seems to have seriously considered launching 'Varsity-Plunder' on short notice in the event of a breakthrough near Wesel but the German forces facing the British Second Army continued to fight with desperate fanaticism and held the west bank of the Rhine. But the morale of the defenders was very low because of Hitler's insistence on a policy of 'no retreat.' Field Marshal Gerd von Rundstedt, commander of the armies on the Western Front was ignominiously dismissed by a desperate Führer, who badly needed a scapegoat for the defeats after Holland.[2]

Field Marshal Albert von Kesselring had been hastily brought from Italy to assume command. He 'inherited' in the words of a British Intelligence report, 'a bankrupt state'. Kesselring had assigned the defence of the Wesel sector to fifty-year old General der Fallschirmtruppe Wilhelm Schlemm who had been given command of the tough professional 1st Parachute Army reinforced with two infantry divisions. Woefully undermanned and short of artillery and other essential materiel, this force was hurriedly moved into the area at the beginning of March to prepare for the Allied attack. At Schlemm's insistence, the XLVII Panzer Corps was also assigned to the defence, being put in reserve about fifty miles north of Wesel. The mood of the German troops, according to Schlemm, ranged 'from suspicion to callous resignation' and even the officers 'lacked confidence and wondered just what were the demands of duty.'[2]

Schlemm was ordered to send a large part of his artillery to the German 25th Army who would be faced with this new offensive. He disposed his limited forces carefully. General Erich Straube's 86th Corps defended Wesel. On Straube's right was the 2nd Parachute Corps consisting of the 6th, 7th and 8th Parachute Divisions - 10,000 to 12,000 fighting men - who prided themselves on the elitism of being paratroopers even if none were jump trained. The area south of Wesel was guarded by Schlemm's weakest corps, the 63rd, under General Erich Abraham. Schlemm's reserve was the 47th Panzer Corps, under General Leutnant Freiherr Heinrich von

Leuttwitz with the 116th Panzer Division and 15th Panzergrenadier Division in reserve. The two divisions had outstanding records but only 35 tanks between them. Behind that, Schlemm had two more reserve formations. One was Volkssturm ('people's storm') a German national militia established in the last months of World War II on the orders of Adolf Hitler, made up of men over the age of sixty and boys under the age of sixteen. Trained hurriedly on Panzerfaust anti-tank weapons, Schlemm had 3,500 of these questionable troops at hand. To defend against the Allied threats, Schlemm strengthened his anti-aircraft defences near Wesel, with 814 heavy and light guns and mobile anti-airborne forces covering all the likely drop zones. Gunners had to sleep fully clothed at their posts. The Canadian First Army and the 120,000 men of 'Big Simp's US Ninth Army, compressed Schlemm's forces into a small bridgehead on the west bank of the Rhine opposite Wesel. On 10 March the rearguard of the 1st Parachute Army evacuated their bridgehead, destroying the bridge behind them. Schlemm was wounded in an air attack on his command post at Haltern eleven days later and command of his forces passed to General Günther Blumentritt.

According to the initial plans the Allied airborne and amphibious assaults were to be launched simultaneously and at night on prepared positions in the depths of the Durch den Diersfordter Wald. Pivotal to the whole enterprise, it lay between three and five miles east of the Rhine on the crest of a gentle rise on the otherwise flat Westphalian plain, consisting of glacial sand dunes, small bogs and heaths, which are largely covered with old, knotty oaks, red beeches and forest pines. Though scarcely one hundred feet above the river, the high ground provided the only good natural observation points in that area that would help the German artillery cover the river from Rees to the north to below Wesel, disrupting Second Army's bridging operations and making any crossing of the river a very costly - if not an impossible - undertaking. But it would be tempting fate to make a night attack on the forest. Also, whereas the river bank would have had to be taken early to aid the surface assault, there was no necessity to take the Diersfordter Wald until bridging operations began. General Dempsey therefore recommended that the airborne attack go by daylight after 'Plunder' had begun. Brereton agreed. Besides a conviction that troop carrier operations would be much more accurate by day, he had a strong expectation that they would be safer. In any event the bad condition and short runways of some troop carrier fields in France made them unsuitable for glider operations at night. By day the Allies ruled the skies challenged only by a handful of jet fighters. After dark the German night-fighter force, conserved for the defence of the Reich, was still a serious threat. Accordingly the plans were drawn for an amphibious assault an hour or two before dawn, followed at 1000 hours by the airborne attack. Since hitherto the airborne phase had ordinarily begun first, this timing offered a fair prospect of catching the Germans in the Diersfordter Wald by surprise. Brereton, Dempsey and General Ridgway decided to drop and land the troops close to the Diersfordter Wald and out of the field of fire of artillery supporting the amphibious assault, thereby eliminating long marches such as had cost the British so dearly in 'Market'.

Aside from the Diersfordter Wald itself, there were five notable features. A double-tracked railway to Wesel cut diagonally across the area from northwest to southeast. A few hundred yards to the east of the railway was a high-tension power line on one hundred-foot pylons, a major hazard to gliders and paratroops. Bordering the eastern edge of the area and running south-southeast was the Issel River, a water barrier sixty feet wide. Just east of the river lay a half-completed autobahn 150 feet wide, heavily embanked at some points and lined with construction equipment, running north from the Wesel to Emmerich and to a number of houses. About a mile inside the northeast corner of the area was the little town of Hamminkeln. There were many minor hazards, tree-bordered roads, local power-lines, windmills and the like, but it was most important to avoid depositing the airborne in the woods, in or beyond the Issel, or against the high-tension line.

The object of 'Varsity' was to land the British 6th Airborne Division and the US 17th Airborne Division on five drop zones and five landing zones on the eastern bank of the Rhine near Wesel. Eight were on or near the east side of the Diersfordter Wald and two, both for paratroops, were set into indentations on the west side of the forest at its northern and southern tips where it was relatively narrow. None of the eastern zones was more than 200 yards from a neighbour and even those on the west side were within a mile of other zones. All ten were packed into an area less than six miles long and five miles wide, an unprecedented degree of concentration. The chance that any airborne unit would be isolated was remote, but the risk of overlapping and confusion was considerable. Almost all of the drop and landing area was firm, level ground and the zones consisted of fields and meadows averaging 200 to 300 yards in length. Hedges were small and fences light, about half of the latter being made of wire. Ditches were few and small. There was no sign that the enemy was preparing landing obstacles. After occupying the Diersfordter Wald XVIII Corps was to push west to make contact with Second Army and then south to the Lippe to seal off Wesel and make contact with the Ninth Army. After that it would prepare to advance eastward as part of Dempsey's forces. The two airborne divisions would hold the territory they had captured until relieved by advancing units of 21st Army Group and join in the general advance into northern Germany. The 6th Airborne Division was ordered to capture Schneppenberg and Hamminkeln, seize the Diersfordter Wald and secure three bridges over the River Issel. The US 17th Airborne Division was to capture the village of Diersfordt and clear the rest of the Diersfordter Wald of any remaining German forces.

The 17th Airborne Division had arrived in Britain in August 1944, too late to participate in 'Overlord'. It had also been absent from 'Market Garden' and the only action it had seen was during the Ardennes campaign. However, no other American airborne divisions were available. The 82nd and 101st, having been held in the line almost continuously since September on what Major General Lewis H. Brereton (who commanded all

Allied airborne forces, including XVIII Airborne Corps with Major General Paul L. Williams, heading its troop carrier component) considered very dubious grounds, had needed several months to retrain and refit for airborne missions. And the 13th Airborne, which was originally selected for 'Varsity' had just arrived in France and had never seen action, although one of its regiments, the 517th Parachute Infantry Regiment, had fought in Italy, Southern France and the Ardennes; besides which, during the earliest planning stages, it became apparent that the 13th Airborne Division would be unable to participate in 'Varsity', as there were only enough combat transport aircraft in the area to transport two divisions effectively. The plan for the operation was therefore altered to accommodate the two remaining airborne divisions, the British 1st Airborne having been shattered at Arnhem the previous September and not considered for 'Varsity' either. Several operations involving the 13th Airborne were planned later, but all were cancelled for one reason or another, leaving it the only American division in the ETO which did not see action in World War II.

As far as the troop carriers and the airborne were concerned the principal participants were IX TCC, 38 Group and XVIII Corps, assisted by representatives of 46 Group, the troop carrier wings and the airborne divisions. On 9 February orders were given to the US IX TCC and IX Engineer Commands to repair and expand fifteen former Luftwaffe airfields in France before 15 March for troop carrier use. On 11 February IX TCC issued movement orders directing the 53rd Wing to begin moving to France next day and be fully established by the Wing had, since late September, been located in territory southwest of Paris. Its headquarters was at Chartres (to where the IX Pathfinder Troop Carrier Group (P) moved, from Chalgrove, on 27 February). The rest of the wing comprised the 439th Group at Châteaudun, the 440th Group at Orléans-Bricy, the 441st at Dreux and the 442nd at Peray (moving to Sainte André-de-l'Eure on 6 November). Colonel Charles H. Young, 439th Group CO, found hangars and buildings on his new field completely demolished. He was later to discover that his younger brother in the 8th Air Force, was operations officer of the B-17 Group that had done most of the damage.

Brereton and his colleagues finally felt certain on 5 March that they had the means to deliver all the airborne troops for 'Varsity' in one lift. Two divisions had never before been flown into battle in one single continuous effort. Larger numbers of troops had been delivered in both 'Neptune' and 'Market', but those operations had been extended over several days so that aircraft and crews could be used more than once.

The British 1st Airborne had only 712 men left in the Glider Pilot Regiment. To provide a pair of pilots for each of the 440 British gliders in 'Varsity' the regiment would have to take 1,500 pilots from the RAF and retrain them in glider flying and infantry tactics fighting as soldiers. They were given a fourteen-day course on small arms at Fargo Camp and a week of assault courses and field training at Bridgnorth, followed by conversion courses on the Hotspur, Horsa and Hamilcar. Colonel (later Brigadier) George Chatterton, the commander of the Glider Pilot Regiment, who was always 'quite ruthless' in enforcing army standards' decided to match rank with rank; the Wings remained under the command of their army commanders, with squadron leaders as seconds-in-command, but the command of the squadrons was divided equally between majors and squadron leaders and Flights between captains and flight lieutenants. Individual crews were made up as far as possible of one army and one ex-RAF pilot. All this was necessary so that the RAF personnel should become versed in army methods. Unlike their RAF counterparts, glider pilots measured their experience not in flying hours but in 'lifts' - the number of successful takeoffs and landings made.

The Americans would have had an adequate number of glider pilots had they not been required to keep a sufficient reserve to fly 926 gliders in 'Choker'. Thus they too had to use converted power pilots as glider pilots. About half of the co-pilots for the Wacos in 'Varsity' were drawn from this source.

Earlier in the war when American glider pilots were badly needed, the new grade of Flight Officer, equal in status to that of warrant officer junior grade had been created on 8 July 1942. The new grade, which also attracted a 20 per cent increase in pay for overseas duty was still not fully taken up and so slowly, entry requirements were reduced. Instead of accepting volunteers up to the age of 26 (the maximum for power pilots) the new requirement was increased to age 35 and the restriction on candidates who had previously failed military flight school was dropped. This applied to men like Bruce Cornelol Merryman and John L. Lowden, a failed power pilot in the 434th TCG. Merryman had become 'hooked' on flying in Corpus Christi, Texas at age ten after riding in a Ford Tri-Motor for the price of fifty cents and a Pepsi Cola bottle cap. He had volunteered for pilot training in the aviation cadet programme in May 1942, was accepted and called to active service in November 1942. He went through the aviation cadet programme lacking approximately one month of graduating from single engine fighter pilot training. Washed out, he was reclassified as a radio/gunner and sent to radio school at Scott Field, Illinois. He volunteered for everything that would get him back into flying and was accepted into the glider programme in late 1943, graduating on 15 June 1944. From Laurinburg-Maxton he went to the ETO via the *Isle de France* and joined the 62nd Squadron in the 314th TCG at Saltby. He was shot loose from his tow plane in Holland after 'Market' while salvaging gliders and made it into the airfield at Eindhoven.

John L. Lowden was invited by the Executive Officer to apply for glider training instead. When he turned down the offer, he found himself assigned to carrying out an inventory of thousands of blankets stacked in a warehouse where temperatures hit 90 degrees by mid-morning. After five days of this, Lowden finally reported back to the Exec. 'Sir, I have given careful consideration to your suggestion that I 'enlist' in the glider corps and I have decided to do so'. The Exec said 'I thought you'd see it my way. 'When I went to check out with the sergeant who was caretaker of the warehouse, he shook my hand and said *Good luck. You held out longer than the others.*[3]

Like all Army Air Corps pilots, the glidermen wore wings on their chests. Theirs were special, with a capital 'G' stamped in the centre. Technically it stood for 'glider,' but they were quick to tell anyone who asked that it really stood for 'Guts.'

Early in March 1945 Major General William Maynadier 'Bud' Miley, commander of the 17th Airborne Division, briefed the glider operations officers of the 53rd Troop Carrier Wing's five groups on the plans for 'Varsity'. His 194th Glider Infantry Regiment would need an extra infantry company if it was to carry out its assigned objective. That company would be made up of glider pilots after landing, making it unique in military history - an infantry company made up entirely of officers. Command would go to Captain Charles Gordon, glider operations officer of the 435th Troop Carrier Group at Welford. The pilots underwent two weeks of intensive training in weapons and tactics with the 194th GIR to prepare themselves. Organized into four platoons, one for each of the group's squadrons (75th, 76th, 77th and 78th), the men were to assist the 17th Airborne Division in securing a crossroads of the Helzweg and Hessenweg north-east of Wesel, establish roadblocks and make contact with British forces north-east of the town. They also knew that this time the LZs would not have been secured by paratroopers first.[4]

In order to test navigational aids it was considered necessary for a rehearsal flight codenamed 'Token' to be made on 17 March. David J. W. Vickery on Flying Officer Ron Langtry's Halifax crew on 296 Squadron at Earls Colne recalls: 'My log book reminds me of the practices: 'MTO (Mass take-off) and formation glider lift.' Six Stirling/Horsa and Halifax/Horsa combinations at Great Dunmow and Earls Colne and one Halifax/Hamilcar combination at Woodbridge took off from Earls Colne ballasted with concrete and made their way via Cap Gris Nez to the Rhine in the neighbourhood of Xanten. They were provided with a high-altitude escort of fighter aircraft and the glider pilots were required to carry side-arms and fifty rounds of ammunition parachutes and 'Mae Wests'. The combinations returned to the UK without incident, no flak or enemy fighter being encountered.[5]

The British with their very limited troop carrier force had great difficulty in finding enough lift for 6th Airborne. The airborne wanted between 406 and 425 aircraft from 38 and 46 Groups to tow their gliders, but the two groups estimated that they could provide no more than 350 aircraft between them. Airborne Army raised 46 Group's quota from about one hundred to 120 aircraft by insisting that SHAEF pry 25 of its aircraft away from transport work for service in 'Varsity'. The Air Ministry gave 38 Group 104 converted Stirlings and Halifaxes to raise his group's contribution from 240 to 320 aircraft. By using every qualified man including those whose tours of duty had expired and those assigned to training units, the two groups managed to scrape up crews for the extra aircraft. Although it would have been preferable to base the RAF troop carriers on the Continent, runways capable of handling Halifaxes and

Stirlings were not obtainable in France but the RAF glider tow aircraft were allowed to land after the operation at Abbeville-Drucat, Amiens/Glisy and Vitry-en-Artois, which were being repaired for use by units of the US 52nd TCW, instead of having to return across the Channel.

Because of the shortage of British troop carrying aircraft, at a conference on 26 February the 6th Airborne Division asked for 275 American aircraft to carry its paratroops. General Williams responded that 243 aircraft was all he could spare and that was all the division got. When, in February-March the 313th Troop Carrier Group at Folkingham and the 314th at Saltby in the 52nd Wing moved to Achiet Le Grand airfield (B-40) near the village of Grévillers and to Poix-de-Picardie respectively, north of Paris, three Groups remained in England to carry part of the 6th Airborne Division. Picked for the task were the 61st at Barkston Heath, 315th at Spanhoe and 316th at Cottesmore, the first two of which had flown British paratroopers in 'Market'. It would have been very difficult for those groups to fly their missions from their home bases in the Grantham area or for 46 Group to do so from its airfields in south-central England so it had been decided that they should stage from East Anglia where they would be near 38 Group, which, early in October had been moved to bases in Essex, northeast of London, a shift which put it about one hundred miles nearer the 'Varsity' area and within reasonable range of its objectives in that operation. On 2 March 8th Air Force agreed to loan Gosfield, Birch near Colchester (which went to 46 Group), Boreham, Chipping Ongar and Wethersfield. The 315th got Boreham. The 61st sent its squadrons to Chipping Ongar. After some doubts about the suitability of Wethersfield, that airfield was assigned to the 316th as a jumping off point for the Rhine crossing operation.

On 13 March the 61st TCG began flying personnel and equipment to a new headquarters at an Advanced Landing Ground at Abbeville-Drucat (B-92) fifteen miles inland from the mouth of the River Somme, but not before 'the boys got in one last bath, visiting nearby towns to drink their last 'mild and bitters' and kiss their sweethearts good bye.' B-92 was previously home for the 'Abbeville kids,' nickname of the German ace fighter Gruppe, said to be the hottest fliers of the Luftwaffe at one time. The field was also said to be one of Göring's favourites, but it reminded men of their first overseas station, Lourmel, French Algeria, as the unit transferred back to field conditions after a year of garrison life.

In the 53rd Wing the 434th Group at Aldermaston began the move to Mourmelon-le-Grand, the 435th at Welford to Bretigny, the 436th at Membury to Melun, the 437th at Ramsbury to A-58 Coulommiers and the 438th at Greenham Common to Prosnes (A-79). These bases were dispersed over a wide area southeast of Paris. For many, aside from a few who had British girl friends or strong attachments to British families, the only thing wrong with the announcement of the move to France was that it had not come sooner. At Membury the mood had been 'pretty high' on New Year's Day, partly because the 436th Troop Carrier Group was pleased with their part in the Bastogne operation. These good feelings evaporated quickly, however. The weather in January 1945 was truly depressing. Men were told that they were living through the worst winter Europe had experienced during the past forty years. And the news from the front lines in eastern France and Belgium made discouraging reading: nothing but costly, inconclusive slugging matches in icy mud. It took the American armies until the end of January to get back the territory they had lost during the Battle of the Bulge.

The silver lining in all those gloomy British clouds was the news that the 436th Troop Carrier Group would soon be moving to A-55. The nearest sizeable town was Melun, six miles away and on the River Seine; but there was a little village, Villaroche, even nearer. Better still, Paris was only thirty miles distant. The distance was an easy two-hour flight, with a chance to spot the Eiffel Tower and some other famous landmarks in Paris on the way. Ken De Blake, a radio operator, reported that on one of these trips his C-47 buzzed the Arc de Triomphe. Paris in March 1945 looked shabby, though there were none of the ruins the Americans had seen in London. So far as sex was concerned, most confined themselves to looking (and to talking about it). We may have made a beeline to the Rue Pigalle (the 'Pig Alley' of World War I fame) to see the famous red-light district, but for the most part we were there to gawk rather than to sample. As glider pilot Ben Ward in the 80th Troop Carrier Squadron reported, 'I saw many strange sights while visiting Paris, including ladies with purple hair. It certainly was true that the classy style of those prostitutes, their boldness and the sheer quantity of them was something about which we were all very conscious. Prostitutes were everywhere GIs were likely to stroll. I remember the shock a bunch of us felt when we emerged from a Metro stop in front of the Paris Opera to be accosted by one who advertised her specialty by asking Suckee, suckee? We were even more startled when one of us took her arm and went off with her.'

Paris certainly held more attractions than nearby Melun - not to mention the tiny villages clustered around the airfield. Still, some found it worth the risk, after work was through for the day, to walk out an unguarded rear gate and stroll a short distance to the villages of Villaroche or Lissy, where there was a charming French barmaid by the name of Suzanne. A less questionable deal was to trade PX rations, not sell them. This way, men could get fresh eggs, wine or cognac and delicious French bread. They could also trade for a bottle of the local potato vodka, guaranteed to make eyes water, made by farmers around Lissy who had emigrated there from Poland during the 1920s.[6]

Unfortunately, the 436th's 'new' base was so thoroughly bombed out that an aerial view taken before the Group arrived showed the field with 'as many bomb craters as a Swiss cheese has holes.' Most of the airfield structures were heaps of rubble piled around twisted steel girders. Only a few buildings were still standing and these were all appropriated for supply storage, vehicle maintenance, parachute rigging and for a briefing building. The advanced echelon's first job was putting up tents for both living quarters and for the Squadron's various departments. The accommodation in the living area were large, four-sided pyramid tents, intended to house six enlisted men or four officers. The biggest problem was trying to keep from freezing. But by 26 February, just twelve days after the first arrivals, Melun was declared 'operational'.

At Coulommiers, Don Bolce, in the 85th TCS, the 437th TCG recalled: 'When we arrived in France I felt that there would be no more large airborne combat missions ahead of us. I thought that our job was now to continue flying needed supplies to the troops on the front line. If they needed gasoline, we would load up our planes with five gallon jerry cans and land in a cow pasture, if necessary, to make the deliveries. It didn't matter what was needed; ammunition, food, medical supplies, we would deliver to any unit that needed our help. But, suddenly rumours about a possible airborne invasion across the Rhine River began to circulate. When we looked at the daily battle maps in the Stars and Stripes newspaper we could see that to cross the Rhine River an amphibious force would need airborne support.

'After flying all the previous missions without self-sealing fuel tanks, all our 437th TCG aircraft finally receive them. The crew chiefs and their assistants worked long and hard for many hours to remove the old wing tanks and install the new self-sealing version. With the installation of self-sealing fuel tanks in progress at an accelerated pace it seemed likely that a combat mission was no longer a rumour but a reality that we must face one more time. For whatever reason, I did not feel good about the upcoming mission. I had a dull, sort of empty feeling in my stomach, which would not go away. Call it butterflies, call it what you like, I guess that I was just plain scared. We had been so lucky on D-Day, the airborne parachute invasion of Southern France, the airborne invasion into Holland, the resupply of the 101st Airborne at Bastogne, but now, I felt that my luck was about to run out.'

The system of multiple traffic lanes used in 'Market' had been proposed for 'Varsity' in November and was embodied in the final plan. There were to be three lanes spaced 1½ miles apart. The contingent bringing 6th Airborne Division from the United Kingdom would follow the northern lane to their Initial Point, head from there for the six northernmost zones and turn north onto a reciprocal course after delivering their troops. Their IP, ('Yalta North') was located beside a railway north of Weeze and east of an oxbow loop in the Nierse River. It lay between fifteen and eighteen miles from the zones. Actually there were two northern routes, lying at different levels. The American C-47s flying paratroops were to fly at 1,500 feet until nearing the IP, while the British glider stream would keep to an altitude of 2,500 feet. This would enable the American serials flying British paratroops at 140 mph to pass under the Dakotas of 46 Group, towing Horsas at 115 mph and make their drop ahead of them. The British had some tug-glider combinations in 38 Group cruising at 135 mph and others at 145 mph. In order to get a continuous stream at the IP the slow units were given a head start at Hawkinge such that by holding to the proper speed the faster ones would catch up with them at Weeze.

The American glider serials would occupy the centre lane and use a bridge over the Nierse on the east side of Weeze as their IP. The paratroop serials of the 17th Airborne would follow the southern lane to their IP ('Yalta South'), a castle beside the Nierse 1½ miles south of Weeze. Although the last two paratroop serials in the south lane would fly for a while parallel to the first glider serial in the centre, the former because of greater cruising speed were expected to pull ahead by five minutes before reaching their Initial Point.[7] All the American airborne were to be dropped or landed on the four southernmost zones, after which the aircraft bringing them would make a 180° turn to the right onto a reciprocal course for the return trip.

These arrangements made it possible to deliver the two divisions simultaneously and, by the use of tight spacing, to compress the whole operation within a period of two hours and 37 minutes. The paratroop serials formed as usual of nine-aircraft 'Vs of V's in trail were to be spaced at four-minute intervals if numbering more than forty aircraft and at three-minute intervals if smaller than that. American glider serials would fly in pairs of pairs in echelon to the right with a 1,500-foot interval between successive elements. Single-tow serials were to be seven minutes apart. Double-tow serials got ten or twelve minutes depending on whether they contained as many as forty aircraft, because the novelty of double-tow made it advisable to allow margin for error. The British glider stream, flying in loose pairs at ten-second intervals, had a time length of only 39 minutes as compared to two hours and six minutes for the American gliders. However, the former had only 440 big gliders to deliver, while the latter had 906 Wacos.

Separate Pathfinder operations were omitted. They were regarded as unnecessary because navigation was so easy, as suicidal because the zones were in a strongly defended area and as harmful because they would forfeit all chance of surprise. However, the lead aircraft in the first serial to pass over each of the four British and American drop zones was to drop a stick of Pathfinder troops who were to set out coloured panels and smoke but no beacons for the initial missions.

Communication between aircraft during 'Varsity' was limited to extreme emergencies and exercise of command functions, at or above wing level until aircraft were at least forty miles along on their homeward journey. Then navigational information might be requested. This air-to-air communication was to be by VHF. A special ground-air W/T station was to be operated by IX TCC Forward. Over it, if necessary, recall signals could be sent to serials anywhere on the route. Two aircraft in each flight were to watch that frequency. Two new organizations, the combat control team and the forward visual control post, had recently been created to remedy the communications deficiencies which had played so serious a part in 'Market'. Both were used in 'Varsity'. The troop carrier command had begun in January to organize combat control teams from its glider pilots and enlisted technicians on the basis of two teams for each American airborne division. The function of the teams was to inform headquarters and incoming serials of conditions in the battle area, particularly weather and enemy resistance and to notify the airborne in turn of any changes in troop carrier plans, especially regarding timing, course or zones. Each team was composed of five men with a jeep and a quarter-ton trailer, modified to hold a power unit, an SCR-399 or 499 for communication with headquarters and an SCR-522 for VHF radio conversation with missions overhead. In the coming operation two teams, one a spare in case of accidents or casualties, were to be landed at opposite ends of LZ 'N' to operate for XVIII Corps. Each was to go in three Wacos; one for the jeep, one for the trailer and one containing equipment for medical evacuation by glider pick-up. Two gliders loaded with wounded had been 'snatched' very successfully from the Remagen bridgehead and the troop carriers were prepared to evacuate large numbers of patients by glider in 'Varsity' under the direction of a combat control team if conditions warranted.[8]

The forward visual control posts were fighter control teams with the primary purpose of directing close support aircraft. They had recently been organized by 38 Group. Each team had a jeep and a trailer and for 'Varsity' was equipped with two VHF sets, one for ground-to-ground communication by which to call for support aircraft and one for air-to-air communication by which to direct the aircraft to their targets. A whole team could fit in one Horsa. In 'Varsity' three FVCPs (Forward Visual Control Posts) were to be flown in to 6th Airborne Division. One would serve that division, one would move south to work for the 17th Airborne and one would act as a reserve. Because the FVCPs had been created only a short time before the operation, their personnel had very little training in either airborne operations or close support. Notwithstanding this handicap they were to prove very valuable.

Remembering the miscarriage of 'Market', to provide against the contingency, however remote, that the Second Army assault might be contained, leaving the airborne cut off from supplies, Brereton and Ridgway agreed that a resupply mission ready to go on 'D+1' unless cancelled, consisting of 440 C-47s of DC TCC carrying 550 tons of materiel and 240 aircraft of 38 Group carrying 530 tons, would be enough to last the two divisions for two days. If bad weather in England or over the Channel pounded 38 Group, a substitute force of 75 Dakotas of 46 Group would take off from Nivelles near Brussels with high-priority items for the British airborne. Likewise, if the troop carrier units on the Continent were grounded, C-47s from England would fly a one-day level of supplies to the 17th Division. In addition, preparations were made to deliver on request an additional two-day level of supplies for 6th Airborne and a one-day level for the 17th Airborne.

Not until after the middle of March were decisions reached on how to protect the troop carrier missions from being fired on in error by Allied gunners, but the action finally taken was very thorough as far as the 'D-Day' missions were concerned. RAF Fighter Command agreed to prohibit anti-aircraft fire near the troop carrier path in England from 0700 to 1500 hours. A representative of the naval commander concerned made a like promise for naval anti-aircraft in the Thames estuary and within a ten-mile belt along the troop carrier route across the Channel. The 21st Army Group directed that on the Continent within a strip thirty miles wide cantered on the route no flak was to be fired west of the Maas between 0700 and 1500 or east of it between 0900 and 1400. Outside the prohibited zone no guns were to fire on aircraft during the period of the missions unless they committed a hostile act. On the Second Army front no guns or mortars near the troop carrier lanes were to fire on trajectories higher than 500 feet between 0958 and 1330 hours. As further insurance the artillerymen were to detail a special watch to report on approaching formations and on such damaged aircraft as might dip low over the guns on their return. Escort and cover were to be provided on a massive scale. The troop carrier stream from the United Kingdom would be escorted as far as the Rhine and back by 11 Group RAF. Units based in France would be escorted to and from the river by fighters of Ninth Air Force. Beyond the Rhine there would be no escort, but a system of standing patrols would be maintained on 'D-Day' from dawn to dark.

As to the German ground forces opposing 'Plunder' and 'Varsity', Allied hopes that they had been shattered in the Rhineland gave way as 'D-Day' approached to a sober conviction that the enemy had extricated much more than anticipated and that there would be a real fight ahead. Aware that Wesel was a logical place to cross the Rhine the enemy had, it was estimated, massed about ten of their best remaining divisions within twenty miles of the area selected for Montgomery's assaults. However, they had been so reduced by attrition as to number less than 50,000 combat effectives. Among them were two or three panzer divisions with perhaps one hundred tanks and self-propelled guns, but these were reported to be near Duisburg and Isselburg on the River Issel, near the border of the Netherlands and Bocholt, more than ten miles away from the assault area. Brereton kept order of battle teams on duty 24 hours a day up to the last minute before 'Varsity' was launched, undoubtedly to prevent panzer units from surprising the airborne at Wesel as they had done at Arnhem. A maximum of 12,000 troops including two divisions and a brigade group were thought to be within a ten-mile radius of the airborne assault. If they concentrated in the Diersfordter Wald to oppose the amphibious landings, the airborne, arriving in their rear and on their flanks would cut them off.

Since the German commanders reputedly anticipated an airborne operation and had even rehearsed defence measures against one, it was more likely that they would place only a holding force in the wood and keep their main strength back of the Issel River to await developments. In that case the airborne might be the ones encircled. Whatever the defence plan, it was evident as little as five minutes after arrival that the paratroops and glider men might be in combat with substantial German forces in well-prepared positions. The initial fighting might be hard. Thereafter the duration and severity of the battle would probably depend on the extent to which the enemy could bring up reinforcements. To stand a chance of winning they would need to get half a dozen of their depleted divisions into the battle area. The Allies proposed to stop any such movement through the use of their superior airpower.

In contrast to 'Market', which had no systematic interdiction, 'Varsity' was the beneficiary of four interdictory operations. The original programme asked for and obtained by Second Army and FAAA was short, small and efficient. It called for bombing a dozen vital communications centres within fifteen miles of the assault area[9] late on 'D-1' or on 'D-Day'. If successful, this would block every good way by which German reinforcements could approach the battle area. On 'D-Day' armed reconnaissance patrols of 83 and 84 Groups and XXDC TAC would sweep the roads clean of military traffic west of Zwolle, Münster, Hamm and Siegen and similar patrols of Eighth Air Force fighters would do so east of that line. To supplement this plan 21st Army Group proposed on 17 March that, since the Germans obviously would not be taken by surprise, they should be softened up by several days of preparatory bombing directed against barracks and military installations within a thirty-mile radius of Wesel. Next day 2nd TAF and the air forces concerned agreed to bomb 26 such targets north of the Lippe and sixteen south of it at least twice every 24 hours from 'D-3' to 'D-1', preferably both by day and by night so that the enemy could get no rest. This programme was aimed solely at German reserves. The assault areas were excluded for fear of damage to zones or river banks. Most of the places already on the interdiction list were included and the general effect was to reinforce the interdiction of the 'Varsity' area. However, about half the targets named were too far away to affect the airborne operation, important as they might be to later phases of 21st Army Group's offensive.[10] The same thing applies to the interdiction patrols flown by the fighters of Eighth Air Force. Their effect was to prevent creation of a second line of defence rather than reinforcement of the front.

Even more remote from 'Varsity', though not without influence on it, was a project proposed early in February by Lieutenant General Hoyt Vandenberg, commander of the Ninth Air Force, to isolate all territory between the Rhine and an arc from Bremen along the Weser and Lahn rivers to Coblenz by bombing eighteen bridges and viaducts and then to paralyze the railways in that area by destroying their rolling stock. The operation was approved, mainly, it appears, for its economic and general strategic value and not as direct tactical assistance to 'Varsity'. It began on 21 February and by 21 March the only remaining serviceable bridges were three at the northern extremity of the arc; twenty out of 25 marshalling yards had been knocked out; and railway traffic was at a standstill. This situation must have hampered enemy efforts to build defences along the Rhine, but, even if the way had been clear, they had almost no reserves east of the Weser. The industries of the Ruhr were strangled, as Vandenberg had intended they should be. The tactical value of the operation as far as 'Varsity' is concerned is uncertain but probably rather limited.

One other air operation was a bombing of Wesel itself. Second Army asked for this very urgently on 17 March and RAF Bomber Command was given the assignment of attacking the city on 'D-1'. Dempsey had decided to take Wesel by a commando assault at 2230 on the 23rd and considered bombing essential to soften up the defenders. Since the flak batteries in Wesel were a threat to the troop carrier missions, this decision to hit the city hard and take it early would be of real assistance to 'Varsity'.

Close support of the airborne troops was to be divided between artillery and air units in much the same way as flak suppression. A 'cab rank' of rocket-firing Typhoon fighter-bombers dispatched in relays of four every fifteen minutes was to be maintained throughout the day over the Wesel area, ready to attack targets on requests received by radio from control parties with the troops. Requests for additional aircraft to fly close support were to be made through the control parties to an advanced control centre of 83 Group.

Artillery support was to play a role never before possible in an airborne operation. At 1000 hours on 'D-Day' XVIII Corps was to receive operational control of 104 guns for direct support of 6th Airborne Division and 88 guns for direct support of the 17th Airborne plus a battery of heavy anti-aircraft guns for each division. An additional 176 guns including 155mm pieces and 240 mm howitzers were to be under corps control for general support. Since only 51 guns were to be flown in for the 17th Division and only 24 for 6th Airborne, it is easy to see that the ability to call on ground artillery multiplied the firepower of the airborne force many times over.

In contrast to the vestigial training for 'Market' preparation for 'Varsity' included a rehearsal, a short period of intensive joint training and, before that, a systematic training programme designed to maintain proficiency, Brereton having insisted that his troop carriers be given adequate opportunity to practice troop carrier operations. Early in January the Battle of the Bulge subsided and during that month and the next about two thirds of the aircraft dispatched by IX TCC were on training flights. Three weeks of intensive combined troop carrier-airborne training for 'Varsity' were to end on 20 March, about ten days before the operation and was to culminate in a rehearsal but when 'Varsity' was moved up to 24 March it became necessary to terminate training on the 15th. No glider exercises were planned or attempted. At most of the fields, facilities for mass glider landings were so inadequate that General Williams had limited non-tactical glider lifts from any base to sixteen at a time. As for the rehearsal, the airborne declined to participate for fear of possible losses. It developed into a mere simulated exercise by a skeleton force to test troop carrier command arrangements and tactics.[11] In the 52nd Wing only one whole group, the 313th, engaged in joint training and it had to, because it was equipped with the new and unfamiliar C-46. General Williams had wanted to have two paratroop regiments familiarized with the Commando and, if possible, to have it tested in an exercise.[12] The other groups of the command did little or no joint training.[13]

Special attention was given to the role glider pilots were to assume after landing. Their status as integral components of the troop carrier squadrons was not changed. However, for combat purposes the glider pilots of each troop carrier group were organized into units equivalent to infantry companies. The wing glider officer and a small staff would act as a battalion headquarters exercising tactical and administrative control of those companies during the ground phase. Training in infantry tactics was conducted by the 17th Airborne Division and the glider pilots were provided with such infantry equipment as compasses, canteens, entrenching tools and light sleeping bags, the lack of which had been felt in 'Market'.

Glider pilot employment was to be much as before. On landing they would assist in unloading, then proceed to the assembly area of the airborne unit carried, assemble there into their own tactical organizations and move as units to a specified wing assembly area. There after mustering them by squadrons the wing glider officer, working in conjunction with a previously delegated representative of the airborne commander, was to assign them to such tasks as guard duty, supply collection and, circumstances permitting, to protection of usable gliders from vandalism. In spite of all the talk of using them to reinforce the infantry, it was specified that the glider pilot units were not to be committed to battle except in extreme emergency and then only in a defensive role. Furthermore, they were to be evacuated from the combat area on the highest possible priority. Evidently Airborne Army had not been convinced that trained pilots were as expendable as riflemen.

The rehearsal, appropriately called 'Token', was postponed by unfavourable weather from 16 March to 17 March. Command arrangements, communications, navigational aids and tactics were like those planned for 'Varsity'. However, each serial in the coming operation was represented by a single element, including the leader and assistant leader of the serial. The 'Varsity' route was used as far as Wavre, after which a similar course with modified headings was used to zones near Montluçon and back on a reciprocal route. No troops were carried and no gliders released, except that two gliders with a combat control team were landed on Villeneuve-Vertus airfield to test the functioning of the team.

While results were generally very good, an unexpected tail wind of 20 mph upset the timing and caused some elements to reach their objectives as much as twelve minutes ahead of schedule. Reception of the M/F beacons along the route was poor in many cases and the signals of the Ruhr 'Gee' chain showed a tendency to fade. There were also failures in land-line communications with the troop carrier forces in England. The signal lines were speedily repaired, since even a brief loss of contact with 38 Group during the actual operation could have been serious. Another significant result of the rehearsal was a decision by General Williams that after passing the command departure point at Wavre the troop carrier serials would adhere to indicated air speeds instead of attempting to reach each checkpoint at a scheduled time. This change was intended to prevent the confusion which might result if some groups interfered with others by excessive slowing or speeding in an effort to meet their schedule.

Because 'Varsity' was a set piece scheduled well in advance, there was ample time to prepare orders and conduct briefings. The briefings, carefully prepared and embodying the accumulated experience of previous operations were generally held to be excellent. The security precautions taken for 'Varsity' were intended to conceal the composition of the attacking force and the exact time and place of the operation. The fact that an assault would soon be made across the Rhine north of the Ruhr was clear to any skilled observer of the military situation and was made even more obvious by Montgomery's massive preparations and by reports in the newspapers. Particular pains were taken to conceal changes in radio traffic from which the enemy might deduce what was brewing. The movement of the airborne divisions to the airfields was done as unobtrusively as possible with identification marks removed from uniforms and equipment. The ground echelons of those divisions were disguised as Communications Zone troops during their move up to the front. At the airfields the precautions taken were like those before the invasion of Normandy, though not quite as stringent. On the arrival of the troops, traffic in and out of the bases was restricted and the troops were sealed in their bivouac areas. Briefed troop carrier personnel were segregated from those un-briefed, telephone service was curtailed and calls monitored and outgoing mail was stored in special bags until after the operation.

At 1600 on 23 March the decision that 'Varsity' should be launched on schedule was made by Brereton and Air Marshal Sir Arthur Coningham, AOC of the 2nd Tactical Air Force commanding all co-operating air forces except bombers on resupply missions, which would be under Brereton's jurisdiction. The meteorologists predicted fine weather for the next day. There would be rather thick haze in the Wesel area during the early morning, but this would clear before the troop carriers' approach, giving them visibility of at least two miles there and over four miles elsewhere. Surface winds would blow at 10 to 15 mph at the bases and about 10 mph on the drop and landing zones. Accordingly the commanders directed that 'Varsity' proceed as scheduled. Montgomery authorized the launching of 'Plunder', his amphibious assault, at 1530 on the 23rd. The operation went with the textbook precision that was his trademark. At 2100, exactly as scheduled, the first wave of assault boats pushed out into the Rhine, carrying the first elements of four battalions of the 51st Division. Their objective was Rees, twelve miles downstream from Wesel. At 2200 the Commando Brigade began its crossing about two miles west of Wesel. At 0200 a crossing in the Xanten area midway between Wesel and Rees was begun by four battalions of the 15th Division. The 9th Army assault south of the Lippe also began at 0200. All these crossings were completely successful. Everywhere the opposite bank proved thinly held, initial resistance was feeble and the initial artillery reaction slight.

Fierce fighting did develop at some points. German paratroops facing the northern prong of the assault held Rees throughout 'D-Day' and kept the 51st Division pinned close to the river. With artillery and mortars still in positions from which they could rake the river in that sector, the enemy prevented any bridge-building there and made ferry operations difficult. No help would reach the airborne from the 51st Division, but it was engaging its share of the German defence force. The commando brigade also had its hands full. Despite the severe pounding received from Bomber Command, the garrison of Wesel clung stubbornly to portions of the town throughout the day. However, in the centre the 15th Division did well and by 1000 hours on 'D-Day' was in a position to capitalize on the airborne assault which was to strike the hilltop positions ahead of it.

Endnotes Chapter 1

1   Rivenhall: *The History of an Essex Airfield* by Bruce Stait (Amberley 2015).

2   *The Glider Gang* by Milton Dank.

3   *Silent Wings At War* by John L. Lowden.

4   *Silent Skies: Gliders At War 1939-1945* by Tim Lynch (Pen & Sword, 2008).

5   *History of the Glider Pilot Regiment* by Claude Smith (Pen & Sword, 2007).

6   *Green Light! A Troop Carrier Squadron's War From Normandy To The Rhine* by Martin Wolfe.

7   All American gliders were limited to the pace of the double-tow serials, 110 mph. Two of the last three paratroop serials were made up of C-46s travelling at 165 mph, the other of C-47s at 140 mph.

8   The Dakota pilot flew the plane so the pick-up hook would shoot between ground poles 12 feet tall, spaced 20 feet apart that held the nylon pickup loop. The glider awaiting pickup was placed off to the side and behind the pickup poles so that the path of the C-47 was not directly above the glider. To reduce the stress on the glider, the pick-up hook was attached to a winch which was like a giant fishing reel with more than 1,000 feet of 3/8-inch diameter steel-wire rope as the line. Once the hook engaged the pick-up loop, the cable on the winch unwound but maintained enough tension to begin pulling the glider along the ground. The glider then accelerated to take-off speed. The whole process was fast, but just slow enough to prevent the glider from being torn apart. In less than seven seconds from the moment of contact the glider would be flying at the same speed as the C-47 as the steel cable played out approximately 600 feet.

9   Artholt, Isselburg, Dingden, Brunen, Raetfeld, Bocholt, Borken, Dorsten, Gladbeck, Sterkrade and a bridge near Sterkrade.

10   Tedder, Spaatz and Vandenberg expressed the opinion on 21 March that this operation should have been concentrated against reserves near the front, omitting several objectives deep in the rear.

11   Counting the pathfinders as a group. During the period of joint training the American troop carriers dropped 19,678 paratroops and carried 26,666 glider troops. Almost all of this, however, was done by eight of IX TCCs 15 groups. The 50th Wing, already established in its French bases, made 4,329 glider tows between 1 and 18 March and on the 9th its A-3 Officer boasted that the wing was giving the airborne three times as much practice as they had asked for. Three groups of the 53rd Wing were also active, especially the 435th, which carried 15,642 glider troops and the 438th, which dropped 6,649 paratroops between 10 and 15 March. The 436th also did its share.

12   Busy until 10 March in moving to Achiet and in competing transition training on the new craft for its crews, the 313th Group then sent out 125 aircraft over a five-day period and dropped 3,246 men of the 513th PIR, its partner in the coming operation, to familiarize them with the characteristics of the C-46, especially its double jump-doors. The group did not attempt any mass drops. On 9 March a dozen aircraft of the 315th Group were sent from Spanhoe to Netheravon to give jump training to paratroops of 6th Airborne. Before returning on the 15th they dropped 4,128 men and the divisional commander expressed himself as well satisfied.

13   The 434th Group was unable to participate because its base at Mourmelon was not ready for it to begin moving there until 10 March. Besides the American units, 46 Group RAF was also very short of training; 90 percent of it was retained on transport work until D-2. Since these seemingly undertrained units did well in 'Varsity', one may hazard the conclusion that joint training with airborne troops before an operation is not essential for experienced troop carrier units. What counted in 'Varsity' was the recovery of proficiency in troop carrier tactics and navigation by hard training during January and February in IX TCC and at regular intervals by relays in 46 Group.

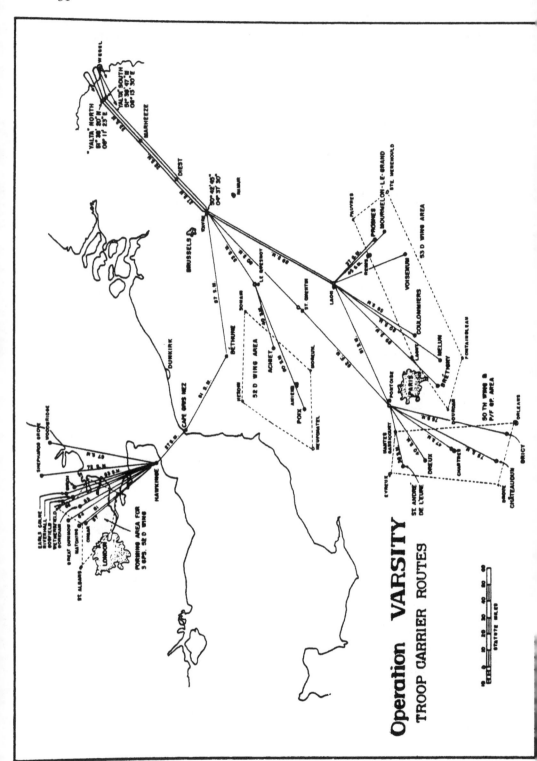

Operation VARSITY

TROOP CARRIER ROUTES

Chapter 2
'Plunder'

The most startling change was that the established sequence of airborne warfare was to be abandoned on Varsity. From Husky through Market, this sequence always started with paratroopers landing behind enemy lines and starting to carve out an airhead. Then gliders, bringing in reinforcements and heavier equipment, would land in areas secured by paratroopers. Finally, the combined airborne troopers would punch through enemy encirclement and link up with a land- or seaborne infantry launched in their direction some hours after the airborne attack began. This time, however, parachutists and glider-borne troopers would be landed virtually on top of each other, or at any rate at just about the same time; in other words, the gliders would not wait until paratroopers cleared out their LZs. Furthermore, this time the land forces were to fight their way across the Rhine first, eight hours before the first troop carriers took to the air. This was supposed to ensure that the British would have at least a small bridgehead across the Rhine before the airborne troopers came in, which would greatly increase the chances of an early linkup between airborne and land infantry. (The amphibious infantry portion of the invasion, mostly a British affair, was code-named Plunder.)

But the biggest and most risky change of all was that the entire operation was to be squeezed into the shortest time frame possible: Varsity was to place two entire airborne divisions - about 21,700 paratroopers and glidermen - into German-held fields east of the Rhine in a bit more than two and a half hours. This would mean 'double-tow': most of the gliders would have to be pulled two to a tug plane.

The decision to put everybody across the Rhine together was a reaction to one of the causes of Market's failure. Varsity planners were haunted by the conviction that if all the airborne troopers could have been dropped or landed together during the invasion of Holland, the Allies could have broken through in September 1944. Planners also hoped that the all-at-once feature of Varsity would deny the Germans time to move in effective supporting defences. By gambling everything on one gigantic airborne lift, the Allies might be losing something in tactical flexibility; but this would be more than offset by not running the risk of unexpected bad weather on successive days, such as had helped wreck Market.

Neptune and Market had also called for delivering two divisions by air, but over two or three days. The number one concern of Varsity planners, therefore, was that by delivering everything at once they faced a traffic problem of gigantic proportions. The armada they proposed to put up - more than 1,550 planes and 1,300 gliders - was going to be crowded together into a tight air corridor. All these planes and gliders had to arrive at invasion sites in the most rigorously orchestrated sequence. Therefore everything depended on each branch of troop carrier doing its job perfectly and on schedule. The ground crews, for example, would have to meet the most exacting timetables for getting planes and gliders into shape and into position. The operation also was totally dependent on the most demanding sort of formation flying FAAA had ever imposed on its pilots.

From tip to tail, Varsity, once airborne, would measure more than 200 miles. It would also be very densely packed from side to side. To prevent jam-ups in such a gigantic airlift, Varsity planners relied on two traffic control devices. They arrayed the aircraft in parallel lanes, three abreast, plus a fourth flying above the other three. And they positioned the more slowly moving planes very carefully in the armada lanes so as not to slow those that were faster. Plans called for seven different prescribed air speeds in Varsity, depending on the plane and its load: British converted Stirling and Halifax bombers towing Horsas and Hamilcars; Dakotas tugging Horsas; C-47s carrying British paratroopers; C-47s carrying American paratroopers; and C-47s towing either one or two Wacos.

Sergeant Martin Boris Wolfe, radio operator in the 81st TCS.[1]

It had been estimated in November 1944 that the Luftwaffe's maximum 24-hour effort against 'Varsity' would be 365 sorties by day and 265 by night. On 16 March 1945 IX TCC rated its capacity as 425 by day and 410 by night. Weak as it was, the Luftwaffe could inflict great damage by night attacks on troop carrier fields during the marshalling period. Action to meet the threat was initiated by IX TCC on 6 March with the result that at least one automatic anti-aircraft battery was stationed at every troop carrier base in France and Ninth Air Force agreed to hold night-fighter units on call during the critical marshalling period after 20 March to defend those airfields.

Responsibility for the 'Varsity' assault area rested on 83 Group RAF, which was to patrol a zone fifty miles deep, bounded by the Lippe, the Rhine and a line touching Emmerich, Enschede, Münster and Hamm. Similar zones to the north and south would be patrolled by 84 Group and the XXIX Tactical Air Command respectively. Fighters of the Eighth Air Force would patrol east of the three zones to intercept enemy aircraft approaching the battle area from other parts of Germany.

The Luftwaffe did have a new and formidable weapon, the jet fighter. About eighty jets had been accumulated during the winter at a group of airfields near Rheine within easy range of the Wesel area. The best way to stop the jets was on the ground. Therefore on 17 March the Eighth Air Force was given the task of bombing the five jet bases and ten others within 25 miles of Wesel which were suitable for jets. This was to be done on 'D-3' or as soon thereafter as weather permitted. Since some damaged fields might be repaired within 36 hours, the bombing was to be repeated on 'D-Day' before 0915, subject to confirmation by 2nd TAF. To make sure no jets got away, fighters of 83 Group RAF would patrol over the jet bases from first light on 'D-Day' until the bombers arrived. On confirmation by 2nd TAF, Eighth Air Force was also to bomb German night-fighter bases just before dark on 'D-Day'. This action, however, was intended to protect the troops on the ground, rather than the troop carriers.

Diversionary feints in the direction of Borkum, an island off the German coast, were to be flown by RAF Coastal Command and certain missions by RAF Bomber Command against targets on the northern edge of the Ruhr had in part a diversionary purpose. These were well suited to draw off interceptors which might be used against the troop carriers. Fifteenth Air Force agreed to send a very large bomber force from Italy against Berlin, Munich and other targets in Central Europe but the direction of approach and the fact that all its objectives were over 300 miles from Wesel make it difficult to regard this effort as diversionary in the strict sense of the word. It may have been meant to discourage redeployment of German fighter units to the western front. A diversionary dummy-dropping mission by RAF Bomber Command was considered but not attempted, partly because that kind of deception was considered useless by day, which was when 'Varsity' would need it most and partly because units previously used in such work were not available.

Flak was the weapon most feared by the planners of 'Varsity' due as much to the nature of the operation as to the weakness of the Luftwaffe. The troop carriers could not fly around the enemy strong points. Those strong points were their objectives. In December the A-3 of IX TCC had warned that anti-aircraft fire might inflict losses such as the command had never before encountered. In March Air Marshal Coningham called flak his chief anxiety. On 19 March intelligence experts reported a very considerable build-up of German anti-aircraft artillery in the 'Varsity' area. The situation had one advantage in that over 2,000 Allied guns were massed within range of the German batteries. Second and Ninth Armies agreed to neutralize flak within range of their field artillery. German batteries further away or masked from artillery fire were to be dealt with by air action. The line dividing the two areas of attack split the drop and landing area approximately in half, providing an opportunity to compare the results of shell-fire and bombardment. Known enemy batteries were to be left strictly alone until 'D-Day' so they would not go into hiding. On the 24th, an hour before the troop carrier columns arrived, medium bombers of the Ninth Air Force and 2nd TAF would begin a half-hour attack on anti-aircraft positions beyond the artillery boundary, using fragmentation clusters and proximity fuses as far as possible to avoid cratering the drop and landing zones. Between the departure of the mediums and the arrival of the airborne missions Allied artillery would hammer flak positions within its sector. Flak-busting fighter-bomber patrols contributed by 83 and 84 Groups and XXIX TAC would arrive at 0930 as the mediums left and would be maintained over the area until 1300 in readiness to silence batteries observed firing on the troop carrier missions.

Interdiction and harassing operations by the Allied air forces between first light on 'D-3' and dawn on 'D-Day' were monumental in size and complexity. On 18/19 March, 66 Lancasters and 29 Halifaxes from RAF training units carried out an operation code-named 'Sweepstake' on Strasbourg in Northern France to draw up German fighters to divert them away from the Main Force which was bombing Wesel just beyond the Rhine in preparation for Montgomery's crossing. One of the Lancasters on 1661 OCU Winthorpe just north of Newark in Nottinghamshire who took part was 'Q-Queenie'. Pilot Officer David 'Mac' McQuitty, a Tasmanian, was second pilot with Flying Officer Paul as skipper. John Joyner, one of the air gunners on 'Queenie' recalled: 'Sweepstake' employed 'Window' which was dropped by the bomb aimer in handfuls according to a pre-arranged plan. I reported a single-engined fighter on our port quarter which I took to be a Focke Wulf 190, but I could have been wrong. I reported it but almost immediately it fell back and disappeared. It was said that fighter aircraft were less likely to attack if their quarry appeared vigilant. Nothing else happened to us before we returned to base. With 'Mac' as skipper, on 23 March we flew our second 'Sweepstake' operation [involving 78 training aircraft on a sweep across France and as far as Mannheim] when we dropped 'Window' at Saarbrücken in support of the main force bombing Wesel just over the Rhine ahead of the alliance.'

On 21 March in morning raids, 1,254 B-26 Marauder and A-20 Havoc bombers of XIX Tactical Air Command in conjunction with aircraft of the RAF and 9th Air Force attacking other targets, bombed ten airfields in north-west Germany, a tank factory at Plauen and a marshalling yard at Reichenbach. Upwards of fifty-one squadrons of RAF Mustangs, Spitfires and Typhoons of Nos. 83 and 84 Groups succeeded in cutting German railway lines at forty-one places. Five Typhoon and three Spitfire squadrons of 84 Group made a successful attack on a camouflaged village near Zwolle, which concealed the depot of German parachute troops and on the same day the same squadrons scored direct hits with rockets and incendiary bombs on the headquarters of the Twenty-Fifth German Army at Bussum in Holland. Meanwhile Bostons, Mosquitoes and Mitchells of 2 Group carried out daylight attacks on seventeen towns close to the Rhine and by night attacked any transport that could be seen. The missions of 21 March were the start of a massive four-day assault on the Luftwaffe, with 42,000 sorties being made over German airspace. On 21 and 22 March, 1,744 Fortresses and Liberators of the Eighth Air Force, escorted by 752 fighters, dumped about 4,000 tons of bombs on the five jet bases and ten other airfields, which they were to put out of action. Almost all the runways attacked were thoroughly cratered. Approximately five bombers and eleven fighters were lost, but reports indicated that at least 62 enemy fighters had been destroyed, most of them on the ground. In 3,471 effective bomber sorties 8,500 tons of bombs were dropped against communications targets. Barracks and other military installations received 6,600 tons of explosive, delivered by 2,090 bombers. In addition to specific bomber missions, fighter bombers swept on armed reconnaissance over the railways and roads, the pilots claimed a total of 215 rail cuts, eighty locomotives, 2,383 rail cars and 318 other vehicles.

On the morning of 23 March fighter-bombers of XIX Tactical Air Command initiated the usual programme of area cover and direct cooperation and kept in the air from first light to dusk. A number of German planes were shot down when the Luftwaffe attempted a slight revival of its aerial campaign against the Third Army. However, fighter-bombers were primarily useful against German gun positions, troop concentrations, command installations and vehicles. US fighter-bombers flew thousands of sorties against German flak positions in the drop zones and protected the long procession of tugs and gliders. Not one plane of any description was lost to air attack during the airborne crossing - an indication both of the effectiveness of the escort and of the success of recent attacks on Me 262 jet aircraft and other airfields by the 8th and 9th Air Forces and the RAF.

Seven squadrons of Mustangs and Spitfires respectively, of Nos. 121 RAF and 126 RCAF Wings of 83 Group attacked anti-aircraft positions beyond the range of the Second Army's artillery. Throughout this period the night fighters of 85 Group RAF made sure that during the hours of darkness the Luftwaffe should not be able to operate. It was so little in evidence, however, that the Group was able to claim the destruction of only two German aircraft.

By rare good fortune 'Varsity' had favourable weather, not only for its grand finale but also for the three days of preparatory air operations but the bombing of flak positions was greatly handicapped by smoke and haze. Although IX Bombardment Division dispatched 433 medium and light bombers (plus eleven carrying 'Window') for that purpose, only 285 bombed their primary objectives and most of them had to rely on 'Oboe' in making their attacks. Of the rest, eight bombed other gun positions, 73 struck at miscellaneous targets and 67 made no attack. In all, 799 tons of fragmentation and thirteen tons of general purpose bombs were dropped on that mission between 0744 and 0904. About the same time 71 medium bombers of 2 Group RAF were dropping 109 tons of bombs on four other anti-aircraft positions. They, too, were hampered by low visibility but claimed hits on two of their objectives.

'For more than a week' recalls Squadron Leader Malcolm Scott DFC a B-25 Mitchell navigator on 180 Squadron in 2 Group, 'the Mitchells and Bostons of 2 Group had been pounding targets in the Rhineland in close support of the 21st Army Group fighting its way to the great river barrier; 22,000 British, Canadian and American casualties had been suffered in clearing the area between the Maas and the Rhine. Xanten, one of 2 Group's earlier targets and more recently the recipient of a devastating night raid by Bomber Command, was now occupied by British and Canadian troops. The last strong bastion of the German troops on the west side had fallen and within a few days the rest of the territory was cleared and the Allied armies stood on the west bank looking at the remains of the Wesel Bridge blown up by the retreating Germans.

'For the six squadrons of 137 and 139 Wings in 2 Group the targets now shifted to the east side of the Rhine. At least two, occasionally three, raids were made each day on marshalling yards, communication centres and bridges, oil dumps, billeting areas and barracks, artillery emplacements and troop concentrations. Some penetrations were deeper to important rail centres, but mostly attacks were concentrated in the Weser-Emmerich-Münster area where 'Plunder', the code name for the overall operation covering the Rhine crossing, was to take place. Maximum effort had been ordered and quite often up to fifteen aircraft per squadron took part instead of the usual dozen aircraft in two boxes of six.

'Montgomery's preparations for the Rhine crossing were, as always, massive and painstaking: troops being ferried to the rear echelons to practice 'boat drill' and the handling of small craft up and down the muddy banks of the River Maas at night in preparation for the real thing. There could be no misleading or attempted feints this time. Within a mile or two, the Germans could estimate where the Allied crossing would be made. As Kesselring wrote, 'The enemy's operations in a clearly limited area, bombing raids on headquarters and the smoke-screening and assembly of bridging materials, indicated their intention to attack between Emmerich and Dinslaken with the point of the main effort on either side of Rees.'

'The only questions facing the enemy were when and how. Always before, the Allies had launched a parachute and glider attack as a prelude to the full force of the main assault. Kesselring could but wait to see where the paras dropped, or so he thought.

'In the meantime, RAF medium bombers and Typhoons and the 9th USAAF Marauders and Thunderbolts carried on with their now familiar role of 'softening up' the area around the chosen points of the great river and the hinterland of the proposed bridgeheads on the east bank. One important road and rail junction town and troop-billeting area was Bocholt, which became the object of almost daily attacks and quickly gained a reputation for providing a very warm reception. On 18 March it was bombed and again two days later. We all got back but with our aircraft and a few aircrew heavily peppered by shrapnel.

'The next morning, 21 March, Bocholt was again listed as the target. On the bombing run No.1 in the box was badly damaged and an air gunner's leg was almost shot away, but the pilot retained control and made an emergency landing at Eindhoven. No.2 in the box received a direct hit as the bombs fell away and virtually disintegrated, taking down No.3, an all-Australian crew, from which one parachute was seen to emerge. This belonged to an air gunner, who, although captured on landing, was freed eight days later by advancing British troops. The pilot of No.4 was severely injured, shrapnel smashing through his right thigh bone, but he managed to retain consciousness long enough to get his aircraft back over friendly territory after bombing, before passing out. The mid-upper gunner then took over the controls and managed, under the pilot's guidance, to crash-land at the first airfield en route without further casualties. The leading aircraft of the second box was seriously damaged by flak, wounding an air gunner, but the pilot pressed on, bombed and led his formation back over the Rhine before breaking away to force-land at Eindhoven. Bocholt deserved its thick red ring on the map as a place to be avoided if possible!

'Of the twelve 180 Squadron Mitchells that had left Melsbroek earlier, only seven returned to base, all with varying degrees of flak damage and some with wounded aboard. Only six aircraft took part in the afternoon show, but the other two squadrons operated 24. The next day they were joined by eleven aircraft on 180 Squadron, attacking an enemy strongpoint near Dingden in the morning and Isselburg in the afternoon. Notification was received of an immediate award of the DSO to the wounded pilot, Pilot Officer Perkins, a CGM to his air gunner, Flight Sergeant J. Hall, who carried out the emergency landing and a DFC to the leading pilot of the second box, Flight Lieutenant Geoffrey Markham Howard-Jones.'

On 23 March the Mitchells and Bostons bombed strong-points near Wesel in the morning and 128 Lancasters of 1 and 5 Groups RAF Bomber Command attacked bridges at Bremen and Bad Oeynhausen and hit both of them, losing two of the Lancasters. Eighty Lancasters of 3 Group dropped more than 400 tons of bombs on the German troops and many strong points were destroyed.

Mosquitoes of 2 Group were heavily engaged all that night against enemy transport opposite the Second and Ninth Army fronts, dropping in all one hundred and thirty-eight 500lb bombs on towns, villages and woods. At Weseke, flames gushed out of the houses and rose to the fantastic height of 1,000 feet.

'On return from a second visit to Isselburg in the late afternoon' adds Squadron Leader Malcolm Scott DFC, we were told at debriefing that this was 'R-Day' and that British, Canadian and American troops would be crossing the Rhine that evening at various points on either side of Wesel and Rees. An early night was suggested and while we slept Bomber Command put in a heavy attack on Wesel.'

At 2230 hours, only a short time before Field Marshal Sir Bernard Montgomery's zero hour, as the 1st Commando Brigade followed by the 51st Highland Division closed in, 195 Lancasters and 23 Mosquitoes of 5 and 8 Groups, known to the Commandoes as 'Arthur Harris and Company, House Removers' followed up the earlier daylight attack with another attack on enemy positions on the northwest side of Wesel only 1,500 yards ahead of the commandoes poised to assault the Rhine. To Commando Major Bartholomew, 'It seemed as if more than mortal powers had been unleashed.' Royal Engineer Corporal Ramsey, with a bridging party on the west bank said, 'It was like fireworks. First a rain of golden sparks as the leading aircraft dropped the markers right over an enormous fire that already lit the town like a beacon. Then we heard the main force. It was a terrific sight. All colours of sparks flying everywhere, red, green, yellow and the fantastic concussion as the bombs went down. On our side of the river the ground shook and we could see waves of light shooting up into the smoke. It was like stoking a fire, the dull red glow burst into flames and it was like daylight.'

Marine Tom Buckingham in 45 Royal Marine Commando recalled: 'Before we crossed, the RAF had a part to play. Spot on 2045 hours, the artillery fire ceased and precisely on time the Pathfinders dropped flares over the town of Wesel, marking the target. More than 200 heavy bombers then plastered the place. We must have had the best ever view of RAF heavies doing their stuff. The ground shook with exploding bombs, but we were surprised to see the Germans fighting back, sending up a barrage of anti-aircraft fire. Then it was our turn. We embarked in Buffaloes (tracked vehicles which could traverse ground or water) and set off across the Rhine. There was little resistance and although some German fire came our way and one craft received a direct hit from a mortar bomb, the landing was relatively unopposed.'

Flight Sergeant Arthur 'Tommy' Thompson and crew on 463 Squadron RAAF at Waddington were one of the first aircraft to bomb. 'Photographs showed that our six and a half tons of bombs were 'spot on' the target markers and we were commended for this. 'Unfortunately we were a minute or so early and we should have delayed our bomb drop. For this we were punished by being sent up the following day on a 1½ hour high level bombing practice; rather harsh we thought.'

'I looked at my watch,' wrote R. W. (Reginald William) Thompson, war correspondent for The Sunday Times in Western Europe.[2] 'It was ten thirty to the minute. A day earlier we had been told that an important key town would be 'blotted'. And now, deluging down out of the sky, an appalling weight of bombs seemed to rip both town and the very earth itself to fragments and at once a great crimson stain of smoke and flame poured up like an open wound so that the puffs of the bursting flak were crimson too and the river seemed the colour of blood.'

Australian born war correspondent Alan McCrae Moorehead, a veteran of war in ten countries, witnessed the bombing from the second floor of a holiday villa on the west bank: 'As we watched, the Pathfinder came in, a single hurrying black moth in the air and he shot his clusters of red flares into the centre of the town, which meant - and how acutely one felt it - that Wesel had just about ten minutes to live. The Lancasters filling the air with roaring and at last the cataclysmic, unbelievable shock of the strike. Great black stretches of the skyline - buildings and trees and wide acres of parkland - simply detached themselves from the earth and mounted slowly upward in the formation of a fountain. As the rubble reached its zenith it suddenly filled with bursting light and a violent wind came tearing across the river...'[3]

No aircraft were lost on the night of 23/24 March due to the lack of German air defences and the work of the Special Duty Squadrons in 100 (Special Duties) Group, which flew 41 RCM sorties. Warrant Officer J. Philipson RAAF and his crew on a 171 Squadron Halifax from North Creake were 'on station' twenty miles west of Wesel carrying out 'Mandrel' jamming and 'Window' duties from 2150 to 2320 hours. 'Great fireworks display as searchlights lit the crossing, laid horizontal and 3,500 guns in a barrage followed the bombing which ended at 2230 hours.'[4] Marine Tom Buckingham recalled: 'The barrage opened up and we set off in single file for the bank of the Rhine. Finding the way was easy because the Royal Artillery had a pair of Bofors guns firing two lines of red tracers to mark our route. We marched under the tracers and thousands of shells screamed over our heads and hit the enemy positions on the far bank.'

In exactly nine minutes, 1,090 tons of bombs went down from 9,000 feet on those troops who had crept back into the ruins to await the British commandoes' attack. The effects on the defenders was devastating; the bombing was completed at approximately 2239 hours and the British Army was crossing the river in assault craft, aided by searchlights before the bombers had left the area. In all, more than 1,500 tons of bombs were dropped in the two attacks - a weight of bombs which had already almost completely wiped out cities eight times the size of Wesel.' A message of appreciation from Montgomery to Sir Arthur Harris was received. It said: 'I would like to convey to you personally and all in Bomber Command my grateful appreciation for the magnificent co-operation you have given us in the battle of the Rhine. The bombing of Wesel last night was a masterpiece and was a decisive factor in making possible our entry into the town before midnight. Please convey my thanks to all your crews and ground staffs.'

'Long before dawn on the 24th, 'R+1'' recalls Squadron Leader Malcolm Scott DFC; 'we were called to attend briefing at 0530. The target was set in the forest of Diersfordter Wald where we would be making the final bombing raid before the airborne assault came in. Our bomb load was six clusters of 20lb

APs. These clusters, large tubular containers, hexagonal in circumference opened at a predetermined height, releasing fifteen fragmentation bombs. In turn, these, dropping on parachutes, exploded approximately fifty feet above the ground - very unpleasant. Bombing was to be under MRCP instructions. The Mobile Radar Control Point ground controller, operating in a caravan a few miles from the target, guided the formations when within range of the release point where the bombs were dropped on his instructions. Bombing by this method was extremely accurate producing an average error of only forty yards. The bombing height was to be between 11,000 and 12,000 feet, approximate heading on bombing run 075, turning right off target after bombing. A mass of information was available and old hands among the navigators had a log sheet already partly completed with all the headings and just filled in the details except the flight plan itself. By 0735 we were checking over our individual equipment in the aircraft and half an hour later we took off leading 'Grey' Box whilst 'Brown' Box tucked in behind as we set course. We picked up our Spitfire escort as we set course for Xanten where we contacted 'Cosycoat', the MRCP controller. Within minutes we crossed the Rhine but the flak was minimal and not particularly accurate. Bomb doors were opened as the pilots followed 'Cosycoat's' instructions on the run in to the target and the six clusters dropped clumsily away from each bomber. Flak was now more accurate but, judged by earlier standards, only moderate. 'Cosycoat' signed us off and took control of another box running in. It all seemed very impersonal as the bombing details were noted in the log and the pilot was given the new course and it was not until we'd made our right turn off the target that I became aware of all the activity taking place below. Even during the Ardennes breakthrough in the snow of the previous December and January I saw nothing to match the scene below us.

'On either side of the river we could see the ripple of flashes from gun batteries and tanks and the occasional puff of dust and smoke as a flurry of shells landed. The little boats (from our height) handled by the Navy were ploughing back and forth across the river and we could see the spans of the demolished bridges lying in the water. Already pontoon bridges were being thrown across the great waterway looking like threads of cotton. We knew, although we couldn't see them, that the Army and Marine Commandos alongside various infantry units were fighting around Rees and Wesel and our tanks were already in action on the east bank, having 'swum' across during the night and early morning. Smoke was still drifting about and we could see Tempests, Typhoons, Mustangs and Thunderbolts diving in to attack enemy positions. We learned afterwards that Churchill was there on a high vantage point with Alan Brooke, Eisenhower and Tedder, but I don't think they got the marvellous view we did.

'As we left the Rhine behind us we could see, coming in from the west, several thousand feet below, the vanguard of the Airborne Divisions. Dakotas, C-46 Commandos and C-47s loaded with paratroopers and their equipment occupied the first waves of the assault, heading three great columns stretching back as far as the eye could see. Following the paratroops came the gliders towed by Halifax, Stirling and Albemarles tugs and of course, the ubiquitous

Dakotas. Our south-westerly course was gradually taking us away from this awe-inspiring sight. We hoped our bombing had been of support and had reduced in some measure the opposition that the Airborne were bound to encounter.

'Our fighter escort left us over Goch and we were all back at base by 1010. There was the inevitable 'turn round' call; the bomb trolleys were waiting to fill the empty bellies of our aircraft as we taxied in. Another briefing was on at 1045 and the Squadron was airborne again by 1250, attacking another strong-point near Brunen. The great colonnade had gone. All that remained of it were masses of 'broken' gliders and splashes of discarded parachutes. Smoke and gunfire were still in evidence, but it was not the same. The morning of 'R-Day + 1' was the only time that I really appreciated to the full our true role in tactical air support.'

On 'D-Day', escort and cover west of the Rhine were provided for the airborne missions by 213 aircraft of 11 Group RAF and by about 330 American fighters under IX Tactical Air Command.[5] Since in most areas relays of fighters were used to maintain protection throughout the operation, no more than a dozen American fighter squadrons and half a dozen from the RAF were guarding the route at any one time. To avoid boundary problems, the RAF fighters kept their patrols on the north side of the troop carrier lanes between Wavre and the Rhine, while the Americans stayed on the south side. East of the Rhine, 83 and 84 Groups had five squadrons on patrol after dawn at altitudes of 5,000 and 12,000 feet over the strip bounded by Wesel, Arnhem, Winterswijk and Dorsten. They added two more at 0930 and kept seven on the watch until after 1300. The Spitfire squadrons which formed the bulk of this force had to be replaced at one-hour intervals because of their limited fuel capacity.[6]

Half an hour after taking off in his Typhoon from airfield B.86, 27-year old Wing Commander Christopher David 'Kit' North-Lewis DFC* of 137 Squadron in 83 Group was shot down near Wesel leading his Squadron in an attack on the fortified village of Krudenburg to the east of Wesel. Born on March 13 1918 into a family of Welsh colliery owners, he was educated at Marlborough, where he performed well in the Officers' Training Corps. Before the outbreak of war he was commissioned into the 2nd Battalion the Queen Victoria's Rifles. Bored with the inactivity of Army service in England, North-Lewis answered an RAF request for Army volunteers to train as pilots. He began flying training in late 1940 and then joined 13 Squadron. On the night of March 30 1942 he was part of a small force of Blenheims sent to bomb German night-fighter airfields in support of the first Thousand Bomber raid on Cologne. North-Lewis evaluated the American-built Tomahawk and Mustang fighters for Army co-operation work and in late 1942 joined 26 Squadron as a flight commander, flying the Mustang. He completed many reconnaissance sorties along the length of the north coast of France, photographing enemy defences. These operations, flown 200-300 yards offshore, provided important information for planning the invasion of Normandy. He also flew many ground attack operations against trains and transport columns in northern France. In March 1943 he was awarded a DFC. He led his squadrons of rocket-firing Typhoon fighters in the fierce fighting during the Normandy campaign and the advance through Holland to Germany. On the Wesel operation he was pulling out of his dive at 500 feet when flak hit his engine. 'I decided to try and reach my own lines which were approximately six miles to the west. When over Wesel, however, my engine stopped; I glided until I was out in the open, put my flaps down and crash-landed on the only bit of flat ground I could see... I made a very smooth landing, not hurting myself at all.'

Setting off, he found a line of white tapes, which he took to have been laid down by commandos on the previous night and followed them in the direction of heavy gunfire towards Wesel, on the east bank of the Rhine. He had gone barely 200 metres, though, when he was challenged by enemy parachutists in a slit trench. 'I walked over to them and found myself to be in the main Rhine defensive trench system of that area. I was warmly shaken by the hand by the first four Germans that I saw and told to get into a small dug-out.' They were not Germans but Austrians and 'wanted to know if they would be well-treated if they surrendered; their main fear being that we would cut their throats.' They even produced a safe-conduct pass signed by General Eisenhower and wanted to know if that would be honoured. North-Lewis was able to assure and to re-assure them on all counts.

With them for much of the day, he watched 'Varsity's mighty airborne assault pass over their heads. Taken away for interrogation he met a very laid-back leutnant who was not in the least bit bothered by the aerial armada, nor even by a squadron or two of Liberators that roared overhead at zero feet. At about 2000 hours the leutnant sent him off to the rear with an escort, but immediately changed his mind when he realised that they were now cut-off and told his prisoner that he was prepared to surrender. Later in the evening another leutnant appeared, altogether of a more warlike disposition, with duelling scars on his cheeks and festooned with weapons and hand grenades. After the newcomer had gone, everyone went to sleep. On the morning of 25 March, North-Lewis attempted to effect a surrender, but failed to contact a passing Auster aircraft which was spotting in the area. Tearing up white towels he spelt out the message 'RAF HAVE HUN POW. GIVE ORDERS' and waving the leutnant's vest, managed to attract the attention of the pilot of an American Piper Cub. 'He read my message but instead of dropping written instructions tried to yell them out of the cockpit.' Needless to say, North-Lewis could not hear a word.

'Walking along the trench system he spotted four friendly tanks on the far side of the Rhine and shouted an explanation of his situation to their crews, who said they would send a boat. When after an hour the boat had not appeared North-Lewis found a canvas canoe and paddled across the river to the British lines. Taken to Brigade HQ he told the brigadier that the enemy opposite wished to surrender. His job done, the wing commander went back to his unit, the enemy surrendered and the war moved on.[7]

Another Typhoon pilot, Flight Lieutenant J. Harrison on 193 Squadron RAAF in 146 Wing was shot down and bailed out. He landed among the American glidermen where his tall frame and fair complexion plus the fact he was wearing a German belt led them to believe he was a 'Jerry'. The Americans set him to work unloading ammunition and supplies until he managed to convince them he was Australian. He was given an American armband and a rifle and spent time helping pick off German snipers until British tanks broke through and he got a ride back to his Squadron on the 26th.

Additional fighter cover south of Wesel was provided by XXIX TAC, which had one fighter squadron on duty from 0630 to 1000 and three during the airborne assault for a total of 72 sorties. All the escort and cover sorties were uneventful. Only a few German aircraft were seen and all kept their distance. During the airborne assault, flak positions in the vicinity of the drop and landing areas were attacked by fighter-bombers of 2nd TAF. Seventeen British aircraft were lost in this anti-flak operation.

Working south of Wesel along the exit route from the southern zones and occasionally attacking guns in the assault area was the 406th Fighter Group from XXIX TAC. This group made 48 sorties in relays of twelve[8] and lost three aircraft but claimed hits on 36 gun positions. As in 'Market' the task of hunting out mobile flak batteries was difficult and dangerous; low-flying decoys had to coax the gunners into revealing their position. Besides protecting the troop carriers with air cover and anti-flak patrols 2nd TAF provided all air support in the battle waged by the airborne troops. Its light bombers and fighter bombers made 412 sorties against prearranged targets, including three German headquarters. Operating partly from 'cab rank' and partly on special request, 254 rocket-firing Typhoons gave close support. Meanwhile, fighters prowling north and east of the assault area flew 212 sorties on armed reconnaissance. Another 180 aircraft made regular reconnaissance flights. East of Münster, the Eighth Air Force made 1,158 sorties during the day in fighter sweeps against air and ground targets. Its pilots intercepted a formation of twenty German fighters about noon and another of thirty about 1530 hours and claimed to have destroyed 53 enemy aircraft in combat. The intercepted formations, which were both headed west, probably represented feeble efforts at air action against 'Varsity'. Some of the sweeps were directed against ground transportation and reportedly destroyed eight locomotives and 132 other vehicles.

The comparative failure of the efforts made by 2nd TAF and XIX Tactical Air Command to quell the anti-aircraft fire of the enemy was in part the cause of the glider casualties on D-Day. The assault was begun by the RAF and American medium bombers, who together dropped 550 tons of 500lb and fragmentation bombs on chosen gun posts. None of them was hit, though the concentration of bombs round several of the batteries were good. The next phase was carried out by Typhoons, which attacked these and similar positions in the dropping zones or near them with rockets, cluster bombs and 20 mm cannon shells. Their activities had to be curtailed owing to the premature arrival of the 6th Airborne Division. During the landing itself there were as many as sixty Typhoons in the air over the landing zones and an average of thirty-seven remained in their neighbourhood throughout the day. The smoke and dust from Wesel made it hard for the pilots to see their targets which were, in any case, extremely small. Only one light anti-aircraft gun was directly knocked out and the crew of one 88mm. gun in a pit were killed by a fragmentation bomb. Many other gun positions showed signs of damage, but that was all. Subsequent statements by prisoners of war make it clear that the German gunners were not unduly perturbed by the assaults of the fighter-bombers. What filled them with dismay was the sudden arrival of the 6th Airborne Division, who appeared in thousands in the air above them.

The armed reconnaissance and close support sorties, flown by Nos. 131,132 and 145 Wings of 84 Group and in the afternoon, by Nos. 121 and 124 Wings of 83 Group also did not achieve any very great result; but there were but few targets to attack. The enemy showed small desire to use the roads and apart from an occasional trickle of cyclists or a lorry towing a gun, there was little at which to fire.

The close support work called for by the 'contact cars' of 21st Army Group was carried out by 83 Group. These were more successful, for in this instance the targets were designated by the Army and the enemy in them were active in defence. The Typhoons were presently joined by 2 Group who attacked three medium gun positions south of Isselburg with good results. The reconnaissance missions made a valuable contribution to the success of the assault. Their photographs and signals provided targets for the artillery.[9]

Another innovation was the employment by the Royal Air Force of two Forward Visual Control Posts which were flown in with the 6th Airborne Division. As a result of their actions directing fighter support sixteen enemy tanks were knocked out by aircraft under their control.

On 'D-Day' 1,452 B-17s and B-24s escorted by 95 fighters dropped slightly over 4,000 tons more. In the morning they hit the jet fields again and during the morning and afternoon they hammered a dozen additional bases, mostly night-fighter fields. Photographs showed that all the targets were badly cratered and apparently out of operation. Somehow the Germans did put jet fighters in the air on 'D-Day', but they were a mere handful of survivors flying not as units but as individuals. The price of the 'D-Day' attacks on airfields was eight bombers all of which, so far as is known, fell victim to flak rather than the Luftwaffe.

Certain bombing missions on 'D-Day' were primarily interdictory. In a morning attack on the edge of the Ruhr, 506 Halifaxes and Lancasters of RAF Bomber Command dropped over 1,900 tons of bombs on marshalling yards at Sterkrade, troops near Gladbeck and industrial plants near Bottrop and Dortmund, in an operation which was at once diversionary, strategic and interdictory. That afternoon 317 medium bombers of IX Bombardment Division were sent on a turnaround mission with the dual purpose of finishing off bridges at Colbe, Pracht and Vlotho under the Vandenberg plan and hitting Borken, Bocholt and Dorsten, these latter being among the twelve targets originally selected for interdiction on behalf of 'Varsity'. The bridges were hit and smashed by 173 of the 202 bombers dispatched against them. For some reason Borken and Bocholt were not attacked, but Dorsten and secondary targets at Stadtlohn, Aalten and Dulmen were severely damaged by 120 tons of bombs dropped by one hundred aircraft between 1500 and 1531. Brunen and Raesfeld, two more of the original twelve interdiction targets, were also hit on the 24th by 66 medium bombers of 2nd TAF with 98 tons of bombs. Troop concentrations in Brunen, which were only five miles east of the

Diersfordter Wald would have been in a particularly favourable position for a counterattack against the airborne.

At 1700 hours on 23 March Field Marshal Montgomery's Twenty-first Army Group launched a tremendous artillery barrage against the sector just east of the Rhine with intense fire sweeping through landing zones and drop zones. At 2100 hours the barrage lifted and under cover of darkness British Commandos opened the assault against Wesel. At 2200 the British VII Corps attacked. At 2330 the British XXX Corps joined the battle. Four and a half hours later, before dawn, General Simpson's US Ninth Army attacked south of the Lippe Canal. It had begun. The drive for Germany's throat was on! By dawn, nine small bridgeheads had been torn out of German hands across the Rhine in the Emmerich-Wesel area and the stage was now set for the aerial armada of Troop Carrier to descend in a vertical flanking movement against the enemy's east bank fortifications as the main Allied forces engaged him frontally.[10]

It was on 13 March that two British infantry divisions took up station along the west bank of the Rhine: the 52nd (Lowland) Division, specially trained in Scotland for mountain warfare but whose first actions against the enemy had been on the flattest possible land in the Schelt Estuary, prior to the opening up of the port of Antwerp for Allied shipping, was occupying a front from Buderich to Vynen - about ten miles as the crow flies, but with two loops in the river and with the town of Xanten on the west bank and the even more important town of Wesel opposite, on the side of the river occupied by the enemy. The division was to be the eyes and ears of XII Corps commanded by Lieutenant General Sir Neil Methuen Ritchie DSO MC while, extending to the north, the 3rd Infantry Division was given a similar role on behalf of XXX Corps commanded by Lieutenant General Sir Brian Horrocks DSO MC.

The work of the two divisions was wide and varied in the tense situation that prevailed throughout the ten days the 'watching' brief was followed. No one knew the real strength of the German forces on the other side of the river or what action they might take at any time.

The Rhine at Xanten is between 300 and 400 yards wide, with a current flowing about six feet per second; the flood bank to which the town of Xanten extends is some 300 yards from the river and the total gap was sufficient cushion effectively to separate the opposing forces, causing each side to be unaware of the other's positions and activities. What surprisingly little air reconnaissance there was apparently did not disclose details of troop movements or their numbers. Nor was anything known about their morale.

Xanten's church tower was a valuable observation post with a panoramic view of the eastern side of the Rhine and the Westphalian plain beyond, but the glimpse of a truck or two, or the odd motorcyclist, was about all the intelligence that could be gathered from this vantage point. The German soldiers were obviously well dug in and hidden; the movements that had to take place were made at night or under cover of smoke. Over the ten days leading up to 'D-Day' the tower and its spire gradually gathered more and more holes from hits and near-missing shells. It seemed rather odd that the Germans did not put a more concentrated effort into taking out the Xanten tower, as the British artillery apparently had little difficulty in bringing down the church towers at Wesel and Bislich on the opposite bank.

The divisional artillery main brief was to make ready for the great bombardment that was to precede the crossing, preparing for themselves the most intricate of fire plans. This is not to say that the gunners missed any chance of firing at signs of movement on the other side. It was dry that spring and moving trucks threw up clouds of dust. All roads on the west side carried the ominous signs: 'DUST MEANS DEATH' - indeed, it sometimes did, as gunners on both sides were playing a similar deadly game. At other times, when the smokescreens were allowed to clear, the gunners would stage a dummy bombardment in an attempt to draw enemy retaliation so the gun positions could be pin-pointed, usually without success, for both sides quickly learned the finer points of the new chess game. The smokescreen was intermittent during the early stages of the watch on the Rhine and was continuous between dawn on 21 March and 1700 hours on 23 March.

For the Royal Engineers Field Companies of the 3rd and 52nd Divisions it was a hectic, tiring and, at times, dangerous period. Theirs was the responsibility to lay tracks to the river for the boats and amphibious vehicles which were to carry the assault troops; to tape routes beyond the flood bank which would be followed by the infantry, routes that were marked at intervals by small cycle-type battery lamps, masked and pointing away from the river so they could not be seen by the enemy. This work had to be done in silence under cover of darkness or smokescreen. The smoke was a mixed blessing, it gave a degree of protection but it was smelly and made the chest ache; it also attracted attention from the German gunners who became aware that something was going on which was not intended for the eyes of their observation posts. Sometimes machine guns opened up on fixed lines of fire or in haphazard sweeps, but bullets caused less concern than the 88 mm airburst shells which Allied soldiers had learned to respect since the earliest days in Normandy and which were to dog forward-area troops until the end of hostilities.

The infantry of the watching divisions had several tasks, none particularly spectacular but nevertheless very necessary. One was to see that no enemy crossed over by boat or raft. This was German soil and, apart from the obvious possibility of reconnaissance parties slipping in from the east bank, it was important to see that no individual agents carried back vital intelligence in the other direction. An infantry battalion could have as many as fourteen section posts at the water's edge. At dusk the men made their silent way to the river to watch through the hours of darkness. It had to be done in complete silence without even the meagre luxury of a smoke. Occasionally deserters would find their way across and, if they survived the first sighting by the sentries, they would be led back to battalion headquarters for interrogation about the disposition and strength of the German forces.

After accumulating such local knowledge and having the place to themselves, it was inevitable that the watchers on the Rhine should feel a little resentful of the newcomers, whose numbers were building up daily. Traffic was constantly increasing and the huge piles of stores, parks of vehicles and the presence of Royal Navy personnel removed any doubt as to the imminent course of events. War plays tricks with time. To the watchers, the vigil on the Rhine seemed far longer than its actual span of ten days. It was obvious that 'D-Day' could not be far away, the DUKWs, Buffalos (12-ton amphibious vehicles known as 'Alligators' to the Americans) and naval craft on trailers parked in numerous assembly areas and in the side streets of Xanten confirmed this fact, but few had an inkling when the moment would come.

The front on which Operation 'Plunder', the ground assault across the Rhine, was launched extended twenty-five miles, from Emmerich in the north to Rheinberg in the south. Some 1,300 guns of the British Second Army were to take part in the prelude to the assault and a total of 60,000 tons of ammunition had to be transported and dumped in readiness for the gunners' use. To build the replacement bridges over the Rhine, 30,000 tons of equipment were needed. Altogether, military stores of all kinds totalled a quarter of a million tons. Throughout 23 March concentrations of men, equipment and vehicles built up behind the continuous smokescreen 'in an atmosphere resembling some vast bizarre fairground in fog'. At around 1730 hours smoke dischargers were shut off; and at 1800 hours precisely, the entire artillery of the Second British Army and the Ninth US Army opened fire, their shells and 'magic carpets' of rockets passing over the heads of the assemblies of men. It was the greatest assault of shellfire since 'D-Day' in Normandy. It was a breathtakingly fearful but, at the same time, exhilarating experience, affording a modicum of comfort in that it would surely soften the enemy's capability and will to fight in the forthcoming battle. The colossal barrage was to be kept up until 0945 hours the next morning, with pauses only in sectors where the assaulting forces were sounding out the strength of the enemy defences.

At 0500 hours on 23 March, the weather being so fine, British tank crews in a forest near Xanten were told that the crossing of the Rhine had been retimed for that night. E. Mallpress in the 44th Royal Tank Regiment, part of the 4th Armoured Brigade, was one of a number of tank crews who 'swam' their amphibious DD tanks across the Maas for the last time on 21 March and lined up for loading on a long line of tank transporters. On 22 March at dawn the 4th Armoured Brigade moved off, riding where they could, back into Germany and to the forest near Xanten, which was reached about midnight. They could not hope that their landing on the other side of the Rhine would be unopposed and Mallpress remembered 'a good deal of noise' as they moved off. Later that night a tremendous barrage was opened, the noise reinforced by RAF bombing of the far bank. Mallpress would never forget what followed, as he was unprepared for it and the memory never fades. 'Hundreds of planes and gliders appeared from the west and what seemed like thousands of paratroopers filled the sky; it was a truly unforgettable sight. Casualties there were and I recall my shock when I first saw ranks of the dead laid out by the road as we passed. Gunfire continued till nightfall and the sky was criss-crossed by lines of red tracer. A heavy, but mercifully short, barrage of artillery landed shells amongst us and our supporting infantry from the 53rd Welsh Division - shells fired by our own RHA who were very vociferously and quickly stopped.'

The artillery bombardment began at 1700 under a precise schedule. Canadian Highland Light Infantry Private Glen Tomlin, aged 21, from Clinton, Ontario described 'an awful noise, the ground just shook, everything shook... The guns started off and then you heard the shells come over and they whistle different sounds for different shells.' As the guns increased their tempo, the sound became a 'continuous roar.' Heavy artillery supported the Allied 21st Army Group crossing of the Rhine during the predawn hours of 24 March. Canadian artillery units joined in the barrage, including their 17-pounder antitank guns and the Cameron Highlanders of Ottawa Machine Gun Regiment, with their powerful Vickers machine guns, chattered with their two-mile range. British and Canadian gunners hammered pre-designated ground targets, which included German bunkers dug in on the riverbank, with a massive volume of fire. The 4th Canadian Light Anti-Aircraft Regiment alone fired 13,896 rounds.

Trooper Albert Bellamy of the 51st Highland Division recalled: 'On the afternoon of 23 March at 5 pm a terrible artillery barrage from numerous guns commenced to pound enemy positions inland. It was the biggest concentration of artillery I have seen over here. The barrage was augmented by several batteries of rockets which went off, hundreds at a time, with a terrifying roar. We, the infantry, boarded the 'Buffalos' at 1900 hours and at 1915 we moved off to the starting point which was one and a half miles from the river. Our troop leader was first and I was in the second craft manning the gun. We reached the river a few minutes before 2100 and at exactly 9 o'clock the first 'Buffalo' entered the water and the rest followed. We manoeuvred into formation and headed for the opposition shore, which was just discernible through the mist. Our hearts were anywhere but in the right place, for we did not know what to expect, but the expected onslaught did not materialise and we touched down at exactly 2103 - three minutes which seemed like three years. We had a very nasty moment when the enemy sent up a brilliant flare and brightly illuminated the whole river, but nothing happened. The operation was a success and took the enemy completely by surprise.

'The flag of the Battalion was carried in the leading craft and was the first flag to cross the Rhine in WW1; thus history repeated itself. The flag is moth eaten and held together by netting. The colours are brown, red and green and mean 'Through the mud and the blood to the green fields beyond'.

'We waited until the infantry had disembarked on the river bank and then returned to the opposite bank. Owing to the bank being very steep at this side, several futile attempts were made to climb it. Meanwhile the Germans had got our range and there were several near misses by mortar and shell fire. Then, after a few minutes we then managed to reach the top of the bank and the proceeded to the loading area, where we loaded up with Bren carriers and other necessary equipment. A few shells dropped in the bridgehead but little if any damage was done. We then crossed the Rhine a second time and proceeded, 300 yards inland to the unloading area. Everything had been arranged so carefully and the organisation was marvellous. On the return trip our craft brought back twenty prisoners - the first to be taken in the operation. For the next three days we worked a ferry service without either rest or sleep, taking across vital supplies until the first bridge was built. Meanwhile a large ferry was taking across tanks to support the advancing infantry.'

Bill Robertson crossed the Rhine at 2100 hours on 23 March, four days after his 19th birthday. 'We crossed the Rhine in amphibious vehicles called buffalos with were run by the Northamptonshire Yeomanry. We were half way across when our tracks locked and we went around in a circle and drifted. We all thought we were going to have to jump or swim for it, but at the last minute the tracks started up again. We were amongst the first people to cross the Rhine. I will never forget an incident in the Netherlands in a place called Kaatsheudal where we were instructed to fix bayonets and charge. I thought this practice ended in WWI but we charged nonetheless. We were assisted in taking the village by Dutch resistance fighters who pointed out the Germans. This was, nevertheless, something of a feat for teenage soldiers.'[11]

In contrast to that of the Highlanders to the north, the Commandoes crossing went almost undetected and they were able to infiltrate the outskirts of Wesel, where the German 180th Division was ready to defend the town. Fifteen minutes later, 200 RAF Lancaster bombers flew in and 'neutralised' the town!

The Commandos were so close to the bombing that they narrowly escaped destruction themselves from the thousand tons of high explosive that were dropped. Many boats were hit by fire. Six Commando's Regimental Sergeant Major Woodcock had three boats shot from under him before he could make a successful crossing. But, attacking immediately, the commandos were able to take possession of almost all of what was left while the surviving defenders were still dazed. Over the radio came the message from the Commandos: 'Noisy blighters, aren't they? We have taken the position and have met no trouble.'

The brigade established its command post only fifty yards from where the Germans had their headquarters. During the night the defenders of the HQ fought as hard as they could; even Major General Deutch, commanding the Volkssturm garrison in the town, tried to shoot it out from behind trees in his garden. He was shot dead by a 6 Commando lance corporal when he said he would only surrender to an officer of equal rank.[12]

By dawn the Commandos had taken 400 PoWs and 45 Royal Marine Commando was dug in at a large factory full of hundreds of thousands of toilet pans. A brigade signals group 'swinging from girder to girder several hundred feet above the Rhine, under spasmodic fire,' managed to lay a telephone line across the river. The elimination of Wesel was achieved with the 1st Commando Brigade suffering only thirty-six casualties, but the very efficiency of the annihilation was later to cause problems. Rubble resulting from the 'over bombing' made passage through the town impossible until US Engineer bulldozers had done their job and bridges had been thrown over some of the craters. Furthermore, the ruined buildings provided excellent hides for snipers - remnants of the 180th Division - making the town and the crossing of the Rhine at Wesel a dangerous undertaking for several days.

Around Xanten the 15th (Scottish) Division, under Major General Colin Muir Barber made ready to spearhead Lieutenant General Sir Neil Ritchie's

XII Corps on to the east bank. The division's H-Hour was 0200 hours and already news of the adversities encountered by their compatriots in the 51st (Highland) Division to the north and of the Commandos' success at Wesel, was filtering through to the men. It was therefore with mixed feelings that the Scots were shepherded into their craft by the Bank Control Group, which had been specifically organised to despatch troops and vehicles from the west bank at the various crossing points. It was an intensely dramatic moment for each man, as he boarded an allotted craft to set out over the mighty Rhine towards the unknown. The LCMs and Buffalos were guided across the river by tracer bullets fired on fixed lines from the 'home' bank and a lull in the bombardment revealed it to be a fine, still and moonlit night. The first wave of Scots 'jumped out on the river meadow to the skirl of the pipes', as one eye-witness historian put it. Resistance was nothing like that being experienced by the other Scottish Division on the left and fighting thrusts were made in the direction of the Diersfordter Wald, where German artillery batteries were hidden, waiting for the dawn light and the opportunity to discourage the build-up landings on the east bank, over which they had a commanding view.

Not everyone who went over the Rhine in the first waves was an infantryman. Beach Masters and their staff had to be conveyed; there were Artillery Fire Control Officers and the odd War Correspondent who needed a lift over so he could claim to his editor to have been in the van of the landings.

Then there was the occasional Civil Affairs Officer with a case full of notices printed in German instructing the civilian population what to do under the Military Government of an occupying power. The Bank Control Group sorted out the 'odd bods', issuing priorities for places in the craft bound for the other side.

There were also reconnaissance sections of engineers whose job it was to try to ensure there were mine-free tracks for the DD and craft-borne tanks and to tape the safe routes. One such section, finding themselves isolated from compatriots, were exploring a narrow track from the river when a machine gun ahead suddenly opened up pinning the sappers in a ditch. Without the means of retaliation - they carried mine-detectors and a walkie-talkie instead of rifles - there was no alternative to sitting it out and waiting for some friendly support. It eventually came. *What are you's doing down there you's dozey barsteds?* asked the infantry platoon sergeant in a strong Glasgow accent. Somewhat shamefacedly the sappers emerged from the ditch, only to return quickly to their hide as the sergeant fell beside them with a bullet in his thigh.

Anti-tank mines were what the sappers sought, but there were other nasty things to look out for: little wooden boxes, packed with explosives that the mine-detectors could not pick up. These anti-personnel mines did not harm tanks and they often had little effect on wheeled vehicles, but they could and did, blow a man's leg off. These weapons were first encountered in Holland a month or so earlier when it was realised that the only way of finding them was to probe with a bayonet and there was not much time to do that on the east bank of the Rhine!

Soon prisoners were being taken as small groups of Germans surrendered to the invaders, turning from a trickle to a steady stream, to be conveyed back to the west bank together with the wounded. LCMs and commandeered launches flying the white ensign, scuttled back and forth across the river giving the impression that the Royal Navy had been familiar with this stretch of water for a long time. At a Field Hospital established behind the flood bank near Xanten, stretcher-bearers in khaki battledress and in Wehrmacht field-grey were bringing wounded into its tents, while both British and German doctors carried on their work of mercy. Prisoners-of-war cages had been set up, their occupants looking shocked and numbed.

Prime Minister Winston Churchill had stayed the night of 23/24 March at Montgomery's Tactical Headquarters near Venlo. 'As 10 am approached' wrote John 'Snowy' Wiley 'Churchill and Montgomery, having enjoyed a sumptuous breakfast under the chandeliers, went out on the balcony to witness the great armada of planes flying over their heads. I hope they were suitably impressed as my mates and I would gladly have exchanged places with any one of them.' Churchill with Field Marshal Sir Alan Brooke (Chief of Imperial General Staff) and Field Marshal Montgomery (Commander of 21 Army Group) were at the 'grandstand' on the flood bank of the Rhine near Xanten when Churchill suddenly jumped up with boyish enthusiasm. 'They're coming, they're coming!' he shouted. It was 1000 hours on 'D-Day' of Operation 'Plunder' (24 March) and the Allied airborne attack over the Rhine had started on time. With triumphant majesty the paratroop-carrying aircraft, gliders and tugs of the XVIII Airborne Corps flew in from the south-west at 2,500 feet, but some at no more than 500 feet.

Winston Churchill, watching the massive assault at the 9th Army's crossing point at Rheinberg saw it all - the artillery barrage, the airborne forces fly overhead, the American and British infantry go across the Rhine. Later in the day Churchill himself crossed the Rhine with Montgomery in a US Navy craft, touring the battlefield, avoiding German artillery fire. Churchill left in Montgomery's autograph book at his Tactical Headquarters: 'The Rhine and all its fortress lines lie behind the 21st Group of Armies. Once again they have been the hinge on which massive gates revolved. Once again they have proved that physical barriers are vain without the means and spirit to hold them. A beaten army, not long ago master of Europe, retreats before its pursuers. The goal is not long to be denied to those who have come so far and fought so well under proud and faithful leaderships. FORWARD ON WINGS OF FLAME TO FINAL VICTORY.'

Endnotes Chapter 2

1   He authored *Green Light! A Troop Carrier Squadron's War From Normandy To The Rhine;* Centre for Air Force History Washington DC 1993.

2   Born in 1904; educated at Merchant Taylors' School; Thompson worked as a Lloyds marine broker from 1921-1925. He began to write professionally while travelling in Argentina and Australia and worked as an author and feature writer on UK depressed areas, 1930-1939. He worked as a special correspondent with *The Morning Post* for which he covered the Gran Chaco War 1935-1936; on the outbreak of war in 1939 he joined the fire brigade and enlisted in the ranks in 1940. Promoted to captain in 1941, he transferred to the Intelligence Corps for training. In 1944 he worked as a censor and a report writer on the mental and physical health of the 'D' Day forces. Later in 1944 he was released from the Army to work as war correspondent for *The Sunday Times*.

3   Born in Melbourne, Australia on 22 July 1910, Moorehead was educated at Scotch College, with a BA from Melbourne University. He travelled to England in 1937 and became a renowned foreign correspondent for the *Daily Express*. During World War II he won an international reputation for his coverage of campaigns in the Middle East and Asia, the Mediterranean and Northwest Europe. He was twice mentioned in dispatches and was awarded the OBE. Moorehead died in London on 29 September 1983 and is buried at Hampstead Cemetery, Fortune Green.

4   *Handley Page Halifax From Hell to Victory and Beyond* by K. A. Merrick (Chevron Publishing, 2009).

5   Both IX TCC and FAAA report that 676 American fighters were used as escort and cover for the troop carriers, but that figure appears to include 273 sorties by XIX TAC in the Mainz-Mannheim area more than 150 miles south of the 'Varsity' objectives.

6   In escort, cover and fighter sweeps, 83 and 84 Croups made 900 fighter sorties that day.

7   *RAF Evaders: The Comprehensive Story of Thousands of Escapers and their escape lines, Western Europe, 1940-1945* by Oliver Clutton-Brock (Grub Street, 2009).

8   Widely accepted reports that 121 American fighters flew anti-flak sorties for 'Varsity' have a basis in Ninth Air Force totals, which probably lumped some other missions under that heading.

9   *RAF 1939-45 Vol. 3 The Fight Is Won* by Hilary St. G. Saunders.

10   *DZ Europe: The Story of the 440 Troop Carrier Group.*

11   This story was submitted to the People's War site by Claire White of BBC Scotland on behalf of Bill Robertson.

12   *Operation Plunder and Varsity: The British and Canadian Rhine Crossing* By Tim Saunders.

Chapter 3

'Red on! Green on! Go!'

The beginning of the end, the great airborne invasion of Germany started out in French boxcars dating from the First World War and bearing the well-known inscription '40 hommes et 8 chevaux.' The US 17th Airborne Division was packed in long freight trains and for forty-eight hours we were shuffled all over France. This was to deceive the enemy spies. After two days of this hocus-pocus, our generals decided that both the troops and the German spies were quite tired enough and we arrived at an enclosed camp next to an airfield, sixty miles from the spot from which we started.

At the camp, we had a short time left for the usual pre-invasion cleaning of rifles and consciences. The day before the jump we were briefed and told that we would be jumping, together with an English airborne division, on the other side of the Rhine, right in the heart of the main German defence line.

From North Africa to the Rhine there were too many D-Days and for every one of them we had to get up in the middle of the night. The end of darkness always brought the beginning of death. But this invasion was different. We ate our double portions of pre-invasion fresh eggs at seven in the morning and took off shortly afterwards.

I flew in the lead plane with the regimental commander and I was to be number two man in the jump right behind him. Before boarding the plane, the G-2 major had taken me aside. If anything happened to the Old Man when we got the signal to jump, I was instructed to boot him through the door. It was a very important and comforting feeling.

Our planes flew low over France. Through the open door of the plane the boys watched the landscape of a now peaceful France pass quickly by. Nobody puked; this was a very different invasion.

Thousands of planes and gliders had taken off simultaneously from fields in England and France and we rendezvoused over Belgium. From there we flew on together in tight formation. Our shadows travelled on the roads and streets of the liberated countries and we could see the faces of people waving to us. Even the dogs were fascinated and ran after our shadows. On both sides of us were planes towing gliders and it looked as if someone had spun strings from the Channel to the Rhine and then had hung from them, at intervals of a hundred yards, a lot of toy airplanes.

I put on an act and began to read a mystery story. At 1015 I was only up to page sixty-seven and the red light came on to get ready. For a moment I had the foolish idea of saying, 'Sorry, I cannot jump. I have to finish my story.'

I stood up, made sure that my cameras were well strapped to my legs and that my flask was in my breast pocket over my heart.

We still had fifteen minutes before the jump. I started to think over my whole life. It was like a movie where the projection machine has gone crazy and I saw and felt everything I ever ate; ever did and got to the end of it in twelve minutes flat. I felt very empty and still had three minutes to go. I was standing in the open door behind the colonel. Six hundred feet below us was the Rhine. Then bullets began to hit our plane like pebbles. The green light flashed and I did not have to kick the colonel. The boys yelled Umbriago! I counted one thousand, two thousand; three thousand and up above me was the lovely sight of my open parachute. The forty seconds to earth were hours on my grandfather clock and I had plenty of time to unstrap my camera, take a few pictures and think of six or seven different things before I hit the ground. On the ground I kept clicking my shutter. We lay flat on the ground and nobody wanted to get up. The first fear was over and we were reluctant to begin the second.

Ten yards away were tall trees and some of the men who had jumped after me had landed in them and now were hanging helplessly fifty feet from the good earth.

A German machine-gun opened up at the dangling men. I began a long, loud Hungarian swear and buried my head in the grass. A boy lying near me looked up.

'Stop those Jewish prayers,' he called, 'They won't help you now.'

At 11 am I had two rolls of film taken and I lit a cigarette. At 1130 I took the first swig from my flask. We were firmly established on the other side of the Rhine. Our regiment had gotten the guns out of the wrecked gliders and we reached the road we were supposed to occupy and hold. We lost many of our men, but this was easier than Salerno or Anzio or Normandy. The Germans of those campaigns could have murdered us here, but these Germans were beaten. In the afternoon we made our junction with the other regiments. I closed my cameras.

War photographer Robert Capa. Born in Budapest in 1913, at 22 he travelled to Spain to photograph the Spanish Civil War and soon established a reputation as one of the greatest war photographers in history. On D-Day, 6 June 1944, he went ashore with the first wave at 'Omaha' Beach. On 24 March 1945 he was dropped by parachute, along with the men of the 513th PIR, 17th Airborne Division, who spearheaded Operation 'Varsity'. On 25 May 1954 in French Indochina Capa was the first American photographer to die in what would become the Vietnam War.

On the afternoon of 23 March 1931, a group of boys were playing alongside a creek that ran through the old St. David's Golf Club in Chester County, Pennsylvania. They dawdled about until one boy suggested that they build a torch. A sturdy stick was secured, and rags wrapped around one end. One boy produced some matches, but the rags were damp and refused to ignite. Another boy ran home and returned with a bottle of rubbing alcohol. As they soaked the rags with alcohol, someone struck a match, igniting not only the rags but the alcohol in the bottle. A jet of fire shot out of the bottle, directly into the face of a boy named Jay Moorehead Phillips. Fortunately, Phillips shielded his eyes. But his face and hands were badly burned, and his sweater was set afire. He was knocked onto his back and lay on the ground, burning. As his friends stood by, paralyzed with fear, Phillips screamed at them, 'Throw me into the creek!' They dragged him into the creek, extinguishing the flames. Several of them then carried him home. His mother summoned the family doctor, who gave Phillips a morphine injection and rushed him to Bryn Mawr Hospital. With the help of the nurse who visited him daily, Phillips was soon on the road to recovery. As the trauma of the incident faded, Jay Phillips liked to joke that 24 March 1931 was the day that 'God had His chance to take me and decided not to.' There was no way he could know that exactly fourteen years to the day later, in a big field along the Rhine, God would have another chance and, this time, would decide to take Jay Phillips.

Having been born in 1920 into a family of artists Phillip's parents were particularly relieved that none of their son's injuries had hurt his ability to be an artist: his eyesight was spared and the tendons in his right hand were undamaged. His father, C. Gager Phillips, was a successful commercial artist whose work included a 1933 *Saturday Evening Post* cover, *Tea for Grandpa* that featured his then seven-year-old daughter, Leaugeay and his father, Dr. John Leaugeay Phillips.[1]

But it was Jay Phillips who possessed an exceptional gift. He started painting at nine and sold his first painting when he was twelve. In 1938 Phillips left school at the Episcopal Academy to work for the artist William Tefft Schwartz, assisting Schwartz as he painted murals for the upcoming 1933 New York World's Fair. Soon, as a student at the Philadelphia Museum School of Industrial Arts, Phillips was painting portraits for lawyers, doctors and other professionals in Philadelphia. He was always setting goals for himself. A sign posted on his bedroom wall in big block letters read, simply, 'I CAN AND I WILL.' It was this determination that would make Phillips a pilot. Just five weeks after Pearl Harbor, on 13 January 1941, he enlisted in Wayne, Pennsylvania as a private in the Pennsylvania National Guard, the 166th Field Artillery Battalion and was sent to Camp Shelby, Mississippi for training. He hated it. What he really wanted to do was fly. But the academic standards for flight training were demanding and Phillips had not completed high school. So he began a rigorous course of study on his own. His studies paid off and in 1943 he joined a class of cadets for primary flight training. He graduated, went on to complete advanced flight training and then qualified as a multi-engine pilot. He was sent overseas for combat duty and on 2 July 1944 Lieutenant Moorehead 'Jay' Phillips was assigned as a C-47 pilot to the 47th Troop Carrier Squadron in the 313th Troop Carrier Group at Folkingham.

In September 1944 he carried paratroopers during Operation 'Market Garden' and was awarded the Air Medal. On one flight, the landing gear of his C-47 collapsed, but Phillips walked away from the crash-landing without a scratch. In late 1944 Phillips' unit began to receive a new transport aircraft, the Curtiss C-46, which unfortunately, had a poor reputation. Known officially as the 'Commando,' the C-46 had earned several regrettable nicknames, including 'The Curtiss Calamity' and even 'The Flying Coffin.' The C-46 was bigger than the C-47 and could carry double the number of paratroopers that a C-47 could carry. The exit time for the paratroopers was the same, as the C-46 had two exit doors, one on each side of the plane. Pilots of 47th who initially flew the C-46 found it easy to handle, but admitted that the plane was somewhat 'fragile' and feared that it would 'not stand the wear and tear and rough handling often necessitated by field conditions.' And, lacking self-sealing petrol tanks, the C-46 would catch fire easily when hit. On 20 March Phillips and his fellow pilots at Achiet le Grand airfield began to hear rumours of an impending mission. Two days later, the 47th was put on alert for Operation 'Varsity', scheduled for 24 March. It would be the first airborne operation where the C-46 'Commando' was used for dropping paratroopers.

By this time, Lieutenant Philip Sarrett in the 313th Troop Carrier Group had flown enough missions and could have sat out this final operation. In 1942 in Ada, Oklahoma his sister, Margaret Sarrett was taking a tennis lesson when her brother came by the court to say goodbye as he left to serve in World War II. They both attended East Central State College in Ada. Philip was in a fraternity and Margaret was in a sorority. They had a lot of dances together. A popular person, a well-rounded young man with many interests, while at East Central State, Philip was able to pursue a new passion; he wanted to fly. East Central State offered classes through the Civilian Pilot Training Program, a government initiative designed to increase the country's pool of aviators. Sarrett signed up for ground school and basic flying lessons. He eventually took an advanced flying class in Texas over the summer. On several occasions, Margaret went flying with her brother to practice his landings. Sometimes, Philip would turn off the engine to perform a 'dead-stick' landing. Margaret was 'scared to death!'

But Philip was always calm. Then came that fateful Sunday in December of 1941. 'We got out of church and we heard about the bombing of Pearl Harbor' Margaret recalled. 'And Mother said, 'Philip, you know what that means.' And he said, 'Yeah, I sure do.'

Sarrett entered the Army Air Corps and was eventually assigned to the 313th Troop Carrier Group. He participated in Operation 'Husky' and probably flew in support of the invasion of Italy. In May 1944 his unit was transferred to Folkingham. The aircraft he was assigned was C-47D 42-32827, 'Chalk 27', which he christened *Ada Red* in honour of his hometown. Early on the morning of 'D-Day', Philip Sarrett flew *Ada Red* on Mission 'Boston'. The sixteen paratroopers he ferried were from the 508th Parachute Infantry Regiment and they jumped into Drop Zone 'N' near Etienville and Beauzeville-la-Bastille. *Ada Red* was hit by flak and small arms fire, but Philip Sarrett managed to fly *Ada Red* back to Folkingham. In the following months Philip Sarrett flew a number of missions, mainly to resupply troops on the ground. 'He had been real homesick' said his sister 'But they asked for volunteers and he volunteered for the Wesel mission.'

The day before Operation 'Varsity', the pilots of the 47th were briefed on their mission. The 72 C-46s in the 313th Troop Carrier Group - 35 in the lead serial, 34 in the second and three substitutes flying many miles behind them - were to drop the 513th Parachute Infantry Regiment and the 466th Parachute Field Artillery Battalion, 2,071 men with 64 tons of supplies and equipment, over DZ 'X', which, set against the east side of the Diersfordter Wald about 1½ miles east-northeast of DZ 'W' and 2½ miles north-northwest of Wesel, was a rough quadrangle, 2,500 yards long from east to west and about 1,000 yards wide, consisting mostly of small, flat fields. The double-track railway to Wesel ran just inside its western boundary, making an excellent checkpoint for the drop. For more than a mile before reaching the zone the troop carrier formations would have to fly over the central portion of the forest. The 49th Troop Carrier Squadron would lead in Serial A-5, followed by the 29th Troop Carrier Squadron. The next serial, A-6, would be flown by the 48th Troop

Carrier Squadron and, as last in the line, the 47th Troop Carrier Squadron.

'On the night of D minus one (23 March)' wrote Milton Dank, 'the briefings began. The combat crews of the 439th Troop Carrier Group assembled in the town theatre at Châteaudun, south of Paris. The doors were guarded by military police to prevent any unauthorized personnel from entering. Crowded into the orchestra and balcony seats of the small hall were the pilots, co-pilots, crew chiefs, radio operators and glider pilots. There was a nervous chatter as they waited to learn what their job would be. The briefing was given in a thorough manner by the Operations officer, a major who had celebrated his 28th birthday over Normandy. Using a huge map that filled most of the stage, he reviewed the group and wing assembly plan. After takeoff the next day, the tugs and gliders would form over the airfield and then fly directly to the rendezvous near Pontoise. There they would meet the three other groups of the 50th Troop Carrier Wing. The four groups would fly directly by way of Sainte Quentin to Wavre, where they would join the echelons of two other troop-carrier wings and the British. The flight to the initial points (where the final turn would be made before the run-in to the landing zones) was traced out and the landing zone (LZ 'S') just north of Wesel was pointed out. The flight was to be made at an altitude of 1,000 feet, dropping to 600 feet after leaving the initial point, at which height the gliders would be released.

'The latest intelligence on enemy dispositions in the area was given and it was pointed out that the elaborate preparations and smoke screen on the west bank of the Rhine, as well as the reports by British newspapers, meant that the enemy was not unaware of the coming assault. The weather forecast was favourable: visibility of at least two miles in the Wesel area and four miles elsewhere, with winds of about 10 mph. There would be a thick haze in the early morning, but this would clear before the beginning of the airborne assault, which had been set at ten o'clock the next morning.

'A captain from Intelligence spoke briefly on escape and evasion techniques. He warned the combat crews not to expect the help that they had received in Normandy, southern France and Holland, for here everyone not in an Allied uniform would be an enemy - civilian and soldier alike. He sounded grim.

'Colonel Charles H. Young, the veteran group commander, talked about the necessity of tight formation flying, in order to get the gliders into their landing zone in good shape. He ended by saying, 'I am sure what you are going to do tomorrow will be an important contribution towards a rapid ending of the war.'[2]

The correspondent of the *Chicago Tribune*, Larry Rue, who was to fly the next day in one of the gliders, remembered the crowded hall: 'There were two solemn occasions at this briefing. The first was at the very opening, when the Protestant chaplain came out on the stage and prayed to God to give those going on the mission the strength, the skill and courage successfully and safely to perform their dangerous mission on the morrow. The second solemn occasion was when the Catholic chaplain, Father John Whelan, closed the briefing. He got on the platform in what cannot be described as a perfect military getup. His pants were too long, so they were rolled up over his shoe tops, which were muddy. His hair was closely cropped. He is one of the most popular members of this group and whenever anyone does him a favour he promises to have him elected mayor of Peoria. He stood for half a minute until dead silence reigned and then began: 'O Father, Your mercy and their courage and skill is all they will need.' He blessed everyone and wound up without a break, looking at his wristwatch: 'I want every Catholic present to have complete absolution. We haven't much time, so I wish all Catholics immediately to go up in the gallery for Holy Communion, while the Protestants can conduct their services downstairs.'

'Half of those below went upstairs, while half of those packing the galleries came down. That such a strong religious spirit pervaded that tough gang of boys came as something of a revelation.'

'Actually, it was not so much 'strong religious spirit' that motivated the men, but great respect bordering on fear. Father Whelan was over six feet tall, weighed two hundred pounds and was an amateur boxer. He practiced a form of 'muscular Christianity' that permitted no arguments.

'In the trucks that took them back to the sealed-off airfield, the glider pilots were very quiet. They were thinking of the red dots that had been so liberally sprinkled over the assault sector, each one indicating a known German anti-aircraft unit. Most of them were veterans and they knew that for every flak unit that could be identified from an aerial photograph, there were a dozen or more hidden in haystacks, in farmhouses and elsewhere, which had not been seen. There was a gut feeling that this would not be the 'milk run' that the English newspapers had predicted.

'In the darkness at the back of one truck, a glider pilot spoke thoughtfully. 'My father was here in France in 1918. He was wounded in the Argonne. When he heard that I was going overseas, he wrote to me and said that if I ever got to the Rhine, I should spit in it for him.' There was a pause and then he continued, unsteadily, 'I just hope I have spit left.'

'There was little sleep at any of the airfields that night; the nervous tension and apprehension that always preceded a mission drove away the desire to sleep. Men checked their equipment, cleaned their weapons, or sharpened knives and bayonets. Some wrote letters home, trying to erase from their minds and from their words the thought that this might be a last message. Some felt the need for company and gathered in their tents or rooms to talk quietly about the coming battle. In one squadron the glider pilots gathered around a guitar player, listening to country music. For others there was an overwhelming need to be alone; in solitude they studied the photographs of the landing fields, as if to discover in the lacework of lines or in the various greyish tints the fate that awaited them. There were those who wandered down to the landing strip, where the planes and gliders had been marshalled and checked their loads again and again. There was little margin for error in the loading of a Waco CG-4A; a shift of as little as four inches in the position of a jeep or a cannon would send the glider and its cargo into a dive from which there could be no recovery. Unwilling to return to the barracks area to face the barrage of wisecracks and jesting with which the men were hiding their fears, some of the glider pilots simply walked in the darkness around and around the inside perimeter of the airfield until it began to get light.

'Someone turned on a radio, trying to find some music with which to pass the time. A broadcast from Radio Berlin blared forth, saying, 'Allied airborne landings on a large scale to establish bridgeheads east of the Rhine must be expected. We are prepared.'

'Switching hastily to the Armed Forces Network, the men heard a commentator reading a proclamation from General Eisenhower to the German Armed Forces: 'The Supreme Commander of the Allied Forces has come into possession of a secret order, issued by the German High Command on October 18, 1943... This secret document orders the execution of Allied airborne soldiers.

'The Supreme Allied Commander thereby addresses to you the following strict warning: 'The execution of uniformed airborne troops and parachutists is an offence against the recognized laws of warfare.... All persons - officers, soldiers and civilians - who have any part in the ordering or carrying out of the above-mentioned order issued by the German High Command will be severely called to account and punished according to military law. ...The excuse of having 'only carried out orders' will not be recognized.'

'Amid a barrage of curses, the radio was hastily turned off.'

'There would be little sleep that night. There was too much to think about.

'Like, how deep is the damned Rhine?'

After the 313th Troop Carrier Group briefing at Folkingham, Jay Phillips went back to his quarters and wrote a short letter home. Mission security prevented him from telling his family what would happen the next day. He could only tell them, *I have a lot on my mind right now* and added, *I promise to write a real letter tomorrow night*. He penned a few more sentences before signing off. *Well, until tomorrow night, I remain in the highest of spirits,* he wrote. It was the last letter his family would receive from him.

At 0725 hours, the lift of the American troops began when a C-47 of the IX Troop Carrier Pathfinder Group, which was to fly the lead serial, took off from Chartres[3] with the group commander, Colonel Joel L. Crouch of Riverside, California as pilot and Colonel Edson D. Raff, commander of the 507th Parachute Infantry Regiment, as a passenger. On the eve of D-Day, 5/6 June 1944, 33-year-old Lieutenant Colonel Joel Crouch who had planned and led pathfinder operations in Italy had flown the lead C-47 that night. As the first pilot in the vanguard fleet, he was, in the words of reporter Lorelle Hearst of the *New York Journal-American*, 'the spearhead of the spearhead of the spearhead' of the high-stakes allied invasion. Before the war, Crouch ('everybody calls him Joe or Colonel Joe,' wrote Hearst), had been a pilot for United Airlines, flying passengers between Los Angeles and Seattle. In the army, he became a specialist in pathfinder operations for aerial assaults and had been the lead pilot in the invasion of Sicily a year earlier and at Salerno, Italy, in September 1943. During the planning for D-Day, Crouch had run the 'Pathfinder School' at North Witham to train both paratroopers and pilots for the job of setting up drop zones.[4] The 507th PIR was the lead assault formation for the 17th Airborne Division and the entire regiment was to be dropped in DZ 'W', an egg-shaped area of fields and bottom land with a main axis about

2,000 yards long parallel to the direction of approach and with a maximum width of 1,500 yards. It nestled against the south side of the Diersfordter Wald east of the hamlet of Flüren and 2¼ miles northwest of Wesel.

The 46 aircraft in 'Colonel Joe' Crouch's serial flashed into the air in less than five minutes and assembled so rapidly that they swept over the field in formation on their way to the command assembly point only ten minutes after the last aircraft left the ground. From Prosnes, Mourmelon and Achiet six other paratroop serials proceeded to Wavre to take their positions behind the serial from Chartres. It was the start of a troop carrier column that would stretch for 420 miles towards Germany.

Over northern France and the Low Countries the sky was clear and visibility unlimited. At Achiet, which had only one usable runway, gusts of wind, blowing at 10 to 15 mph across the runway caused 'Chalk 13' to swerve and crash on take-off. Only deft handling kept others from a similar fate. Engine trouble and a flat tyre kept two C-46s from taking off and another with engine trouble had to return after take-off. 1st Lieutenant Robert 'Bob' Wilson managed to take off safely on full power but at about 1,500 feet the left engine began to cut out. Wilson immediately reduced the power to the left engine, but found that the left engine was still able to pull twelve to fifteen inches of manifold pressure. On board the aircraft were a battalion commander and his staff. The commander went forward to the cockpit and asked Bob Wilson what he planned to do. Bob said that he planned to continue with the mission. The commander put his hand on Bob's shoulder and said 'Good, those boys up there need me.' They then proceeded on their way with reduced power on the left engine and increased power on the right engine. Except for three men injured in a crash, all troops in the aborting aircraft were transferred to four substitute aircraft, which were standing by and flew after the rest. The last left Achiet about 0930, half an hour behind schedule. As the big lumbering C-46s flew toward the drop zone, the mood was one of cautious confidence. There was a sense that the war was winding down and pilots had been told to expect only moderate anti-aircraft fire. Yet while the Germans were certainly close to being defeated, they still had a lot of fight left in them. The area around Wesel was bristling with over 350 anti-aircraft guns and the C-46s were headed directly into a firestorm.

The C-46 serials were scheduled to reach Wavre at 0934 and 0938. In order to take their place in the right-hand lane, they would have to cross the path of the leading American glider serial, which was to enter the centre stream from their right at 0936. The remedy prescribed for this awkward situation was to have the C-46s fly in the left lane, then temporarily free of British traffic, until their greater speed put them well ahead of the gliders, after which they would shift to the right-hand lane. Ingenious as it was, the arrangement left too little margin for error, considering that two very different types of formation, employing different types of aircraft, were to converge on the Wavre area from widely separate starting points.

As Lieutenant Jay Phillips flying C-46 44-77595, carrying 35 paratroopers of the 513th PIR, together with the rest of the C-46 pilots in the 313th approached Wavre, they beheld the glider column crossing directly in front of them. As briefed, the lead serial turned left, outpaced the gliders and swung around them into its assigned lane, but it had had to make a considerable detour to do so. The second climbed to 2,000 feet and went over the gliders without changing course. Though the Achiet serials quickly recovered their proper course and altitude, Colonel James 'Lou' Coutts, Commander the 513th Parachute Infantry Regiment, believed that the first serial at least never did get fully reoriented and that the subsequent inaccurate drop of his men was a result of this episode, though the error would prove providential.

The first four paratroop serials, a force of 181 C-47s of the 438th Troop Carrier Group at Prosnes carried 2,479 troops of the 507th PIR and the 464th Parachute Field Artillery Battalion to DZ 'W'. Colonel Lucion Nelson Powell's crews were awakened at 0400, had breakfast, picked up their escape kits and other equipment and reported for final briefing at 0600 hours. Colonel Powell, was born 7 January 1913 the son of a coal mine superintendent, in Cardiff, Alabama and grew up in Carbon Hill. He went to work in the mines at the age of seven and was driving trucks by the time he was ten. When he was seventeen, his father consented to his enlistment in the Army where he served as an aircraft mechanic. After he separated from the Army, he was an amateur prize fighter in Chicago. He enlisted in Army Air Corps in 1933, entered Aviation Cadet training in 1934 and graduated from Kelly Field, Texas, in 1935 as a pursuit pilot. He was commissioned as a Second Lieutenant in 1936. He left service in 1936 to fly for United Airlines while he also flew for the Army Reserve. He told his crews to expect German jets to attack their formation. The map at the front of the briefing room giving the order of battle showed many enemy flak positions. To reach DZ 'W' the 438th's troop carriers would cross the Rhine at a sharp bend in the river near Xanten. From there would fly east-northeast for about three miles to the zone. During most of the run-in they would have on their right a natural pointer, the Alter Rhein, a long, straight, narrow lake in an old riverbed parallel to their course. Shortly before reaching the zone the fliers would pass for a few hundred yards over a hook of woodland projecting from the southwest corner of the Diersfordter Wald.

The two serials apiece in the 437th, 436th, 435th and 439th Troop Carrier Groups flew the 194th Glider Infantry Regiment, the 680th and 681st Field Artillery Battalions and four batteries of the 155th Anti-aircraft Artillery Battalion to their landing zones.[5] Pfc Jack Trovato in the 1st Squadron, 'A' Battery was carried into battle by the 438th TCG. He and his buddy Jim Murphy had met in an infantry replacement depot in France. Both were eighteen years old and were eager volunteers. 'We had been in the Battle of the Bulge with everyone killed or wounded except the squad leader' says Trovato. 'After two weeks of torturous physical training, inter-dispersed with piling in and out of airplanes and gliders, we received our wings and a raise in pay. Within three days, we were in a marshalling area looking over maps of a little town named Wesel and a bridge that crossed the Rhine into Germany.' After a thorough briefing on the route, speed, drop zone and the turn and route back after the drop, the 438th TCG crews joined in a prayer with Chaplain Lusher and then went directly to the flight line where they checked their load list, their parabundles and their transports one final time. They then went over the jump serials with the paratroopers and spelt out, again, the emergency duties of each crewmember. Those flying their first combat mission, especially co-pilots, had many last-minute questions.[6]

Austin J. 'Buck' Buchanan's crew was entirely 'green'. The co-pilot, Lieutenant R. M. Schow, crew chief, Corporal Stielow and the radio operator, Corporal Henegar, had never been on a combat mission before. The fourteen paratroopers led by jumpmaster, Lieutenant L. J. Liles boarded their new C-47, at 0745 hours. Beneath the wings of the transport were six bundles filled with ammunition, machine guns and other equipment. The all up weight was 5,375lbs; nearly 600lbs over the maximum recommended weight. Colonel Powell was in the lead C-47 of the first serial of 45 transports. Lieutenant Colonel David E. Daniel, 87th Squadron commander piloted the lead aircraft of the second serial of 45 C-47s. 'Buck' Buchanan took off at 0815 hours and the formation was on course in the regulation twenty minutes. The serials hit their first checkpoint, the Command Departure Point, at 0918 hours. At 0930 'Buck' Buchanan ordered his crew into their heavy flak suits and at about 0940, the time for the twenty-minute warning signal, he handed over to Schow and put on his own cumbersome flak suit. When they saw the light in the dome of their flight leader's C-47, Corporal Stielow relayed the information to Lieutenant Liles. As they approached the Rhine the crew could see the tremendous smoke screen that had been created by Field Marshal Montgomery's men. For three days before the opening gun, 'Monty' had stoked a sixty-six-mile smoke screen in hundreds of chemical generators strung along the river. With four minutes to go 'Buck' Buchanan reached up and flicked the red warning light on. Immediately he could feel the weight shift as the paratroopers crowded toward the door in response to the order Liles gave them to 'stand up and hook up.' The moving of their weight to near the door made the C-47 very tail heavy.

Just before he crossed the Rhine, 'Buck' Buchanan glanced to his left and saw a B-17 go down in flames. Soon they saw the crew and passengers safely out in chutes and felt better about that. Buchanan crossed the Rhine flying in thick smoke and haze. At 1011 hours he flicked the green light on. They were directly over the left-hand side of DZ 'W' with its wooded areas north and west and the 1,354 paratroopers tumbled out of the C-47s and began landing close to the trees on the left side of the transports' formation. Given even passable visibility the drop by the 438th Troop Carrier Group was almost bound to be accurate, but DZ 'W' lay under a pall of smoke blown by the southeast wind from the bombed ruins of Wesel and from Second Army smoke pots along the river, only a mile south of the run-in. The pilots could glimpse coloured panels at 'Last Lap' and see the Rhine. Beyond the river the ground was invisible except through an occasional rift in the smoke.

'Buck' Buchanan made a fast turn out of the DZ and back across the Rhine; the dangerous part of another mission completed. It was a moment of sheer relief to be able to take off their flak suits. Buchanan was much amused when Schow announced 'Why, I didn't see anything!' Buchanan had given him many things to do to keep him from being too nervous but he did not got all of them done. Schow had heard a noise while in the drop area but did not know that it was machine gun and ack ack fire. Of the 89 C-47s that returned, eleven would have damage from rifle or machine gun bullets. Those that arrived back over the IP at Brussels, one hundred miles distant, could not see the end of the long formation of transports stretching clear across the Channel back to England and this was only the southern line of the two lines of C-47s in the sky.

Enemy action had little or no effect on the drop. Since the Germans had already been driven from the open land near the river, ground fire was negligible west of the woods. The first two serials found it everywhere very slight, probably because they took the enemy by surprise. The 438th lost only one transport. 1st Lieutenant Donald P. Sundby's C-47 in the 88th Squadron was hit on its homeward turn. It went down in flames, hit a building and exploded, killing all four crew. The other two serials received more fire, mostly from small arms, but, although 29 aircraft were hit not one was shot down. There was no air opposition although one or two hostile aircraft were seen on the way back.

The lead serial, which carried the 1st Battalion, lost its way in the smoke and at about 0950 its first three flights dropped Raff and most of his 493 men on the western edge of the Diersfordter Wald, more than two miles northwest of DZ 'W'. This placed them in the sector allotted to the 513th PIR and a little way northeast of the fortress known as Schloss Diersfordt, a major objective, the taking of which had been delegated to the 3rd Battalion of the 507th. The rear elements of the serial held closer to course and dropped 200 men of the 1st Battalion somewhat to the south of the castle.

Private Robert Vannatter of Headquarters, 1st Battalion, 513th Parachute Infantry, was one of the troopers unable to avoid landing in the trees. Amid the smoke and din of battle, Vannatter plummeted through the branches of two tall trees near the edge of a wooded area. As the unlucky trooper took stock of his situation, suspended 20 feet above ground, he was horrified to see a lone German soldier kneeling on the ground only about thirty feet away. Apparently the noise of battle had masked the sound of his landing and the German was unaware of his presence. As Vannatter considered what to do, the chute suddenly slipped through the branches, dropping him to only five feet off the ground. The sound alerted the German, who whirled around in surprise. Vannatter levelled his carbine at the man and ordered him to drop his weapon and raise his hands. The German obeyed, but then Vannatter realized he had failed to insert a magazine into his carbine. Not only did he have to load his weapon before the German realized it was empty, he also had to find a way to get out of his chute and onto the ground. Vannatter managed to free himself with the help of his prisoner and then delivered the German to a prisoner-of-war collection point. By the end of the day, the 513th had taken more than 1,100 prisoners and the division had captured nearly 3,000. Handling such a large number of prisoners became a major logistical problem for the Allies.

Staff Sergeant Robert L. 'Lendy' McDonald, a trooper in 'A' Company, had a close call while still airborne. As he was next to last in his stick, his assigned seat was near the crew compartment. Once the plane took off, he sat in the vacant navigator's seat of the new C-46. The plastic observation bubble afforded him an excellent view of the vast air armada all around him. As soon as the troopers had responded to the command, 'Stand up and hook up!' the sharp crack of German anti-aircraft fire filled the air. A loud ripping noise filled the plane and McDonald and the troopers around him were covered in a shower of plastic. Looking back into the navigator's compartment, McDonald saw a jagged hole in the metal seat where he had been sitting and the observation bubble was gone except for a few jagged pieces. Evidently, a German round had come straight up through the plane, failed to explode and exited through the bubble. McDonald did not have time to reflect on his good fortune, however, because the plane was on fire. Peering through the doors, he could see nothing but flames. But on the command to jump, the troopers began to pour out the doors, plunging through the fire. McDonald sucked in a deep breath, closed his eyes and followed them out. In a fiery split second, he was free of the doomed plane.

The 438th TCG glider pilots later informed the transport crews that Flight Officer Grenable was killed by flak on the way in for a landing and Flight Officer Lamson was seriously wounded. Flight Officer Bruce Merryman, who had joined the 62nd Squadron in the 314th TCG at Saltby in the summer of 1944, recalled: 'For this mission we were to drop right in on our objectives - not like in the past when we were to land near them. The whole damned Allied airborne force, about 22,000 men, was to be on the ground in less than three hours.

'We cut loose over our landing zone and started down through heavy flak and smoke. Only moments after I popped the tail chute to slow our descent - we were now down to about fifteen feet - we took a direct hit to the rear of the cargo section from an 88. The concussion blew the jeep forward, which snapped the rope tie-downs. The cable attached to the jeep did its job and released the nose hatch, which raised the nose section to the up-and-locked position. This left John W. Heffner and me strapped in our seats with our feet pointing heavenward - and we were still airborne! The jeep, with the trooper still in the driver's seat, flew out of the glider and landed upright with no damage to it or injury to the trooper. Heffner and I crashed nose down immediately behind the jeep. We looked like two guys sitting in chairs that had been tipped over backwards. Then a second 88 round tore off the left wingtip and we released our seat belts and smashed our way out of the glider.' Merryman and Heffner suffered shrapnel wounds and other injuries and were treated at various hospitals in France before returning to fly the 101st Airborne Division's glider troopers in July and August in Salzburg, Austria in order to get the troopers their flight time before being rotated home through the 351st Bomb Squadron in the 'Bloody Hundredth' Bomb Group, arriving in the US in December 1945 in time to spend his first Christmas with his wife Evelyn and Bruce Jr since their marriage on 1 August 1942.

Colonel Raff rallied his separated paratroopers and led them to DZ 'W', engaging a battery of German artillery en route, killing or capturing the artillery crews before reuniting with the rest of the regiment. Raff's men drove confused and wavering German troops out of good positions in the nearby woods, killing 55, taking over 300 prisoners and capturing a battery of 150 mm howitzers. Then they marched south to attack the castle where at about 1100 they found the rest of the battalion already engaging the German occupants. The 2nd and 3rd Battalions of the 507th, commanded by Lieutenant Colonel Charles Timmes and Lieutenant Colonel Allen Taylor, respectively, along with Lieutenant Colonel Edward S. Branigan's 464th Parachute Field Artillery Battalion, landed on their assigned drop zones, assembled quickly and set out to seize Diersfordter and the castle that dominated the area.

By 1400 the 507th had secured all of its objectives and cleared the area around Diersfordt, having engaged numerous German troops and also destroying a German tank. The actions of the regiment during the initial landing also gained the division its second Medal of Honor, when 21-year old Private George J. Peters of Cranston, Rhode Island posthumously received the award. Peters and a group of ten other troopers landed in an open field near the town of Fluren. Raked by enemy machine gun fire the troopers laid there helplessly.[7] Peters armed with only his rifle and a few grenades took it upon himself to charge the German machine gun nest. After receiving several wounds and bleeding profusely he crawled to within fifteen feet of the gun emplacement and pitched two grenades into the enemy stronghold. The ensuing explosion silenced the machine gun and its crew.

The second and third serials approached DZ 'W' accurately in good formation and placed the 2nd and 3rd Battalions of the 507th squarely on the zone. The 2nd Battalion came down under heavy fire from German troops concentrated in the woods north and west of it. Nevertheless, the paratroops assembled quickly into platoons and companies, moved against the enemy strong points and by 1100 had taken them in a series of short, fierce actions. Their biggest prize was a battery of 81 mm mortars which had been zeroed in on the zone. The 3rd Battalion also had to conduct a fighting assembly, in the course of which it took about 150 prisoners. However, within 45 minutes after its jump, 75 percent of the battalion had been concentrated in readiness to move to Schloss Diersfordt. Altogether, the regiment is reported to have had 90 percent of its personnel assembled within an hour and a half after its jump.

The fourth serial, which reached the zone about 1005 was fairly accurate, but its drop of the 464th Field Artillery Battalion was somewhat dispersed. Elements of the battalion were dropped as much as 1,500 yards northwest of the DZ. Under brisk fire from the woods as they hit the ground, the artillerymen hastily set up three 50-calibre machine guns and three howitzers and laid direct fire on the most troublesome enemy positions. After the fighting around them died down, they moved according to plan to the northeast end of the zone and by 1300 hours had nine of their twelve howitzers set up there. The other three had been damaged in landing because the parachutes did not open properly. The battalion only fired fifty rounds that day, most of them during the afternoon in a difficult but successful duel with an 88 mm gun, two 75s and a mortar located around a house which the 464th had intended to use as its command post. Major General 'Bud' Miley, the 17th Airborne divisional commander, who had briefed the 53rd Wing's five groups three weeks earlier, jumped with the artillery, but was little more than an observer during the initial stages of the battle. High-level coordination of the innumerable small-unit actions was neither possible nor necessary.

The 435th Troop Carrier Group's 144 gliders came under ground fire as soon as they released from their tugs, causing heavy casualties among the infantry and glider crews. The survivors made their way to their objective - half a dozen brick houses in the middle of a wide, open area. The men dug in during the afternoon and evacuated the civilian inhabitants to the rear. All but one family had left and, in appreciation of their not being evicted, the remaining family, an elderly couple with their pregnant daughter, had prepared a meal of stew and potatoes for the Americans. Towards dusk, a force of about 150 Germans with two or three tanks and self-propelled guns emerged from no-man's land between LZ 'S' and Wesel. The first German patrols ran into the glider pilots of the 75th Platoon in the 435th Group, who, organized as an infantry company and with the help of a couple of anti-aircraft batteries, defended a crossroad north-east of Wesel. Flight Officer William Horn remembers that, 'all of a sudden, the German infantry started hyping themselves up with a weird sort of yelling and cheering and came at us in a Japanese banzai charge and we really poured it into them'. One of the Germans, a teenager of around 17, began to plead in English that he was wounded and had an uncle in Milwaukee but, thinking it may be a trap, the pilots left him where he was. He died during the night.

Around 2355 hours, a Ju 88 bomber crashed into a field next to the crossroad, coming to rest against the wreckage of a Waco. Flight Officer Oliver Faris was the first to reach the wreckage. Unable to see any markings in the darkness, he asked if the crew were British. 'No', answered one, 'we are Germans, but the war is over for us'. As the Americans rescued the trapped crewmen, a barrage of mortar fire fell around the site, heralding the start of an attack which became known as the 'Battle of Burp Gun Corner' (as the forces newspaper *Stars and Stripes* first called it). Much of the German fire came from Schmeiser submachine guns that always fired in long bursts, which to Americans sounded like an enormous 'Burp!' At about midnight, the first attack by a German tank supported by a large number of infantry hit the crossroad north-east of Wesel. Thirty minutes later a German tank and approximately 200 German infantry, supported by two 20 mm flak guns, attacked the position defended by the 77th Platoon. The defenders held their fire until the enemy troops were in close range before opening fire and then smashed the attack with a single volley, which killed about fifty men and knocked out the tank. The Germans stumbled off into the darkness, ran against a position manned by glider infantry. Murderous small-arms fire took a heavy toll on enemy infantry during the hour-long battle.

Flight Officers Chester Deshurley and Albert Hurley held their positions, firing their machine guns until the tank came within fifteen yards of them, as did Flight Officer Robert Campbell, armed with a Tommy gun. At that point Flight Officer Elbert Jella severely damaged the tank with his bazooka. A tank round hit a .50 calibre gun emplacement and another set fire to a crashed glider. By the light of the flames, Flight Officer Joseph Menard watched in horror as the barrel swung slowly towards him and began to fire his rifle at it, hoping against hope that a round might enter the muzzle and explode the shell before it could be fired. Then suddenly, an explosion rocked the tank and its gun fired early, hitting the ground and ricocheting over Menard's foxhole, missing him but leaving him with a slight wound and temporarily deafened. Flight Officer Elbert Jella's bazooka round had been enough to make the tank fall back, running over the 20 mm flak gun it was towing and, seeing what had happened, a second tank behind also withdrew and was captured by the glider pilots.[8]

At daybreak the glider pilots defeated several smaller attacks and joined up with British forces coming out of Wesel. Flight Officer William Horn saw a lone German medic out in front desperately trying to minister to a number of his wounded comrades 'but' he said 'it was a losing battle'. Thirteen enemy dead lay around the crossroad and a sweep later recovered forty-five wounded. The glider pilots' job was done with the professionalism of veteran infantry troops. They soon were relieved from further duty as ground soldiers. Overall they suffered 31 casualties in the operation, killed a large number of enemy troops and captured several hundred prisoners.

During the afternoon German morale weakened and resistance in the 507th's sector almost vanished. The last big fight was at the castle. The 3rd Battalion arrived there at 1200 hours after a rapid march through the woods, relieved the 1st Battalion, excepting Company 'A', which was already deployed and launched an attack. Within an hour they had taken the fortress but an isolated turret, bagging 500 prisoners and five medium tanks. The paratroops knocked out one tank with a Gammon grenade and two with shoulder-fired recoilless 57 mm guns, the first successful use of the weapon in combat. The other two were destroyed by the fire of heavy artillery from across the Rhine. Evidently German hope and fighting spirit were vanishing together. By 1500 resistance in the castle ended after Company 'G' cleared the structure room by room. The troopers collected over 300 prisoners, including a number of senior officers from the German LXXXVI Corps and 84th Infantry Division. Within 3½ hours after its jump the 507th had taken all its assigned objectives and it appears to have done so in the face of numerically superior forces. It captured that day approximately 1,000 prisoners belonging to three regiments of the German 84th Division, an artillery regiment, a GHQ battalion and an anti-aircraft battery. What remained to be done was to link up with the ground forces and other airborne units.

Because of the speed of the C-46 the verbal warning was given fifteen minutes before the jump instead of twenty and the red light three instead of four minutes in advance. There was much jostling within the serials, probably because the 313th Group had had insufficient opportunity to fly their new aircraft in large formations. The jam which occurred as they approached the Rhine may have played its part in throwing them off course. The pilots all appear to have believed that they crossed the Rhine at the proper point, but their crossing place was not particularly distinctive and it is perhaps significant that only one crew reported seeing the panels set out near the west bank to mark it. East of the Rhine the visibility was about half a mile, very bad, though a little better than that on the approaches to DZ 'W'.

Moderate and rather inaccurate light flak and small-arms fire met the two serials as they passed over the Forest of Diersfordt. Several aircraft, including the lead ship, flown by Lieutenant Colonel William L. Filer, commander of the 313th TCG, burst into flames. As the 47th Troop Carrier Squadron got over the drop zone, anti-aircraft fire was intense. One pilot later described how 'the Germans really began to give us the works' and how C-46s 'were burning and exploding all around us.' Another pilot said, 'the flak was the worst that I have ever seen.' Here, in the thick of battle, the weaknesses of the 'Curtiss Calamity' became evident. Just short of the drop zone, Jay Phillips' C-46 was hit by flak, went into a dive and exploded as it hit the ground. Phillips, his co-pilot, 1st Lieutenant William C. Simmons, the radio operator, Staff Sergeant Harold Power and crew chief/flight engineer, Tech Sergeant Homer Lundine and all 35 paratroopers were killed.

Seconds after the last paratrooper had jumped from Philip Sarrett's C-46, the plane was hit by flak and caught fire. Sarrett attempted to turn the transport but flames began to spread over the right wing and he ordered the crew to bail out. One by one, they exited the burning aircraft until only he and his navigator, Captain Richard Ketchum remained. As Ketchum prepared to bail out, he turned and saw Sarrett leave the cockpit and pass the radio operator's station. Relieved that his pilot was right behind him, Ketchum jumped and pulled his ripcord. Sarrett, however, never got out. In an after-action report, the pilot of a nearby plane described how he watched Philip's big C-46 as it 'nosed into a clearing and exploded.'

Philip Sarrett was only 23 years old. Forty-five days later, the war in Europe ended. For several weeks, Leaugeay Phillips Weber and her family remained unaware of Jay Phillips' fate. Then, on Friday 13th April, Leaugeay returned home to find her father waiting for her at the door. 'I could tell that something was very wrong,' she recalls. Her father told her that Jay was missing in action. After several weeks of agonizing uncertainty, the family received the devastating news that he had been killed. 'It was so painful, so difficult,' says Leaugeay Phillips.[9]

At 1008 the first serial of the 313th TCG reached what appeared to be the drop zone but instead of being dropped on DZ 'X' the 513th PIR had been dropped in the British 6th Airborne Division's area directly on batteries of 88 mm guns which were wreaking havoc among the gliders. The Americans were able eventually to silence the guns and the battalions of 6th Airlanding Brigade were thus able to secure the small town of Hamminkeln but at no small cost to the C-46 serials in the 313th Group. As they let down to make their drop the C-46 serials were raked by intense and accurate light flak and small-arms fire from positions on their left and received some heavier flak from the right. Suddenly the sky seemed full of burning and exploding aircraft. The formations began to break up and congestion forced some pilots to slow to as little as 80 mph. The C-46s displayed remarkable resistance to stalling, but one, apparently un-hit, did dive into the ground with all its crew and troops. The other 68 in the serials dropped their troops from heights of 600 to 1,000 feet. Of three stragglers, two dropped behind the seventh serial at 1023 hours and the other after running into interference in two passes over the zone dropped its troops on the west bank of the Rhine. On one C-46 a bundle stuck in the door prevented a dozen men from jumping and eight others were brought back, most of them because of wounds. Several paratroops made the jump in spite of being already wounded.

Accurate and intense ground fire, especially from positions along the Issel, continued while the C-46 serials in the 313th Group made their right turn after the drop and some shooting followed them until they got back to the Rhine. The 48th Troop Carrier Squadron, who led the second serial, approached the drop zone and overtook the 47th Troop Carrier Squadron as they made their slow up prior to dropping their load of paratroopers. Bob Wilson dropped behind and to the right of the 47th Troop Carrier Squadron. As the last paratrooper jumped from his C-46 the first 20 mm round went through the fuselage. In an effort to dodge the flak coming up Wilson dived down and right. Whilst diving, his aircraft was hit three more times by 20 mm rounds, once by 40 mm round and was also hit several times by machine gun fire. Whilst pulling out of the dive he discovered that the trim tabs and the hydraulic boosters were not working and that he had very little aileron control. After regaining control of the aircraft, the pilots flew back to Achiet Le Grand flying right wing low to hold the aircraft straight, the crew experimenting with slowing the aircraft to 120mph to determine whether it would be safe to land. Wilson was going to ask his radio operator and crew chief to bail out but discovered he needed their weight to hold the tail of the aircraft down but he could not use the flaps to slow the aircraft during landing because it would have pitched the aircraft down and they would have crashed. With the radio operator and crew chief braced for a crash landing in the tail of the aircraft Bob Wilson put the C-46 down on the runway at 110mph but soon discovered that the brake system had been damaged and was forced to ground loop to avoid hitting other aircraft already parked on the airfield.[10]

The 48th Squadron lost eight C-46s (a loss of 44%) on the mission. Captain Leroy L. Bryand filled in a report as a witness of what happened.

'After completing the drop I did a turn and proceeded back across the Rhine. On crossing the Rhine I sighted a C-46D with the left wing on fire behind the gas tank. I put on power to catch up with the aircraft to call the pilot over the VHF to tell him he was on fire. As I was catching up with the aircraft the pilot started down in a slow glider as if preparing to crash land. Instead of putting the aircraft down straight ahead, the pilot started a low turn at what seemed to be a slow air-speed. When the aircraft went into the turn the fire spread to the extreme end of the left wing, burning the aileron off almost immediately. Unable to straighten the aircraft out the left wing struck the ground followed by the nose and then the right wing. The aircraft then exploded and the tail section was thrown clear of the wreckage. I went down to a low altitude and buzzed the wreckage and was able to read the call letter on the tail section. The call letter was 'Q for Queen'.

'Upon returning to the squadron and checking with the other squadrons, all of their aircraft with marking 'Q' had returned. From this check it can be assumed that this aircraft was 'Bubbles Q for Queen', piloted by 2nd Lieutenant Donald D. Shire, which crashed between 1020 and 1025 hours in the vicinity of Bonninghardt. Tech Sergeant Norman E. Rhoads escaped with only slight lacerations and contusions. The British immediately took him to an aid station and he was back to duty five days later. 1st Lieutenant Joe T. Henderson, who crashed in the same vicinity, stated that he came upon the wreckage and noticed two or three bodies.'

Richard Curt Hottelet, a Brooklyn-born American broadcast journalist and a Combat Camera motion film unit flew on a B-17 piloted by Lieutenant Colonel Benton R. Baldwin to witness the airborne operations at first hand. Baldwin was born on 11 December 1908 at DeLand, Florida. Hottelet was born in Brooklyn on 22 September 1917, the son of German immigrants who spoke no English at home. His father had an import-export business that failed during the Depression. Before the Americans entered the war, Hottelet worked as a correspondent for United Press and he was arrested by the Germans under suspicion of being a spy. He was released in 1941 during a US-German prisoner exchange. In January 1944 the young reporter became one of Ed Murrow's 'Boys' tutored and/or encouraged by Edward R. Murrow at CBS. On D-Day, 6 June 1944 Hottelet aired the first eyewitness account of the seaborne invasion of Normandy; he rode along in a 386th Bomb Group B-26 Marauder that attacked 'Utah' Beach six minutes before H-Hour. Hottelet was deeply air sick from the rough return to Great Dunmow and made it back to London with a slop bucket at the ready to describe the pre-dawn raid! On 'Varsity' worse was to happen to him, as he revealed in his article, *Big Jump Into Germany for Colliers Magazine:*

'The sky above was pale blue. Below us, golden soil and bright green meadows were cut by long morning shadows. Flying at a few hundred feet, banking steeply to let the cameramen get their shots, we saw the solid phalanxes of olive-green troop carriers and tow planes and gliders nose to tail on the perimeter tracks of the ground bases. From one field to another we went until it got monotonous, until we sat down on our flak suits and parachutes in the waist and just watched the sky. I no longer even felt worried that I was not worried.

'On my right was Colonel Joel O'Neal, the Deputy Chief of Staff of the US Carrier Forces, come to see the execution of what he had helped plan. He chewed gum and looked at his map. Tech Sergeant Clarence Pearce and Staff Sergeant Fred Quandt sat silent, with their knees drawn up and smoked. We all watched dark-bearded Sergeant George Rothlisberg, who sat and slept on the upended little khaki suitcase that carried his equipment. He just sat upright, with no support and slept.

'It was warm, despite the fact that we had taken the windows out of the waist and the wind was rushing through. Outside, the sun was climbing and you had just about absorbed the roaring of the four great engines and the screaming of the slipstream into the open fuselage as a thoroughly acceptable part of a perfect day, when someone nudged you and pointed out of the side. 'You got up and looked and there they were - hundreds of C-47s flying along in tight formation. This was the realization of months of training and planning. It was an airborne dream come true. It was a mighty olive-green river that surged steadily and inevitably over Germany and over the Germans crouched behind their last great defence line below. It was a mightier river than the German Rhine and this day would prove it. From now on in, it was business, strict and cold. The troop carriers looked sleek and well fed, bobbing up and down in the air currents and propwash like fat men in a gentle surf. But inside them there were thousands of desperate young men, trained to a fine edge and armed to the teeth. Slung under the green bellies of the planes were the bundles of explosives and ammunition and supplies for dropping to the paratroops. They nosed ahead inexorably and behind them came other serials and behind them still others, until the procession disappeared in the thin March mist.

'Colonel O'Neal put his flak suit on over his parachute harness and strapped the steel flaps of his flak helmet down over his ears. We all did the same. The three photographers, their cameras clocking away, jostled one another at the waist windows as we swooped around the drop ships.

'P-Hour, the drop hour for the paratroops, was 10 am. Just after 0945 we passed the last check point. It was called the IP or Initial Point, the same as a bombing run. Its code name was 'Yalta'. All of a sudden the ground below us, which had been golden in the morning sunlight, turned grey. For a moment I thought that we had run into clouds. It seemed impossible. Then we caught a whiff. It was chemical smoke. Below us and around us was a bank of misty smoke that ran for miles up and down the west bank of the Rhine, across the river and over the east bank.

'Here there was no sunlight; here in the centre of green and fertile land was a clearly marked area of death. The smoke seemed a shroud. Outlines below us were indistinct. What had seemed warm now appeared ominously cold and almost clammy. On our left was the first serial of paratroop pathfinders. We were flying at 700 feet.

'Below us there was no sign of life. We looked for troops going across, for the familiar invasion LCVPs and LCMs of our Rhine navy. We saw none. The river below us was a slate-grey ribbon winding through a dull grey land; on our left the troop carriers, pregnant dolphins in an eerie sea; and down to our right, straight into the sun, the dark mass of the city of Duisburg. From its broad, regular inland harbour the sun reflected panels of light into the battle area.

'Over the roar of the engines and the screaming of air in the waist windows we heard a faint thumping. Colonel O'Neal grabbed me by the shoulder and pointed. The intercom crackled and a dry voice said, 'Flak at twelve o'clock; and nine o'clock. But they're off the beam.' Outside, coming up from Duisburg, were the shells from Nazi 88s. Black puffs of smoke feathered pretty far off to our right. All of a sudden I felt how tense I had become. There was no more flak for a moment and I began to relax.

'And just at that moment we were over the first drop zone. It was 0950, ten minutes early. On our left, paratroopers were tumbling out of the C-47s, their green camouflage chutes blending with the dark grey ground. The troop-carrier serial seemed like a snail. And it was crawling indeed - about 115 mph. Our big Fort seemed to me to be close to stalling speed.

'We were watching the bright blue and red and yellow supply parachutes mix with the falling paratroopers, admiring the concentration of that first jump, when we first got it. I was surprised and pained. The ground, as far as we could see it through the smoke, was torn up as if a gigantic seed drill had passed over it. It was an insult that anyone should be left down there to shoot at us.

'It sounded like a riveting machine, a heavy one. For a split-second I didn't catch on. Then I smelled the explosive - a stench that always nauseates me. You get it in outward-bound bombers when the gunners clear their guns. But we had no gunners. Our turret guns were taped up and our waist guns had been unmounted. We were here to photograph and record, not to fight. There was a sharp rap on the ship somewhere. We had been hit.

'The drop run was finished. So we swung up in a banking climb to our left while the first serial turned sharply right and headed out. I listened to the engines. They roared healthily on. The sound of the slipstream was the same and the crackling of the aluminium skin.

'I looked around the waist with new eyes. I noted the sheet of armour below each waist window and decided to stick close there. The men were busy with their cameras, their knees bent and hunched slightly over to keep balance. I hung on to one of the innumerable pipes that run down the top of the fuselage, like a strap-hanger in a New York subway, swaying slightly as we banked and heeled. I looked at Quandt. He looked back and nodded his head with the corners of his mouth turned down. I knew exactly what he meant, so I did likewise. Colonel O'Neal's Irish face remained impassive.

'We turned and circled for a minute or two and then joined another serial going into the drop zone. On the ground we could see occasional gun flashes, but no signs of life apart from them. No flak was coming near, so again a gradual relaxation made me see how tense I had become in every muscle. We watched the serial, with its fifteen tight little three-ship 'V' formations, drop its load.

'A hundred yards away from us, one of its ships, spawning parachutes from the rear, suddenly blossomed with yellow light up forward. It was not the reflection of the sun on the windshield. It was flame. And the ship turned off to the left in a steep glide. I remembered that two ships in the first serial had also slipped away, but with no apparent damage. Probably the pilots were hit by flak.

'This bunch finished its work and turned for home. We turned off and joined a third formation, flying level with them at their speed and altitude. One of the photographers, crowded away from the window, was probably thinking along identical lines with me. There were a couple of extra flak suits back with us and he stretched the double aprons flat out on the wooden floor.
'It suddenly seemed extremely silly to me that we should be there, because we were a huge bright silver B-17 flying along at almost stalling speed. We were probably the most conspicuous thing in the sky.

'The Germans must have arrived at the same conclusion. We had been over the drop zone twenty or twenty-five minutes. We were turning again to pick up the first incoming serial of C-46s.

'We were banking to head back to the Rhine and pick them up. Hanging from my pipe, I could look almost straight down through the waist window through the tattered smoke at the ground. By now, there were several blobs of drop zones where the coloured parachutes reminded you of a Mardi Gras sidewalk strewn with confetti.

'And then we really hit trouble. It may have been the same gun. I did not see it. Radio Operator Roy Snow watched the tracers come up from the ground and lifted his feet to let the shells pass under him. In the waist we heard the riveter again; a short burst and then a longer one. The heavy steel-scaled flak suit and the heavy flak helmet, which had been weighing me down, now felt light and comforting. Then we got hit in a ripple. The ship shuddered, I grabbed my pipe. And then, as if it had been rehearsed, all five of us in the waist stepped onto the flak suits, spread on the flooring.

'Over the intercom, Snow was telling our pilot, Lieutenant Colonel Benton Baldwin, that the left wing had been hit and that fire was breaking out between the engines. The flak stopped. Baldwin was gaining altitude in a climbing turn. Smoke began to pour down through the plane and in the left waist window. A tongue of flame licked back as far as the window and the silver inner skin of the ship reflected its orange glow. The crew chief told Lieutenant Albert Richey that gasoline was sloshing around in the bomb bay.

'Sitting in a plane that is being peppered by flak and being able to do nothing at all about it is a miserable feeling. But even that is nothing to the sensation of sitting in a burning plane. Baldwin used both extinguisher charges in a vain attempt to put out the fire. There was nothing to do but bail out.

'As we staggered out, we watched the C-46s come in and apparently walk into a wall of flak. I not could see the flak but one plane after another went down. All our attention was concentrated on our own ship. It could blow up in mid-air any moment. We moved close to the windows. From the pilot's compartment came streams of stinging smoke. The intercom went out.

'Up in the cockpit, Colonel Baldwin was keeping the ship under control, watching the fire eat a larger and larger hole in the left wing like a smouldering cigarette in a table-cloth. Looking down one wing from above, he could not see a large fire. The flame was mainly below the wing.

'Suddenly we went into a sharp dip. Back aft we did not know what was happening. All we had was the smoke and the deafening noise and the tiny fragments of molten metal which the wing was throwing back and which twinkled in the sun as they raced past the waist window.

'We pulled off our flak suits and helmets. I reached down and buckled on my chest chute. It was obvious we would have to jump. But down below was still the cold, grey smoky country east of the Rhine. Impossible to tell what was happening down there. If it was not in enemy hands, it was a battlefield.

'As we went into the dip, I thought the pilots had been hit and I put my hands on the edge of the window to vault out. But the colonel brought her back under control and we hung on. There was no movement among the men in the waist. We stood and waited - for flak, or more flames or explosion or the Rhine to slide below. There was nothing else to do. After what seemed hours, the Rhine was below us at last. The left wing was blazing but three motors were still running.

'We were hardly across the river when Roy Snow came back and told us to jump. That and the Rhine River were all we had been waiting for.

'Colonel O'Neal went back and began to struggle with the handle that jettisons the rear door. I jogged my chest pack up and down; made sure it was secure. The other men did the same. Colonel O'Neal was still wrestling with the door. I went back to help.

'There was no panic. But if this telling sounds cool and collected, the actuality was not so. Uppermost in everyone's mind was just physically getting out of that ship. We were still flying at less than a thousand feet, which left not much time. I abandoned, with hardly a thought, my recording equipment and typewriter and notes and jacket in the radio compartment. Of the cameramen, only Quandt thought to take the film out of his camera. There was no point in trying to jump with anything in your hand because the opening of the chute will make you drop anything that is not tied to you.

'The colonel got the door open and crouched in it for a moment. I shouted, 'Okay Colonel, get going.' He didn't hear but tumbled out. I got into the doorway.

'All my life, one of the sensations I have disliked most had been the feeling of falling. As a boy I avoided the big slides in the amusement parks at Coney Island. Even now, working at the front, when I go up in a Cub or observation L-5, I always hope fervently that the pilot will not do those steep banking dives they like so much. The sinking feeling in my stomach when I fall is sickening.

'Stranding in the doorway of the burning Fortress, I somehow hardly thought of that. Down below, the ground was green and golden and friendly again. We had left the smoke zone, the sun was bright and the air was warm. Everything seemed friendly. It was the most natural feeling in the world to want to leave the doomed plane and, anyway, behind me were three men waiting to jump too. So I simply let myself tumble forward on my face. As I left the ship, the slipstream caught me and it was like a big friendly hand that I could dig my shoulder into. The black rubber de-icer on the stabilizer was above me. And then all was confusion.

'We were jumping at about 600 feet so I pulled the rip cord almost immediately. I pulled it so hard I almost jerked my shoulder out. There was more confusion. I felt as if I had come to a dead stop. The harness straps were digging into my flesh. My main thought was to save the ring and I put it in my pocket. My next thought was gentle surprise that I should have been successful in parachuting the first time I tried.

'For a moment there was relaxation and enjoyment of the wonderful quiet that the departing Fort had left me in. Up above my head, the chute was glistening white, billowing like a sail full of wind. I began to sway, so I turned my attention to the ground.

'I tried to remember everything I had read about parachuting - like pulling the shrouds to stop swaying. But I was afraid to try anything that might spill the chute. So I concentrated on worrying about where I was going to fall. Below me were a farmhouse, some open fields, a clump of trees and a pond. Men were running in my direction from one side of the house. Away in the next field, Colonel O'Neal, who had also been swaying, had just come down.

'I landed in a pasture. Trying to gauge my height to brace myself for the fall, I kept opening and closing my eyes, but was barely able to keep pace. I remembered to flex my knees. The next second I hit with a grunt. I snapped off the parachute and got to my feet. To my surprise I stayed there, getting my wind back.

'It was the British Second Army area and - true to the old Battle of Britain tradition - the parachuting visitor was promptly filled with tea and whisky.

'I reached in my pocket for the ring. It is a parachuting tradition to keep the ring to prove you have been in command of the situation at all times. The ring was not there. I had obviously been out of control.

'Word came that the colonel was all right but that Pearce, who jumped right after me, had been killed when his chute streamed like an exclamation mark instead of opening. Our pilot pulled his rip cord in the cockpit by accident while putting his chute on after we had all got out. So he rode the Fort into a crash landing and came out safe.

'All around us, as we stood on this approach route for the airborne forces, burning and disabled C-47s crashed into the fields. In every case the pilot stayed with his ship until his crew and passengers were out before bailing out himself. In some cases he stayed too long. It was a thrilling demonstration of the highest kind of courage to see a burning troop carrier come gliding in, to see two or three or four chutes blossom out under it, a pause as the ship turned away and then another lone chute as the pilot got out. We stood looking up and cheered.

'After a while, I noticed that my eye was hurting and found that the chest chute had given me the start of a beautiful shiner as it was ripped up past my face. On hitching my way back to Paris next day, I found a telegram from my boss in London saying: 'Better a purple eye than a Purple Heart.'

'By that time, there was good news from the front. Some 6,400 Nazis had been taken prisoner in the drop zones; the whole operation was a great success and the British Second Army was slashing across the top of Germany - east of the Rhine.'

General James Gavin, whose 82nd Airborne Division was not in this battle, was flying above 'Varsity' as an observer; he counted twenty-three aircraft on fire at one time, all trying to make it back to the west bank of the river. Later Gavin called 'Varsity' 'the highest state of development attained by troop-carrier and airborne units.'

As the remnants of the 313th trickled into Achiet between 1110 and 1147 hours it became evident that the group had suffered a disaster, which proved only too tragically that those dreadful C-46s deserved the label 'flaming coffins' that was pinned on them.[11] One of the C-46s crashed on takeoff. The German guns had taken a toll of nineteen aircraft destroyed and out of these fourteen went down in flames, while the rest were fit only for salvage. Another seven made emergency landings west of the Rhine River. Another 38 damaged; many of them severely. Personnel losses, though less than at first expected, stood a week later at one dead, 22 wounded or injured and 33 missing. Of the nineteen aircraft lost, fourteen had gone down in flames. Participants in the mission agreed that the C-46 seemed to catch on fire every time it was hit in a vital spot. The Group blamed this flammability on the plane's complex hydraulic system. The technicians of the 52nd Wing attributed it to the arrangement of the wing tanks which, when they were hit, caused gasoline to travel along the inside of the wing toward the fuselage. In other respects the C-46 showed it could endure punishment very well. One Commando received a direct flak hit on the left engine and then three in the fuselage and glided to a landing after another hit stopped the right engine. The crew tried to count the small holes in the plane from bullets and shrapnel, but quit when they reached 200. Another plane landed safely at a friendly base with two large shell holes in the left wing, one in the right stabilizer and major flak damage to the left propeller, the controls, the fuselage, the tail wheel nacelle and the wheel itself, not to mention numerous bullet holes, some of which had punctured a gas tank.

Unlike the pilots of Colonel Joe Crouch's serial, who were vaguely aware that they had missed their mark, those of the 313th TCG were sure that they had either hit their zone or come extremely close to it. Actually they had deposited their paratroops between 1½ and two miles north of DZ 'X' in fields southwest of Hamminkeln. Where they crossed the Diersfordter Wald the forest was about as wide as on their proper course and the relative position of the double-track railway beyond it was similar to what it was on the true zone. Thus such glimpses as the fliers had of these landmarks merely confirmed them in their error. Indeed, Colonel 'Lou' Coutts commanding the 513th PIR was equally deceived and supposed himself to be on the drop zone for quite a while after he reached the ground. The puzzling aspect of the situation is not the failure of visual navigation but the failure of radar to correct it. The 313th reported that its navigators made frequent and successful use of 'Gee' both along the route and in the DZ area, relying principally on the Ruhr chain. As observed earlier, pinpoint accuracy in the use of 'Gee' was not easy to attain, but in this case a single good fix should have sufficed to show that the 313th was too far to the north.

Some of the 513th Parachute Infantry had been dropped two miles away from their intended zone, DZ 'X'. Most came down within an area approximately the same size as the drop zone and the drop pattern was such that they were able to concentrate within an hour into about six large groups.

The greater part of the 2nd Battalion assembled and organized within thirty minutes under intense small-arms fire. The paratroops then engaged the enemy in their vicinity and disposed of them effectively. The British airborne into whose sector they had descended testified that the Americans were excellent fighters and very helpful. Because the regimental objectives in the Diersfordter Wald had already been cleared by the 1st Battalion of the 507th PIR and those east of the wood had been taken by members of the 194th Glider Combat Team, the 513th PIR was able to deploy almost unopposed into its assigned positions in the northern portion of the 17th Division's sector. Fighting and reconnoitring in the drop area occupied a majority of the 513th PIR until after noon. Not until after 1230 did three groups of its men, one from the 1st Battalion, one from the 2nd and another led by the regimental commander, join forces about a mile southwest of Hamminkeln. They then reorganized and prepared to fight their way south into its assigned area. The movement was sharply contested and had to be interrupted several times for operations against strong points along the line of advance. However, the main body of 513th reached DZ 'X' about the middle of the afternoon. Other portions of the regiment made their way to the zone independently against opposition varying from fierce to feeble. A group from the 3rd Battalion reached the drop zone about 1300. By 1400 Colonel 'Lou' Coutts reported to the Divisional Headquarters that the 513th had secured all of its objectives, having knocked out two tanks and two batteries of 88 mm guns and captured about 1,150 prisoners during their assault.

One question which had perplexed the leaders of the 513th PIR during the morning was the whereabouts of their supporting artillery unit, the 466th Parachute Field Artillery Battalion commanded by Lieutenant Colonel Kenneth L. Booth. The reason was that the battalion had come down where it was supposed to, on DZ 'X'. The last parachute serial, a formation of 45 C-47s of the 434th Group at Mourmelon-le-Grand, had flown accurately to the drop zone and dropped 376 artillerymen and twelve howitzers there at 1023.[12] Nine over-eager men had jumped west of the Rhine and two wounded men were brought back. Ground fire against that serial was nowhere more than moderate. It caused the loss of only one plane and damage to seventeen. This record suggests that if the two preceding serials had followed the proper course their losses would have been much less than those they did incur.

At first the fighting in the drop area was severe and the artillerymen with only a couple of sticks of infantry to assist them were in a difficult position. All the officers in one battery were killed or wounded within a few minutes after they hit the ground. However, the 466th fought manfully to clear its zone and was greatly aided when glider troops landed north of it on LZ 'N' and south of it on LZ 'S'. The last seven American glider serials went to LZ 'N', the most northerly of the two landing zones selected for the 17th Airborne, which was about 1¼ miles long and half a mile wide, laying against the east side of the Diersfordter Wald about four miles north of Wesel. It was tightly sandwiched between DZ 'X' on the south and two British landing zones to the north. Once again the principal landmark on LZ 'N' was the ubiquitous double-track railway, which slanted across its western end. Here is a case in which the closeness of the zones and the decision to bring in the gliders immediately after the paratroops was beneficial and may have saved the artillerymen from heavy losses. The amount of infantry fighting that the artillerymen had to do is shown by the fact that they killed fifty Germans, took 320 prisoners and captured ten 76 mm guns, eight 20 mm guns and eighteen machine guns.

The load going to LZ 'N' amounted to 1,321 troops and 382 tons of supplies and equipment, including 143 jeeps, 97 trailers and carts and twenty guns and mortars. The troops consisted of the 139th Engineer Battalion and a melange of medics, signal men and staff personnel. These specialists had been protected as far as possible by sending them last and by providing that the 513th PIR should occupy the landing zone before they arrived. However, at the time of the landings the 513th was still pulling itself together after its unexpected drop near Hamminkeln.

Within thirty minutes after its jump the 466th Field Artillery Battalion had some howitzers in operation. Except for one piece which had been damaged by enemy fire, all its twelve howitzers were in position and ready to fire by 1300 hours. Radio contact with the 513th Regiment was made about noon and during the regiment's move south the 466th gave it effective artillery support against several German strong-points. The gunners' performance was the more creditable in that they were in the strange situation of firing from behind the enemy toward their own attacking infantry.

Twenty-year old Private First Class Stuart S. Stryker of the 513th Parachute Infantry Regiment was posthumously awarded the Medal of Honor after leading a charge against a German machine gun nest, creating a distraction to allow the rest of his platoon to capture the fortified position in which the machine-gun was situated. His citation reads, in part, 'His gallant and wholly voluntary action in the face of overwhelming firepower ...so encouraged his comrades and diverted the enemy's attention that other elements of the company were able to surround the house, capturing more than 200 hostile soldiers and much equipment, besides freeing three members of an American bomber crew held prisoner there. The intrepidity and unhesitating self-sacrifice of PFC Stryker were in keeping with the highest traditions of the military service.'

The 17th Airborne Division gained its fourth Medal of Honor in the days following the operation, on 28 March, when 26-year old Technical Sergeant Clinton Monroe Hedrick of the 194th Glider Infantry Regiment received the award posthumously after aiding in the capture of Lembeck Castle, which had been turned into a fortified position by the Germans. Hedrick made a charge straight at the German positions while firing a Browning Automatic Rifle (BAR) from his hips. This inspired the remaining members of his company and they followed him overrunning the enemy positions. Some of the German forces retreated into a castle with Hedrick close behind. Then a German soldier lured Hendrick and his men into a trap by attempting to surrender. Hedrick sensed the trap but was mortally wounded. He was able to signal his men to pull back however, while he single-handedly engaged the enemy forces. By the time that his BAR was silenced he had wiped out the remaining German forces. Bleeding profusely Hedrick died shortly after.

Endnotes Chapter 3

1   Jay Phillips' older brother, C. Gager Jr., would later become a freelance artist, and younger sister, Leaugeay, a talented painter.

2   *The Glider Gang* by Milton Dank.

3   For a time the role of the US pathfinder group in 'Varsity' remained in doubt. The objectives were so close to friendly territory that it was felt that the pathfinder teams' participation would hardly be necessary and so close to German positions that an advance drop by such teams would be suicidal.

4   On 14 September 1944 the Pathfinder School became the IX Troop Carrier Pathfinder Group (Provisional). Lieutenant Colonel Joel L. Crouch continued in command. The change reflected growing recognition of the value of pathfinder tactics in airborne missions and also Crouch's conviction that the pathfinders would be more efficient as an independent organization.

5   'A' Battery was attached to the 507th PIR 'B' and 'E' Batteries were attached to the 194th GIR; 'C' Battery to the 513th PIR. 'D' and 'F' Batteries were landborne echelon who must catch up with the Division once the Rhine had been bridged.

6   *Into Fields of Fire: The Story of the 438th Troop Carrier Group during World II* by Austin J. Buchanan.

7   22-year old Staff Sergeant Isadore Seigfreid Jachman was posthumously awarded the MoH for defending the town of Flamierge in Belgium from a German attack on 4 January 1945.

8   Although it received coverage in the 1 April edition of the *Stars and Stripes,* the fight soon faded into obscurity. It would not be until fifty years later, at the 435th Troop Carrier Reunion in October 1995 that Jella, Deshurley, Campbell and Hurley were each awarded the Silver Star for their defence against the tanks at a range of only fifteen yards. All the others who fought in the battle were awarded the Bronze Star, but many of the more than 280 men had died before their heroism was finally recognized. *Operation Varsity* by John L. Frisbee, *Air Force Association Magazine 79/3* (March 1966).

9   After the war, American families were given the choice of bringing the remains of their loved ones back home, or burying them in Europe. The Phillips family knew that Jay loved flying and was close to the men he served with, so they decided that he should be 'buried with honour' in Europe. Phillips was laid to rest in the American Cemetery at Margraten, Holland.

10 Bob Wilson was recommended for the DFC for this mission but the recommendation got lost in the system and he forgot about it. That is until his daughter in law found Bob's original copy of the recommendation and resubmitted it. The US Air Force upgraded the recommendation to the Silver Star and Bob Wilson was presented with his medal in July 2007, 62 years after he flew the mission the medal was recommended for. From an article by Mr. Richard Chancellor.

11 Martin Wolfe.

12 Three howitzers landed by glider on LZ N joined the battalion later.

Chapter 4

'All Was Clockwork'

Several slugs go through your glider fabric sounding much like a dull drum beat, but no one is hit. Tensely, your eyes dart about as you look for a landing place, for high-tension wires and for other gliders. Now you are down to one hundred feet and out of the corner of your eye you see a transmission tower, but no wires. Just ahead is a pasture with barbed wire fences and there are two gliders touching down... Ahead a glider rolls to a stop, disgorging troops on the run. Just past it is a burning glider with smoke and flames billowing into the air. Glancing to your right, you see a small wood and approaching it, two gliders on the ground, but rolling too fast. The first hits the trees, crumpling the nose and stopping abruptly. The big tail lifts up and then drops. The second glider pilot tries desperately to ground loop, but the right wing catches a tree and his glider is drawn into the woods also, with its parts flying all over... But you are concentrating on the approach and landing, you flare, touchdown, put it up on the skids and quickly come to a stop. You have accomplished your primary mission. But while you were still moving, a rifle slug whined through the glider and the airborne troops started scrambling out of the doors.

A 17th Airborne Division trooper describing the flight. The *Stars and Stripes* **headline on the day after 'Varsity' proclaiming that 'All Was Clockwork' in the American glider operations was only partly true. Successful though the American glider operations certainly were, like most combat missions, they did not go with metronomic smoothness. The glider contingent would have had a much harder time had it not been for the presence of British paratroops on DZ's 'A' and 'B' and of American paratroops dropped by mistake on zones west of Hamminkeln. However, the gliders did bring into the assault area a force of 3,383 airborne troops with 271 jeeps, 275 trailers, 66 guns, ranging in size from 6-pounders to 25-pounders and a wealth of other equipment including trucks and bulldozers.**

At Melun flight chiefs like Grover Benson were supposed to take the place of crew chiefs in their flight when a crew chief became ill before a mission. Cloyd Clemons, the crew chief on Captain Bill Frye's plane was sick and Benson was to take his place. 'I had all my things in the plane ready to go. But he came down to the line and said he felt better and that as it probably would be our last combat mission he wanted to go. And I let him go.' Operations clerk, Bert Schweizer was very close to Clemons' pilot. 'I had tremendous respect for this kind, soft-spoken gentleman.' Before taking off in his C-47 on the morning of 24 March, Frye left his wallet, ring and other personal items with Schweizer for safe keeping. Lou Kramer the 81st Squadron Intelligence Officer had the chance to fly with Bill Frye. He had flown with Frye on one of the Holland missions, to Eindhoven, but this time Colonel Brack, the squadron commander, did not want Kramer to go.

Melun was now stuffed to bursting, not only with paratroopers, but with gliders, ammunition and supplies. In order to provide each glider in the 436th TCG with a co-pilot, 124 glider pilots from the 434th and 438th Groups at Mourmelon-le-Grand and Prosnes respectively (Groups that would be flying paratroopers, not towing gliders) were transferred to the 436th Troop Carrier Group. As a glider pilot, Roland Minot in the 74th Troop Carrier Squadron had secondary duties as Group Mess Officer. 'After consultation with the Mess Sergeant, we proceeded to change how breakfast was served. The Mess Sergeant lined up three field ranges and his crew served hot pancakes, french toast, fried eggs, etc right off the grill. No more cold stuff in large pans.... a great success. Dinners and lunches were served the same way.'

When 2nd Lieutenant John L. Lowden, the former failed power pilot and latterly a glider pilot, in the 434th TCG, attended the briefing, he recalled being ordered to 'take no prisoners for at least seventy-two hours' after landing. Asked what to do if Germans surrendered, they were told 'take them someplace out of the way, like a house or a barn and get rid of them. Either knife them or strangle them. But for Christ's sake, don't shoot them. Some of their comrades might hear that and decide to fight it out, rather than surrender.'[1]

The operation would also be a landmark for the American pilots. The glider pilots finally had much of the equipment so grievously lacking on previous missions: entrenching shovels, good compasses, sleeping bags and canteens. For once all glider pilots had enough good maps and photos of their LZs. Those who wanted them could carry bazookas rather than carbines into battle. Even more important improvements were the protective steel bumpers (Griswold noses) and arrester parachutes fitted to almost all the gliders. IX Troop Carrier Command had finally realized the danger to glider pilots from flak exploding directly under their cockpits and indeed it was known that Germans tried to fuse their ack-ack shells to explode just below the gliders rather than level with or above them. Finally, glider pilots were provided with enough 14-inch square flak pads to sit on: some glider pilots used two of these. Some went even further and managed to scrounge from fighter or bomber depots squares of scrap armour plating that could be installed to really protect their behinds and their legs. On the other hand, glider pilots had to listen to stern lectures aimed at insuring that they would be of maximum use to the airborne infantry once landed. Glider pilots still had high priority for being evacuated; but until it was certain they were no longer needed on the battlefield, they were to report to assigned command posts and remain under the strict orders of a senior glider pilot from the 53rd Wing. Once assembled, glider pilots would serve, in effect, as provisional infantry companies; they were not to let themselves be enticed singly or in small groups into volunteering for some sideshow by junior airborne officers who might need help.

'Supper was with the airborne boys', recalled Adelore Chevalier, one of the CG-4 glider pilots. 'They gave us a good one. Spam and Vienna sausage were prohibited from this mess. They gave us steak. I had no appetite that day and even steak had to be pushed in. After supper a priest said Mass outside. There was good attendance, everybody kneeling on the grass. The feeling surrounding that service was different from anything you will ever experience. It was mighty solemn. The men - boys, I should say - were all in battle dress, Indian haircuts and all, but during that Mass they knelt and bowed their heads more reverently than I'd ever seen it done before. They were going over the Rhine the next morning and they weren't all coming back. I didn't sleep well that night; in fact, I didn't sleep at all.'

Tension was building up fast. Base restrictions were now in effect: no more passes; in fact, no unauthorized entries or exits at all from the bases. Extra guards against saboteurs were posted on both the north-south and east-west runways where the transports and gliders were already lined up.

At each base the carefully rehearsed Group security plans swung into operation. A restriction was slapped on. Special passes were given to all outstanding vehicles. At the veteran 440th Troop Carrier Group's base at Orléans-Bricy (A-50) warning signs appeared all over the compound and quarters... *Home Alive in '45, Don't Talk! ... Enemy Ears Are Listening! ... What You See and Here, Leave Here...* On D-2 the ball was passed to the Squadron Staffs and throughout the day preliminary briefings were held. Questions and answers flew thick and fast inside the guarded briefing rooms... *Those orange pins represent flak positions, but they expect to clean out most of them before Saturday (laughter) ... No, we make a flat right turn...You're damn right the pattern will be crowded...Don't forget to wear GI shoes.* No one was overlooked. Everybody got his instructions.

In the late afternoon of 23 March, C-47s and gliders were marshalled on the runway at A-50 Orléans-Bricy. Behind locked doors inside the War Room of the 440th Troop Carrier Group Headquarters, Lieutenant Colonel Frank X. Krebs, his staff and intelligence officers got down to the 440th's task in the complicated maze of the mammoth plan contained in the terse, clipped phrases of Field Order No. 5. Major Young L. Watson's Intelligence staff sweated over the newly arrived 'Top Secret' material. 'One more river to cross and I'll take me and my damn air medals home,' was in everyone's mind as they eagerly scanned situation maps day and night as excitement mounted. The 440th was to send two serials each of 45-tug-glider combinations filled with a IX Troop Carrier Command Control Unit, a Reconnaissance Platoon of the 17th Airborne Division, together with their equipment to LZ 'N'. At the controls of the lead ship would be Lieutenant Colonel Howard W. Cannon with Colonel Krebs as co-pilot. Both men had flown C-47 *Stoy Hora* to the drop zone near Sainte-Mére-Église on 6 June 1944. Born in St. George, Utah in 1912, Cannon became intrigued by the budding aviation industry while attending Dixie Junior College in the 1930s. He was more than just a little impressed by the glamour of flying in those days. 'Lindbergh had recently made his epic ocean-crossing flight and that added to the pilot mystique that dominated that era.' On 17 September on 'Market-Garden' Cannon and Krebs were again flying paratroopers behind enemy lines, this time in *Miss Yank*. After they had dropped the troops, a C-47 in the 441st TCG collided with their C-47. Except for the navigator, who was captured by the Germans there followed a 42-day odyssey during which they evaded their captors with the help of Dutch civilians.

The 441st TCG was to send one serial of 48 from Dreux, the 442nd one serial of 48 from Sainte André de l'Eure and each would contribute half of another 48-plane serial from Chartres. The three 50th Wing groups would fall into line at Pontoise, the wing departure point. Two forty-plane serials of the 314th Group at Poix in the 52nd Wing area would take position behind them at Wavre. All were to haul Waco gliders in single-tow. Bricy had a giant runway 7,700 feet long, but the other bases were unsuitable for double-tow operations, either because of short runways or lack of marshalling facilities.[2] Simple enough - on paper. Finally, on 'D-1' at ten o'clock in the morning, a mass briefing of power and glider pilots by the 440th Group Staff was conducted at the Royal Theatre.

At 0953 hours the first Pathfinder serial would appear over the target. It was the first link in a Troop Carrier chain over four drop zones and six landing zones that included seven American and six British parachute serials and thirty glider serials divided equally between the two members of the Allied team. The 17th Airborne Division would ride into battle from airfields in the Paris area aboard 1,800 C-47 and C-46 aircraft and CG-4A gliders in both dual and single tows. The British 6th Airborne Division jump off in England would be made with the entire paratroop lift of 240 C-47s. To join the American glider assault, the RAF would contribute 381 Horsas and forty-eight giant Hamilcars, singly towed by C-47s Stirlings and Halifaxes. The two great serial task forces were to converge at a point south of Brussels, while Allied fighters buzzed about protectively.

At Melun after lunch, David Brack and Harold Walker, accompanied by Colonel Williams went on a fast inspection. Born in Shelby County, Kentucky in 1916 Adriel Newton Williams went directly into pilot training following his high school graduation, received his wings in 1939, became an officer and in 1942 assumed command of the 436th Troop Carrier Group, a position he held until the end of World War II. At 1 o'clock all glider pilots attended a Group briefing and were given new 'escape and evasion' kits. Finally, at 4 o'clock, David Brack briefed all combat crews in front of the Operations tent.

In the velvety darkness before dawn on 24 March fresh winds had blown across dozens of airfields in France and England. By the thousands, sleepy-eyed, yawning warriors climbed into their big-pocketed jump suits and pulled on high combat boots. It was another fateful morning of: well, here we go again! May your dog tags never part! This time they were going beyond the Rhine. When assembled a Troop Carrier force of almost 3,000 planes and gliders in a 420-mile-long stream would be aimed squarely at the Ruhr defences. If the aircraft had been strung out in a single file they could have stretched in unbroken line from Paris to Berlin! Altogether the procession across the target would continue for three hours and twelve minutes. The last plane would wheel homeward at 1304 hours.

The 440th tow comprised two serials (A-16 and A-17), each serial containing forty-five tow planes and forty-five gliders. For the first serial, twenty-two C-47s of the 95th Squadron, twenty-two C-47s of the 97th Squadron and one of the 96th Squadron assigned to Group headquarters for the lead ship in the 440th formation, were assigned to transport the Reconnaissance Platoon, the Control Unit and elements of the 139th Engineering battalion. In the second serial there were twenty-one C-47s of the 96th Squadron, one of the 95th and twenty-three of the 98th and would carry the 517th Signal Company as well as elements of the 139th Engineers. Gliders were loaded with a total of 193,433lbs of equipment. Five hundred and thirty-two airborne troops were to board the craft.

At Melun at 0500 hours 19-year old 2nd Lieutenant Clifford Underwood in the 79th TCS, 436th Troop Carrier Group was aroused from a restless sleep. He made his way to the mess tent and was surprised to find waiting for him a steak and egg breakfast. Clifford had trained as a C-47 pilot but in October 1944, just prior to being transferred to the ETO, he had been among hundreds of power pilots who were sent to either Lubbock, Texas or Laurinburg Maxton, North Carolina to make ten landings in a CG-4A glider including one night landing and one check ride. Eleven landings and they were trained glider pilots. They were given some more infantry training to augment what they had received in basic. It had been mandated by the 9th Troop Carrier Command that all power pilots assigned to the ETO after 1 November would fly as co-pilots in CG-4A gliders.

At 0800 hours, the teenager and fellow pilot 2nd Lieutenant James D. Hammett climbed into the cockpit of their CG-4A glider loaded with Troopers from Company 'M', 3rd Battalion of the 194th Glider Infantry Regiment. At 0815 hours they lifted off the runway at Melun and joined the other seventy two gliders and thirty six C-47 tugs of the 436th Troop Carrier Group heading to LZ 'S' a crude rectangle more than two miles long and more than a mile wide, with its long axis tilted east-southeast. It was about half a mile southeast of DZ 'X' and about two miles northeast of Wesel. The double-track railway ran just to the west of it. The most obvious landmark on the LZ itself was the Issel, which curved across the zone, isolating the eastern quarter from the rest.

When Rex Selbe, a C-47 pilot in the 81st TCS at Melun had woken up it had been a bright, sunny, early spring morning and only a few clouds flecked a pale blue sky. 'Most of us had been up for hours. After breakfast - for those who could choke something down - we had a final weather briefing in front of the control tower, plus good luck wishes and a short prayer from the Group Chaplain. Our sixteen C-47 crews, our thirty-two glider crews and the airborne troopers were on board by 0730 hours. Fifteen minutes later it was: engines on! Our Group's lead plane, with Colonel Williams and his two gliders (one piloted by Group Glider Officer William Brown, the other by the 81st TCG's Purl Stockton) took off at 0754 hours. Colonel Williams, in the lead plane with the shortest runway takeoff distance, had to bounce his plane in order to get enough altitude before he ran out of runway. Forty-three minutes later our entire Group was off the ground and manoeuvering over Melun into formation. We were headed for LZ 'S,' just three miles north of

Wesel.'

'Even with full power, it seemed to take forever to get to takeoff speed' wrote Roger Krey, another of the glider pilots in the 436th TCG. 'We literally staggered into the air, just above stalling speed, because of the tremendous load we were pulling. Even maintaining full power, it seemed to take forever to get up a hundred feet off the ground. If, during the first few minutes of flight, one engine would have merely faltered, we would have bored right into the ground. Only after we got up to 500 feet or so was the danger from engine failure reduced; we then could slack off the power somewhat and know that in an emergency we could cut the gliders loose, since they would now have a chance to pick a safe landing spot.

'No collisions; only one glider aborted; no planes down with engine failure! A good beginning for what we hoped would be our last assault mission. We circled Melun once, the usual airman's goodbye. Flying in echelons of four to the right, our plane-glider tandems headed northeast toward Brussels and a rendezvous with the rest of the huge air armada. For a while nothing indicated that this mission would be rougher than the last - certainly not the vast British formations passing to our left with their four-motored planes and huge Horsa and Hamilcar gliders that carried over thirty men or even armoured cars. To me it simply spelled invincibility.'

Though the skies were clear in the early morning, promising a sunny day, Clifford Underwood knew that it would not be 'a walk in the park'. This was the first time in the ETO that double-tow would be used in combat making the two and a half hour flight difficult with all the prop-wash caused by the 36 C-47s flying in formation in their serial. And 10,000 German infantry were ready for them at LZ 'S'. For the first time in the war the landing zones would not be secured on their arrival. German 88 mm anti-aircraft guns were waiting to be lowered on the gliders as they landed.

'After cutting loose over LZ 'S' Hammett and Underwood's glider received light and heavy flak causing a ten inch hole in the right side of the glider as they were landing. Fortunately none of the 'glider riders' was hit. They then received rifle and 20 mm small arms fire but they 'landed without damage to glider or crew.' Due to heavy enemy activity they were ordered to stay with the airborne and dig in for the night. They remained with the airborne until relieved the next day. Immediately after 'Varsity' pilots like Clifford Underwood transitioned from flying two to three missions a week to flying two to three missions a day. For a four week period, from 25 March to 20 April he was flying resupply missions in hostile Germany and bringing out the wounded. It was during this time that he really found out about the atrocities of the war as the forced labour camps were discovered in the many concentration camps. Some forced labourers did not make it home and died in the plane on the return to their country.

At Coulommiers the 437th TCG lined up all 72 of its C-47s on the runway and began its take-offs at 0734. Its first serial assembled and was swinging over the airfield onto course at 0823. The rest would follow it to Wavre and down the centre lane to the Rhine. 'We had two CG-4A Waco gliders attached to each C-47' recalled Don Bolce on Captain Floyd Kelly's crew, who after the briefing had gone to church. 'I prayed that I would survive the mission but if I did not, that God would forgive me my sins and take me to heaven. At the service I met a young 2nd lieutenant, a pilot, who had just joined our outfit. He told me that he would be flying the mission too and that he was really frightened. He said that he had been checked out to fly as a co-pilot on a C-47, but because there was a shortage of glider pilots, he was going to be flying as a co-pilot on a CG-4A glider. He said that he had never been in a glider before and that he had not had the infantry training that the regular glider pilots had completed. This was his first mission. I don't know whether he made it or not, but I truly hope he did!

'The marshalling of so many airplanes and gliders left us with a lot less runway length to get two gliders off the ground at the same time and to be able to get up sufficient speed to get the C-47 into the air. There were a lot of tall trees at the end of the runway and I knew that we had to get both gliders and the C-47 into the air before reaching that point. I watched from the astrodome as the first C-47 and its two gliders lumbered down the runway at full throttle, fifty inches of mercury! When the combination reached the end of the runway, both gliders were already in the air. Then, the C-47 lifted off the runway at a speed just a little bit above stalling and barely cleared the trees. The mission was underway.

'When it was our turn to take off, we pulled forward until the towropes had no more slack. Then Captain Floyd Kelly and co-pilot Major Joe Antrim gave us full throttle and the airplane began to move slowly and gradually picked up speed. Two fully loaded gliders plus the gross weight of the airplane was a challenge for our two Pratt and Whitney engines to get us all into the air before we reached the trees at the end of the runway. The two gliders were into the air relatively soon as our C-47 struggled to pick up sufficient speed to get airborne. As we neared the trees, Kelly pulled back on the controls and we sort of 'mushed' into the air. We gained altitude and joined up with our formation on its way to Germany.

'It was to be a long mission. I don't remember how many hours it took to get to Germany, but I remember that the turbulence from so many aircraft flying together at the same time made our gliders bounce around violently, which caused their towropes to constantly jerk the tail of our aircraft in all directions. The C-47 pilots had their hands full trying to keep the airplane straight and level but the glider pilots were having a life and death struggle to control their gliders in the worst turbulence that any of them had previously experienced. It seemed that we would never get to the Rhine River and the LZ.'

At Poix at 0930 hours Colonel Clayton Stiles, the 314th TCG commander and crew in chalk #1 was rolling with Majors Allen and Kenady flying the first glider tow. Stiles had begun his flying career in 1928. From the summer of 1931 until May 1942 he gained valuable flying experience; first with Delta Airlines, dusting cotton in Texas and then flying commuter flights in the east and Midwest for United Airlines. Colonel Stiles led the 314th TCG on one of the few accurate paratroop drops during Operation 'Husky' and on the night of 5/6 June, upon seeing the wall of clouds that separated and disoriented so many troop carrier units that night, Stiles made a critical decision to go under, rather than through, the cloud bank. The decision kept the formation together and resulted in another accurate drop for the 82nd Airborne Paratroops on board.

Using opposite sides of the runway, the next three followed and the first element was airborne. In the second element the towrope broke on the lead ship piloted by Captain Jack Downhill and a standby crew took their place. Downhill, however, was determined to carry out his assignment and returned; found a glider that needed a tow, hooked up and took off an hour and twenty minutes late to catch the formation at the IP. Chalk #2 was towing Captain Emil Crozier, 62nd Glider Operations Officer as pilot with Flight Officer Wesley J. Hare in the right seat and eight passengers. 'Everything looked peaceful' Hare recalled later. Elated, he turned to say to the airborne troops in his glider, 'Gee, this is a 'milk run,' there's nothing to this!' Then he realized that the glider was diving straight toward the ground. Crozier wore glasses that resembled the bottom of a coke bottle. The battle haze did not help his vision and as they approached their landing spot Wes Hare was watching a farm house directly in their flight path. Wes Hare said, *Do you see that house?* Crozier looked but could not determine the distance and dived the glider into the ground from twenty feet in the air at about 100 mph.

'There was no chance to do anything' Hare said. 'As soon as I turned around and looked, the ground was there and we hit. And then the fire started. We were being shot at from three different farmhouses.' The nose section was pushed into the cargo bay and all on board were injured. Captain Crozier, seriously injured in the crash, was helping Wes Hare and Private Alverez remove another injured trooper from the glider when enemy fire killed Crozier and Alverez.' Wes Hare continues, 'they had us pinned down for two or three hours. Finally the paratroopers and the rest of the airborne troops linked up and went in and cleaned out the houses. One paratrooper had come up over the rail tracks with a Tommy gun and five German prisoners. As he came up the rise in the road at the tracks, some Germans from one of these houses started shooting at him, so he just opened up with his Tommy gun and shot the five German prisoners dead and dropped to the ground, staying by the ditch.' Medics treated the seven survivors and directed Wes Hare to a field hospital.[3]

Of the 610 C-47s and 906 Wacos scheduled to go, eight aircraft and fourteen gliders had to be replaced by substitutes, either because of unfitness to take off or because they aborted soon after starting. An additional 21 gliders dropped out along the route, principally on account of loose or ill-balanced loads, but also because of structural weaknesses and towing difficulties. Three pairs of Wacos flying in double-tow had the short-tow glider foul its mate's rope, with the result that two lost wings and crashed and three had to be cut loose. Aside from these accidents, double-tow worked well.

Take-off and assembly was punctual and without serious accidents, although the strong wind created difficulties; especially at Sainte André-de-l'Eure, where it blew at right angles to the runway. The 442nd Group's

48-plane serial began its take-offs at 0900 and swung over the field in full formation headed for Pontoise at 0935. At Orléans-Bricy the 440th Troop Carrier Group's C-47 propellers whirled impatiently, while the gilders waited submissively in neat rows on both sides of the runway. Pilots sniffed nervously at the cross-wind coming from the left as they climbed into their flak vests. That might cause trouble. Throughout the dawn hours trucks had snarled their way up from Orléans through the still sleeping town of Bricy, carrying the yawning crews. Now all were ready. It was time. But they did not like the way that cross-wind swept across the battered airfield.

Lieutenant Colonel Cannon and Colonel Frank Krebs took off from the long, concrete runway at 0831 with the first glider in tow, piloted by Major Robert Wilson. One after another, at twenty-second intervals, the tow planes moved into line, gently tightened the rope and then poured on the power and roared down the runway into the sky. The drift from the wind was evident at once. Crews still on the ground swore softly as they waited their turn. The take-offs continued with stop-watch accuracy. At 0848 the 96th TCS Commander, Lieutenant Colonel Johnson with Captain Roberson as his co-pilot led the second serial off. In thirty-eight minutes all ninety of Krebs' tug-glider combinations were airborne. Men on the ground heaved a concerted sigh of relief as they watched the skytrain come back over the field to form in groups of four, echeloned to the right. And just as they had resigned themselves to the seating-out stage, one of the C-47s dropped out, released its gilder over the field and landed shortly afterwards. An engine was cutting out. Hurriedly, the business of getting a spare ship into action began, for there was still time to catch the formation. Some minutes later, with the formation already out of sight, another abort winged back over the field. This C-47 had developed a runaway propeller that refused control. Another spare was called on as the Commanding Officer of the 139th Engineers, Lieutenant Colonel Johnson, raged and fumed with impatience and worry for he had been aboard the abortive glider. The second spare got into the sky about a half hour behind the Group formation with the uncomfortable prospect of a lone flight ahead of them. The 346-mile flight to the target, later reported as 'uneventful' had begun.

It was seventy-five miles north northwest to 'Slate' the Wing Departure point near Pontoise and then eighty-two miles northeast to the next checkpoint, 'Jasper', a spot near Sainte Quentin. Then straight on for another eighty miles to the Command Departure Point 'Marfak' where astonished inhabitants of Wavre had a choice ground view of the entire Troop Carrier train flying 1,500 feet above them. On the transports ploughed battling the wind drift. Descending to an altitude of 1,000 feet, the 440th drove on twenty-seven more miles to 'Vega' thirty-two miles to 'Kingston' and thirty-three miles more to 'Yalta' lying twelve miles from the banks of the Rhine and seventeen miles from the target. Down went the C-47s to 700 feet, the prescribed altitude for the release. Nerves tightened as the yellow smoke and yellow panel appeared on the ground, signalling the alert just before the river appeared. Wind, turbulence, prop-wash and the unduly slow air speed specified in the orders gradually distorted the glider formations and caused the rear elements of the serials to stack up until they were 400 feet or more above the leaders. In the 442nd Group formation all but one glider, which was cut loose because of structural weakness, arrived at the Rhine squarely on course within sighting distance of the white panels and yellow smoke which marked the point where they were to cross the river. Excellent fighter cover, both above and below their level protected the formation as it approached the battle area. Between Wavre and the Rhine eight flights of fighters were seen and protection by one flight or more was continuous. No German fighters came forth to challenge them.

Ground fire between the Rhine and the landing zone was remarkably meagre and ineffective. There was only an occasional rattle of small-arms fire as the serials crossed the concave waist of the Diersfordter Wald. Most of the enemy in that part of the wood had already been dealt with by the 507th Parachute Infantry. Fire from the zone itself was hot enough to make Lieutenant Colonel William H. Parkhill of the 441st Group describe it as a 'flaming hellhole' but the shooting was directed at the gliders. The aircraft were mostly left alone.

The first American glider crossing the Rhine was flown by Major Hugh J. Nevins, the glider officer of the 50th Troop Carrier Wing and his co-pilot, 1st Lieutenant 'Bob' Bunks; it carried the inscription *Kansas City Kitty-Mary Lou*, which he had put on in honour of his hometown and his wife. Nevins remembered that the flight from Chartres to the Rhine had been very choppy and that his airborne passengers had become deathly sick. 'Ten minutes out from the initial point on the friendly side of the Rhine I turned the glider over to 'Bob' my co-pilot and went aft to put on my flak suit and helmet with far from steel-nerved hands. We turned right at the initial point and were on 'Last Lap' - the alarming code name given by higher Headquarters to that section of the run-in from the initial point to the Rhine. It was here that Bob and I first saw Marshal Montgomery's unannounced smokescreen at Wesel, billowing north-east to cover the movement of his troops across the river. Unfortunately, the smokescreen was cloud-like and in penetrating it we encountered horizontal visibilities as low as one-quarter of a mile all the way to the drop zone. The north-south railway indicating the release point loomed up ahead. The 'light to moderate' flak and small-arms fire increased to 'intense.' A later remark that the fabric-covered glider sounded like 'a paper sack full of popcorn kernels' aptly fitted the situation. Unfortunately, we were above and parallel to the rail track and embankment, which was infested with Germans and their efficient weapons. While keeping my left eye on my landing zone I put the nose down and we were doing a whistling 120 mph.

'We were doing 100 mph as I turned into the final approach and had to do an immediate nose-high stall and left side-slip, which dropped us from 100 mph to 50 mph instantly. Bob rode the controls with me and we managed to get the left wing up just before contacting the ground some one hundred yards beyond a flaming C-46. The left landing gear sheared off in a ditch and we ground-looped left and stopped. We were 'safe.' Bob and I jumped out of the glider onto the ground and were followed by the dull, airsick troops.

Preoccupied as we had been while flying, it was not immediately apparent that we were receiving fire - accurate fire - from twelve snipers in a nearby building. Our position was untenable unless we silenced the systematic fire so I commenced pumping lead from my rifle into the four nearest windows. Bob reinforced me with his carbine. Fire also was coming from the Red Cross Hospital steeple above us, 100 yards away.

'The stunned airborne troops, perhaps from my lurid demands or from their intensive training, came to life and by judicious use of grenades, Tommy guns and carbines disposed of our immediate enemies. We unloaded the glider and started with three prisoners towards the previously designated assembly area.'[4]

Flight Officer Karl F. Harold was flying his first combat mission. 'It's hard to adequately describe a glider landing,' he later wrote home, 'particularly when it is made in the heart of enemy territory, with fighting going on all about. Too much happens too fast. Some lucky gliders made it without a scratch; others became funeral pyres. One glider, ripped through and through with ack-ack crashed nose first deep into the earth. Not a man came out. In a few seconds, fire started by tracers roared through the fabric. Trying desperately to land before they are destroyed, other gliders smashed through fences, ripped through wires, crashed into ships already on the ground. Men who were unhurt tumbled out of the last ships. Despite the losses, the number of glider troops in the area increases.' Harold and his co-pilot, Flight Officer Bill Waterman, brought their cargo, which consisted of three airborne troopers, a jeep and a supply of artillery shells, in safely, but they were pinned down by sniper fire for over an hour. After the jeep was unloaded, it was driven over to another glider to pick up the British six-pound gun for which it was the carrier. At that point, the glider pilots started out for their prearranged assembly point.

'Bob' Wilson, struggling to land his glider amid the heavy smoke and ground fire, was barely able to lift his glider above a sixty-foot tree before it started to shake as though it were about to stall out. He finally managed to put it on the ground safely and then motioned for his co-pilot to leave the aircraft. 'He was a nice guy and I was a nice guy,' he said later, 'so we unhooked our belts and I said to him, 'Go ahead.' He said, 'No, you go ahead,' and all of a sudden, we're both waiting for the other one to get out of that glider and we realized that they were shooting at us! So now we both went at once and we bumped helmets right there in the cockpit and knocked each other back into our seats! Believe me, I got out first after that and we both jumped into a little ditch that was there and put our noses right in the dirt.'

Flight Officer Oscar 'Joe' T. Rains in the 71st Troop Carrier Squadron, 434th Troop Carrier Group had delivered gliders under combat to landing zones in Normandy and Holland with the chances of being killed by the Wehrmacht. However, it was not the German army but a jeep that now threatened the lives of the men in 'Chalk 132' that he and Lieutenant Richard S. Batlon were flying. Born in Alabama on 15 May 1920, 'Joe' was the fifth child of Oscar and Lula Rains. He had flown a glider on the Normandy 'Chicago' mission, Southern France and the September 18th flight during

'Market-Garden'. Now, 'Chalk 132' was taking men of the 17th Airborne and that jeep. 'At approximately 0910 the formation was already on course, we hit some rough air causing the chocks underneath the jeep springs to jar loose. We continued on, calling to the airborne in the jeep to attempt to tie the load more securely, but they were unable to leave their seats as the jeep was starting to bounce severely so that their helmets were hitting the main bulkhead. When some more rough air was encountered the load started to shift forward against the pilot's and co-pilot's seats causing the nose latch catches to springs. As we had an hour and forty minutes more to the LZ, Batlon thought it best to cast loose. Before doing so he asked my opinion and that of the airborne members. We all agreed. So picking a field in the area we released, approaching a ploughed field on our left - 180 degree approach. As we touched down the load came forward, split the pilot's seat but no further damage was done to the glider. The field was located outside the town of Dampleaux about 45 miles northeast of Melun. We left one Airborne sergeant in charge of the glider and returned as best we could to base.'

Formation flying along the way to the LZ was made more difficult by extreme turbulence, which Colonel Williams in the 436th TCG called the worst he had ever experienced. So strenuous was the task of holding the gliders in position that many of their pilots and co-pilots were glad to be able to alternate in fifteen-minute stints at the controls. As a further complication, the prescribed air speed of 110 mph turned out to be too slow, causing some near stalls and much jockeying for position.

'The picture worsened quickly after about 1015' wrote Thayer Bonecutter, one of Williams' glider pilots. 'We had been pushed along by an unexpected tail wind and our Group was too close to the serial in front of us. Colonel Williams tried to slow us down by 'S-ing,' that is, manoeuvering in large curves from right to left. But such curves were limited by the columns of planes to our left (the British) and our right (the paratrooper planes). We crossed the Rhine when the serials in front of us were still launching their gliders over Wesel. To avoid a jam-up, Williams had to take us up over the prescribed height. This meant our gliders would be released higher than planned - and therefore subject to more flak on the way down. To make matters worse, the British commandoes who had crossed the Rhine some hours earlier had been protected by a thick chemical smoke screen; this was still in the air and it, plus the bombing of Wesel, raised so much dirty smoke that it was really hard to make out our landing zone. And it was not encouraging, either, to be looking ahead and to see that several tow planes already were in trouble and seemed about to crash'.

Just as Thayer Bonecutter was circling for his final approach his glider was hit by flak. 'I was able to land OK; and we came down in a freshly ploughed field, which kept us from rolling too far. But when we came to a stop the airborne troopers there were just frozen in their seats. I yelled, 'Get the hell out!' and the glider emptied quickly - except for one lad who was dead. That flak had exploded right underneath him. And the same shot had wounded the troopers seated to his left and his right. We got the dead and wounded out and did our best to make things easier for the wounded until the medics arrived.

'We dug in around a German house. To our left there was another group of glider pilots. During the night those fellows had to beat off a German attack with tanks. By now glider pilots had enough fire power so they could give a good account of themselves. During that attack I kept thinking that if it moved over in our direction I would have to use my bazooka. But, thank God, I never had to fire it, because - as I found out later - I had positioned its batteries the wrong way! Geary, another glider pilot fixed up my bazooka the next morning. But I never had to use it at all.

'The next day we were relieved and ferried back across the Rhine. There we saw a field with lots of tanks lined up, waiting to cross the Rhine on a pontoon bridge British engineers had just put down. But above the other side a German plane, a lone Ju 88, kept trying to knock down that bridge while our artillery, time after time, sent up a cone of fire around him without knocking him down. That Luftwaffe plane finally had to leave without getting that pontoon bridge.'

Thanks to the clear skies, the simple course and the effective system of beacons no serious navigational problems appeared until the formations reached the Rhine. The intercom sets, as usual, proved unsatisfactory. In the 50th Wing less than half of them functioned. The run-in from the bend in the Rhine near Xanten to LZ 'S' was about six miles long. There the column was to split in two, one line heading for the northern part of the landing zone and one for the southern part, so that the gliders in each serial could avoid congestion by landing in pairs in two separate patterns. In order to land into the wind they were to make a 270° turn to the left after release. As usual that day most of the serials appear to have reached the zone between five and ten minutes ahead of schedule. An exception to this was the 436th Group, which was fourteen minutes early. It overran the rear formations of the 437th Group, causing a jam. As a result about half the pilots of the 436th had to climb and release their gliders from altitudes between 1,000 and 1,700 feet. The other serials maintained safe intervals and with few exceptions released in formation from heights of 400 to 800 feet.

Roger Krey again: 'We sailed over the Rhine at 1,300 feet. Where was the war? I asked myself as I peered down through smoky murk, seeing only some British assault boats on the river and more burning plane wrecks on the ground. In seconds the Kraut gave me my answer: four or five heavy reports from a big flak gun below is enough to tell anyone he is in a war. Bill Lane [the other pilot] gave me a grin: *That's us they're shooting at!* he said.'

Adelore Chevalier continues: 'The Krauts knew when we were coming and they knew just exactly where and they were ready. They had machine guns, antiaircraft and rifles set up in every house, barn, pillbox and slit trench, all over the area. So when our gliders started coming in we caught hell all the way down. A heckuva lotta nice guys died right there in their seats before their gliders touched the ground. Some got it as they were piling out the doors. Some came in on fire and got roasted. I never thought a glider could catch fire from an incendiary bullet, but some did. My glider was one of the very few that didn't collect a mess of lead, even though I flew right through a whole pot full of the stuff making my landing pattern. I had to come in over a high tension line, side-slip like everything and plop it down hard to stop before I went ramming into a woods. Even then a telephone pole got in the way and chopped off ten feet of wing - that was nothing, we hardly noticed it. Then I lay down in a ditch and watched the show. It was the show of a lifetime - I kid you not.'

The glider formations met with the same smoke and haze which had proved such an obstacle to the paratroop echelon. Visibility over parts of the run-in area was reported to be as low as an eighth of a mile and the landing zone itself was very hard to see. However, only a fraction of one or two serials appear to have gone off course. Possibly the pilots could observe the landmarks better than the faster-moving paratroop formations, or possibly the zone was far enough to the southwest to be somewhat in the lee of the smoke.

Roger Krey recalled: 'Looking back, it seems a miracle any of our glider pilots got out of LZ 'S' alive. Practically every glider coming into this landing zone was hit by flak or machine gun fire. German 'flak wagons' of 20 mm guns held their fire until gliders rolled to a stop; so enemy fire, deadly enough as the gliders were coming in, was even more murderous once the troopers tried to get out of the gliders and unload their equipment. The next second we saw smoke coming out of the left engine of our tow plane. The prop slowed. That engine was gone. But even though that plane could have exploded any minute, the crew - on one engine - continued to pull us and the other glider deeper into Germany. But all three aircraft were losing altitude rapidly. Bill Lane of course was anxiously scanning for a place to go down; but the smoke was blocking any clear view. He did know that we were far enough beyond the Rhine to be able to hit our landing zone. And if the gliders got off right away the tow plane crew might have a chance to stay airborne. With a mild curse, Bill hit the rope release. I relaxed my hold on the controls and he took over in a beautiful peel-off. The other glider cut, too. A quick look backward gave me a last look at our tug as it disappeared westward into the haze with the towropes still attached. They looked as though they might make it.

'Now we began to have glimpses of the ground through the smoke. The Kraut, of course, had glimpses of us, too. Gliding silently at 80 mph we seemed to be able to hear every 'crack-crack' of rifles and every 'pup-pup-pup' of machine guns aimed at us. You could see the gun flashes, too. Later I heard that sight described as like flying over a junk yard with hundreds of tin cans glistening back at you in the sun.

'In our glider, our eleven airborne glider troopers began to sing, very loudly, *Hail, hail, the gang's all here!* And I joined in. But after the second series of *hails* a 20 mm shell exploded right in front of the glider and the singing had to stop. Shell fragments got me in the head, face and neck and Bill was hit in the foot. The glider troopers thought we had had it; but the glider wasn't badly hurt and the two of us were still fully effective.

'The smoke now was gone. The sunshine seemed brilliant. My God: there, directly in front of us, was a tall transmission tower and all its wires. No way

A six pounder gun being loaded into a Halifax for 'Varsity'. Using parachute clusters whole jeeps and artillery pieces could be dropped from the bomb bays of Halifaxes.

Above: Glider Pilot Regiment briefing.

Below: Halifax and Horsa glider tow.

Above: Troop Carrier briefing.

Below: 17th Airborne at the 440th Troop Carrier Group base at A-50 Orléans-Bricy loading para-packs under the wing of a C-47.

Above: C-47s of the 32nd Troop Carrier Squadron, 314th Troop Carrier Group lined up for 'Varsity'.

Right: British paratroopers preparing to board their C-47, possibly at Boreham, home to the 310th Troop Carrier Squadron and so the men are most probably from either the 7th or 12th Parachute Battalions.

Below: C-47s in the 50th Troop Carrier Squadron, 314th Troop Carrier Group preparing to board troops for 'Varsity'.

Above left: Bruce Cornelol Merryman, a glider pilot in the 62nd Squadron in the 314th Troop Carrier Group at Saltby.

Above right: Believed to be No.5 Platoon, 'B' Company, 8th Parachute Battalion shortly before take-off for Operation Varsity. Left to right, back row: Unknown Private, Privates Gibbons (KIA 24.3.45) and Thomas, Captain Belson, Privates Russell and possibly 'Paddy' (who later became mayor of Saskatoon, Saskatchuan, Canada) and Sergeant Bryan (KIA 24.3.45). Middle row: Possibly Jimmy Stagg and David Gooding (KIA 24.03.45), Privates Witchett, Donaldson and Maskell (KIA 24.3.45). Front row: Private Fisher, Fred Potts, Unknown, Sergeant Glover. Lying down at front: Privates Bean and Sam Rafferty. (Nick Rafferty)

Below, left: Colonel James 'Lou' Coutts, Commanding the 513th Parachute Infantry Regiment.

Right: Colonel Edson D. Raff, commander of the 507th Parachute Infantry Regiment.

Above: C-47s in the 440th Troop Carrier Group at A-50 Orléans-Bricy

Right: A young British paratrooper en route to Wesel during Operation 'Varsity-Plunder'.

Below: Glider tow ropes being prepared by British ground troops.

Above: 17th Airborne Division paratroopers march to their waiting C-47s.

Left: 17th Airborne paratroopers board a C-46 Commando that will drop them over the east bank of the Rhine during 'Varsity' on 24 March. (National Archives)

Below: Glider pilot's view of his Stirling tug aircraft on takeoff.

Halifaxes and Stirlings tow Airspeed Horsa gliders over the French countryside shortly after crossing the English Channel, en route to the landing zones east of the River Rhine.

Above: Major General Eric Louis Bols CB DSO and Brigadier Stanley James Ledger 'Speedy' Hill, commanding 3rd Parachute Brigade (in passenger seat).

Below: American glider troops of the 194th Glider Infantry Regiment after landing near Wesel.

Above Left: A dead US paratrooper whose parachute got snagged on telegraph wires. (Robert Capa)
Above right: A dead US paratrooper hanging limp from a tree.

Halifax IIIs and VIIs of 298 Squadron with 644 Squadron's IIIs at Woodbridge on 24 March. On the runway are 48 Hamilcars with twelve Horsas at the far end. Unlike the gliders, none of the Halifaxes have invasion markings because of involvement in bombing and SOE drops at night.

Right: Corporal Clinton M. Hemsley of San Diego, California pictured on 22 March 1945 replacing the windshield in a glider which is equipped with a new type Griswold nose at Coulommiers-Voisin (A-58) from where the 194th Parachute Infantry Regiment took off on 24 March. This heavily armed glider is one of 25 that transported the HQ Company, 2nd Battalion. (US Army Signal Corps).

This famous photo was realised by Robert Capa in the morning of Saturday 24 March just prior to the jump over the Rhine. The soldier is James 'Jim' P Conboy Jr from Company HQ. Jim was born in 1925 in Philadelphia, PA. He was inducted on 14 January 1944 in New Cumberland, PA. Just after the jump, a 20 mm shell hit his right leg, shattering it. His leg was amputated. (National Archives)

Left: Waco CG-4 gliders carrying 17th Airborne Division troopers in the 507th PIR to Wesel behind a C-46 Commando transport during a Double tow.

Below, right: Two German soldiers, one dead and the other seriously wounded photographed by Allied forces during Operation 'Plunder'.

Waco glider 43-41084 in the 83rd Troop Carrier Squadron, 437th Troop Carrier Group, which was towed by C-47 42-100572 that was flown by Captain Thomas F. Rataiczak and 1st Lieutenant James R. Youngs Jr. The glider was piloted by Flight Officers Arthur R. Johnson and Carl E. Jones, both of whom were KIA in the crash near the farm at the cross-roads of Molkereiweg and An Der Lackfabrik.

Above: The C-46 Commando was bigger than the C-47 and could carry double the number of paratroopers that a C-47 could carry. The exit time for the paratroopers was the same as the C-46 had two exit doors, one on each side of the plane.

Below, left: Corporal Frederick George 'Toppy' Topham VC of the 1st Canadian Parachute Battalion.

Below, right: Lieutenant Ellis 'Dixie' Dean MC who commanded the Vickers Medium-Machine Gun Platoon in the HQ Company, 13th Battalion (Lancashire), The Parachute Regiment.

Below and inset: Private George J. Peters MoH. When Peters and a group of ten other troopers landed in an open field near the town of Fluren they were raked by enemy machine gun fire and, armed with only his rifle and a few grenades, he charged the German machine gun nest. He was badly wounded but, crawling to within fifteen feet of the gun emplacement, threw two grenades, which killed the machine gun crew.

Inset, right: Technical Sergeant Clinton Monroe Hedrick of the 194th Glider Infantry Regiment who was awarded a posthumous MoH.

Below: The body of a 17th Airborne Division trooper.

Above: C-47s in formation over the Rhine.

Below: 78th Troop Carrier Squadron, 435th Troop Carrier Group C-47 landing at Welford.

Practice para drop.

to go over it at our airspeed; Bill dived the glider under the wires and swept around the tower. This increased our airspeed - something we truly did not need, now that we were about to land. But I yanked the red handle for the arrester chute and our speed once more was under control. I pulled the yellow handle to release the chute as Bill flattened the glider for a landing. We skimmed half across a large field - and we were in. We were under fire; but there was no panic as all thirteen men on that glider piled outside in an instant.

'Hell in the air over Wesel that day had lasted about fifteen minutes for our airplane crews; for our glider pilots, hell coming down and hell on the ground lasted another twelve hours. Those who came through with only minor injuries carry the emotional scars of those terrible hours. With a load of infantry in your glider, it is the pilots who leave last. The glider's doors are in the rear. Pilots have to unbelt and pick up their weapons before running for those rear doors. But this can have its advantages. With a glider on a landing zone, the enemy may wait to fire until they see men pouring out the doors. Another matter of luck is - which is safer, the right or left door? That depends on which side is facing the enemy. In our case, the door on the right was the lucky one - that's the one Bill Lane and I used. German rifle fire did not get either of us.

'I was last out and went through the doorway in a fiat dive, clutching my submachine gun. I hit the ground and looked around. What I saw was bad. Three or four of the airborne men had been hit. Their lieutenant and sergeant were taken out of the fight right beside the unlucky left door; neither could move. All the lieutenant could do was yell at us not to draw any more fire. Bill and I could do nothing but keep very flat along with the infantry and hope that the fire would remain over our heads. Nobody could spot where the Germans were shooting from. It seemed as if the two or three gliders now down in this field had the whole Wehrmacht to contend with. But soon the situation changed. As more of our big birds floated in, the Germans' fire seemed to get more dispersed and confused. One of the airborne men near me thought he could make it to a safer place. He shouted my way: 'Lieutenant, wanna get out of here? I'll try if you cover me. Follow behind with your grease gun and every time you see me hit the ground and roll back up, you do the same!'

'Let's go!' I yelled back.

'OK, but first I gotta get back into the glider for mortar ammo!' I saw this guy had been hit; but he was not about to give up. He went back in, crawled out of the glider with a bag of mortar rounds, slung the bag over one shoulder and took off. I followed about fifteen feet behind and we both made it to a nearby patch of woods. I never saw that airborne guy again; but I may well owe my life to him.

'Bill Lane also made it somehow out of that German fire. I was glad to see him the following day in the same field hospital where I ended up. That field hospital, by the way, had itself been brought in by gliders.'

'As soon as I took off my boot to see what damage that piece of flak had done, my foot started to swell up' recounted Bill Lane. 'It was a small wound but I could not get my boot back on. We walked out along a ditch, looking for an aid station. Then, standing on top of the ditch, we saw the same lieutenant and his squad who had been in my glider. Back in Melun, when they had been loading up, I had noticed some equipment I never saw before; but when I asked about it the lieutenant had told me it was classified. Now that we were down on the battlefield he could explain: it was a new recoilless rifle just arrived in the ETO. This would be the first time it would be used in combat. He and his men were watching three German Tiger tanks they knew were behind a farmhouse. The tanks, just then, started to move out; and the troopers got all three tanks with just four shots.'

The luck of the 81st TCS had deserted them. During the approach ground fire brought down two aircraft in the lead serial, forcing their gliders to cut and land about a mile short of their destination. Their glider pilots accounted for seven percent of those sent by the 53rd Troop Carrier Wing into LZ 'S' that day; but they took 14 percent of the 53rd's glider pilot casualties. Among them, Ray Gephart and John Hampton were known dead; John Kearns, Tom McGrath, Pierson Metoxen, George Pittman and John Sweeney were all missing in action; and Lee Personius, Jim Pritchett, Rex Cook, Roger Krey, Bill Lane, Fred Tuck, Harry Zonge and Chauncey Clapp were either wounded or injured. Ellery Bennett, a C-47 pilot in the 81st TCS recalled that 'Chauncey Clapp caught a burst in the legs and the back; but he had a piece of metal under him, a sheet cut out of the kind of armour plating they had in fighters. I finally found out he was in a hospital in Paris and a batch of us went up to see him. When we walked in, the first thing he said was: 'Well, they didn't get my family jewels!'

Several men were spectators of that most terrible drama - seeing some of their buddies facing death in front of them. Gale Ammerman had to watch while Ray Gephart's and John Hampton's glider was riddled by machine-gun fire; no one, neither pilots nor airborne troopers, got out of the glider alive. Several saw Captain Edward J. Vosika's C-47 with one engine on fire. (One of the gliders this plane tugged was piloted by Bill Lane and Roger Krey). Vosika reported: 'The run-in was started at the IP and proceeded uneventfully until we crossed the paratroop drop zone. About 800 yards after crossing the DZ we were fired upon and hit in the left main tank and left engine. The left engine wasn't giving very much power and I didn't feather it, as it would be an invitation to more fire from the ground. The gliders hung on and with absolute full power I pulled the gliders to the LZ. My gliders cut in the same spot as did the three ships in front of me. It was the LZ, as I saw the canal in front. I made my turn and at that time my crew chief told me that we were burning underneath. I told him to watch the fire's progress and told the co-pilot to pull the fire extinguisher on the left engine. At this time I feathered the left prop. When I had reached a heading of 240° (the reading out) I put the ship into a steep dive so that I could regain my air speed and also if anything worse should happen, we would be on the west bank of the Rhine. Just as we crossed the Rhine at low altitude, the crew chief reported that the fire seemed to be out as the smoke had stopped; but that the gas fumes were strong in the cabin. I had remembered the field at B-100 as we went by going in and I headed for it. Landing was single engine with wheels down. None of the crew was injured. Looking over the plane upon landing I found the following damage: Left engine: out and burned and covered with fire extinguisher fluid. Left prop: had a bullet hole. Left main tank: bullet went through tank, floor boards in cabin and through top of ship. A couple of holes in left wing; holes in tail and horizontal stabilizer, a hole in the right engine but don't know where it came out.'

1st Lieutenant Stuart J. Anderson was flying on Captain William M. Frye Jr's right wing. 'We split for the 'run in' and I was flying parallel with him at a distance of about 400 yards, when I noticed flames coming from one of his engines. I called him and told him he was on fire, but there was no reply and he kept on flying his course. The gliders released over the LZ and he immediately started a steep climb. I watched him in his climb until he was out of my line of vision due to my forward flight. The last attitude I saw him in was this vertical climb.'

2nd Lieutenant Harry W. Zimmerman, co-pilot for Captain Wolf in another C-47 added: 'Captain Frye was behind us leading an element. We had cut our gliders and climbed up 400 to 500 feet to make our turn. During the turn I looked out the right hand window and saw a ship pull straight up in a vertical climb. The gliders cut loose when the ship went into this climb. The ship was going over on its back and started to drop. I saw two men jump at this time but can't be certain whether the chutes opened or not. The ship was falling down, tail first and gradually the nose came down and it went into a dive. The ship pulled out of this dive and started into another climb. It was going up as in a chandelle when it fell off on one wing and went straight down. I saw the ship crash and burn and saw no one else bail out. In my opinion the ship was out of control at all times indicating a hit in the cockpit.'

Ken De Blake, the radio operator on the C-47 that had once buzzed the Arc de Triomphe, wrote: 'The Wesel mission shook me up badly. Willard Cooke, who had been my co-pilot all the way through transition training and for the flight overseas, was Frye's co-pilot on this mission.'

2nd Lieutenant Willard Richardson Cooke Junior was a Texan, who was one of two brothers, born on 16 June 1922 at Galveston County. His brother, John R. Cooke, was a power pilot also, in the 81st Squadron.

De Blake was looking out the navigator's window at the time to keep track of any hits they might get in or behind the engines. 'Lieutenant Frye's plane, apparently, took an incendiary hit, or anyway, I saw a fire starting up right by one of his engines. I had to sit there and watch while the fire must have melted off some of the control surfaces on that side, since the plane went into a dive. The pilots pulled it out, though and they followed through with their approach pattern, going right straight ahead toward the landing zone. Then they must have gone into another dive, since I lost sight of them.'

Ellery Bennett, C-47 pilot, wrote: 'Going over the Rhine we saw at least three British bombers used as tow planes and five Horsa gliders going down out of control in front and to our left... Bill Frye was right in front of us. I watched him get hit. That plane must have caught it right in the cockpit. In his death agonies a pilot probably would pull back on the wheel; and that plane just went straight up, turned over on its left wing and then went straight down. It didn't look as though it went into any spin whatever.'

Jerome Loving, crew chief added: 'As we were coming in for the glider release I could see the British planes getting hit one after the other. Just as we crossed the river, one of our own flight leader's planes [Frye's] was hit and one of its engines caught fire. We called to him on the radio to tell him that fire was streaming out behind him. We were worried he couldn't see it. After cutting off his gliders he snapped his plane up and down trying to blow out the fire; but on the third attempt he went down and crashed.'

Hal Friedland, radio operator, could see that Captain Frye's plane was on fire. 'I knew that Eugene Davis who had flown with us several times as navigator was on that plane. I heard somebody yelling over the radio to them: 'Whip it! Whip it! The fire will blow out!' As if in answer the plane started a steep climb. But suddenly it broke off, flipped over on its back and plunged down. I could see the cockpit escape hatch on top of the plane pop open; but nobody got out that way.'

In all, out of 295 aircraft entering the battle area on their way to LZ 'S', twelve were lost due to anti-aircraft fire, one lost by accident on its return and a further 140 were damaged by the same fire. Although fourteen of the damaged aircraft were forced to make emergency landings and about that many more needed 3rd or 4th echelon repairs, a great many had nothing but harmless bullet holes. Of the crews, four men were known to be dead, seven wounded and 23 missing at the end of the month. The lead serial made its release at 1036, the last at 1140. Within little more than an hour they delivered approximately 572 gliders containing 3,492 troops and 637 tons of cargo, including 202 jeeps, 94 trailers and 78 mortars and artillery pieces, to the vicinity of LZ 'S'[5]. In accuracy and concentration the glider landings compared favourably with those in previous operations.

Pfc Jack Trovato in the 155th Anti-aircraft Artillery Battalion recalled: 'We had squeezed into this egg crate in what seemed to be the middle of the night. At dawn's light, the view through the window was both awesome and majestic. The sky was filled with planes and gliders as far as the eye could see. Strangely, I felt more like a spectator then a participant in this event. The ride got bumpy and I could feel my stomach turning. I fought this feeling until I saw Murphy throwing up, followed by the rest of the squad and myself. It was one big stinking mess. I was in a state of disgust with myself, but was shaken out of it when I saw these big, black puffs of smoke all around us. The realization that this was flak from enemy AA guns brought me to the ready; someone was trying to kill me! We jumped out of that stinking mess in what seemed a split second.

'The next two hours in and around the drop zone, was confusing and chaotic. The events flashed through my mind like a kaleidoscope: the squad spread out all over the place, crawling on our bellies trying to get together. Enemy small arms fire was picking off men who dare to kneel or stand up. Mortar shells were opening up the ground here and there. Gliders were landing in every direction, tearing themselves up by hitting houses, telephone poles and power lines. C-47s were being shot down like sitting ducks as they exposed their bellies in banking manoeuvres after dropping their cargo. I was to see many men get killed or wounded that day. I saw a trooper who had his cheek torn open by small arms fire. He stood there, his helmet down around his neck, blood running down his face and body. With a boiling anger in his eyes, legs spread apart, he began pumping lead from a grease gun into a house one hundred feet away. Within seconds he was blown away by small arms fire. Whoever he was, I will never forget him. The 155th suffered 30% casualties in that first two hours.'

Lieutenant Kenneth Tudor and co-pilot Lieutenant Richard Beck in Serial A-18 were assigned glider #2 (45-6489) with a few, no more than seven, infantrymen of Battery 'A' and a 75 mm Howitzer gun destined for LZ 'N'. They landed late morning and were greeted by flak and small arms fire. 'On the approach we received small arms fire', reported Richard Beck. 'We made a 360 degree turn and stacked right behind Major Morris in NE corner of the LZ. No.4 Glider was undamaged on landing but another glider later landed between us and tore up the wing. We helped get the 57 mm gun out and then stated for the GP assembly point to shelter in the embankment. During the night we helped repulse an enemy counter-attack and when we encountered German gun fire we fired upon a group that did not answer appropriately to the call signs. The enemy suffered heavily in men captured and killed. One German approached my foxhole with a knife and I shot him in the chest and leg. My squad captured 38 Germans and all the prisoners were marched to the stockade the following morning. Second Lieutenant Baker and I stood guard around the perimeter track. Baker was shot through the head. He was dead. He was only about ten feet from me. No doubt he was killed instantly. The next morning we moved the prisoners to an area near the Rhine and handed them over to the MPs. Around 0900 hours on 25 March my squad was evacuated to Helmond airfield to catch a flight back to B-86, Dreux airfield, arriving back on March 26th.'

A total of 72 C-47s of the 439th Troop Carrier Group and 144 Waco CG-4A gliders had taken off from Châteaudun. Larry Rue, the *Chicago Tribune* correspondent, flew in one of the lead planes of the 439th Troop Carrier Group. 'Miles before we came to the Issel Canal and to the Rhine, we passed over rubble heap after rubble heap, blasted or burnt out towns and buildings... here and there, around deserted barnyards, there seemed to be some stray chickens, but there was no sign that any of the civilian population remained in that area at all. There was a slight ground haze as we crossed the Issel and approached the Rhine. Through the window, to the south, I could see that there was still some fighting going on at Wesel. ...It was immediately after we crossed the Rhine that the flak came up at us. Pilots cannot take evasive action when towing gliders. In the plane, the bursting shells outside - this was small stuff - sounded as if someone were pounding on the bottom of the ship with a heavy hammer... the tree-tops over a long distance were covered with parachutes. Flashes from guns and smoke indicated a battle was going on here as well as in Wesel. The flak subsided when we got to the drop zone, but beneath us we could see that some of the preceding gliders had not fared too well. One was burning and another had crashed headfirst and there were some bodies and equipment scattered around it... our gliders unhooked in a good position and the last I saw of them they were gliding under control, in the centre of the drop zone.'[6]

Of 157 loads delivered by the first two serials, 139 were well concentrated at their proper destination, the east end of LZ 'S'. A sequence of fifteen gliders at the tail of the lead serial achieved the feat of packing themselves into a strip a quarter-mile long and the first dozen of the next serial did equally well in a neighbouring area. In the four middle serials the Wacos were spread loosely all over the zone, about a dozen outliers were scattered up to a mile away from it and two landed more than two miles off in the British sector. After the last two serials split at DZ 'W', part of the left-hand line deviated too far to the north. In consequence, of 141 gliders brought across the Rhine by those two serials, only 58 landed as they were supposed to on the west end of the zone. This error by the 439th Group, the only significant inaccuracy by American glider formations in 'Varsity', was less serious than it might have been. Since most of the territory for three miles northwest of LZ 'S' was occupied by other drop and landing zones, most of the misplaced glider men found themselves among friendly troops.

As the gliders swooped down in their 270° turn, they ran into savage fire from flak and small arms. According to one prisoner, the Germans had fused their shells to burst at 500 feet, a little low for most of the aircraft but effective against the gliders. Also, it was observed that the gunners seemed to concentrate on the gliders rather than on the aircraft. LZ 'S' was infested with entrenched riflemen and machine gunners. Every building in sight seemed to house snipers. There were several batteries of 20 mm flak guns, at least four 75 mm and 88 mm pieces and innumerable mortars in action. Over fifty percent of the descending craft were hit by flak and a similar proportion by small arms. Less than a third were not hit. The gliders given high releases by the 436th Group seem to have suffered a little more than the rest from flak, but otherwise all serials fared approximately the same. Though most of the Wacos were hit, only perhaps half a dozen were shot down. Many were wrecked on landing, usually by collision with trees, telephone poles or other gliders. Wounded pilots and damaged controls were contributing factors in some cases. At least nine gliders were destroyed on the ground by shells and tracers. Several other Wacos were so raked by machine guns and rifle fire that all or most of the occupants were hit before they could take cover. Under the circumstances fighting came first and assembly second.

At first the landing zone was a scene of the wildest confusion with at least 150 small battles raging at various points. In these fights concentration counted heavily. Troopers of the 194th Glider Infantry Regiment landed accurately in the midst of a number of German artillery batteries that were engaging Allied ground forces crossing the Rhine and as such many of the gliders were engaged by German artillery pieces that had their barrels lowered for direct-fire and their gliders and tow aircraft took heavy casualties. Private Vitautas Thomas of Headquarters, 1st Battalion, 194th Glider Infantry, was especially nervous as his glider banked hard and came in for a rough landing. His brother, a member of another unit in the 17th Airborne, had been killed in action during the Battle of the Bulge. Vitautas wondered if his own time had come. The glider carrying Thomas, his five fellow squad members and their jeep loaded with ammunition made a typical crash landing. Smashing through a barbed-wire fence, the glider hurdled a large ditch and ploughed into an embankment. The men inside were thrown around and the jeep broke partially free from its lashings and jammed against the side of the glider fuselage. Thomas lost his helmet and rifle in the crash. Under intense machine-gun fire from a nearby building, the glider troopers scrambled out and dived into a ditch. The German gun raked the glider and the men held their breath, fearing that the ammunition on the plane would explode at any minute. Later, when things had quieted down a bit, Thomas decided to crawl back to the glider to get his rifle and helmet. He swallowed hard when he found that a German round had passed through his helmet, leaving two gaping holes. Thankful that his head had not been in the helmet, he inched forward to recover his rifle. Just as he reached it, a sniper put a bullet into one of the jeep tyres right beside his head. The noise of that tyre deflating was enough for Thomas. He scrambled back to the ditch and there he stayed until other troopers had cleared the building.

The role of the 194th Glider Infantry and its attendant artillery was to occupy the southeast corner of the divisional sector bounded on the east and south by the River Issel and Canal. It was to make contact with the British commandoes on the southwest, the 507th PIR to the west and the 513th PIR on the north. Thanks to exemplary performances by pilots and glider pilots in the 437th Group in the second serial, the 194th Glider Infantry was able to assemble within a quarter of an hour, taking fifty prisoners in the process. The 2nd Battalion with 90 percent of its gliders on the zone, most of them well grouped, was off to the best start. Its companies had assembled and were advancing on their objectives within 45 minutes after landing. Fastest of all was half of Company 'E'. Shortly thereafter it and part of Company 'F' converged upon a German regimental CP and took it with a rush. So bewilderingly swift had been their onslaught that as the German commander was going out the door of the dugout under guard, an orderly, unaware that the CP had been captured, dashed out of an inner room calling 'Sir, you forgot your maps.'

The most graphic account of what might happen to a glider pilot once he joined the battle on the ground comes from Sherman 'Bull' Ryman in the 81st TCS, 436th TCG; a rather heavy man with a build like a wrestler.

'Several of our troopers were hit on the way down. The Germans were still firing at us after we got out of the glider; but we were able to haul out the wounded and dive into a nearby empty canal. Pretty soon we were able to get the wounded men to medics. When all of us glider pilots showed up at a rendezvous point, we were given an assignment to go down a road and set up a roadblock at a railroad crossing. The road went into Wesel. Down the road we could see a German tank half up a sidewalk: it was on fire, looking as though it was about ready to blow. There was no way to get around that tank by going in back of the buildings, because the Germans out in the woods behind the buildings then would see us. Those stone and brick houses were separated by alleyways about ten or twelve feet apart; so we had to run by the alleyways, one at a time, to stay out of the field of fire from the Germans behind the town. By the time I got by that tank I could feel the adrenaline pumping pretty good. Sure enough, after we all got by, the tank blew up.

'Further down the road things got quieter - too quiet to suit us. As much as we could, we kept behind the scattered small houses and trees while we kept on going. Around here some houses had white sheets hanging out of the windows - what did all that mean? Pretty soon we realized the people were showing they wanted to surrender, or maybe that they didn't want their houses shot up. By now it looked as though we had gone too far, past the perimeter we were to set up. We stopped and got out the maps; and sure enough, we had walked too far! We could spot ourselves by a railroad track running parallel with the road.

'We decided to walk back along the railroad instead of the road; this was safer, out of view of the houses. It was then we saw how the Germans had coped with the endless bombing of their railroads by Americans and British. On one side of the track they had dug a continuous trench - in a zigzag pattern to protect themselves as much as possible from strafing - so that when bombers or fighters came along everybody on those trains could scramble into a trench. Most of us were walking along the track on the side of that trench; but Tommy McCann and I were on the other side.

'All of a sudden machine gun and rifle fire started to come our way. The guys on the other side of the track jumped into that trench. Mac and I hit the ground. Luckily, the path we were on had a slight rise beside it; but this rise was only about a foot high and about fifteen or twenty feet long and after that the land flattened out. When I looked to my left I could see bullets hitting the top of that rise and chewing it up. The dirt was showering down on us and that rise seemed to be getting smaller and smaller. We moved forward about six feet; but they must have guessed what we were doing, because they started to work on us again in the new position. The same thing happened when we moved back again.

'Now we were really pressing our faces into that dirt. The thought flashed through my mind: this is it. I remember thinking 'So long, Ma.' The machine gun that seemed so anxious to make our acquaintance wasn't firing continuous bursts, but rather with pauses in between - I suppose to prevent it from overheating. During one pause we heard this loud clanking - and there through the bushes we could see a tank coming down toward us. It had to be a German - our people didn't have any tanks around yet.

'The way he was going, if that tank crossed the road we would have seen my big butt lying on the other side of the tracks. Now we could see it was a Tiger tank with a big 88 gun on the turret. We yelled at the guys in the trench to give us some covering fire; they did and the machine gun stopped. Mac and I jumped up, dashed across the track and dove into that trench.

'When the tank reached the tracks, not far from where we had just been, it stopped; they must have realized there was trouble around. But the tank was tightly buttoned up; and they couldn't really see too much. They turned that turret down toward the trench where we were, but they couldn't see us; then they straightened out the turret. Finally the tank and the rest of the Germans moved on up the road.

'Our glider pilots were committed to help hold a defence perimeter between LZ 'S' and Wesel. This was aimed at repelling an expected German attack from the direction of the town toward that landing zone. The same LZ might have to be used by gliders the following day.

'During the afternoon, several hundred American glider pilots from several squadrons moved into this perimeter and did what they could to prepare for what the night might bring. From where they were digging in they could see the Diersfordter Forest and hear the scattered fire still coming from that direction. Mac and some of the others said they were going to sack up in an abandoned building. But [Julian] Hoshal and I decided that a better bet was a two-man foxhole. We found a nice spot hidden by a couple of bushes. In front of the bushes was a huge bomb crater that gave us a good field of fire. It was getting dark. We broke out our K-rations and tried to get comfortable. It had been a long day. The next thing I knew I was waking up with a hand across my mouth. Hoshal's face was inches from mine and he had a finger across his lips. 'Krauts!' he whispered. Now I could hear them, maybe three or four. I slipped my 45 out of my holster and felt for the handle of my trench knife strapped to my boot. But before long those Germans moved off.

'When morning came the Germans let fly what we called 'screaming meemies.' These were mortar shells with a whistle or a screamer attached that made them sound as though they were coming down right on top of your head. They kept this up for about twenty minutes. Pretty soon some of the shrapnel from those mortars were coming right down into our foxhole. Hoshal reached down and picked up a good-sized piece; luckily for him he had leather gloves on, because that piece of lead was so hot it sizzled on his hand. Meanwhile, there wasn't anything to do but lie there in that hole and take it.

'Finally, the barrage stopped. Thank God! Hoshal and I just sat there looking at each other. He said, 'Bull, I don't know how you can be so calm!' I said 'Hosh' I was thinking the exact same thing about you!' We broke out laughing - pretty hysterical, I guess.'

The first artillery support received by the 194th Glider Infantry came not from the guns landed with it but from British guns across the Rhine, against targets given them over the radio of the 681st Field Artillery. They went into action soon after the landings, at a time when assistance was particularly welcome and continued to good effect throughout the day. As the convoy flew over the river, the 680th Field Artillery reported that 'all Hell seemed to break loose.' The flak and smoke made such a solid wall around the aircraft and gliders that it was almost impossible to see the drop and landing zone below them. Then the green lights flashed, the troopers rushed outside the transports and the gliders cut loose and floated earthward. The first members of the 680th to land were those in the Liaison Party led by Captain Joe T. Payne who jumped with the 3rd Battalion of the 513th PIR. Some gliders were shot to pieces in the air but most landed miraculously on the ground where upon the men inside burst out, ran for cover and began to organize 'in a hell of a hurry'. It was approximately 1140. Before taking up their role as gunners, the men of the 680th were obliged to fight as infantrymen to secure the perimeter. The artillery loads were spread among 97 gliders with only 321 enlisted men and officers to handle them but in less than three hours the first howitzers were in position and ready to fire. In all, the 680th managed to get eight guns into position after a dispersed landing and some hard infantry fighting. Two of its guns had been landed too far away to reach the unit and two had been destroyed by enemy fire. All of the anti-aircraft guns appear to have arrived safely.

Major Dantes A. York of the 680th Field Artillery wrote that: 'Crossing the Rhine we had no difficulty in locating ourselves, as we were familiar with the outline of the river from our map studies, but we were soon in a cloud of smoke which blotted out much of the detail on the ground below and kept us from being sure of our ground location. The Germans cut loose with everything they had. On signal the pilot cut loose, stood the glider on its nose and came in for a quick landing. We cleared the glider and hearing nothing but small arms fire, started unloading our jeep. Then it happened. Our glider took a direct hit from a German field piece in the vicinity and both men with me were badly wounded. I got first aid to the men and proceeded to orient myself and collect men and material. We discovered we were over a mile from our pre-designated landing area. As additional gliders landed, enemy artillery took them under direct fire and systematically destroyed about eight of the sixteen or more gliders which landed in the same field. With Lieutenant Zimmerman I located one of our howitzers, moved it to a point of vantage and took the German battery, now located, under direct fire. We had a muzzle burst on our fourth round which wounded all the crew but me. A direct hit from the German battery then destroyed our piece. I got the wounded under cover and taken care of, then started to gather personnel together to flank and capture the German battery. En route we captured six enemy soldiers and gathered several glider loads of our material and personnel. Meanwhile Lieutenant Price was attacking the enemy battery from the flank and rear. By direct fire at 300 yards he neutralized the position and then personally led the charge which killed or captured all 25 of the cannoneers manning the guns.'

Captain Thomas F. Magner of Battery 'B' said: 'At 1145 hours our glider was cut loose over the town of Blumenkamp. The pilot managed to manoeuvre through intensive anti-aircraft fire and landed in the field to the south of the town. Immediately upon landing, we ran from the glider, took shelter in a shell hole and surveyed the area. The field was rapidly filling up with gliders, some crashing into the trees and telephone poles, some turning end over end. About twenty yards to the north-east, three gliders and their loads were disappearing in flames - direct hits of German artillery. The continuous crack of enemy small arms and the chatter of their automatic weapons from nearby strong points made the open field a death trap for standing personnel. Immediate assembling of units and orderly movements were rendered impossible because of the enemy's excellent observation and fire power. Two needs were uppermost in our minds: exact orientation and neutralization of enemy fire so we could move to pre-designated areas. Captain Greenfell reconnoitred to our west and determined the location of a single track railroad, one of our check points. All this while, glider crews were unloading howitzers and prime movers and attempting to move northward. I dispatched Sergeant Angetaed to clear the woods to the northeast corner of the field. His men concentrated their fire into the woods and upon charging the strong point found four German artillery pieces camouflaged by the bushes, which the enemy had hastily abandoned. The cannoneers for these pieces had been driven away by our fire and rapid closing on the position.

'Houses along the railroad track sheltered German soldiers and hostile civilians; the battalion commander organized small detachments to storm these points and knocked out all resistance. Men seized whatever weapons were at hand, poured terrific and effective fire into enemy strong points and dugouts and closed with the enemy rapidly to destroy him wherever he appeared. These actions were all simultaneous and in an incredibly short time elements to the battalion were moving rapidly toward their position areas.

'My jeep towed the first howitzer into a position designated by the battalion commander. Fire was coming from a building to the rear which he desired to be used as a battalion CP. He directed me to take this building under direct fire. After my gun crew shelled it, Captain Davis with a squad of men charged the house, cleared it and started organizing the CP and fire direction centre. Meanwhile, Captain John H. J. Featherstone, Battery 'A' Commander who was moving his battery into position to the west of the railroad track, was receiving a great deal of automatic weapons fire and small arms fire from his west flank and especially from a strong point about 300 yards to his north. It consisted of a well dug-in position around a large house. We were being hit by this fire and it was impossible to serve the pieces without first raiding this strong point. Featherstone moved a howitzer up to point blank range; about fifteen yards from the strong point and started pouring direct fire into the trenches and dugout. He then led the group which closed with the enemy from the flank and captured twenty prisoners. He gave his life in this gallant deed.'

Featherstone was killed while he led a patrol to neutralize some small arms fire that came from a group of nearby houses. After clearing the houses, the men discovered the sniper: a twelve year old German boy.

Featherstone was replaced by Captain Edward H. Geiger who reported: 'My glider landed completely outside the landing zone. Immediately upon landing, we were surrounded by Germans and only by the most devious means were we able to extricate ourselves. We received small arms fire immediately and took cover in a ditch. After locating ourselves on the map we proceeded to fight our way back to our unit. With me I had two pilots and three enlisted men. As we moved eastward from our cover we came upon three Germans searching for us. At point blank range we fought it out with them killing all three. However, we attracted attention. Fire on us increased in intensity and the Germans began a systematic search for us. By crawling away from the point and making a long circuitous manoeuvre we were able to avoid the bulk of the estimated company in this area. Finally, making a dash at dusk, we evaded the trap, storming an outpost of the strong point; killing one German and capturing the other. By dark, we had made our way to the battalion CP with the prisoner.'

Captain L. Q. Stewart of the Medical Corps, the 680th Glider Field Artillery Battalion Surgeon wrote: At 1135 hours glider #59 in our serial landed in an area picked out by the pilot and co-pilot as being within our pre-designated landing zone. On the outskirts of Wesel we ran into flak and small arms fire, some hitting the glider, mostly in the tail position. This continued until we landed. There was much smoke and haze over this area, which, with the now plainly audible firing, made picking out a clear area extremely difficult. We all piled out immediately and spread out, taking cover as best we could. Mortar shells as well as small arms fire landed all about us. In a field just east of us, three gliders, one after the other, sustained direct artillery hits and caught fire. After about five minutes we unloaded the glider. One of my men had crossed a small road to take care of some casualties. Fortunately the glider carrying our trailer had landed about 150 yards north of us and as we moved north we came upon it and hooked it onto the jeep. The battalion commander helped unload and was collecting other personnel and directing them towards our assembly area. We took cover in the ploughed rows off and on when the firing got close and took advantage of what few hedgerows there were. I picked out a farmhouse near the gun positions and set up an aid station approximately 1,000 yards north of where we landed. Almost immediately the casualties began coming in, we soon filed the house and then we put them outside. Most were severely injured but we treated many who were immediately returned to duty once their wounds were dressed. No contact was made with our clearing station until 1600 and between then and 1930 we transferred about one hundred patients to them. We were about 400 yards north of the battalion CP. Throughout the afternoon we received sporadic fire around the aid station. By evening the snipers and strong points nearby had all been cleared out. Many drivers and other personnel brought us portions of the medical resupplied dropped by B-24s. This was transferred to the clearing station as soon as we had available transportation, along with much captured German medical supplies. We took care of men from many units of the division, a number of glider pilots and a few British. We evacuated over one hundred cases and treated a great many more. I feel that the important factor that enabled us to function that day was the outstanding, aggressive and efficient way every man in the unit performed.'

Medics treated over a hundred casualties. The 680th Field Artillery lost nineteen killed, including both howitzer battery commanders and 56 men wounded in action in securing its objective including the capture of 150

German prisoners, a battery of 105 mm and a battery of 155 mm artillery. The Commanding Officer Paul Oswald declared later that 'these troops were the very best that I had the fortune and privilege to command.'

By noon the 194th Glider Infantry Regiment was 73 percent assembled and German resistance was beginning to crumble. The 507th PIR made contact with elements of the 194th Glider Infantry Regiment under the command of Colonel James Pierce east of DZ 'W' was achieved early that afternoon. At 1300 Company 'D' met advance elements of the 15th Division and Company 'F' reported contact with that division at 1434. Other bodies of men arrived at 1330 and 1530. At 1803 the paratroops joined forces with the British airborne on the northern boundary of their sector and at 0200 hours next morning a patrol to the southeast reached the British troops in the Wesel area. In contact with friendly forces on all sides the 507th had nothing more to do in its sector except a little mopping up. The Regiment had taken about 1,150 prisoners and had destroyed or captured ten tanks, two flak wagons, 37 artillery pieces and ten 20 mm anti-aircraft guns and five self-propelled guns.

The airborne units on LZ 'S' had over fifty dead and one hundred wounded or injured during the landings and the initial assembly period. Of the glider pilots accompanying them, eighteen were killed, eighty wounded or injured and thirty still missing three weeks later.

The 437th Troop Carrier Group's performance en route had been good but by no means perfect. Before they reached the Rhine, Don Bolce could tell that the combat area was not far away. 'I stood up in the astrodome and could see lots of action up ahead. We were not encountering any ground fire, but I could see that we would soon be crossing the Rhine with our two gliders bouncing around behind us. All of a sudden it was like Normandy again. The ground fire was extremely intense and I thought to myself that this is worse than 'D-Day' as this time it was daylight and the Germans can see us! It was extremely smoky and visibility was limited, but we reached the LZ and our gliders cut loose. They were just as glad as we were to be finally free and no longer a sitting duck at the end of a towrope. We made our turn, dropped our towropes in the assigned area, crossed the Rhine and headed for home. We had made it! I couldn't believe that the German gunners were not able to shoot us down since we were flying so low and so slow. We were very lucky.'

Five other C-47s in the 437th TCG were not so lucky. They were destroyed with seven crew members lost. In the 85th TCS, Second Lieutenant John Rauch, co-pilot of a C-47 named *Asphodel*, which means 'Lily of Hell', a name chosen by the pilot, 1st Lieutenant Richard Dean, recorded his memories of that terrible day's events: 'At approximately 1100 hours we were towing two Waco CG-4A gliders, one on a 700 foot rope and the other on a 500 foot rope. The extra drag caused us to fly at about 90 to 105 mph indicated airspeed just a few hundred feet about the ground. The plane was hit in the right engine. As soon as Dick Dean saw smoke and flames coming from the engine he gave orders to jump. At about the same time he cut the gliders loose. Staff Sergeant Charles Salerno, radio operator, was gone in a wink of an eye followed by Tech Sergeant Warren Horr, crew chief and then myself. Dean was the last one to leave the plane. The time period from being hit to total evacuation was probably three or four minutes.

'I was not all that high above the ground when I hit the silk and as I floated down I recall seeing German soldiers running away from the area I was headed so I hung limp in the chute, playing dead, just in case a German was looking for a 'turkey shoot'. Dean and I landed about seventy-five yards apart. I went through an apple tree and Dean got hung up in the branches of a larger tree. We were both unhurt. The apple tree was on a farm owned by a Monsieur Wagner. As I approached the farmhouse someone presented a white flag. One of the first questions the family asked was, 'did I know a Hans Wagner from Missouri!' I said, 'No! I don't'. Obviously they had no idea how big the United States' was! Soon the troops that had been riding in the gliders that we'd released earlier showed up and, with little conversation, locked the Wagners in a barn. This done, they helped us to a marshalling area for 'shot down' airmen. Whilst with the troops we came across the remains of Asphodel. She had made a perfect landing but was burned out except for the outer third of each wing and the tail section. Several days later, after crossing the Rhine, we arrived in Helmont before returning to Coulommiers. We decided to name our replacement aircraft *Asphodel II*.'

Thick smoke of battle was everywhere when the 440th plunged into the conflict at its raging height. It was late in the airborne attack. Most of the glidermen and all of the paratroopers were already on the ground, at grips with the enemy. 'The smoke and haze were so thick, I hardly knew I was over the Rhine,' said one pilot. But Landing Zone 'N' was still clear of combat. At 1155 hours, the first C-47 released its glider over the LZ and Major Wilson began his perilous 270-degree descent to the left, while Colonel Krebs' tug made its flat 180-degree turn to the right to head for the rope drop area on the west side of the Rhine. Then came the withering hail of enemy flak which damaged fourteen of our planes and destroyed two. Heeding the order for no evasive action, every one of the ninety C-47s released its glider over the target area.

As on LZ 'S' the formations were to split as they approached LZ 'N' and release in columns of pairs 600 yards apart. The first glider release was made at 1155; five minutes ahead of schedule and subsequent releases ran from three to six minutes early. The seven-minute interval allotted each serial proved a little too tight for 48-plane formations and one or two of them overran their predecessors. This happened to the 441st Group's serial from Dreux and probably accounts for the fact that it released too soon and too high, at the west end of the zone instead of the east and at 1,000 to 2,000 feet instead of 600 feet above the ground. In other serials the lead elements generally came in at about the right height, but the rear usually slanted up to over 1,200 feet and in the last serial as high as 2,500 feet. Such differences in altitude made it impossible to follow a uniform landing pattern. Many gliders were so high that their pilots felt it necessary to make more than the prescribed 270° left turn and some in the 441st Group made one or even two complete circles before beginning that turn. Haze and smoke, which still held visibility to about half a mile, also disrupted the landings. The glider pilots could see the ground beneath them quite well but could make out very little ahead of them or to the side until they were about 200 feet from the ground. Men who did not know exactly where they were on release needed a rare eye for terrain to orient themselves on the basis of a few fields and farm buildings. Many had no idea where they were when they landed. Intense fire, mainly from small arms, met the gliders as they coasted down. As a rule, whether by design or because they could not see through the smoke, the Germans held their fire until the Wacos were below the 500-foot level. The enemy appeared to have a detachment in every building or patch of woods and although loath to venture from cover, they maintained a steady fire. Many glider men were slain in their seats and many loads were burned or destroyed by mortars. In several cases the airborne were pinned down for as much as two hours. The defending force in the vicinity of LZ 'N' appears to have been relatively small and lacking in artillery[7] but its opponents, not much more numerous, were mostly semi-combatant specialists and rather widely dispersed.

Only one glider is known to have been shot down, but at least a quarter of them were hit, producing some damage and several casualties. Of 302 gliders, about 200 landed on LZ 'N'. The south wind combined with the low visibility produced a tendency to land further north than was proper. The last two serials released over or outside the edge within sight of panel markings and smoke set out on DZ 'X'. As a result none of their gliders came down north of LZ 'N' but about 31 landed south of it. Although there were some complaints that the glider pilots had lacked air discipline and had gone on the principle of every man for himself, the prevailing view was that they had landed as well as could be expected. Those in the later serials had the added excuse of having found the best of their assigned fields already occupied not only by American gliders but by several British Horsas. Unwilling to serve as targets any longer than necessary, a large proportion of the glider pilots dived down in tight spirals and made fast, rough landings. Over fifty percent of the gliders were damaged in accidents, but once again almost all their loads came through intact. While some gliders landed among friendly troops north or south of LZ 'N', the zone itself was enemy territory. No advance party of paratroops had arrived to neutralize it. Fighting lasted until about 0530 with the 139th Engineer Battalion doing the lion's share of the work in clearing the zone. That day its men killed 83 Germans and captured 315. As of early April, glider pilot casualties stood at fourteen dead, 26 wounded and 51 missing, a ratio indicating resistance almost as severe as that on LZ 'S'.

In the 440th TCG narrow escapes were plentiful. The 95th Squadron got through with aircraft piloted by Major Budd and Lieutenant Davey severely shot up. In the 97th Lieutenant Sharkey returned with holes in his cabin large enough for one to crawl through. By then, farmhouses and dugouts in the LZ were alive with bursts of light flak and small-arms fire. The second serial met it head on and was hit much harder. The hazy sky swarmed with escaping tug planes, grim-jawed pilots' manoeuvering feverishly to get out without hitting the feared Issel Canal line, eyes of crew chiefs darted everywhere searching for signs of critical damage to their planes.

2nd Lieutenant William Jean Hamrick, born in St. Mary-of-the-Woods, Terre Haute on 27 November 1924, navigator and flight leader in the 96th Troop Carrier Squadron who flew with Krebs, recalled: 'The C-47 flown by Lieutenant Colonel Johnson, our squadron commander caught a 20 mm shell smack in the nose while we were dropping over the Rhine. Captain James Roberson was the co-pilot and he was trying to use the fire-fighting equipment to get the flames out. Captain Aldo Tombari got so excited that Johnson had to tell him to sit down because he had to make an emergency landing. He made it back across the Rhine while the crew chief fought fires in the cockpit area and they managed to make an emergency landing in a field at Eindhoven, Holland. 2nd Lieutenant Aymon Prudhomme in the 96th Squadron was the pilot of the right wingman plane and 1st Lieutenant Joseph Turecky was the co-pilot. They were forced to drop out of formation after two gasoline tanks had been hit. Trailing gas, they had to set it down at another emergency airdrome.'

The 98th Squadron, trailing the second serial, was hit the hardest, with two aircraft losses. Lieutenant Walters, his plane afire after being hit by three successive bursts of flak, found himself fighting for altitude in the dangerously crowded aircraft pattern. The 'Bail Out!' order was given. As the crew parachuted to safety, they saw their ship blaze up in mid-air. Back over the Rhine plane number 774, piloted by Lieutenant Decou in the 98th TCS was in serious trouble. The right engine was on fire and a radio message from another ship told the pilot that his tanks were on fire. Decou ordered the crew to jump. 'When I got to the door,' related co-pilot Eastman, 'the crew chief and radio operator were struggling with the door, which had jammed at the lower right hinge. After trying unsuccessfully to release it, the crew chief and I pushed against it as hard as we could to allow the radio operator to squeeze out the restricted opening. I then did the same for the crew chief and finally squeezed through myself. It took me at least fifteen seconds to get through the opening. The pilot had stayed in the cockpit all this time. Too low to jump himself, with one engine dead Decou elected to ride the stricken plane into a ploughed-up field. 'Along the field's north edge,' said the lieutenant, 'was a highway which had heavy military traffic on it. Wishing to avoid piling up the ship across the highway and also to avoid a large herd of sheep on the north of the field, I dragged the right wing through some posts on the south edge of the field which caused a ground loop to the right and the ship came to a halt about two-thirds of the way across the field...I immediately removed the top escape hatch and went out over the nose, not knowing when the ship would blow up, having fully expected it to on first impact. Captain Thompson then buzzed the field and I waved an 'OK' to him.'

Once Wesel was passed, the return was unopposed. The aircraft swept back across the Rhine, dropped their towropes in a specially designated zone five miles south of Xanten and headed home on the prescribed reciprocal course.[8] In the 436th TCG the first transports of the lead serial reached

Coulommiers on schedule at 1225 and by 1345 most formations had landed. The flow of stragglers continued until 1500. At least 37 of them had simply stopped at authorized emergency fields to refuel.

Between 1404 and 1505 the serials returned to their bases almost intact amid a festive atmosphere. Out of 313 aircraft winging over or near LZ 'N' only three were lost and 44 damaged. Moreover, only nine of the damaged craft needed 3rd or 4th echelon repairs. Not a man in their crews was killed or missing and just three were wounded. All losses and most of the damage appear to have been incurred during the turn, a mile or more beyond the zone at points where the formations came temporarily within range of enemy positions beyond Issel.

By 1411 hours, the last 440th transport had returned to the home base at Orléans-Bricy. In the entire operation, but one C-47 pilot, Lieutenant Raftery of the 97th, received slight wounds in the arm.[9]

Return of the glider pilots on Tuesday 27th March revealed that they had had it much rougher on the ground. In all, five of them were killed and six wounded, largely by enemy shellfire. One glider, loaded with demolitions, exploded in mid-air when hit, killing all aboard. Gliders were widely dispersed on landing and assembly of the Airborne was initially by squad and two squad groups. Immediate contact was made with the enemy, but the tough Airborne Engineers set about their task, the clearing and defending of the zone from armoured attack from the north. Every house, patch of woods and haystack had been fortified by the Germans and for hours the invaders were under heavy fire. One of the two gliders carrying the Battalion medical personnel landed immediately adjacent to a German house sheltering forty German soldiers. Withering small-arms fire and a direct mortar fire hit greeted them. The medical officer and non-com escaped unhurt, but their driver was killed and burned with the glider. With equipment from the other glider, the battalion surgeon set up an aid station and immediately began treating casualties.

By 1730 hours, the battalion had taken all of its objectives and had consolidated its position. During the day, eighty-three Germans were killed or wounded and 315 captured, along with an entire battery of 105 mm artillery.

The 440th glider pilots holed up in their assembly point in the woods guarding prisoners and the next morning assisted in marching them back to the Rhine where they were turned over to the MPs. Evacuation was made by DUKWs (colloquially known as 'Ducks'),[10] to the west bank of the Rhine, where the glider pilots were picked up at airdrome B-68 and brought to Bricy in C-47s on the evening of D+2, March 26th.

At Coulommiers Don Bolce, radio operator on Captain Floyd Kelly's crew, recorded that 'after a very long and dangerous flight, it felt good to get something to eat and head for our tents. Many of our C-47 crews had still not returned to base. Radio operator Chuck Salerno's cot was empty in our tent that night. The following day we discovered that he had bailed out over Germany, but it was several days before we heard that he had survived. Radio operator Jim Lyons had been shot down and was in a hospital with the rest of his crew, all badly injured. My friend, Captain Victor Deer and his co-pilot, Second Lieutenant Eldred Trachta were shot down and killed. Radio operator Staff Sergeant Earl C. Nordgren and navigator 1st Lieutenant Bryce C. Gibson also died. The only survivor was crew chief Tech Sergeant Paul B. Lefever who managed to bail out moments before the aircraft crashed. Crew Chief Gerry Cataline and his crew crash-landed in a schoolyard in Bonn, Germany. Radio operator George Babich and his crew made an emergency landing with the fuel control valve shot out. There were so many more, but I do not know all their names. When 'Monty' (George Montgomery) our crew chief, removed the metal strap holding the old gasoline tank in the left wing, a spent bullet that had penetrated our plane on D-Day was found. I have always wondered what would have happened if that bullet had gone into the tank, instead of just wedging between the tank and the steel strap.'

At Melun, Operations clerk Bert Schweizer waited for news of Bill Frye's crew. 'Before long it became clear that Ben Smith and Cloyd Clemons had not managed to jump safely from the plane and that John Kearns and George Pittman also were dead. As the days went by and the status of one after another was changed from 'missing in action' to 'killed in action' the thought that these men had had their lives snuffed out during our very last combat mission became harder and harder to bear. Bad as I felt, I couldn't even write Bill Frye's wife at the time. Everything had to 'go through channels.' I remember she was from Kelly Lake, Minnesota.'

When it became obvious that Frye's C-47 was overdue, John R. Cooke waited anxiously in front of the Operations Office waiting for news of his 22-year old brother, Willard, asking crew members coming in: 'Did they see that plane actually crash? Did they see any parachutes coming out? Were they sure it was Frye's plane they saw on fire?' Ellery Bennett sorrowfully remembers telling him that he wasn't sure whether this plane's tail letter was 'O' or 'Q.'

When Jesse Coleman, the 81st Squadron Flight Surgeon, learned the co-pilot's name he asked if he was related to the Dr. Willard Cooke who had taught him in medical school in Galveston and it turned out it was his father! 'I thought the world of young Cooke' wrote Coleman. 'I guess we tend to feel that the fellows who got shot down were the best ones of the batch. It's only human to feel that way.'

'Was it [all] worth it?' wrote Marty Wolfe in the 81st TCS of the 436th TCG. 'At that stage in the war, should Eisenhower have granted Montgomery the right to launch 'Varsity'? Many of us would say no; that 'Varsity' should never have gotten off the ground. Some military historians agree.'

Adelore Chevalier, 81st Troop Carrier Squadron glider pilot, was in no doubt what had brought about the successful conclusion to 'Varsity'. 'The thing that whipped the Krauts was the suddenness and the size of the attack. Each C-47 was pulling two gliders and that was a lot of gliders. They came in so thick and fast that the Krauts were swamped. All of a sudden, a pin-pointed section of Germany was swarming with Yanks who weren't there five minutes before.

According to Tim Lynch, author of *Silent Skies: Gliders At War 1939-1945*

'American pilots of the 440th Group established themselves in a Parisian brothel and cut cards to determine who would get the unit's allocation of medals for the operation'). After 'Varsity' the 440th Group was engaged in carrying supplies to the front line and evacuating casualties. 2nd Lieutenant Bill Hamrick recalled that on one particular day, he flew as a navigator with 1st Lieutenant David Brown, 1st Lieutenant James Murphy and Sergeant Thomas Pinto on a mission to deliver five-gallon jerry cans of fuel to the Third Army. 'The flight was a routine we made our way back to Metz. I didn't fly with them the next day but Murphy and Brown slid in a little too close on takeoff and they started to roll out to the left. I could tell the pilot was trying to pull up but the weight of the cargo shifted to the left and they couldn't pull it up. They came down but didn't make it out. The plane hit and went off like a bomb had exploded. When I got there, their bodies were already taken off. Murphy was a guy who always liked to fly with jump boots on. I saw his leg with a boot by the tail of the aircraft. Pinto, the crew chief, was a Brooklynese kind of a fellow. I saw his coveralls there. He was the only one still with his body in good condition, the rest were consumed by the flames. We lost other guys but seeing that was hard. I did get a week's pass on the Riviera to get over the shock of it, but it never really went away. They were all nice young men.'

Endnotes Chapter 4

1   *Silent Wings At War* by John L. Lowden.
2   The 437th, 436th, 435th and 439th TCGs all used double-tow and were the only ones to use it.
3   See *War Stories:The Men of the Airborne* by Earl Hagerman (Turner Publishing) and *The Glider Gang* by Milton Dank.
4   Quoted in *The Glider Gang* by Milton Dank.
5   The initial load had been 592 Wacos with 3,594 troops and 654 tons of cargo including 208 jeeps, 101 trailers and 84 mortars and guns.
6   Quoted in *The Glider Gang* by Milton Dank (Cassell Ltd, 1978).
7   A single 88mm gun is said to have been the only piece of sizable artillery on the zone.
8   Similar areas had been designated for other glider missions, but this was the first in which friendly territory could be used for the purpose. Tow ropes were too valuable to be dropped at random or over enemy territory if it could be avoided. At the same time, falling ropes were too dangerous to allow their being dropped on the zones or near the troop concentrations on the west bank of the Rhine.
9   *DZ Europe: The Story of the 440 Troop Carrier Group.*
10   'D' for designed in 1942, 'U' for 'utility', 'K', all-wheel drive and 'W' for tandem rear axles; a six-wheel-drive amphibious modification of the 2½ ton CCKW trucks.

Chapter 5

The British and Canadian Lift

As the great battle for the Rhine crossing approached, everyone felt that it would mark the beginning of the end. I myself looked with amazement at the progress that had been made in airborne warfare since the days when I had led 1st Parachute Battalion in its drop in North Africa in October 1942 from thirty-two American C-47 aircraft whose crews had never dropped parachutists before and which were not equipped with radio communications equipment. On that occasion I had sat in the cockpit with the American commander. The Dakotas were flying in line astern and aided by a quarter-inch to the mile scale French motoring map, the navigators located our DZs in Tunisia 400 miles away. On seeing the leading aircraft disgorge its load, the remainder followed suit.

Two-and-a-half years' later lessons from previous operations had been learned and I had the choice of dropping 3rd Parachute Brigade on a small DZ, measuring approximately a thousand yards by 800 yards, which was located in a clearing in a wood amongst enemy positions manned by German parachute troops. The alternative was a far more ideal DZ three miles away but with the prospect of fighting all the way to our objective. The choice for me was simple - land on top of the objective and take the risks of a bad drop.'

Brigadier Stanley James Ledger 'Speedy' Hill, commanding 3rd Parachute Brigade. The airborne troops were required to capture the high ground forming the western edge of the Diersfordter Wald in order to neutralize the enemy troops and artillery positioned there, who would otherwise be able to cause havoc among the four divisions forming the assault forces on the ground. They were also to capture two road bridges and one rail-bridge over the River Issel across which the main break-through into Germany would be made.

No.1 Sniper James N. Corbett of 19 Platoon, 'D' Company, 12th Battalion (Airborne), The Devonshire Regiment or the 'Red Devons' as they liked to be known, had first set foot on the continent as a 19-year old on D+1 in June 1944. Understandably frightened and fearful for his personal safety; at the same time, he had also been apprehensive about being able to deal with the rigors and horrors of total war. Nevertheless, he felt privileged to be a member of the famous 6th Airborne Division and nothing had changed except that at the time of the Normandy landings the Devons had arrived in France by sea. Now all twelve parachute battalions, five British, one Canadian and six from the US, closely followed by 1,300 gliders, packed with troops, would go by air in RAF transports from eight airfields in East Anglia. All parachute drops would be made from 540 C-47 aircraft in three American troop carrier groups in the 52nd Wing using Chipping Ongar,

Boreham and Wethersfield as their staging points for the Rhine crossing operation.

'We had dispersed to our departure airfields in Essex about a week before the battle', wrote Jim Corbett. The 12th Devons found facilities at Gosfield airfield to be quite inadequate for their purposes on every level, yet they did not take-off from here, as parts of the 1st Royal Ulster Rifles and 2nd Oxford and Bucks known as the '52nd'were scheduled to do; instead they had to travel a considerable distance to three other airfields. All three battalions, therefore, would have to rise and leave their camps hours before what should have been necessary on 24 March. 'We were given a basic plan of the operation by the 'Top Brass'. The Commandoes and 51st Highland Division were going in at 3am to form the Bridgehead and we would land seven hours later, approximately eight miles ahead of the land troops to complete the rout. To boost morale one commander described the operation as, 'a piece of cake'. Nothing was said about air defences; perhaps they hoped it would be non-existent, or that it was all guarding German cities from bomber attacks. After basic briefing, we were given personal briefing as to our individual objectives from our CO [Lieutenant Colonel Paul Gleadell CdeG]. This turned out to be the small country town of Hamminkeln. My company's objective was the centre crossroads, which we were to hold until relieved by land troops. There was a paper-mâché model of the town showing most of the houses and a church with a tower overlooking the crossroads. We were then introduced to the two glider pilots who would take us in. As they informed us of their flight-plan, the phrase, 'your life in their hands' came to mind.'

The 12th Devons' orders were to land at 'LZ R', to the south-west of Hamminkeln and then proceed to secure the two western roads leading out of Hamminkeln, thereby cutting off the possibilities of retreat or reinforcement of the garrison, before assaulting the town itself. To assist them in this endeavour, the 3rd Airlanding Anti-Tank Battery, minus three of their 17-pounder guns, was placed at their disposal.

'Well' they said, 'We are going to try and get you in as close to the crossroads, as we can.' wrote James N. Corbett. 'Coming in from the southwest, we can hop over this wire fence, land in this potato field and run the glider towards the gap between these two houses which are right on the crossroads.' It all sounded so simple. We were reassured by the scale model and the superb aerial photography. It not only showed the number of weapon-slits guarding various points, but also their depth. The photos even showed the height of each strand of the five-barbed wire fence that we were to 'hop over'! When they asked for questions, I ventured to ask, 'what if we lose our landing-gear in the ruts of the potato field? With no brakes, we would just slither towards the gap between the two houses completely out of control.' I was thinking that this gap was only the width of a car. The pilots replied with absolute confidence. If that happened they said, they might lose the wings, but the fuselage would finish on the crossroads. 'It's all expendable' and added 'we are not intending to fly it again'. Then someone else shouted, Yes, but your passengers ain't and we all laughed. The glider pilots turned out to be first-rate and we grew to have a lot of respect for them, especially when, on landing, they both grabbed a Tommy-gun and jumped out of the pilot seats to fight alongside.'

Another soldier in 'D' Company, Edward A. Horrell, recalled: After our disastrous experience in the Ardennes when we lost Charlie Humphries, Freddie Harvey and Dennis Richmond with four others badly wounded we spent two hectic weeks reorganizing the platoon. Reinforcements had to be accommodated and new equipment and stores allocated and checked. I didn't have time to breathe, never mind contemplate what lay ahead. But here we were at Capsfield in Essex, ready to go. We had a most excellent briefing and knew exactly where we were landing - the exact field, the exact corner of the field - provided, of course, everything went right. We had loaded our Horsa Mark I, an older type of glider at Great Dunmow airfield the night before. Nick Hillier's and my job on landing was to throw a ring main charge around the tail of the glider and blow it off, so that the hand trailer loaded with ammunition and explosives could be quickly removed from the aircraft.'[1]

While some paratroop regiments were housed at their departure airfields other units in 'Varsity' were billeted in remote transit camps; some more palatial than others. Brigadier Geoffrey Kemp Bourne's 6th Airlanding Brigade Headquarters and the 810 men of the 1st Royal Ulster Rifles who were to take off from Gosfield and Birch were billeted on the 2,300 acre estate at Chadacre Hall at Shimpling in south Suffolk. Unfortunately, accommodation was described as 'overcrowded, lacked sanitary facilities and entertainments and was so badly administered that a significant number of airborne personnel, who should have been in a briefing or resting, had to provide guard duties to seal their own camp'. The Main body of 265 men of the 53rd (Worcestershire Yeomanry) Airlanding Light Regiment RA at Chadacre also were to take off from Earls Colne and Shepherds Grove, while another detachment of 55 men at Mushroom Farm Transit Camp would go from Dunmow and sixteen other troops at Glevering Hall would take off from Woodbridge, as would two detachments of the 6th Airborne Armoured Reconnaissance Regiment at Mushroom Farm and Glevering Hall. Two hundred men of the 2nd Airlanding Anti-Tank Regiment RA at Glevering Hall would take off from Great Dunmow and Earls Colne and 168 men of the same unit at Shudy Camp would leave from Woodbridge.

Twenty-three year old Lieutenant Ellis 'Dixie' Dean MC who commanded the Vickers Medium-Machine Gun Platoon in the HQ Company, 13th Battalion (Lancashire), The Parachute Regiment who had jumped into Normandy on 6 June 1944 as Machine Gun Officer recalled: 'The transit camp this time was to be at Shudy in Suffolk - convenient to our takeoff airfield of Wethersfield. It was a long trek from Salisbury Plain and not surprisingly took all day; the later part spent driving along country lanes, devoid of all habitation except small villages and hamlets. It was a bright spring day and the scene at one of the two hourly halts, is still firmly etched in my memory. The convoy halted deep in the country where there was a wide grass verge on which to stretch our legs and alongside it ran a neatly trimmed hedge just coming into leaf. Beyond this a field of winter wheat, several inches high and a brilliant emerald green in colour rose gently to the horizon. To one side in a slight hollow could be seen the red tiled roof of the farmhouse and buildings and running away at an angle was a line of washing, fluttering in the breeze. Shudy was a Nissen hutted camp in a parkland setting of fields and small woods and beneath the trees was a carpet of violets and primroses. Compared with the green field site at Keevil prior to 'D' Day this was luxury. Everything was under cover, the cookhouses manned by permanent staff. There was electricity and ablutions with hot water - there were even beds for us all.'

Throughout the campaign in Normandy Lieutenant Dean commanded his platoon, affectionately known as 'the Oily Rags' by the CO, Lieutenant Colonel Peter J. Luard DSO because whenever he would visit the platoon in training, he could be sure that at least one of them, would have an oily rag in his hand. In Normandy 'Dixie' fought with outstanding skill, courage and devotion to duty. In the Battle of Bure in Belgium on 3 January, a Royal Tiger Tank with infantry escorting, was advancing down the village street covered by the guns of Dean's platoon. A gun team was hit and all killed or wounded. At point blank range, 'Dixie' crossed the street. He carried the only survivor to safety and then, in spite of heavy fire from the tank not one hundred yards away, he returned for the gun. He returned to command his platoon as imperturbable as ever.

'We still had no notion of when 'Varsity' was to take place, but thought it couldn't be far away since the first morning parade was a drive to the airfield to draw and fit chutes. After half an hour's drive along country lanes, the transport dropped us at dispersal sites around the perimeter of Wethersfield where the Dakotas were parked and numbered to match the stick 'chalk' numbers. No air crew were about and we also waited for the wagon carrying the chutes to arrive. The four planes allocated to the Platoon were all together, with the mortars waiting at the adjacent one.

'We were busy fitting our chutes when the wagon carrying the crew arrived and they introduced themselves to us, saying what a great honour it was for us to be carried into battle by such an illustrious squadron. They certainly were very experienced. Apart from the Normandy operation, they had participated in the South of France drop and also flown twice during 'Market Garden' and what they didn't know about dropping parachutists wasn't worth knowing. Boy would they come in slow and give us the best jump we had ever had from no more than 500 feet. Once chutes had been fitted to the satisfaction of Sergeant Kenny (stick commander), we placed them on our seats in the plane, said 'Goodbye' to our intrepid flyers and then returned to camp to receive the first of our briefings. This was only a general one and was given to the whole Battalion by the CO himself as we sat on the grass in front of a large scale reproduction of the battle area. The DZ was in flat open country, some four miles west of the river and close to the town of Hamminkeln. All necessary features were pointed out on the large scale reproduction.

'After lunch, along with the Company Commanders and other Specialist Platoon Officers I reported to the briefing hut prepared by the Intelligence Section. In the centre of the hut was a sand model of the Hamminkeln area, while on the walls, large scale maps and enlarged air photographs of the district were displayed. The Colonel started his detailed briefing with the assault across the Rhine by the infantry, which was to be made between the towns of Rees to the north and Wesel further south. Great emphasis was put on the amount of artillery support we were to receive - after all we were going to drop right on top of the Boche guns and our minds had to be set at ease on that score. For the two hours immediately before 'P' Hour, every known German gun site was to be engaged by the massed artillery of 21 Army Group under the code name 'Apple Pie'. The machine gun positions would be in 'A' Company location, providing covering fire to the Battalion's left flank and since we were to dig in alongside the 'A' Company rifle platoons, we would be amply protected. It didn't sound too dangerous an undertaking - at least there was no 21st Panzer to worry about this time and I left the briefing fully confident of the Platoon's ability to successfully carry out the task given us.'

The 9th Parachute Battalion set up their models and air photos in a specially guarded room. The Commanding Officer, Lieutenant Colonel Napier Crookenden, born 31 August 1915, the son of Colonel Arthur Crookenden CBE DSO gave out his orders to the company commanders. 'We were to drop last on Drop Zone 'A' after the 8th and 1st Canadian Parachute Battalions and, while they secured the landing highest part of the Diersfordter Wald and the Schneppenberg, destroying several batteries of German guns on the way. Then the whole battalion crowded into the same room, all 600 of them and I explained to them our drop and our tasks in some detail. It was an exhilarating and a sobering experience, talking to so many men of such quality and realising how intently each one of them was following my words and their tasks, as the plan unfolded. I must have spoken for twenty minutes or more with hardly a sound, a cough or a movement from the men. Afterwards each company and each platoon took its turn in the briefing room and each man had to confirm, on the model in front of his own platoon, his rendezvous, his task and the objectives of his company and of the battalion.'

Medic James Byrom who had seen it all before and a pacifist by conviction and refused to serve in the combat arms of the military, was much encouraged by the Brigadier 'Speedy' Hill's morale boosting briefing to the 600 men of the 1st Canadian Parachute Battalion and other units in 3rd Parachute Brigade before departure: 'Gentlemen, the artillery and air support is fantastic! And if you are worried about the kind of reception you'll get, just put yourself in the place of the enemy. Beaten and demoralised, pounded by our artillery and bombers, what would you think, gentlemen, if you saw a horde of ferocious, bloodthirsty paratroopers, bristling with weapons, cascading down upon you from the skies? And you needn't think, just because you hear a few stray bullets flying about, that some miserable Hun is shooting at you. That is merely a form of egotism. But if by any chance you should happen to meet one of these Huns in person, you will treat him, gentlemen, with extreme disfavour.'

Brigadier Hill was a strong believer in the importance of optimal physical and mental condition, as the key to survival in an action context. His programme is a simple one, based on four principles: 'Speed: Speed in action: paratroopers must move twice as fast as anybody else must on the operation theatre; speed in decision making: paratroopers must always be ten minutes ahead of others. Simplicity: Simplicity allows speed and eliminates the possibility of mistakes. Control: Tight control is essential to optimize resources and keep units organized, since paratroopers battalions are small units (some 500 men) and have little ammunition. They may also find themselves scattered over the drop zone. Fire Effect: A paratrooper must also be a sharpshooter and proficient with a wide range of weapons, including those of the enemy. And as paratroopers carry little ammunition and equipment they must make sure that their fire is on target. They go by the following: wait until you see the white of their eyes before shooting.'

Brigadier 'Speedy' Hill's troops would fly from Chipping Ongar in gliders towed by C-47s of the 61st Troop Carrier Group at Chipping Ongar and the 316th TCG at Wethersfield. Others would fly with the 315th TCG from Boreham. Plans to have the 315th and 316th Groups land in France had been abandoned on 22 March because their new bases there were not ready, so they would have to make the long flight back to their home fields at Spanhoe and Cottesmore respectively. For many 'Varsity' would be their last big operation. Colonel Harvey A. Berger, commanding the 316th would die in action over Germany on 3 April while on a flight carrying paratroops from England to the German front.

Lieutenant 'Dixie' Dean of the 13th Battalion waiting at Wethersfield where C-47s in the 316th TCG would fly them to the Rhine, wrote: 'The weather had been set fair all the week and it must have been the same on the continent, since we knew early on the Friday that the operation was definitely on and there wasn't to be a 24 hour postponement this time. It was a very busy afternoon, now we knew it was on - the final check of the guns was made and 'kit bags' loaded, magazines of personal weapons filled, grenades primed, water bottles filled and 24 hour ration packs broken down. We were only carrying one - so confident were the higher authorities that the link up with supply chain being quickly made. There would not be time in the morning, so all had to be ready that afternoon. Then there were last letters to be written.

'The final event of the day was to be an open air Church Service in the evening and after that, there was a Frank Sinatra film in the main dining hall. Knowing that it would not be possible on Saturday morning to have a final little pep talk with the Platoon, I went along before the Service and found them lounging about on the grass in the evening sunshine. They gathered around informally and I said my little piece, hoping to allay any fears they might have. Earlier we had received copies of Field Marshal Montgomery's Order of the Day, which started with the statement '21 Army

Group will now cross the Rhine'. Stirring words and if Monty was so confident it could be done; then so were we. Some senior Officers I know didn't like him, but as far as I know, we all had complete confidence in his leadership. I also emphasised again how important it was to get to the RV as quickly as possible and how dependent the Battalion was on our supporting fire in the early stages of digging in. Finally I wished them all 'Good Luck' and *I'll see you all in Germany.* But even as I said it, I couldn't help thinking; this is the last time I will be speaking to some of them.

'It was still not time to fall in for the Service, so I stayed talking to them, moving from one little group to another as I did so. I was just moving away from one lot of men, when I was approached by Private Bill Colquohon, one of the reinforcements who joined us earlier in the week. 'This is only an exercise we are going on, isn't it Sir?' he asked in all innocence. As gently as I could, I explained that this was the real thing, 'but there was nothing to worry [about as he] was with some first rate soldiers, the rest of the Platoon would look after him and show him the ropes'. I then spoke to Sergeant Fred Drew, his Stick Commander, asking him to keep an eye on the youngster as far as possible. The service which followed was something special, with us all gathered informally in front of a make-shift altar. Brigadier Poett [since 1 July 1943, commander, The 5th Parachute Brigade] and his staff who were sharing the camp, also attended and Padre Whit Foy again rose superbly to the occasion. He was blessed with the ability to involve his congregation emotionally in his services and yet at the same time satisfy our involvement. Hence you came away, spiritually and morally uplifted and on that sunny March evening, he was at his best. His text that night was *In my father's house are many mansions,* which he used to prepare us for the dangers and even death which we would all be facing the next morning.'

On 24 March elements of the 6th Airborne Division began to rise as early as 0200 for their breakfast, before climbing aboard the lorries that would take them to their allotted airfields; of which there were many. Divisional Headquarters and a part of the 12th Devons headed to Rivenhall. The remainder of the Devons went to Dunmow and Matching, with elements of the 53rd Airlanding Light Regiment, 2nd Airlanding Anti-Tank Regiment and 6th Airborne Armoured Reconnaissance Regiment joining them at the former. The remainder of these latter units took off from Woodbridge, alongside the heavy Hamilcar gliders of the 3rd and 5th Parachute Brigades. 6th Airlanding Brigade Headquarters made its way to Earls Colne, whilst the 1st Royal Ulster Rifles and 2nd Oxford and Bucks Light Infantry each sent a half of their formations to Birch and Gosfield. The Horsa gliders carrying vehicles and equipment for the Parachute Brigades left from Shepherds Grove, whilst the main body of the 3rd Brigade, including Headquarters, the 8th and the 1st Canadian Parachute Battalions made their way to Chipping Ongar. The 9th Battalion, with the detachments of the 3rd Parachute Squadron and 224th Field Ambulance in tow, went to Wethersfield.

5th Parachute Brigade Headquarters and the 13th Battalion were to take-off in 33 Dakotas and two Horsas from Wethersfield and Boreham respectively, whilst the remainder of the Brigade; the 7th and 12th Battalions with elements of the 591st Parachute Squadron and 225th Field Ambulance, were assigned Boreham. By dawn, all the men were waiting beside their allotted aircraft. They had visited these 24 hours earlier, when, to ensure that all would go smoothly on the day, they had arrived to draw parachutes, load the aircraft and the gliders so that all would be ready for them when they arrived.

After what must have been a fitful sleep, at Boreham Captain Richard L. Adams in the 34th TCS figured 'It's a day's work. He was not a fatalist. However 1st Lieutenant Charles Voeglin in the 43rd TCS recalls, 'I'll never forget the night before. You know you're supposed to get crew rest and we all had these crews, 15-20, sleeping in one room. All of us were frightened. Someone would wake up, light a cigarette at two in the morning and say, 'I can't sleep.' Then nobody would sleep and here you've got to take off on a mission in a few hours.' Then the standard joke was 'the condemned men ate a hearty breakfast'. The administration instructions for Normandy had stipulated the serving of a fat free meal at least two hours before emplaning. No such orders were issued for operation 'Varsity'. Breakfast consisted of porridge, bacon and fried potatoes, bread and marmalade and the inevitable tea laced with tinned milk. For the Americans there was bacon, orange juice, powdered eggs, milk, toast, fruit, pancakes, SOS (shit-on-a-shingle, creamed beef on toast); then it was one last mug of strong 'Java' (coffee) to wash everything down. The 315th's CO, Colonel Howard B. Lyon, recalls that 'while the combat crews had breakfast, the dance band, *The Dakotans*, played music. We knew the war would soon be over and we were in good spirits.'[2]

All of the airfields in East Anglia were a hive of aircraft and glider activity for the mass of flights to the far bank of the Rhine. Apart from the British airborne troops of 3rd and 5th Parachute Brigades flying from England, conveyed by 243 aircraft of the three American Troop Carrier Groups, thirteen RAF transport squadrons were fully employed in delivering the 6th Airborne in 392 Horsas and 48 Hamilcars. Six squadrons of Stirling tugs - 295 (motto: 'Help from the Skies') and 570 (motto: 'We Launch the Spearhead') at Rivenhall, would tow 21 gliders containing the 12th Devons; 196 and 299 at Shepherds Grove, were to tow 32 gliders to LZ A' and LZ 'B' and 190 and 620 at Great Dunmow, would tow 24 gliders.

Of the transports and glider tugs, 416 were British. 46 Group, under Air Commodore L. Darvell carried the paratroops while 38 Group under the command of Air Vice-Marshal James Rowland Scarlett-Streatfield delivered the Air Landing Brigade of the 6th Airborne Division into action.[3]

Thirty-five C-47s of the 61st Troop Carrier Group took off from Chipping Ongar at 0730 hours and formed up for the two-hour flight to DZ 'A', an irregular area about 1½ miles in diameter on the west side of the panhandle which formed the northern end of the Diersfordter Wald. With the British paratroops embarked in almost perfect weather, clear skies and excellent visibility, takeoffs went away about on schedule; the first transport taking to the air at 0709 and the last shortly after 0740. Of 243 aircraft detailed to go, only one failed to depart and that because no load had been provided for it. Aboard the rest were close to 3,900 troops and 137 tons of supplies.

At Birch a large number of Horsa gliders had been landed and Dakotas of Nos. 48, 233 and 437 Squadrons in 46 Group arrived on detachment from Blakehill Farm and Down Ampney. On 19 March the 800-strong 2nd Battalion Ox and Bucks had joined the armada of gliders and tugs at Birch where 65 gliders were waiting to transport them to LZ 'O'. Captain Richard Smith would be in the glider which carried much equipment, including a jeep, a lot of 3-inch mortar ammunition in a trailer plus full petrol tanks on board.' Many in the 2nd Battalion Ox and Bucks, including the CO, Lieutenant Colonel Mark Darell-Brown DSO, a big and hefty man; and Private Denis Edwards, in No. 25 Platoon in 'D' Company, were not only veterans of Normandy but had participated in the very first attack of 'D-Day', the assault on the Caen Canal bridge (subsequently renamed 'Pegasus Bridge'). Now they were going to do it all over again.

The Ox and Bucks' lift began at 0630 hours. Denis Edwards, who would fly in the glider piloted by two RAF sergeant pilots; Stan Jarvis and Peter Geddes, recalled: 'A strange event occurred at this time. One of the corporals who had been with us in the Normandy campaign had by this time been promoted to sergeant of his platoon. While waiting to enplane he had a premonition that the aircraft was fated and doomed. He ran off, only to be later detained, tried, stripped of his rank and sentenced to military detention. He might well have received a more severe sentence than a few months' detention had it not been for the fact that his premonition was justified. The glider in which he would have travelled took a direct hit and was destroyed with no survivors.'

Edwards' glider was in fifth place to take off but the towrope snapped while they were on their takeoff run, this being a not uncommon occurrence, since the tension in the rope was at its greatest as the glider accelerated while being dragged along the runway. A tractor was quickly sent down the runway to drag the glider back to the start line and eventually they were ready to go again, but now at the back of the queue. 'We were thus the last combination to leave, travelling towards Europe in grand isolation', wrote Edwards. 'Our [Dakota] tug pilot, Wing Commander (later Group Captain) Alex Blythe [commanding 233 Squadron] did not follow in the wake of the airborne armada. After a chat on the intercom with Stan Jarvis he had a new course plotted by his navigator in order to reduce the journey by a few miles and thus to arrive earlier. He intercepted the other aircraft exactly where he expected, close to the destination and reinstated us close to our correct position in the formation.'[4]

Four squadrons of Halifaxes made up the rest of the RAF transport squadron strength with 296 and 297 at Earls Colne and 46 Halifaxes on 298 and 644 at Tarrant Rushton. 298 and 644 would operate from their jumping off airfield at Woodbridge in Suffolk where they were split into two flights, most of which being used to tow Hamilcars to the far side of the Rhine in what was to be their last wartime mass glider operation. 298 and 644

Squadrons were commanded by 34-year old Wing Commander Hubert Law-Wright DSO DFC[5] and Wing Commander Ernest Leonard Archer AFC respectively. 298 Squadron had the distinction of operating the first seven Mk.VII Halifaxes to go into action during 'Varsity'. Additionally, three Halifaxes were specially equipped with extra radio facilities and acted as master supply aircraft to direct the American 'Eureka' and compass beacon operations. As a result of experience gained from previous operations, every possible aid was provided to identify the four Allied dropping zones precisely with 'Eureka' and compass beacons set up at the various turning points. Additionally and immediately prior to crossing over the Rhine, 'Eureka' beacons and coloured strips with distinctive letter panels were set up as a guide for the airborne component of the crossing.

At Earls Colne 296 and 297 Squadrons' Halifaxes would tow a combined force of sixty Horsas between them to LZ 'P' and LZ 'R'. On the night before the operation, 50% of the combinations had their tows in place and were lined up along approximately one-third of the length of the runway while the remainder lined its perimeter from where they were fed into the take-off sequence. The Horsa skippered by veteran Glider pilot Staff Sergeant Norman Harold 'Andy' Andrews in No.2 Wing would carry Lieutenant Colonel Jack Carson the Officer Commanding 1st Battalion, The Royal Ulster Rifles and the tactical headquarters of the battalion due to capture bridges over the River Issel near Hamminkeln. In 1942 22-year-old 'Andy' Andrews volunteered for the newly formed Glider Pilot Regiment to escape the boredom of waiting for the German invasion that never came. He had served with the Royal Engineers in France but, after evacuation from Dunkirk, he found service in England unexciting. He was by now one of only six glider pilots to take part in all four major operations; one of whom was fellow Horsa pilot Warrant Officer Lawrence Turnbull.[6] He had picked up the nickname 'Buck' during a winning streak at a 'Crown & Anchor' pub game just before Dunkirk, where a drunk Geordie who he had never seen before or since kept slapping him on the back and yelling, 'All right, Buck!' to all and sundry. By morning, the name had stuck.

David Vickery on Flying Officer Ron Langtry's crew on 'N-Nan' on 297 Squadron recalls: 'On the afternoon of the 23rd we had a pre-briefing for pilots, navigators and air bombers for 'Varsity' involving our two squadrons, 296 and 297 and, no doubt, the other squadrons in the group: 17,000 men, with 600 tons of ammunition and 800 vehicles and guns were to be carried in 1,500 aircraft and 1,300 gliders in support of Ground forces' big push to cross the last great natural frontier of Nazi Germany. The camp was sealed.'

Tom Staniforth, a flight engineer on 296 Squadron recalled: 'We were the headquarters squadron of 38 Group. Our aircraft were Halifax GT Mk.IIIs with Hercules engines. Our Squadron Commander, Wing Commander T. C. Musgrave had been put in charge of our part of the lift. He was a remarkable man in the same mould as Douglas Bader. Though Wing Commander Musgrave had lost a leg in North Africa in a glider accident in August 1943 he flew the Halifax just like any other pilot. It must have been difficult sometimes, especially when towing gliders; not that this prevented his crew from making sarcastic remarks if a take-off was erratic. I am also told that they usually lit their post take-off cigarettes from matches struck on his legs.

'At this time, operations carried out by 38 Group were many and varied; dropping SAS men behind enemy lines on special operations; supplying the underground forces in Norway; a task which invariably involved trips of twelve to fourteen hours in the air and a heavy reliance on long-range tanks. These operations usually called for twenty canisters in the bomb-bays and a couple of 300lb panniers - huge rectangular baskets - which had to be literally kicked out of the parachute hatch when the red light came on; one of my jobs as flight engineer. We also kept in practice towing gliders, but it wasn't something we had to do operationally very often. We had done it at Arnhem but that was before I joined the squadron. On the Rhine crossing each Halifax towed a single Horsa glider - we called them 'matchboxes' - which carried twenty fully-equipped airborne soldiers. With all the practices, we got to know our bunch very well. We lined them up the night before on the runway at Earls Colne; an incredible sight. At 0730 hours we took off for the LZ near Wesel on the German side of the Rhine.'

At other Essex airfields were the 12th Battalion, the Devonshire Regiment; at Matching Green where a dozen gliders would be dispatched to DZ 'R', at Rivenhall where six more would be towed to LZ 'P' and at Great Dunmow where 24 more would be dispatched to LZ 'R'. The 1st Battalion, the Royal Ulster Rifles destined for LZ 'U' were at Gosfield where 28 gliders would be dispatched; at Birch where 27 more would be towed into the air and at Rivenhall where eleven more would be dispatched.

Horsa pilot Sergeant Tony Wadley, second pilot to Sergeant 'Tug' Wilson from Doncaster, recalled: 'We were woken very early with tea brought to our hut by WAAF cookhouse staff.' At 0200 hours the Stirling crews were called, given breakfast of bacon and eggs and received a last briefing which included final weather reports. 'Each glider crew received a low-level photograph of their landing zone at the briefing, close to a farm house near Hamminkeln, which was to be used as Divisional HQ. Our Horsa was loaded with a jeep and trailer carrying radio equipment together with five troopers from the Devon regiment.'

Twenty-six of the thirty gliders towed by Stirlings of 570 Squadron at Rivenhall carried a total of 275 troops plus many vehicles. The HQ Staff of the operation was commanded by the 6th Airborne Divisional commander, Major General Eric Louis Bols CB DSO, and 295 Squadron's thirty Stirlings at Rivenhall carried 222 troops of the 12th Battalion, The Devons and the 1st Battalion, Royal Ulster Regiment, plus many vehicles were in its towed gliders. On the advice given by Brigadier George Chatterton, Major General Bols had decided that the gliders were to make many small, separate, precision landings as close as possible to tactical objectives instead of the massed landings employed hitherto. Speed was to be sought at the expense of concentration. However, two coup-de-main parties, in eight gliders at Birch and seven more at Gosfield, were to land the Ox and Bucks and the

Royal Ulster Rifles' on the eastern edges of LZ's 'O' and 'U' to seize the road bridge and the rail bridge over the Issel at Ringenberg and make preparation for demolition in case their recapture by the enemy appeared certain. The new Mark II Horsas were a distinct advantage in the execution of this concept because, like the Hamilcar, they had a hinged nose, allowing vehicles and other stores to be unloaded immediately on landing.

Lieutenant Dixie' Dean wrote: 'Reveille was 0300 hours and as I made my way through the trees to the ablution block, the silence was broken by the raucous roaring overhead of a V1 'Doodlebug', which must have been one of the last to be launched against this country. Daylight came as we drove to the airfield and on our way we passed the gates of another camp, whose occupants must only just have departed, since the permanent staff were still waiting there and gave us a great cheer as we passed.

'Wethersfield seemed deserted and we drove directly to the dispersal point where the Dakotas were parked. At Keevil on the evening of 5 June the aircrew had been there to welcome us - a move much appreciated, but now there wasn't a soul about. There was still time to go before chutes were to be fitted and so, as if we wanted to delay such actions until the last possible minute, we hung around and watched as a mighty armada of 'Flying Fortresses' collected overhead.

'At last things couldn't be delayed any longer. The door had been removed from the plane, but we required the ladder to enable someone to get inside and hand the chutes down. We all gathered round the door, Frank Kenny was given a leg-up into the fuselage, on the floor of which were several bundles. These came to life and revealed the ground crew, who hastily dressed. Then one said 'Gee fellars, what about chow?' Then they disappeared cross the tarmac in search of their breakfast.

'Before we emplaned, Sergeant Cope of the Mortars came across. He had three men refusing to fit their chutes. He wanted me to try and change their minds. I said that at this stage, I wasn't going to start giving direct orders. They had been isolated from the rest of the stick and I emphasised the difference between refusing to jump on an operation and on an exercise, stressing what a serious Military offence it was. I then asked them individually if they understood and were they prepared to continue their action. They all knew what they were doing, but were not going to change their minds. By now it was time to get on board, so they were left for the ALO's staff to deal with.

'Our crew was still missing. Sergeant Kenny checked us over and gave the order to emplane. We sat inside and waited. All around engines were being started and run-up. Eventually a jeep came screaming up, out jumped four bodies who climbed aboard, pulled in the ladder and disappeared into the cock-pit cabin. Within seconds the engines coughed and spluttered into life and only moments later we started to roll along the perimeter track towards the runway.

'From my seat in the fuselage I could look out of the door and watched as the aircraft neared the runway from both directions of the perimeter track in a constant stream. As they reached the end of the runway, they turned along it, staggered on either side and crawled forward, until all forty aircraft of the Battalion group were lined up. We waited a few minutes, engines ticking over and then with a mighty blast all engines were revving at maximum, planes straining at the leash momentarily, brakes off and down the runway raced the complete Battalion group. Faster and faster as if in a race and then the feeling of relief as the plane lifted off the tarmac, upwards climbing engines at full throttle to get you airborne and finally that feeling in the pit of your stomach as the pilot eased back and assumed normal flying speed. I was always happier once takeoff was safely accomplished since an incident in 1942 at Netheravon, when the brakes of a Whitley seized and the plane ran into a hangar, killing half the stick. Once airborne the 'jump master' came out of the cabin and handed round cigarettes, but on learning that few of us smoked, disappeared and returned to hand round candy. He then went back into the cabin and we saw no more of him for two hours and more.'

'Take-off' recalled Sergeant Tony Wadley 'was soon after seven o'clock, but as we gathered speed down the runway our towrope broke before we were airborne. A waiting tractor towed us clear of the runway and we were eventually connected to LK351 E7-N, a 'spare' Stirling on 570 Squadron piloted by Flight Sergeant Sabourin. We finally took off at 0855 long after the remainder of the Rivenhall serials had departed.'

David Vickery on 297 Squadron was awakened on the morning of 24 March very early (0530). 'After eating a massive breakfast the Air Minister, Sir Archibald Sinclair was present at the squadron briefing, standing beside our squadron commander 'Dixie' Dean [Wing Commander E. G. Dean DFC]. After delivering a brief exhortation, he moved along us, no doubt absorbing our feelings of mass excitement and pre-op tension. Walking out to the crew wagons I recognised the novelist, Ernest Hemmingway; a large, genial man with a large hat, intent on being in on the action. The Horsa gliders, containing troops of 6th Airborne Division, were positioned at the end of the main runway in close formation, whilst our aircraft were parked further up, on either side, facing inwards and at an angle.

'Each crew was deposited by its own kite and we were completing pre-flight checks when the first Halifax taxied out, turned to face the runway, the towrope was attached and it trundled slowly forward until the rope tightened and the Horsa started rolling. The organisation was admirable; the atmosphere taut and purposeful. The Halifax on our left taxied out to the centre of the runway, the trolley acc was plugged in to our kite and the engines run up as we watched another glider go from stationary to 60 knots in a few tenths of a second and follow its tug before leaving the concrete. The aircraft opposite us taxied out and the process was repeated.'

439 Horsas and Hamilcars of No. 1 Wing, led by Lieutenant Colonel Iain Murray, took off in perfect flying conditions between 0600 hours and 0750 hours. One tug had failed to take off because its undercarriage collapsed.

David Vickery again: 'The first Halifax to take off had to fly almost up to Bury St. Edmunds and back, the second to a point a few miles less and so on; so that the last aircraft to take off turned directly onto course - almost exactly 090° as the squadron, with its gliders, formated into a tight box. Then it was our turn. Flying control ordered us out. We taxied out, turned 90° port, 'Pinky' from the tail turret called 'Tow line attached' and we were off. As our glider, piloted by 'Baldy' of the Glider Pilot Regiment, became airborne and went into high tow, I could see the combination preceding us about two miles ahead and climbing.'

Flight Lieutenant Malcolm Guthrie on 296 Squadron recalled: 'The job of flying the aircraft with a glider on was very much simpler than the job the glider crews had in actually controlling their glider while they were being towed. On take-off one had to hook up and then inch forward very carefully until you got a taut rope. It necessitated an extremely long take off. The glider was airborne at about sixty or seventy knots, long before the aircraft was and that assisted in bringing the tail up. The glider went to the 'high tow' position - that was above the aircraft and stayed there during take-off speed. Then the other problem was engine overheating. You had to watch the engine temperature very carefully because you were flogging them at full-rated boost for almost twice as long as you would in a normal take off. On top of that, if you had the slightest drop in power you had to make a pretty rapid decision whether to cast off the glider. We had an intercom cable running down the centre of the tow-rope, so the tug was in communication with the glider.

Before leaving from Earls Colne, Major Ian Jodrell Toler DFC, Officer Commanding, 'B' Squadron, 1 Wing Glider Pilot Regiment visited his niece, Flight Officer Rosemary Britten, an RAF intelligence officer who as well as being a pianist, played cello and flute and asked her to come and watch his takeoff. During Operation 'Market-Garden' on 17 September Toler and his Horsa co-pilot, 25-year old Staff Sergeant Arthur 'Shack' Shackleton had flown Lieutenant Colonel Derek McCardie, commanding the South Staffordshires, five of his men and a jeep and trailer. 'Shack', who had transferred to the Glider Pilot Regiment after initially joining a heavy artillery regiment in Derbyshire, was to recall: 'At dawn we started the attack. But they were waiting for us with Panzer tanks. Three hundred and fifty of us were killed in one hour.' Toler and Shackleton (who acted as the former's bodyguard) established a command post in a cellar close to the Hartenstein Hotel. By 25 September, after days of relentless shelling and mortaring, mounting casualties and no sign of reinforcements, it was clear that the position was hopeless. Toler, by then in command of the regiment, was ordered to make a strategic withdrawal across the river during the night. He put Shackleton in charge of a file of airborne troops who were leaderless. At about 2200 hours Toler and Shackleton set off towards positions in a forest where they acted as guides during the evacuation to the south side of the Rhine. They spent two or three hours directing men along a safe route and when there were no more arrivals they decided to go to the river. They came across a small group of stragglers and Toler told Shackleton to stay with them while he found a way to the river. 'Shack' recalled: 'Suddenly I heard a burst of machine gun fire and I felt like someone had hit my arm with a sledgehammer. When I turned I saw that the others were dead. Then I felt my hand was sticky and blood running down my sleeve.' He set off in the direction of the river and there he met Toler again. Toler helped Shackleton into a boat but while crossing the river it was hit by a mortar shell and Shackleton was thrown into the water. He was a non-swimmer and resigned himself to the inevitable. 'Suddenly I was in the river on my back. I felt my leg bump down into some mud and I heard someone say 'here's a body washed up' and I shouted, 'I'm not a body, I'm alive.' His rescuers were probably Canadian engineers, who took him to a field dressing station. The medics first attempted to remove the bullet and pieces of shrapnel from his shoulder and the rest of his body. At Toler's insistence, 'Shack' was evacuated with other wounded. From then on he was admitted to successive hospitals, finally being put on a hospital train to St. Elizabeth's hospital in Birmingham to recuperate.

During the winter of 1944-45, based at Chelsea Barracks, 'Shack' was part of a demonstration unit established to train recruits in the art of street fighting. They were equipped with German army uniforms and taken each day to the battle school site at Battersea, where they fired Spandau machine guns to add a touch of realism to the exercise. One Friday afternoon, when they were due to go on weekend leave, no vehicle arrived to collect them. Shackleton and a comrade decided to walk back to barracks. The two uniformed 'Wehrmacht unteroffiziers' marched down Queenstown Road, past Battersea Power Station and over Chelsea Bridge carrying their machine guns without once being challenged!

'Shack' was not crewed with Major Toler on the 'Varsity' operation but instead he had as his co-pilot, John 'Willy' Williamson, an old colleague from early 'B' Squadron days. Toler, who by now was the only officer in the squadron to have survived Arnhem, would fly in another Horsa with his RAF co-pilot, Flying Officer George Telman.

Rosemary Britten however had no time to watch a take off; she was determined to be part of the operation too! She later recalled, 'I kept well out of the way of the senior officers present and the aircrew carried my Mae West and parachute so that I would just look like a love-sick WAAF officer seeing off her boyfriend. An awkward moment arrived when my uncle came up to say goodbye and asked me to come and see the take off'.' Rosemary got on board Halifax NA698 'D for Dog', 17th aircraft in the serial lift, piloted by Flying Officer Ron Lamshed. Alongside her escape kit, she had packed powder and lipstick because she 'wanted to look like a German girl in case of bailing out'.

John Cooper, a medic, occupied one of thirteen gliders at Earls Colne, each carrying eighteen members of the 195th (Air Landing) Field Ambulance RAMC destined for LZ 'R'.[7] 'We'd been warned that the weather was poor and to expect a bumpy ride. At the briefing we had been told to be careful not to cause unnecessary damage to the gliders, that it might be wise to recover them for further use. Did these people who came out with these stupid ideas even have an indication of what it is like on an LZ when you're under fire?'[8]

'Reveille was at 3am' wrote Jim Corbett 'and we tooled up with all our fighting gear: with crossed bandoliers of ammo and a grenade (suitably taped to avoid accidents in the aircraft) hanging from each lapel. Our weapons were loaded with full magazines and one 'up the spout'. Just as dawn was breaking, we were ferried to the airfield. All the heavy bombers were lined up on one side of the runway and the gliders on the other with the coiled tow-ropes between them. Tension was high and hardly anyone spoke. The last-minute briefing was not reassuring. Apparently, while the land-forces assault was going well and a bridgehead of some sort had been established, the unwelcome news was that some big guns had been brought up to stop the advance into the Fatherland and they were likely to be used to shell the landing zones. It was hoped to bring in Typhoon fighter aircraft for close support. Most of the RAF personnel, including the WAAFs, got up to see us off. Lastly, the tow-plane pilot poked his head around the door and wished us luck, adding that he was glad he was not landing with us. A nice touch!

'The take-off by RAF personnel was a model of quiet precision and organisation. Picture, if you can, fifty heavy bombers, one after another, pulling to the centre of the runway, followed by its glider. A quick word of confirmation between the two pilots and we soared into the dawning sky. There was one casualty and it happened to be one of our Company's platoons. The tow-rope broke on take-off and the flight aborted. Unfortunately, the glider couldn't attempt a normal landing on the runway as it was being used by other aircraft taking off. Without much height, it drifted around to find a suitable spot and crash-landed on the edge of the airfield. There were no serious injuries and the platoon joined us later in Germany.'

On another glider Eddie Horrell in the Devons recalled: 'On our way to deliver the last heavy blow of the war, we felt great elation and great apprehension. There was no doubt in our minds that Germany would soon be beaten, the war would be over and we would be able to go home after six long years, but would we all survive this last battle? I never had any doubt that I would, but some were not so confident. Sid Carpenter from Bovey Tracey, with whom I had shared a civilian billet in Exeter in 1940 said to me on the way back from loading the glider, 'I wish I could see my wife and baby daughter once more.' I told him it was our last 'do' and we were all going to survive and go home for good, but he wouldn't be consoled and was killed in the landing.

'With last minute preparations made we were in our gliders lined up behind our tug-planes, Short Stirling bombers ready to go. It was a perfect morning and a cloudless blue sky as we formed up and crossed the Channel, an unforgettable sight as we passed the coast of Belgium and flew on over Brussels, with tug-planes and gliders as far as the eye could see. We joined up with the 17th American Airborne Division to make a total of 2,796 aircraft over Belgium; what a sight we must have been from the ground. The American 17th used Waco gliders, much smaller than our Horsas, so one of their tug-planes towed two Wacos.

'The Rhine soon came into view and we passed over it and on to our destination, the town of Hamminkeln, which was an important road and rail junction. Our job was to capture and hold it until the land forces crossing the Rhine could join us.

'Conversation dropped off and everyone became strangely quiet as we neared our target. The inside of a glider is dark, with a few very small windows, but looking out we could see thick walls of smoke obscuring the view. The smoke-screens the army had been using to hide their movements from the Germans had drifted across our landing zone and it was difficult to see the ground. Then there was complete silence apart from the swish of the wind as our tug cast us off. This was it; no going back or opening up the throttle for another circuit! If things don't look good you just sit there and hope the pilots will do a good job, with a bit of help from the Almighty.'

Staff Sergeant Leonard David Brook, a Horsa pilot in 'E' Squadron of the Glider Pilot Regiment recalled being told at briefing at Birch that the 7th Parachute Division and the 84th Infantry Division were waiting for them together with a few thousand Volkssturm and a Panzer Division available in the vicinity of Bocholte. Brook had volunteered for the Army in February 1942 and joined the 58th Training Regiment Royal Armoured Corps at Bovingdon, Dorset. His first six months of initial training included instruction on driving and maintenance, gunnery and wireless radio. He was then posted to the Green Howards Armoured Car Regiment stationed in Scarborough and spent time training on the Yorkshire moors with the armoured cars and firing live ammunition. In May 1944 he volunteered for the Glider Pilot Regiment and underwent infantry training before being posted to RAF Booker on 25 May to undergo basic pilot training at 21 Elementary Flying Training School until 27 July. He was subsequently posted to RAF Stoke Orchard Glider Training School northwest of Cheltenham where he trained on the Hotspur glider before going to the Heavy Glider Conversion course at North Luffenham on 1 September. On the 13th he flew to Ouistreham, Normandy and flew one of the 'D-Day' Dakotas back to Netheravon. In November he was posted to 'C' Squadron at Tarrant Rushton and flew the Horsa and Hamilcar.

David Brook took off soon after dawn from Birch with a small group of Ox and Bucks Light Infantry. 'Our sixty formations of Dakotas and Horsas slowly wheeled round gaining the 2,500 feet flying height and forming up until we had joined with the other 1,000 odd combinations forming one continuous line and heading out for the Channel. In number 52 in the seemingly endless stream, the leading gliders and their tugs disappeared over the horizon as we headed towards Brussels and we knew that behind us the stream continued, the tail of which would take half an hour at 120 mph before it reached our current location. High above us could be seen the silver spots of escorting fighter cover and we changed direction at pre-determined places three or four times in order not to make our destination obvious. That we need not have bothered was shown to us later by the strength of the welcoming committee that awaited our arrival!'

At 0800 the American 17th Airborne Division at seventeen airfields in the Rheims and Amiens areas of France and almost all tugs and gliders of

38 and 46 Groups carrying the 6th Airborne were in the air. The only exception was the 6th Airlanding Brigade commanded by Brigadier Hugh Bellamy DSO, which took off at 0600, over an hour ahead of the paratroop aircraft, because it took about an hour to get a batch of sixty gliders into the air and more time still to haul them up to the prescribed altitude. Some 370 gliders were to carry Divisional Headquarters and 6th Airlanding Brigade to four landing zones, LZ's 'O', 'R' and 'U', bunched within a one-mile radius around Hamminkeln and LZ 'P', an irregularly shaped area about 1½ miles long from north to south which was just west of those zones and just south of DZ 'B'. Another seventy gliders were to land reinforcements for the paratroops on DZ's 'A' and 'B'. Only one of the tugs failed to take off. However, the heavy Horsas and Hamilcars were very apt to abort and in this case, despite the superlatively good weather, 35 broke loose or had to be released prematurely. Two of them ditched in the Channel, but all aboard were speedily rescued. The brigade was tasked with landing in company-sized groups and capturing several objectives, including Hamminkeln.

As usual the aircraft assembled into elements, the elements into flights and the flights into serials, which then swung over their bases and headed for the departure point at Hawkinge in Kent, which was reached approximately on schedule after sighting more robot missiles en route which were immune to anti-aircraft fire because they were in the troop carrier lane. The whole armada met over Wavre (close to the site of the Battle of Waterloo) near Brussels, to make their combined way towards the Rhine. As the British gliders flew over Waterloo, one officer-pilot turned to his sergeant co-pilot, a soldier who had been retrained as a glider-pilot after the heavy losses suffered by the Glider Pilot Regiment at Arnhem and said: *My great-great-grandfather fought at Waterloo.* The unimpressed working-class non-com looked down at the old battlefield below and grunted: *So did mine and it was probably your great-grandfather who my great-great-grandfather killed. Try not to do the same to me today![9]*

The weather was near perfect, with only the smoky haze from the artillery bombardment obscuring the view from the air. Sergeant Dan Hartigan of the Canadian 1st Paratroop regiment observed: 'As we flew inland from the coast at about 1,200 feet I looked down and saw a strange countryside. As far as the eye could see were hundreds of thousands of crater rings. There they were, sullen on the surface of this ravaged landscape ... Then it dawned on us that we were flying over the World War I battlefields. A sobering sight. Yet here we were 26 years after that last war ended, going to fight the same enemy.'[10]

The C-47 piloted by Major Thomas C. 'Doc' Cargill, the 14th Troop Carrier Squadron CO in the 61st TCG, carried elements of the Canadian 1st Paratroop regiment to DZ 'A'. 'Doc', born 6 June 1919 in Montgomery, Alabama excelled in sports in high school. He was the starting quarterback on the varsity football team and he also ran in track. Upon graduation from high school, Doc accepted an athletic scholarship from Clemson College to play football and run track while majoring in textile engineering. He played halfback on the varsity team for his first two years and would have been on the squad through his senior season had he not left school. Even though he was in school only two years, he set a school record in the 440 yard dash. On 9 July 1943 he participated in Operation 'Husky' which dropped paratroopers into Sicily. This was the first combat mission for Cargill and the 15th. All planes and crews returned safely. His second combat drop during Operation 'Husky II' on 11 July would have quite a different outcome. The communication between Patton's Army and the US Navy supporting the invasion were not clear. The route the airborne troops would be taking carried them over the supporting US fleet. Nervous US Navy gunners mistook the troop carrier C-47s for the German twin engine Ju 88 bombers which had just bombed them shortly before the C-47s appeared overhead and opened fire. A total of 24 C-47s were shot down, two of which were from the 15th. Among the crews of the 15th, only one pilot was seriously injured.

On 6 June 1944 (his 25th birthday) Cargill and the 15th took off at 0232 for the assault on the European Continent. The 15th carried elements of HQ Company, 2nd Battalion, 507th PIR of the 82nd Airborne Division to DZ 'T' just outside of Sainte-Mére-Église. Although the weather deteriorated badly as the troop carriers reached the continent, seventeen of the eighteen C-47s in the 15th put their troops within one mile of the DZ. Cargill was deputy leader on the 'D-Day' mission which would have put him in command of the 61st Troop Carrier Group if Colonel Willis W. Mitchell, the group commander in the lead ship, was shot down or in any other way incapacitated. Cargill cared deeply about his squadron and its men. 1st Lieutenant Claude Breeden was shot down on 'D+1' and had to ditch in the English Channel. The crew received only minor injuries. Breeden remembered that Cargill personally flew down to Exeter to pick up the lucky crew and return them to Station 483 at Barkston Heath.

As the C-47s of the 61st TCG exited the DZ on the 'Varsity' drop they were to make a left bank to turn and head back to base. As Major 'Doc' Cargill banked, the C-47 flew into what looked like a stream of tracer fire and was seen to start puffing smoke from around the left wing. Shortly after, there was smoke seen coming from the cockpit. Cargill's plane never came out of the bank and quickly lost altitude. The left wing hit a house as it neared the ground tearing it off and the rest of the ship hit the ground and exploded. There was evidence of one parachute coming out of the plane at about tree top level. The parachute was shredded in the trees and all aboard the plane were killed.

Captain James E. Drake of the 14th Troop Carrier Squadron who was flying as Deputy Leader of the right wing of Major Cargill's ship recalled: 'After dropping our troops on the DZ, Major Cargill dropped the nose of this ship to pick up speed. He went, I imagine, about 3/4 of a mile and then went into about a 30° bank for a 180 degree turn for our return heading. As he was rolling out a heading of about 220 degrees he was hit to the best of my knowledge in the left engine, or left side of cockpit the plane immediately left a trailing stream of smoke seemed to make a dive for the deck. I, sensing his trouble, pulled up over him and to the left of him. From that time on, my co-pilot, Lieutenant Theodore Walker saw the rest. Major Cargill had just dropped his troops and nosed his ship down for the turn out of the area. When he completed his turn, his ship seemed to have been hit. Smoke started puffing from his left engine and from the roots of his left wing. The ship seemed to nose down even further, as if to be going down to hit the deck. At that time smoke seemed to come from the roof of the cockpit. When the plane was at about tree top level, a man and parachute came out. The parachute streamed out in the trees and was torn to shreds. The left wing tip hit a house, driving the nose and engine into the ground. The plane skidded along the ground in flames. The tail came up and the fuselage snapped at the trailing edge of the wing and the tail and went crashing into the line of trees along the road.' Major Thomas C. Cargill was buried at the Netherlands American Cemetery in Margraten.[11]

Two C-47s in the 53rd Troop Carrier Squadron in the 61st TCG made two passes over DZ 'A' to get all paratroopers on the drop zone. One of the C-47s was flown by Captain Victor A. Anderson, who recalled: 'My load consisted of sixteen paratroopers, together with their equipment and other equipment carried by six pararacks attached to the underside of the aircraft. On the run in to the DZ we encountered no enemy action and immediately after crossing the road which was the west boundary of the DZ, I gave the green light. It was about the geographical centre of the DZ when the first of the paratroopers (B-1) left the aircraft. The eleventh paratrooper fell down near the door after the first ten had apparently made a successful jump. This caused the remaining six paratroopers to become more or less entangled which necessitated a second pass to enable the remaining six to drop in the designated zone. Of the first ten paratroopers, all were well within the DZ.

'Leaving the target I then made an 180° turn to the left and again approached the DZ crossing the road at approximately the same point but at a different heading. I again gave the green light immediately after crossing the road and shortly after, the remaining paratroopers had jumped well within the designated area but more to the southwest than the first ten. On my second pass, I went in after our serial had completed its run and immediately preceding the second serial (B-2). It was after completing my second pass at the DZ and on my turn to the left from the DZ that I received concentrated small arms fire. One of the shells penetrated the cockpit on the right side and shout out a hydraulic pressure gauge, releasing hydraulic pressure also. The point of penetration of the bullet was to the right and below 2nd Lieutenant James A. Oien, the co-pilot's seat. Before takeoff he and I noticed two extra flak suits in our aircraft. We used them to improvise additional armour by placing them under the seats and the two sides of the cockpit. It was that portion of the flak suit that Oien placed to the right of his seat and next to the side of the cockpit that ultimately stopped the shell thus preventing a possible casualty. The shell was recovered. It was a German thirty calibre. The flight home was accomplished without incident. The radio operator, Thomas J. Dittman, busied himself on my instructions with setting up a parachute to use as an emergency brake. However we found that it was not necessary for I was able to land short on the runway and rolled to a stop without any brakeage. The engineering department made an examination of the ship and found hits in the elevator, the rudder, the belly and creased main gas lines. An engine cylinder that had been hit had to be removed in addition to the punctured hydraulic lines.'

The 5th Parachute Brigade, commanded by 37-year old Brigadier Joseph Howard Nigel Poett DSO, had a hard time landing on DZ 'B'. All the aircraft, forty from the 316th Group and 81 in the 315th, are believed to have reached the zone and dropped at least some of their troops, although at least two aircraft were hit and burning before the jump began. The drop zone, an irregular area 1½ miles long on the east side of the wood about two miles beyond DZ 'A', came under heavy fire from German troops stationed nearby and was subjected to shellfire and mortaring which inflicted casualties in the battalion rendezvous areas. Poor visibility made it more difficult for paratroopers of the brigade to rally. However, 7th Parachute Battalion soon cleared the DZ of German troops, many of whom were situated in farms and houses and the 12th Parachute Battalion and 13th Parachute Battalion rapidly secured the rest of the brigade's objectives. The brigade was then ordered to move due east and clear an area near Schneppenberg, as well as to engage German forces gathered to the west of the farmhouse where the 6th Airborne Division HQ was established. Captain David Tibbs, medical officer to 13th Parachute Battalion found 24 men of his own battalion hanging dead in their harnesses in the forest they had been dropped in.

After dropping the 5th Parachute Brigade the formation of Dakotas swung away to port for the flight home but met heavy anti-aircraft fire from units of the 7th Parachute Division in the area of Mehr to the west of the drop zone. The 315th Troop Carrier Group had ten transports shot out of the air in the few minutes after they had dropped their sticks and were making their turn, crashing on the east bank of the Rhine; seven others were damaged so badly they had to make forced landings west of the Rhine. Seventy more aircraft were also damaged.

The drop zone also came under fire almost immediately after the drop began, whilst mortar and artillery fire was brought down on the battalions' RV areas. Brigadier Nigel Poett was as usual jumping with the leading element of his brigade.[12] With the rest of his 'stick', comprised of men of his brigade headquarters, he was standing at action stations in one of the leading Dakotas as it neared the battle already raging ahead. 'As we approached the Rhine, we could see ahead of us the battlefield covered by haze and the dust from the bombardment. At 1,000 feet we passed over the administrative units and the supporting arms and then the crossing places themselves. However, there was no time to interest ourselves in the troops on the ground, or in the craft upon the river because the red light was on and almost before we realised it we were over enemy territory. We were being shot at and the aircraft bumped and shook. Then we were over the

DZ, the green light was on and we were out.

'As we dangled from our parachutes we tried, in the very short time available, to pick up the landmarks. These had seemed so very clear and simple on the sand models and in the air photographs, but now they appeared somewhat different as we came down rapidly amongst the firing and into the dust and smoke caused by the artillery bombardment which had finished more than ten minutes previously. Although this had been heavy, ten minutes was ample time for the enemy not knocked out to recover sufficiently to be a considerable threat to our parachutists as they swung in the air or disentangled themselves from their parachutes and got their bearings.

'We felt very naked but this was where the battle experience of the brigade became evident. All three of my battalion commanders had taken part in the landings in Normandy. Together with our gunners, sappers and field ambulance, we had fought with the division in France, Belgium and Holland. Our officers and men all knew one another well and this was to prove an enormous advantage in this operation that was going to require a high standard of leadership right down to junior NCO level.

'Assembly at RVs was always a tricky business and a landing in broad daylight, in an area covered by fire of enemy troops who were fully alert, meant that very rapid rallying and high standards of leadership on the DZ were essential. Moreover, the concentrated drop meant that the different sub-units of the battalions were inevitably mixed up. They had been shot at on their way down from the aircraft to the ground and they were under considerable harassing fire as they struggled out of their parachute harnesses, unfastened their kitbags, extracted their weapons and got their bearings.

'Although all three battalions had been dropped accurately, individual officers and men experienced considerable trouble in working out their exact positions. This period on the DZ was where most of our casualties occurred. Once enemy positions had been located and action taken to deal with them, the troops in them generally surrendered without putting up a serious fight. However, until they were spotted, they were extremely troublesome.

'Just as our chaps were reaching their RVs, the glider-borne element of the brigade group began to approach its landing zone. To the south the gliders of 6th Airlanding Brigade also began to come in. This caused a considerable diversion of enemy artillery fire and provided a most welcome relief for us. It was, however, a most tragic sight to see gliders picked off in the air and on the ground. Their losses were very heavy and thus only a comparatively small proportion of our anti-tank guns and vehicles carrying the machine guns, mortars and ammunition reached the battalions at their RVs. There is no doubt that, had a strong enemy counter-attack developed later in the day, we would have been seriously embarrassed by these losses of anti-tank guns and ammunition reserves.

'It was about one hour after the drop that our three battalions were sufficiently complete in their RVs to be able to report that they were ready to start on the second phase of the plan, the securing and consolidating of the brigade objective. Considering the circumstances of the landing, our casualties had not been unduly heavy. Our losses were approximately twenty per cent of those who had jumped. I lost my Brigade Major, Major Mike Brennan and my Signals Officer, Lieutenant Crawford on the DZ. My DAA and QMG, Major Ted Lough, was in a glider and also became a casualty when he was very badly wounded. As a result, my brigade headquarters had to be considerably reconstructed when we reached our RV.

'One lesson I had learned in Normandy was that of wireless communications. On the night of D-Day I had lost the wireless team that jumped with me and I was without any proper communications throughout the whole night. This time, therefore, I and all my battalion commanders carried our own American walkie-talkie sets strapped inside our parachute harnesses. These radios were intended only to maintain control until proper communications had been set in the RV or on the final objectives but they proved to be a huge success.'

By 1530 Brigadier Poett reported that the brigade had secured all of its objectives and linked up with other British airborne units.

The American pilots dropped the 1st Canadian Parachute Battalion nine minutes early and many of the aircraft failed to throttle back over the DZ, which resulted in a scattered drop, mostly to the east. As expected the Canadians landed on a 'hot' DZ, experiencing heavy flak and crossfire from the firmly entrenched German positions. Unfortunately, there were many Canadians who landed some distance from the intended target just north of the Diersfordter Wald and they met severe machine-gun and sniper fire. Twenty-three Canadians were killed and 42 wounded. Regrettably, one of the few soldiers to be dropped into the surrounding trees was the Officer Commanding 1st Canadian Parachute Battalion, Lieutenant Colonel Jevon Albert 'Jeff' Nicklin OBE a native of Winnipeg, born in 1914, had won the Grey Cup with the 'Blue Bombers' football team in the 1930s.. This was not the first time he had been hung up after a drop. On D-Day, 6 June 1944 he landed in the midst of a German position at Varaville and his parachute was ensnared on a rooftop. Nicklin received fire from German soldiers before he cut himself free and took cover. He eventually rejoined his unit and was later wounded by shrapnel. This time he was immediately shot and killed before he could get down from where he was hung up. Nicklin left a widow, Mary Eileen Nicklin, in Port Credit, Ontario.

The Battalion's orders were to seize and hold the central area on the western edge of the Diersfordter Wald, which was believed to be held by German paratroopers. 'C' Company's objective was to clear the northern part of the woods near the junction of the roads to Rees and Emmerich. Once this area was secure 'A' Company would advance through the position and seize the houses located near the DZ. 'B' Company would clear the southwestern part of the woods and secure the battalion's flank. The Canadians helped capture the village of Schneppenberg and three of the bridges over the River Issel in partnership with the 513th PIR.

Notwithstanding this, all of the Canadian companies were able to organize themselves and take their objectives within two hours of the landing. No doubt the exceptional leadership and battle experience helped tremendously with the reorganization on the ground. Once dug in, the Battalion was successful in beating off the inevitable German probes and counterattacks, which began almost immediately. The Canadians were facing a tough and resourceful enemy, including battle-hardened paratroopers who were now fighting for their homeland.

The Canadian drop witnessed supreme gallantry. At about 1100 hours a cry for help came from a wounded man in the open. Two medical orderlies from the 224th Parachute Field Ambulance went out to this man in succession but both were killed as they knelt beside the casualty. Without hesitation and on his own initiative, 27-year old Corporal Frederick George 'Toppy' Topham, born in York Township on 10 August 1917, a medic treating casualties sustained in the drop, went forward through intense fire to replace the orderlies who had been killed before his eyes. As he worked on the wounded man, he was himself shot through the nose. Fighting the pain, blood pouring from his mangled nose and cheek, he stood his ground, gave the solider first aid and then picked him up and carried him through the hail of bullets into the woods to safety. Then he turned around and headed right back out again, to help more of the wounded men. For the next two hours, he refused to stop working, refused to let anyone take care of his bloodied face until the entire area had been cleared of casualties. On his way back to join his company, he came across a Bren gun carrier that had been hit by a shell. Mortars were still landing all around it. Flames leapt from it; there were explosions. An officer warned everyone to stand back. Topham rushed in. He found three men inside and carried each of them to safety. One died of his wounds almost immediately after. Topham arranged for the evacuation of the other two, who undoubtedly owe their lives to him. For six hours, most of the time in great pain, he performed a series of acts of outstanding bravery and his magnificent and selfless courage inspired all those who witnessed it. According to the *Canadian Gazette* of 2 August 1945, Frederick Topham was awarded the Victoria Cross in recognition of 'sustained gallantry of the highest order'.[13]

The outcome of the Canadian operation was the defeat of the I. Fallschirmkorps in a day and a half. In the following 37 days, the Battalion advanced 285 miles as part of the British 6th Airborne Division, encountering the Bergen-Belsen concentration camp on 15 April and taking the city of Wismar on 2 May to prevent the Soviets from advancing too far West. It was at Wismar that the battalion met up with the Red Army (the only Canadian army unit to do so during hostilities), other than a Canadian Film and Photo Unit detachment. The armistice was signed on 8 May and the battalion returned to England. The Battalion sailed for Canada on the *Isle de France* on 31 May 1945 and arrived in Halifax on 21 June. They were the first unit of the Canadian Army to be repatriated and on 30 September the battalion was officially disbanded.

Endnotes Chapter 5

1   The Pegasus Archive.

2   *Airborne Troop Carrier Three One Five Group* by George F. Cholewczynski / *The Last Drop* by Stephen E. Wright.

3   When the German forces capitulated in May 1945 Scarlett-Streatfield was given the honour of accepting their surrender in Norway. With his Norwegian liaison officer Major Petter Cato Juliebø, he took off from RAF Great Dunmow at 0355 hours flying to Oslo aboard Short Stirling IV (LK297) of 190 Squadron RAF. On 10 May 1945 his aircraft disappeared without trace in extremely bad weather conditions. On 21 June 1945 the wreckage of his aircraft, the remains of its crew, AVM Scarlett-Streatfield and the paratroopers accompanying him were located at Andtjernåsen in the hills near Oslo, it had crashed into the hillside and exploded.

4   *The Devil's Own Luck: Pegasus Bridge to the Baltic 1944-45* by Denis Edwards (Pen & Sword, 1999, 2001, 2009).

5   Law-Wright was the pilot of a Halifax which took off from Tarrant Rushton at 2235 on 2 April 1945 for 'Stirrup 14' an SOE mission to Norway. The aircraft was shot up over Lista and crashed at Kalleberg near Farsund. The crew were all killed and are buried at Vanse Churchyard.

6   Staff Sergeants Nigel Brown, Jimmy Wallwork, Bert Holt and Brian Taylor were the others.

7   Of the seven airborne field ambulances formed during the Second World War, two were glider borne (the 181st and the 195th); the other five (the 16th, 127th, 133rd, 224th and the 225th) were parachute trained.

8   Quoted in *Paras: Voices of the British Airborne Forces in the Second World War* by Roger Payne OAM (Amberley, 2014 and 2016).

9   Quoted in *The Gliders: An Action Packed Story of the Wooden Chariots of World War II* by Alan Lloyd (Leo Cooper, 1982).

10   *A Rising of Courage, Canada's Paratroops in the Liberation of Normandy* by Dan Hartigan (Drop Zone Publishers, Calgary, 2000).

11   Researched and written by Randall W. Lewis.

12   In Operation 'Overlord', the 5th Parachute Brigade was assigned the task of securing two road bridges across the River Orne and the Caen Canal, Operation 'Deadstick'. Poett jumped on D-Day at 0019 hours with the pathfinders and a small team. At 0050 hours Poett made contact with Lieutenant Sweeney at Horsa Bridge, he then made his way to the Pegasus Bridge and Major Howard.

13   Working for Toronto Hydro, he died in an electrical accident on 31 May 1974 at the age of fifty-six.

Chapter 6

Winged Pegasus

I really enjoyed the sensation of flying; then came the day when we had to put into practice all that glider training. The early hours of 24 March; a lovely, warm spring day. We were transported to an airfield crammed with gliders and their towing Halifaxes and Stirlings. We made our way to our big, black, rather beautiful glider, past jeeps and trailers and other gliders and aircraft and everywhere miles of towropes; and full of the bravado we needed to demonstrate to each other, we sang a stirring and comforting ditty to the tune of the 'Volga Boatman', the first, second and fourth lines of which went, 'The fucking rope broke'.

Horsa pilot, Alan Spicer, whose glider was towed by a Dakota on 24 March 1945.

'Takeoff. The roar of the Dakota's engines as it slowly moves off, the jerk of the towrope's slack being taken up and we are away and gathering speed. First, the Dakota slowly lifting while we still race along the runway as if unconnected, then we feel the ground suddenly drop away as we climb into the sky behind the towrope bending up into the distance, our umbilical cord. Gradually our towing plane levels off and now our suddenly fragile-seeming glider is in level flight, now rising, now, alarmingly, falling, every now and again buffeted against the force of the slipstream on our way up or down. Then, as we approach our dropping zone, the towrope is released, the umbilical cord cut. We are free, no longer dependent on that lumbering Dakota, suddenly and miraculously still sailing along without power, a new sensation of smooth, effortless movement through the air, the thin whistle of the wind over the wings the only sound apart from the idle chatter of the few too insensitive, or nervous, to appreciate the beauty of silent flight even though we always take a steep dive for several hundred feet, practising to get below the German flak and machine guns that can bring down a wooden glider with ease.'

When Alan Spicer had found himself part of the 6th Airborne and was introduced to gliders he had found the prospect of his flight exciting. 'It was not till after our first training flight that we could have refused to go up and thus been considered for a transfer to a more down to earth unit. But since nobody had refused, not altogether surprising since nobody was aware of the option (although I wouldn't have refused a chance to fly even if they'd charged a fare!), we were deemed tacitly to have accepted the posting as glider-borne infantry, a sort of retroactive volunteering and we were paid an extra sixpence a day for the privilege. Still, I was now qualified for the glamorous and famous combination of red beret and Pegasus flying horse shoulder flashes and as long as no-one was shooting at me it felt good to be part of the 6th Airborne. And one of my ambitions had, up to a point, been realised: I was involved with flying - although with thirty odd men to a glider, it was not unlike travelling by tube, but with a better view. And you did get a seat.

'We climbed aboard our Horsa and sat in our two rows, making jokes and laughing a little too heartily, trying to pretend we weren't worried about what was ahead as we waited for our turn to move off. Between us, at awkward intervals, were our trailers lade with assorted ammunition and weaponry. Ahead of us was the biggest airborne crossing of the war, over the Rhine and into Germany, while on the ground the Rhine would be crossed by thousands of other poor sods, on foot. Then we were off, part of this awe-inspiring armada of aircraft towing their gliders, stretching as far as the eye could see.' Thirty-five gliders in the 6th Airborne contingent failed to reach their destination through accidents but the 213 aircraft of RAF Fighter Command guarding that part of the route had little to do, for not one enemy aircraft was seen that day. The only flaw was an error in timing which caused the various serials to arrive from six to ten minutes ahead of schedule. The crews were aware of their true position and the red warning lights flashed as usual four minutes before the actual arrival time. However, this premature arrival did cut out nearly a third of the artillery bombardment of German flak batteries which had been scheduled to last from 0930 to 1000 hours'.

Near the Rhine an unexpected navigational difficulty arose. Montgomery had shielded his amphibious operations with a huge smoke screen extending for nearly fifty miles along the Rhine. Although the generators were turned off early on 'D-Day' after reconnaissance pilots reported that unfavourable flying conditions were developing, the smoke did not have time to clear. Borne on the southeast wind it covered the visual aids at Last Lap so they could be seen only from directly overhead and combined with local haze to reduce visibility between the river and the drop zones to one mile or even less. Fortunately the distance was short, less than three miles to one zone, five miles to the other; landmarks on the run-in were plentiful and not such as to be readily obscured by haze; and good 'Gee' fixes were available in case of need. In addition some pilots were helped by the visual aids set out on the zones by the pathfinders from the lead serials. At any rate both supplies and troops were dropped with great accuracy. Of the first three serials all except two C-47s, which had to turn back for mechanical reasons, reached DZ 'A'.

Lieutenant 'Dixie' Dean of the 13th Parachute Battalion recalled: 'We had a long flight ahead, in the region of three hours' duration. Initially we flew over southern England, crossed the North Sea to make a landfall in Belgium and somewhere over that country linked up with the American Division, flying from airfields near Paris. They must have been ahead of us, since they were never in sight, but later on over Holland we under-flew the tugs and gliders of the air/landing forces involved in the operation. There was plenty of time for contemplation and I wondered just how much longer my luck was going to last. I carried no St. Christopher's, rabbit's feet or sprigs of white heather - nor on this occasion did I have any premonitions of any sort.

'On we flew, with quite a wide river passing below. 'Surely that's not the Rhine', I thought; it's wider than that and besides there were no sign of battle on either bank but soon burning buildings indicated that it was the Rhine after all and we were approaching the time for action.

'Look at that', was the cry from behind. I turned my head. Number 2 was pointing to the starboard windows. A large group of Dakotas, lower than us flew past in the opposite direction and from one a long tongue of orange red flame streamed from one engine. Through the starboard windows were seen the homeward bound Dakotas which had dropped 3 Brigade. I didn't want to be reminded that such things could happen, so I turned to look out of the door again and what an impressive sight it was and one which I will never forget. How long all this took, I have no idea, but looking out there was no signs of any military activity, only peaceful farmland and we were flying much too high for dropping.

'Whatever other criticisms there were of American air crew on 'Varsity', the airmanship of the pilots could not be faulted, as we flew in a tight box nine abreast in three 'vics' of three. Our aircraft was the left hand one of the right hand 'vic' of the second flight of nine. Back and front, left and right, Dakotas gently rose and fell as the pilots expertly kept formation. But my eyes were on one plane only - the one in the centre of the leading 'Vic', because I knew that when bodies started falling from it, it would not be long before I too would be taking that one, inevitable step forward. Nine abreast in three 'vics' of three they flew, with only yards separating individual aircraft which constantly rose and fell a few feet as the pilots worked hard to maintain position. In every plane by now, Number Ones were standing in the doorway taking in the spectacle, for it was an unforgettable sight to see all 33 Dakotas in close formation.

'When we first boarded the plane, we noticed four 'flak suits' of body armour and now the jump master came and collected the same, returning to the air crew cabin. He next reappeared, to announce 'twenty minutes to go' and he proceeded to the rear of the fuselage. We busied ourselves with the standard drills. We were all jumping with 'kit bags' so we fitted these first and then hooked up and went through the usual procedure of checking and reporting before moving to the door. All was in order and the next orders would come from the jump master, but when I looked for him he was hardly visible. Dressed in his 'flak suit', he had gone into the Elsan closet cubicle at the rear and pulled several inflatable rubber dinghies the plane carried in case of ditching, across the doorway in front of him so only his face was visible. He now announced 'OK you guys, I'll despatch you from here''.

'Frank Kenny would have none of this. He came forward to act as despatcher and we all unhooked. Sergeant Kenny took No.1 hook and moved to the rear of the door while the rest of us moved down one hook. After a further check that we were all hooked-up correctly I again positioned myself in the doorway.

'I was thinking 'Surely it's time the planes descended to the dropping height of 500 feet?' (We were flying somewhere near 1,000). The ground below was littered with discarded parachutes as we passed over 3 Brigade's DZ. The 8th, 9th and Canadian Battalions must all have reached their RVs in good time - there wasn't a soul in sight, but I knew now we were on our correct course for DZ 'Baker' and there were only two miles to go and the drop was a little over one minute's flying time to go. Two questions the Number Ones were asking themselves; when are the pilots going to descend to 600 feet and when are they going to reduce speed? Normally the wing flaps were half lowered, as was the undercarriage and the pilot flew at just above stalling speed, but this was not happening. The height was nearer 1,000 feet and there was no slackening in the pace of the run in. But now we were all at 'action stations' and the open farmland of the drop zone clearly visible ahead. Butterflies were fluttering in all tummies as we awaited the green light.

'I would be dependent on the 'red and green' light signals, since our jump-master and his communications with the pilot were not available to us. We were still flying high and faster than normal dropping speed too. Standing in the door, you could watch as the under-carriage was lowered and 'half- flap' applied to reduce the flying speed, but this wasn't happening as we ran in to the DZ. Now we were over the woods and ahead I could see the open farmland on which we were to drop. It couldn't be long and my eyes were riveted on that lead aircraft. A blob appeared underneath it, then another and another and soon all the planes in the leading flight were disgorging their human cargoes. On came the 'red' - a last look down to make certain we were clear of the trees and I was tensed ready to jump 'Green on - Go' - whether Frank Kenny gave the order or not, I don't know, but I am sure the Dakotas were nowhere near stalling speed and flying nearer 1000 than 500 feet.

'The impact of the former was immediately apparent once my chute had developed and I had released the 'kit bag' and lowered it to the end of the recovery rope. Instead of dropping below me, it swung upwards level with my head, before running backwards, as my chute oscillated wildly. I didn't look down or around, my efforts were concentrated on curbing the pendulum effect of the swinging parachute. I realised the ground was coming up fast and I was in for a backward landing. My feet didn't touch - at least not to begin with. Only feet from the earth, something caught my legs at ankle height and I was thrown over onto my right shoulder. There was no wind and my chute collapsed slowly around me.

'All was quiet, apart from the departing planes - seemingly the 'apple pie' treatment applied to the Boche guns had been successful. I tried to get to my feet and there was a sharp jab of pain in my right shoulder - the arm was useless and just hung at my side. Using the left arm and hand only I got out of my harness, but couldn't unpack the 'kit bag', so I hid it under a bush at the side of the track, adjacent to which I had landed. In order to do this simple task, I first of all had to negotiate a post and wire fence. This type of fence criss-crossed the part of the DZ. I had landed and was responsible for the bad landing I had made. Coming in backwards, my heels had caught the top strand of wire, pitching me onto my shoulder. These fences can't have shown up on the air photos and we had not been warned of their existence. Fortunately, I only had to cross one such obstacle - once over the track, I was in open fields.'[1]

Norman Mountney in 'Dixie' Dean's stick had celebrated his nineteenth birthday in Holland. Shortly afterwards the Americans arrived to relieve us. One of them remarked: *What's holding you guys back? That little drop of water?* On reflection I reckon I crossed the Rhine before he did. I was jumping with a kit bag carrying two liners of ammunition (500 rounds of Mark VIIIZ). Before take off the pilot said he was going to drop us as low as possible and as slow as possible. But his good intentions were forgotten when waiting for the 'green', we were hit by flak and he climbed increasing speed as he did so. I made a good exit there were chutes all round and I noticed two Dakotas on fire but I couldn't see the ground for smoke or dust. I hit it hard and rolled into a hollow as a mortar bomb exploded nearby. There was also sporadic machine gun fire. A short distance away I saw some men hung up in the trees, but when I got closer, I could see they had all been shot, still in their harness. I linked up with my Platoon Commander Lieutenant Dean and as we neared the RV a glider still trailing the towrope nearly caught us.'

Fred Beddows wrote: 'While we were standing up waiting for 'Action Stations' I saw black puffs of smoke appear among the planes, this was the German welcoming committee. The day we went to draw and fit chutes I had spoken to the pilot who said he would drop us bang on target. The American jump master was standing beyond the open door, wearing a flak suit and steel helmet and smoking a big cigar. *OK you guys, let's go* were his instructions and we all shuffled forward. I watched as the light turned from red to green and out we all went. I was a long time coming down. By the end of the day I had learnt what an SP was.

'The trouble on the ground was to find the RV. Smoke or early morning mist reduced ground level visibility to little more than one hundred yards and very few men picked up the land marks of the planned rendezvous. Everyone had painted on the back of his jumping jacket a black rectangle surrounded by a white strip. We all turned to face the line of fly in, as instructed and moved back in that direction. Consequently the Battalion funnelled towards a dog leg bend in the road bordered by woodland. At last the enemy woke up and machine guns opened up on the right flank. No particular targets were being engaged but the bullets were whistling overhead. Some of the young soldiers who had not been in action before threw themselves down when the first bursts were fired, but were quickly on their feet again at the urging of the experienced soldiers.

'Prisoners were already being rounded up. Clearly they had no stomach for a fight and took the first opportunity to surrender their weapons. There must have been a considerable number of Germans in the copse towards which the Battalion were streaming, with an excellent field of fire, but Sergeant Arthur Higgins and others disarmed them very quickly and offered later arrivals Lugers and Schmeissers if they wanted extra fire power.

'To begin with, all was rather chaotic at the impromptu rendezvous with a couple of hundred bodies milling around as Officers and NCOs endeavoured to sort out Companies and Platoons. Some alert individual must have kept a look out for suddenly, in the midst of all the disorder came the cry *There's a jeep coming*. This had to be an enemy vehicle since the gliders had not yet landed. Every one dived for cover in ditches and hollows and behind trees, with weapons cocked and covering the road. The sound of the approaching jeep grew louder and louder and we were all geared up to give it a hostile reception when the call came: *Don't shoot, it's Sergeant Webster*. And indeed it was. A beaming sergeant reported to the CO with a recaptured American Army jeep.'

Bill Webster tells his own story: 'I made sure the plane had stopped flying over the forest before I jumped as No.1, with tile Yankee jump master yelling *Go, Go, Go* all the time. I landed close to a cottage alongside the road and standing outside watching the drop were an elderly couple. I could hear a vehicle approaching so I motioned with my Sten for them to get inside in case there was going to be any shooting. Hearing the vehicle stop, I swung round with my weapon pointing towards it. *You can't shoot me* the officer standing up in the front seat of a jeep called. *I'm a doctor.* The others with him must have been medics too because they made no attempt to fight. Despite the angry protests of the doctor, I commandeered the vehicle and drove on along the road until I came to the wood where the Battalion were gathering. Later I drove the CO and Captain Fred Skeate, who was wounded, to where we had been briefed to dig in.

'Not all the members of the Battalion were in a position even to reach the temporary RV and it soon became apparent that some of the pilots, in addition to flying high and fast, had also given the signal to jump before they reached the drop zone. Consequently not a few men landed in the woods along the line of fly in, some of them to be shot dead, hanging helplessly still in their parachute harness.'

A member of the anti tank platoon, Private Dave Robinson, landed off site in some woods with his chute in one tree, his kit bag in another and him hanging in between. Two men pulled him down. 'I had a hole in my cheek, three teeth missing, a swollen face and a black eye, resulting from shrapnel as I jumped. No permanent damage so I did not get any treatment until two weeks later, when an Army dentist took out what was left of the three teeth, hurting me more in the process than the shrapnel.'

CSM 'Taffy' Lawley MM who had parachuted on the very first operation carried out by British parachutists, now jumped on the last one: 'I took up my place in the door. There was much flak bursting around and while I was watching intently for the signal to go, a burst exploded a short distance from me. But for the fact my hands were gripping the outside of the door, I would, most probably have been blown across the fuselage. The next second the green light came on and I was away. It seemed a long time before I landed but I was quickly out of my chute harness and made for some buildings, where I found some members of the Company. My Company 2nd in command Captain Fred Skeate was wounded. I took his hunting horn and blew the Company call, mustering most of them. While this was happening a truck load of Jerries drove round the corner of a wood, no more than 200 yards away and we soon dealt with them. Taking the Company to the RV we met the OC Major B. C. E. Priday. Soon the whole area was cleared of the enemy, large numbers of prisoners being taken, some of whom we made dig our slit trenches. They thought they were digging their own graves.

'There were some nasty sights; burnt out gliders, complete with their passengers. Paratroops shot as they hung in the trees. It was sad for me to find the body of our young Colour Sergeant Charlie Wrigley, a great friend of mine.

He had landed in a wood and been shot in the back.'

Dave Beadham was another who was dropped from a greater height than planned: 'Our plane must have been flying 1,000 feet up, rather than the 500 we were supposed to drop from, because I was a long time in the air and there were those 20 mm flak guns blazing away at us. There was a small wood near where I landed and some of the lads were hung up in the trees. I dropped in the open in an area of post and wire fences just like in England, but it was quite a job having to keep climbing over them before I could reach any cover. The first thing I can remember seeing was a German farmer standing in a two wheeled cart lashing the horse with a whip to get away from us.'

'As things turned out, there was no need to put the CO's plan into operation, since the objective had already been captured by men of the Battalion who had landed close by and led by Lieutenants Harry Pollack and 'Topper' Brown attacked the position. The Germans here also surrendered and seventy of the enemy, including the major commanding that sector were put in the bag. They looked very disconsolate, sitting in a line on the roadside as the Battalion passed.

'There was a new hazard now; the gliders as they came in to land, for their pilots too were troubled by the bad visibility after they cast off and started their downwards glide. The German flak guns, many of which had not been put out of action by the artillery bombardment, had the easiest of targets, while the cumbersome gliders were in flight. Corporal Jack Carr and Lance Corporal Tommy Howell of the MMGs landed close to the objective and set up the Vickers alongside the road and watched the gliders as they were landing in front of them. They realised that a giant Hamilcar was bearing down upon them and ran clear as the glider caught the gun, knocking off the traversing handles. Yards to their rear the Hamilcar buried itself in a wooden farm building which collapsed about it. But even before the roof tiles had stopped falling, out drove a Bren Carrier, apparently undamaged.

Captain Reverend A. L. Beckingham of the 224th Parachute Field Ambulance RAMC recalled: 'The crossing of the Rhine was a completely different drop from the Normandy invasion. That had been in the dark in the early hours of the morning before the invasion by sea took place. In Germany the Brigade dropping was timed for 1020 hours. Our Brigade [the 13th] was to seize and hold a spur in the dropping zone. It was much pleasanter coming down in daylight but the drop itself was from rather high up, estimated I believe between 800 and 1,000 feet, with the result that we were in the air for what seemed a long time. This increased the casualty rate as the Germans were bursting AA shells amongst the parachutists. The visibility on landing was not as good, as the dropping zone was largely obscured by smoke. Some of our men actually fell into German gun pits and were in fact firing on the enemy before landing. I was fortunate to land in a rather healthier spot and as soon as we had reached our RV with Dr. Wagstaff and his RAMC orderlies, I was amazed and delighted to be presented with a hot cup of tea by my batman! He had dropped into Germany carrying amongst his kit a flask of tea! There was little time during the rest of the day for food or drink as casualties soon needed the attention of all available hands. But though the shelling and mortaring went on all the time it was not as intense as I had expected it would be. We had 93 casualties in the Battalion on the first day, including seventeen killed.'

The troops testified that the American pilots flew straight and true and gave them an accurate and generally excellent jump. Only seven soldiers were returned, all because of fouled equipment. Brigadier 'Speedy' Hill commanding 3rd Parachute Brigade wrote: 'The American pilots performed brilliantly, although they dropped us nine minutes early. Apart from the loss of Lieutenant Colonel Jeff Nicklin, a splendid battalion commander, I recall two other incidents. The first took place near my command post on the edge of the DZ where there was a small belt of trees. At the end of this was a spinney which was held by some Germans who immediately engaged our troops as they landed. I saw Major John Kippen of 8th Parachute Battalion who was one of the best company commanders in my brigade, which was tasked with clearing the DZ. I told him to collect some men and eliminate the enemy position which he proceeded to do with considerable gallantry but was unfortunately killed in the process. The second incident occurred when I was watching the approach of a Horsa which was obviously going to crash into the wood on the edge of which I was standing. It banked steeply and flew along the side of the wood until it caught its port wingtip in the trees twelve feet above the ground. To my amazement, I discovered that it contained, amongst other things, my batman, jeep and wireless operator as well as a motorcycle. Regrettably, the pilot broke his legs but the other men in the aircraft survived.'

Eighty aircraft of the 61st Troop Carrier Group and 39 in the 316th carrying Brigadier 'Speedy' Hill's Brigade approached DZ 'A' in good order, albeit, at 0951, nine minutes ahead of schedule and for the next quarter-hour, dropped 1,917 men on or near the drop zone from altitudes between 700 and 1,000 feet. The Germans manning the anti-aircraft batteries in the area had yet to recover from the shock of the 2nd Army's softening-up bombardment and so the first troops of the Brigade were faced with only a loose scattering of flak as they jumped. The 8th Parachute Battalion's task was to secure the drop zone and in particular to clear the enemy dug in around it. 'B' Company's objective was 'Axe Handle Wood', so named for its hatchet-like appearance on the aerial photographs, situated in the centre of the southern-half of DZ 'A' and dominating it and two small copses which commanded the open area of the DZ itself. Only four minutes had been allowed to complete this task. Meanwhile, the remainder of the Brigade, arriving four minutes later, landed and attacked the main objectives. By 1030 'A' Company had captured their assigned wood in the north-eastern corner of DZ 'A', meeting little resistance and capturing a few prisoners. 'C' Company with Battalion Headquarters and the Mortar Platoon in tow similarly encountered no problems in taking their objective in the south-east.

Lieutenant Colonel Hewetson commanding the 8th Battalion later described the events that took place: 'The stick of the Anti-Tank Platoon with the platoon commander had jumped to the east of the DZ owing to a failure in the light signals in the aircraft. Returning to the DZ, they had a short sharp engagement in a house and captured an officer and fifteen men of a German signal unit together with their 3-ton lorry. This vehicle was invaluable later when the DZ had to be cleared. The gliders began to arrive at 1100 hours. One of the first down, a 9th Parachute Battalion glider, overshot the LZ but although it was badly damaged there were no casualties. My second in command, Major John Tilley had gone off to see Brigade Headquarters and 'B' Company. I was standing on the edge of the wood briefing Lieutenant England my Intelligence Officer to keep in touch with Brigade Headquarters on the wireless while I went down to see how 'B' Company was faring and to see if it would be necessary to put in an attack with 'C' Company. Two sergeants, one from 9th Parachute Battalion, were standing a few yards away. Suddenly, with a terrific crash, a glider came through the trees and I found myself lying under the wheel of a jeep. I managed to crawl out from the wreckage to find the glider, one of the medical Horsas of 9th Parachute Battalion, completely written off.'

Hewetson, in obvious discomfort and anger, emerged from beneath the wreckage, exclaiming, *How now you whoring bastard shite!* The two pilots, two 8th Battalion sergeants and Lieutenant England had been killed.

'At about this time my second in command reported back from 'B' Company. The wood had been taken by a platoon attacking from the north-east using 36 and 77 grenades and covered by the fire of the platoon which had earlier attempted an attack from the south. The last phase of the attack was a hand-to-hand fight down a trench, led by the platoon commander. A considerable number of the enemy had been killed and one officer and twenty six soldiers were taken prisoner.'[2]

As Henry Bagley flew in over the drop zone his platoon commander kept looking out of the door. 'Even we could see the amount of flak that was curving up toward us and it was obvious to a blind man that we definitely hadn't surprised old Fritz. Then we had another shock in store for us. Our lot who were waiting to cross the river after we had secured Fritz's side were putting out an enormous smokescreen to cover their crossing. It was doing its job all right; it had partially covered our landing zones, making it extremely difficult for pilots to see exactly where to drop us. The aircraft shook as the flak bracketed us for about a minute, trying hard to shoot us down. It was the last shell that caused us no end of grief. It exploded right alongside us and literally threw the thirty ton monster to one side as if it were a child's doll. We were all watching the red light; the next moment we were all thrown on to the floor of the aircraft. By the time we got up the pilot had to do a wide turn and run in a second time, something I am sure he wasn't too happy about; for that matter, neither were we as the shrapnel from the shell had ripped huge holes in the fuselage.

'When I dived out of the aperture the sky was a veritable mass of tracer and explosions. I felt sure I would never get through it all. Well I did, but I had drifted over a large wood and looked like I was going to come down in it. I crossed my hands in front of my face and prepared to hit the trees. With over 50lbs of equipment in my leg bag, I literally crashed from the top branches through to the lower ones, but luckily, except for a few minor scratches, I was unhurt. Unfortunately, when I stopped I ended up hanging about four feet off the ground with the plate in the centre of my harness pushed up in my face. I was just about to cut it with my fighting knife when above the sounds of battle I heard German voices. My Sten gun was fixed inside my harness, but I did have a Colt pistol that I had won in a card game with some Yanks and it was tucked inside my smock. So I at least had something to defend myself with.

'I fumbled with the smock and after what seemed like hours I got it out and pointed it toward where the voices were coming from. Not a minute later two Fritz's moved into my vision. They were both crouched down as they moved, clearly trying to find where we had landed. How they missed me I don't know, but I dare not let them get out of my line of sight as if I did they could easily kill me.

'In the end I shouted *Hande Hock* in rudimentary German and pointed the pistol at them. Shocked, they both turned and looked up at me and then they slowly dropped their machine pistols and stood up. Some ten minutes later they had helped me down to the ground and I had relieved them of their stick grenades and was now holding my Sten gun while they stood with their hands up. My leg bag had been kindly unpacked by one of them and they seemed relieved they were prisoners. It was at this point I found out that my pistol didn't have a magazine in it, nor did it have one up the spout and I was so glad the Germans didn't think it important enough to recognise the characteristics of our weapons, whereas we had to learn the characteristics of all theirs.'[3]

The British troops showed a tendency to become entangled, with the result that some jumped late, others required a second pass and at least thirteen were brought back. Some formations, probably in the rear, came in much too high and dropped their troops from heights up to 1,150 feet. Until after the drop, flak was insignificant, but thereafter it thickened and brought down three aircraft and damaged about thirty. The C-47 piloted by 1st Lieutenant Joseph W. May in the fourth element in the 53rd Troop Carrier Squadron in the 61st TCG made a second run in on the DZ at 0955 hours. May gave the green light to go and British paratroopers of the 8th Battalion began leaving the aircraft, number one, two and three; the fourth trooper fell in the doorway and his kit bag went flying out, effectively preventing a quick recovery. The stick was jammed and by the time the passageway was cleared the aircraft was well out of the drop zone and in a shallow left turn. In the interim May asked his co-pilot, 2nd Lieutenant Alvis O. Back to check the plane to see if all the paratroopers were out. Back replied, 'No, they're not all out!' Sixteen still remained. The pilot shunted his aircraft from the outside of the turn to the left of his squadron's formation and began gaining altitude to 900 feet indicated.

Back asked if he was going to go in again and May replied, 'Yes, we've got to get 'em out somehow.' He noted the approach of serial B-2 on its run-in to the dropping zone and decided to tack on to the rear. May made a 180° turn to the left and dropped in behind at 700 feet. The moon-shaped flooded area came at them and then the roadway. Green light; and the balance of the stick mushroomed out over the centre of the littered field. Machine gun and other small arms fire scattered up towards the aircraft at the end of the dropping zone, but a quick turn out of the target was made and direct course set for home.

At 1115 hours the 8th Battalion's Hamilcar glider arrived, bringing in a very welcome load of a Bren carrier, spare 3-inch mortars, Vickers medium machine guns and some radio sets. Shortly afterwards, the enemy began to bring down shell and mortar fire on the drop zone. However, the battalion continued to clear it of equipment and containers, almost completing the task by 1200 hours at which time it was ordered into brigade reserve. It subsequently moved off from the DZ, leaving one platoon from 'C' Company to finish clearing equipment from the DZ and to guard the equipment dump. En route to its new position, the battalion encountered two 88 mm guns, one of which was firing into the trees and causing casualties from shrapnel bursts. Both guns, however, were attacked and knocked out. Finally, at 1830 hours the battalion was ordered to move again to a position covering the rear of divisional headquarters at Kopenhof.

9th Parachute Battalion was the last to jump. The CO, Lieutenant Colonel Napier Crookenden later described the scene in his aircraft as it neared the final stages of the flight: 'There had been some singing in the early part of our three-hour flight but most men had gone to sleep or relapsed into the usual state of semi-conscious suspended animation. The yell of *Twenty minutes to go!* from the crew chief woke us up and sent the adrenalin pumping through our veins.

'We were over the battle-scarred wilderness of the Reichswald and the terrible ruins of Goch when the order *Stand up! Hook up!* brought us to our feet. Each man fastened the snap-hook on the end of his parachute strop to the overhead cable, fixed the safety pin and turned aft, holding the strop of the man in front in his left hand and steadying himself with his right on the overhead cable. The stick commander, Sergeant Matheson checked each man's snap-hook. We all checked the man in front and, beginning with the last man of the stick, shouted out in turn, 'Number Sixteen okay - Number Fifteen okay!" and so on down to myself at Number One.

'Just aft of the door stood the crew chief in his flying helmet and overalls; listening on the intercom for our pilot's orders. I was watching the red and green lights above the door and I am sure that the rest of the stick were too. The red light glowed, the crew chief yelled *Red on! Stand to the door!* And I moved forward, left foot first, until I was in the door with both hands holding the door edges, left foot on the sill and slipstream blasting my face. Then the great, curving river was below me and seconds later, a blow on the back from the crew chief and a bellow of *Green on! Go* in my left ear sent me out into the sunlight. Once the tumbling and jerking were over and my parachute had developed, I had a wonderful view of the drop zone right below me. I could see the double line of trees along the road to the west and the square wood in the middle of the DZ. The ground was already covered with the parachutes of the 8th and 1st Canadian Parachute Battalions and I could see them running towards their objectives. There was a continuous rattle of machine gun fire and the occasional thump of a mortar bomb or grenade and during my peaceful minute of descent, I heard the crack and thump of two near misses. It was clearly a most accurate and concentrated drop and I felt a surge of confidence and delight.'

In the 3rd Brigade, the 9th Battalion landed without any major mishap and after three quarters of an hour was almost fully assembled in the area of its RV. By 1300 hours Lieutenant Colonel Crookenden's battalion was in position on its final objective on the Schneppenberg and the forward edges of the forest commanding the approaches to the Rhine. Crookenden directed the advance with the greatest vigour and as a result quickly seized the first objective with a large haul of prisoners. On approaching the second objective, the battalion was held up by the enemy in strongly dug in positions. Crookenden immediately took the leading Company round to a flank. He then personally led the assault. Although enemy fire was very heavy he pressed the attack with such vigour and determination that complete success was rapidly achieved, many Germans being killed and nearly 500 captured. Shortly afterwards Crookenden was given the task of capturing the village of Lanchenoffer. This necessitated a final advance of 500 yards across open country in daylight. Fire was heavy, both from infantry in the village and from two self-propelled guns to a flank. Crookenden decided to rush the objective. He himself again took the lead. The garrison was routed, 200 prisoners being taken and both self-propelled guns knocked out.

As the troop carrier formations swung left onto a homeward course after leaving the zone, sudden blasts of intense and accurate light flak swept the serials. Of the 121 aircraft which had reached DZ 'B', ten were shot down east of the Rhine and seven others crash-landed in friendly territory in such condition that only one or two of them were ever repaired. An additional seventy were damaged, most of them severely enough to make them temporarily non-operational. Troop carrier casualties amounted to only six dead, twenty missing and fifteen wounded or injured. However, many crews came down just behind the front; others were rescued by the rapid Allied advance after a brief term as prisoners of war. The high ratio of aircraft losses were inflicted in a comparatively small area from which flak had supposedly been eradicated by the systematic use of overwhelmingly superior airpower. The batteries doing the bulk of the damage were too far east to be affected by the artillery barrage. Some may well have been mobile pieces brought in at the last minute in spite of the elaborate interdiction programme. Others may have eluded observation or been unsuccessfully attacked.' The 61st Group returned to Abbeville-Drucat, the first C-47 landing at 1125.

In 5th Brigade 7th Parachute Battalion's initial task was to establish itself at the northern edge of the drop zone, which was northwest of Hamminkeln and to engage any enemy whilst 12th and 13th Parachute Battalions captured the brigade's objective which was the ground astride the road leading from the drop zone to Hamminkeln, thus preventing the movement of any enemy reserves through the area. The 7th Parachute Battalion's Commanding Officer was 37-year old Lieutenant Colonel Geoffrey Pine-Coffin DSO MC, whose troops, amused by the unusual applicability of his family name, referred to him as 'Wooden Box'. He was very tall and insisted on wearing cowboy boots during combat, making him easily recognisable to his fellow Allied soldiers in battle. Pine-Coffin later gave an account of his battalion's landing and the events on the DZ: 'The drop was at 1010 hours and was from rather higher than we liked for an operational drop; it must have been from nearly one thousand feet. This would normally have been an advantage as it seems that one is in the air for longer than one expects and thus gets a good chance of spotting a landmark as one comes down, but in this case everyone was getting pretty anxious to get down quickly because it was far from healthy in the air. The German flak gunners weren't getting much success in shooting down the Dakotas so a lot of them switched and burst their shells amongst the parachutists instead; this was most unpleasant and we suffered a number of casualties before we even reached the ground. There was mortar bombing and shelling on the ground but it was a great relief to get there just the same.

'The suddenness of the drop had the desired effect and we found the Germans slow to react. The battalion was in this position for five hours and during that time there was no really serious attack put in on us. There were various attacks on 'B' Company's position by parties of about platoon strength or slightly more and at one point, 'C' Company took on a company that was working its way round towards them. However, it was 'A' Company who came in for the worst time. They had arrived late and found their area was a very nasty spot. Their casualties were high and so were those of the mortars and machine guns who were with them.

'The trouble came from a small wood seven hundred yards away. There was a troop of 88 mm guns located there and they were commanded by an officer that one could not help but admire. When the drop took place it appears that the gun crews panicked and ran away but this officer managed to turn enough of them back to man one of the guns. He was, of course, in a hopeless position but he kept that gun firing and did an immense amount of damage before he was rounded up. Although 'A' Company suffered badly, 12th Parachute Battalion and Brigade Headquarters got it worse. It was 12th Parachute Battalion that sent out the party that rounded him up; 'A' Company, of course, should have done it but they were late getting in and it had to be done quickly. We got our share of it in Battalion Headquarters and had quite a few casualties, as well I know because I got a splinter in the face myself.'

Despite sustaining serious wounds to his face Pine-Coffin refused to leave for treatment and continued to move around his battalion's positions encouraging his men. He was (according to the citation for the bar to his DSO) instrumental in rallying his battalion to hold out against German counter-attacks, which played a pivotal role in the successful completion of the Brigade's main objectives. The brigade arrived in the second wave of aircraft, after the 3rd Parachute Brigade and the German anti-aircraft gunners were waiting for them. The parachute descent was made under fire and the DZ itself was also subjected to artillery and mortar fire. The 7th Parachute Battalion suffered casualties from air burst artillery shells. Their section of the DZ was only 700 yards from a battery of German 88 mm guns, which also targeted the brigade headquarters and the assembly areas of the 12th Parachute Battalion. The 7th Parachute Battalion secured the DZ, while the 12th and 13th Parachute Battalions headed for the brigade objective, the road from the DZ to Hamminkeln. By 1500, despite fierce opposition, the brigade had secured its objectives, with a large number of prisoners taken, but had suffered around 700 casualties. The 7th Parachute Battalion was ordered to start withdrawing at 1545 hours.

In 5th Parachute Brigade the 12th Parachute Battalion, along with the other battalions in the parachute brigades, knew that speed and surprise were going to be essential to the success of the operation. The Commanding Officer, 35-year old Lieutenant Colonel Kenneth Thomas Darling, born in India, educated at Eton and Sandhurst, was smallish in stature but tough and resolute and believed passionately in the British soldier. He would stand no nonsense from anyone, particularly the enemy who was soon made aware of his presence. Darling later described the measures he had taken beforehand to ensure that his battalion went straight into the attack as soon as possible after landing: 'We were dropping in broad daylight on top of the enemy positions and also on to our objective. The essence of the plan was rapid action, taking risks early and rushing our objectives before the enemy could recover from the preliminary bombardment and the surprise of a mass landing of parachutists.

'We were flown in by thirty-three Dakotas of the US Ninth Troop Carrier Command whose practice was to fly in tight formation of V's which produced a tight concentration of parachutists on the ground. During the short time that we had for training and rehearsals in England before the operation, we paid great attention to parachuting techniques and especially the handling of kitbags. As a result there were very few losses of equipment on the drop. In addition, we took drastic steps to cut down weight on the man and this was an important factor in respect of movement and success. Entrenching tools and No. 75 Grenades were not carried; one man in two carried a toggle rope; no spare clothing, except socks, was taken and the time-honoured custom of every man being equipped with two No. 36 Grenades was abandoned.

'Finally, because of the tight flight formation of the aircraft, the positioning of a platoon and its jumping order was determined by where we wanted the men on the drop zone rather than in the air. Thus a platoon could be allotted to, say, the last ten places in each of three aircraft (a Vic) with the platoon commander travelling in the middle Dakota, another platoon occupying the remainder of the same three aircraft. All of these measures enabled the battalion to act with speed and they paid off handsomely.

'Towards the evening, an eerie silence fell over the DZ which had been such a noisy battleground. Enemy resistance had been completely flattened and thus I was able to ride a horse, found on one of the farms nearby, around the battalion area. Special mention must be made of the sterling work of our medical staff: Captain Wilson, who was our Medical Officer, Corporal Houghton and the stretcher-bearers and our most respected Padre, The Reverend Joe Jenkins, all of whom tended our casualties under fire. These amounted to twenty-one killed, forty-five wounded and twenty-five missing. Many of the latter rejoined the battalion later.'

When 13th Parachute Battalion landed on the drop zone it found the entire area covered with smoke, dust and haze. This made identification of land marks and thus estimation of position, very difficult despite the fact that the battalion had been dropped with reasonable accuracy. Added to this problem was the considerable amount of small arms and artillery fire which was being brought down on the DZ at the time. Nevertheless, the battalion was assembled in its RV location by about one hour after the drop. There were enemy troops dug in on the edge of the DZ and these caused casualties amongst the battalion which was very exposed as it moved across the open ground to its RV. The enemy positions were difficult to locate but once they had been pinpointed and attacked, the enemy troops surrendered without putting up any determined resistance.

Private Tom Backshell RAMC recalled: 'While many of the Medics dropped off the mark and had colourful times hiding in woods, fighting for their lives or being taken prisoner, others like my self had a very ordinary time with the crowd. My first memory is of my neighbour in the plane stuffing an orange into my kit bag as we stood in the door. My next of hovering over a pylon, but finally landing a considerable distance away. As I emptied my kit bag I wasted no time groping for the orange.'

Major John Bernard Robert Watson MC, always known as 'Jack' born at Scarborough, Yorkshire on 14 January 1917 commanded 'A' Company. 'We flew over the Rhine in broad daylight, something a lot of us weren't too happy about as the Germans could use us like ducks on a shooting gallery. I was standing in the open doorway of the Dakota carrying the members of my 'stick' and christened the river by throwing an orange down on it. The next thing I noticed was the American dispatcher putting on his flak suit, which was slightly worrying! Then I didn't see any more of him. As we got to the drop zone I could see where we were going. The thing that struck me most at the time was the amount of flak that was hitting the aircraft - the Germans really were pumping a lot of it into the Dakotas and Halifaxes and no doubt they'd have a field day with the gliders, but that did not deter me; I simply had to conquer my fear once again.

'The Red light came on and then the Green and my batman, Private Henry Gospel, was right behind me shouting, 'I am right behind you Sir!' and out we went! Although I felt the loud zip of machine gun bullets coming right by me it didn't seem very long before I was on the ground and out of my harness. I threw away my helmet, put on my red beret and grabbed my Sten gun. The Commanding Officer had told us to put on our berets as soon as we had landed in order to 'put the fear of God into the Germans'. As I moved off, I found myself with a platoon of Americans who had dropped on the wrong DZ and they now joined my company as we started to move off the drop zone towards the farm, which was our objective. The most amazing thing was watching the whole battalion in the air in one go - in fact, the whole brigade. The entire division, including the gliders, was on the ground within forty-five minutes in what one would call a saturation drop. But I have to say there were a lot of casualties in the air in both aircraft and men.

'Once we were on the ground we were immediately faced with the enemy. One of my platoons to my left captured a machine gun position and we started taking prisoners - the Germans were giving themselves up all over the place. There was a lot of firing going on - even 88 mm and 20 mm guns were firing on a level trajectory at ground targets. Yet one seemed to be oblivious to what was happening because once you had landed, it was into action straight away and your mind focused on what needed to be done rather than worrying about getting shot. There was the objective and that is what we went for - in many cases wearing our red berets and shouting our heads off. Like Lieutenant Colonel Peter Luard DSO and all the company commanders in the battalion, I had a hunting horn.[4] We each had our different calls to muster our men. I blew mine, calling my company as we went for specific objectives. My batman was still with me, saying, 'Right behind you, Sir!' as we took a farm with no problems. We then secured the place and it was all over pretty quickly. Whilst we were at the farm the Commanding Officer and the divisional commander joined us. We invited them for breakfast and my batman cooked us all bacon and eggs.

'The ground was covered in mist and haze, which had been created by the bombardment from our guns and the smoke generators from the other side of the river and was very difficult to see. This caused a lot of problems for our gliders. I think that the saddest thing I saw was when we were moving towards our battalion objective, in the direction of Hamminkeln. There were glider pilots still sitting in their cockpits, having been roasted alive after their gliders had caught fire. One pilot and co-pilot were melted into unrecognisable pieces of flesh and bone, still sitting there with their hands on their control columns. A lot of people were lost like that. Although we lost a quite a lot of casualties in the air, it was nowhere near what those poor devils in the gliders had.

'One of the major problems, as far as we were concerned, was that 3rd Parachute Brigade was the first to go in and they had been dropped about ten minutes too early. Consequently, the artillery bombardment had to be lifted so that, by the time that 5th Parachute Brigade and the remainder of the Division arrived, the enemy were able to recover and organise themselves. That's why there was such a God awful lot of flak on my aircraft. However, there was nothing that could be done about it. It was then a question of rooting the enemy out of all the buildings. They put up some stiff resistance for the first few hours but once they could see it was the 'Red Devils', as they called us, they started to give up pretty quickly.'

In the 6th Airlanding Brigade the flight to Germany was peaceful and uneventful. However, as the fleet of gliders and tug aircraft approached the Rhine, a great pall of smoke rising from the area of the battle could be seen. Once across the river, enemy anti-aircraft fire became heavy and several gliders were hit, with casualties being suffered and equipment damaged.

The first fifteen gliders to land contained the coup-de-main parties of the 2nd Ox and Bucks and 1st Royal Ulster Rifles. 'B' Company, 2nd Ox and Bucks under Major Gilbert Rahr supported by two anti-tank guns and a detachment of sappers of No.1 Troop, 591st Parachute Squadron, landed on LZ-O1 to seize and hold the road bridge over the Issel but they had suffered very serious casualties before they had even reached the ground. The Horsa carrying No.17 Platoon received a direct hit from a heavy flak gun and broke up at 2,000 feet, scattering men as it plummeted before finally crashing in woodland; all aboard perished. No.18 Platoon's glider lost half of its left wing through flak and with many controls inoperable and the wounded pilots unable to alter their course without destablising the craft it overshot the landing zone and similarly crashed into woodland, killing more than half of those inside. Only two gliders, therefore, carrying Company Headquarters and No.19 Platoon were able to participate in the coup-de-main raid. Although under considerable enemy fire, both landed safely and on target at 1024. No.19 Platoon were out of their glider almost immediately and quickly brushing aside a lone sandbagged machine-gun which delayed them momentarily, they pushed forward, making such violent and rapid use of their Sten guns and grenades that all opposition quickly evaporated and the bridge was captured.

Meanwhile, 'C' Company in the Ox and Bucks commanded by Major James Molloy, landed on LZ-O2 and established itself in defence of the railway bridge just 200 yards to the north of the road bridge. 'C' Company soon overcame the token garrison around the railway bridge and captured it intact. To ensure that both the road and rail bridges remained that way the sappers crawled over the superstructures, removing demolition charges and cutting any wires that they could find. With this done, they later placed their own explosives around the bridges to blow them in case a determined enemy counter-attack threatened to take them back. Major Harry Styles' 'A' Company occupied the area of the road junction to the west.

Coming into land CSM John Stephenson in 'D' Company under Major John Tillett saw the anti-aircraft barrage. 'It was like Guy Fawkes Night, only in the daytime. It didn't seem possible that so many aircraft could get through it. It didn't seem possible that there was so much flak and ground fire considering the bombing and artillery barrage that had taken place just before we arrived either. The sky around us was full of aircraft and puffs of smoke that signalled the flak and lines of tracer fired from the MG34 and 42 machine guns. The parachutists dropped and not long afterward the gliders went in to land, right in the east side of the battle. The sky seemed to be just bright red with flames coming from aircraft that had been hit, or grey and black with smoke from the other side of the river, making it difficult to see the ground, except that the unfinished autobahn was clearly visible. For a split second it seemed as if every glider had been wrecked on landing. As we touched down and halted, 'D' Company HQ was soon out of the glider. We flung ourselves on to the ground, but not too close in case it got targeted. Major Tillett finally figured out where we were and after a dash across the road to a house, we secured it and then we were on our way to Hamminkeln railway station.'[5]

Born on 4 November 1919 at Ipswich and educated at the town's Grammar School, during a hockey tour of Germany in 1936 Tillett saw at first hand something of the Hitler Youth organisation and was made an 'honorary member'. Convinced that war was coming, he joined the Territorial Army, was commissioned and posted to the 2nd Battalion Ox and Bucks Light Infantry. Major John M. A. Tillett MiD was closely involved with the glider-borne operation to capture 'Pegasus Bridge' on D-Day.

CSM John Stephenson gave Lieutenant Fox the company rum bottle. 'It saved me carrying it - I think it was a gallon. Eventually we moved to take over positions near 'C' Company, close to a rail bridge that carried the railway line over the Issel River.

At around midnight, 'B' Company, by far the weakest element in the 2nd Ox and Bucks, were attacked on the road bridge by a force of thirty infantry supported by armoured vehicles. The Battalion's 6-pounder anti-tank guns fired upon the latter but failed to make much impression on their heavy armour. One of 'B' Company's positions on the eastern bank of the Issel was overrun, but a counter-attack pushed the enemy back and the ground was retaken but German infantry supported by Tiger tanks continued to press, so Lieutenant Colonel Darrell-Brown received permission from Brigadier Bellamy to destroy the bridge if it seemed likely to fall. At 0240 neither the anti tank guns, nor 'B' Company could deny the enemy the bridge any longer and it was blown as the leading tank appeared to be upon it.[6]

Lieutenant Colonel Mark Darell-Brown of 2nd Battalion Ox and Bucks HQ was with his jeep and trailer together with his men in a Horsa piloted by Squadron Leader V. H. Reynolds DFC OC 'F' Squadron with Flying Officer Bayley as his co-pilot. On his approach to his landing target, Reynolds saw a German four-gun 20 mm anti-aircraft battery shooting at other gliders. He ordered Bayley to take control of the Horsa while he engaged the Germans with a sub-machine gun, firing through the cockpit canopy. He killed or wounded all of the gun crew and took the survivors prisoner after Bayley had landed the glider. Reynolds then came under fire from a nearby four-gun flak battery and he ordered Bayley to attack it with a PIAT (Projector, Infantry, Anti Tank) a man-portable anti-tank weapon.[7] Bayley crawled off and after three close shots, scored a direct hit killing the gun crew in the position. Meanwhile, Flight Lieutenant Ince and an NCO had worked their way around the back of a windmill, which gave them cover from another anti-aircraft pit and charged at the crew, killing all of them. The officer at the other gun hoisted a white flag. The glider had landed beside the enemy guns and Darell-Brown and his men disembarked at speed, attacking the German gunners and overpowering them. As they did so, other gliders were landing around them with varying fortunes.

Further south, 'D' Company of the 1st Royal Ulster Rifles under Major Tony Dyball, following on a minute behind the coup-de-main parties of the 2nd Ox and Bucks landed at LZ-U1 to take the rail bridge over the Issel whilst 'A' Company, commanded by Major Charles Vickery, landed on LZ 'U2' to seize the area of the station and the level crossing. The rest of the Battalion landed on LZ 'U3' to move up to defensive positions incorporating the objectives already taken.[8] The haze, smoke and heavy anti-aircraft fire made landing extremely hazardous. Some pilots were unable to pick up their bearings and several gliders landed in the wrong place. Seventy-five per cent of the gliders were hit by flak or small-arms fire. Some disintegrated in midair while others went up in flames as the flak hit them whilst others crashed on landing or were set ablaze after being hit on touching down.[9] Dyball's Horsa landed heavily at 1025 hours about 150 yards from the bridge. Some of its passengers were ejected through the wrecked nose of the glider, immediately came under fire from a machine gun position at a range of seventy-five yards.

Major Dyball takes up the story: 'My wireless operator had been killed and the set having received part of the burst, I could not get in touch with any of my leading platoons. One good thing about the crash was that one of the wings had made a small trench in the ground, into which some seven of us crawled. In a matter of seconds we had a Bren in action and it silenced the machine gun but another started up some thirty yards to its left. I could still see no signs of my other platoons. I decided I would make a dash across the open and get into a small wood and see if I could contact anyone there.

'The Bren covered me across and I contacted two glider pilots, two men from the Ox and Bucks and a few sappers. They had got into a good firing position covering the house that I wished to assault. I then moved the rest of my headquarters into a wood and we cleared it, killing two Germans. We then took up defensive positions. From where we were, a continuous trench ran up to the house and bridge. The Germans were still holding the house, although we could see a few retiring. A small party of enemy advanced towards us; we let them come until they were within twenty yards and then threw a 36 grenade. Unfortunately it did not fall into the trench, though it exploded by its side. At once all hands went up. With two glider pilots and another two men, I went off down the trench towards the house. As we got to it, No. 21 Platoon arrived from the other side of the road in fine form, having cleared the house and captured twenty-five prisoners. About another twenty-five were also rounded up.

'I then went across the bridge and found that No. 22 Platoon had done their job in clearing the houses. Although the platoon commander had been killed, the platoon sergeant, despite being wounded in the head, arm, leg and thigh, had led the platoon against strong opposition which was dug in. The bridge was in our hands and an all-round defence was quickly organised, consisting of four groups made up of the two platoons; Company Headquarters, some glider pilots, anti-tank gunners without their guns and a few men from the Ox and Bucks. Although it was originally planned to capture the bridge with four platoons, this was the force which actually did so - some fifty men in total.

'During the attack five German self-propelled guns came down the road. One was hit at twenty-five yards range by a PIAT but it was not knocked out. However, they showed no fight and retired as quickly as they could. About fifty prisoners were taken and about twenty Germans were killed.'

The enemy had been surprised by the scale of the landings but when the remaining Royal Ulster Rifles contingent landed at LZ 'U' south-east of Ringenburg to take up defensive positions with 'A' and 'D' Companies it met stronger than expected opposition, immediately coming under a very heavy volume of fire. All the farmhouses in the area had been converted by the enemy into strong points and a number of armoured vehicles, including self-propelled guns brought fire to bear on the landing zones, causing a number of casualties. One of the glider pilots, Lieutenant Desmond Turner, later recalled: 'We were flying at roughly 2,900 feet to avoid slipstream. Three checkpoints were marked on our maps: points 'A', 'B' and 'C' which were all five minutes flying apart and with point 'C' being the release point. Point 'A' was easily seen but from then on nothing could be distinguished on the ground. The flak was extremely heavy and concentrated and flying in position behind the tug became harder as the surrounding air was more than a little bumpy. As we could not see our own LZ or anybody else's, we remained on tow. Suddenly we saw the autobahn below us and, as a result of previous careful study of air photographs, we knew where we were. We released and did a tight 270 degree turn to port and saw the church spire of Hamminkeln in front of us. Owing to the immediate vicinity being rather crowded with gliders, we applied full flap and went down on to the LZ as briefed. Our passengers were none the worse after this unorthodox approach and proceeded to unload.'

The Horsa flown by Staff Sergeant 'Andy' Andrews carrying the

Commanding Officer, Lieutenant Colonel Jack Carson had a rough landing after flak wounded his co-pilot and badly damaged the controls of his Horsa soon after cast-off. The Horsa had been towed by a Halifax, which developed engine trouble over the North Sea and all surprise had been lost by the time he reached the landing zone, which was obscured by smoke. Andrews found he was descending too steeply and too fast. Because of the smoke, he could not see the ground until down to 500 feet. At 250 feet he saw a small field beyond some trees, which he brushed through, half tearing off the undercarriage. The glider clipped the wing of another glider and was sent cartwheeling across the DZ, disintegrating on impact, the tail being catapulted over the debris to face the remains of the cockpit. 'I was thrown through the front and finished by sliding along the left side of my face, slightly cutting the corner of my left eye, but was otherwise unhurt. I went round pulling out people from the wreckage, all of whom were in a heap under the wings, on top of each other, with seating harness still strapped to their backs with part of the seat. I still cannot discover what happened to the three in the back. There were no bodies and they were not in their seats.' The infantry scrambled clear of the wreckage and formed a defensive position astride the local railway line.

Andrews stated: If Arnhem had been one of my best landings, then this was one of my worst. With some difficulty due to a faulty tug engine we struggled across the North Sea and got over the target as number one hundred. The element of surprise was completely gone and there was very active German ack-ack fire to greet us. Smoke obliterated the LZ and I had to pull off blind. Eventually I saw the canal running north to south and turned in approximately in the right direction. We had lost valuable height in free flight and the ack-ack had damaged something. In any case the descent and the gliding speed were too fast. Until we got to 500 feet I couldn't see the ground and, when we did, there was no place to land. Flying straight ahead, I made for a small field but knew that at 250 feet I would have to go through some tall trees to get in. I got through the trees but the undercarriage was half off. The next thing I knew was that the Horsa II was disintegrating around me and the tail detached itself to fly over the nose and land facing me. All seemed OK except for Colonel Carson, who was injured. We organized a successful defensive position astride the railway line.

When the Adjutant Captain Robin Rigby, landed, his glider touched down about eighty yards away from the enemy positions. The Horsa was badly smashed up and it was impossible to unload the jeep and equipment inside. Here he recalls the scene on the landing zone:

'I got everybody out of the glider into a ditch on the side of the road. Between ourselves and the houses a 'C' Company glider was burning, the ammunition inside it exploding. About two minutes later, half a platoon of 'C' Company came across the open ground towards us from the direction of the houses. On questioning these men I was told that they had crash-landed and that their glider had caught fire almost immediately. About two thirds of their platoon had got out alive and had moved towards the houses but had met considerable opposition and had been forced to withdraw. Very shortly after this, another platoon of 'C' Company and one from 'B' Company arrived with twelve prisoners from the houses on the west side of the road. One or two men from 'B' Company's headquarters were also with them but Major Ken Donnelly had been killed.

'As this appeared to be the total sum of the battalion which had landed so far on this LZ, I decided to leave a small fire group in the ditch and to move round to the right and attack through the orchard. However, just as I was about to move, I saw Lieutenant Colin O'Hara-Murray's platoon of 'B' Company starting to advance through the orchard. I therefore had some 2-inch mortar smoke put down and put in an assault on the houses from where we were, going in at right angles to O'Hara-Murray's line of attack.

'Fire was spasmodic and a very half-hearted defence was put up, most of the Germans throwing their weapons away when we got to within forty or fifty yards of them. Quite a lot of Germans were killed by grenades and Stens in and around the houses and barns and in about fifteen to twenty minutes they had all been rooted out. The whole area appeared to be fairly clear so I sent 'B' and 'C' Companies to the position laid down in the original plan and put a few glider pilots that we had, about sixteen in all, in charge of the prisoners who numbered about a hundred.

'By this time it was about 1115 hours and I established wireless communications with 'D' Company and heard that they were on the bridge. However, I could not get in touch with 'A' Company. I decided to wait until midday in case any more of the battalion should arrive and very shortly two 6-pounders and some of the Machine Gun Platoon turned up. The machine gunners went to 'C' Company and the two 6-pounders took up positions to cover the road running south from Hamminkeln. They had been in position for about two minutes when two armoured cars came up the road from the south. These were promptly knocked out and the crews taken prisoner.

'Shortly after this the Liaison Officer and Signals Officer arrived with a 62 Set link to Brigade, accompanied by some members of Battalion Headquarters and followed by our Medical Officer who had been collecting casualties on the LZ. Prior to this, we had been in touch with brigade headquarters via the FOO's set. As there appeared to be no sign of any more of the battalion on the LZ I decided to move at 1215 hours along the original battalion route to the dispersal point from which 'B' and 'C' Companies would move to their positions as given in the original plan. As there was no sign of the Recce Platoon, one platoon of 'C' Company acted as left flank guard and another platoon acted as rearguard, with the two anti-tank guns moving in bounds on the left flank. The right was by now safe as American gliders were landing on our immediate right during the move. Lieutenant John Wright joined the column en route and we also met two platoons of the Ox and Bucks. On arriving at the level crossing, we met Major Paddy Liddell who had a platoon of 'A' Company and two of our Vickers machine guns on the level crossing.'

After the coup-de-main parties had landed, the remainder of the 2nd Ox and Bucks and 1st Royal Ulster Rifles arrived on the main zones and once again all the anti-aircraft guns in the vicinity concentrated their fire on this fresh wave of gliders. The Germans fully recognised the vulnerability of the craft, particularly when they had landed and come to rest, the men inside being utterly at the mercy of nearby machine-guns in the crucial seconds that it took for them to get out and to comparative safety. Some were lucky and emerged unscathed, others were cut down before they had a chance to defend themselves. The scene across LZ 'O' in the first hour was one of utter chaos, as small groups of survivors, plunged immediately in action, attempted to win control of the zone by attacking whatever enemy positions were to hand. To add to the confusion, three enemy tanks with accompanying motorcyclists drove across the zone at this time, shooting on the move at the wrecked gliders, causing further misery to the casualties still inside them. These were SS troops of Kampfgruppe Karst, whose pre-planned role in the event of an airborne landing was to race amongst the enemy and cause as much damage to them as possible whilst they were at their most vulnerable. These particular raiders, however, became a victim of the very confusion of which they had intended to take advantage, for they ran straight into one of the 1st Royal Ulster Rifles anti-tank guns which promptly knocked-out one of the tanks. Small groups of armoured vehicles made similar attacks around the Hamminkeln area during the first hours. Although they made a considerable nuisance of themselves, they nevertheless achieved little, chiefly because airborne troops are very aggressive by nature and they eagerly took on the German armour with whatever weapons were available, by and large causing them damage and thwarting their efforts.

Endnotes Chapter 6

1   Major Dean MBE MC became the archivist of the 13th Battalion after the war and wrote an unpublished account of their exploits: *13th Battalion The Parachute Regiment: Luard's Own.*

2   Lieutenant-Colonel Hewetson was awarded the DSO.

3   Quoted in *Paras: Voices of the British Airborne Forces in the Second World War* by Roger Payne OAM (Amberley, 2014 and 2016).

4   Luard had been commissioned into the Ox and Bucks in January 1931. When he landed in Normandy on his 33rd birthday in June 1944 he rallied his men at the RV by sounding his hunting horn. Compared to the other parachute battalions of the 6th Airborne Division, the 13th Battalion Assembled tolerably well after the drop with 70% of their strength accounted for.

5   Quoted in *Paras: Voices of the British Airborne Forces in the Second World War* by Roger Payne OAM (Amberley, 2014 and 2016).

6   In a battle with the German 1st Parachute Brigade the Ox and Bucks lost 101 men killed and 356 wounded; one platoon being over-run and captured trying to blow up the bridge.

7   The PIAT entered service in 1943. It possessed an effective range of approximately 115 yards in a direct fire anti-tank role and 350 yards in an indirect fire 'house-breaking' role. The PIAT had several advantages over other infantry anti-tank weapons of the period, which included a lack of muzzle smoke to reveal the position of the user and an inexpensive barrel; however, the type also had some disadvantages, a difficulty in cocking the weapon, the fragility of the barrel, powerful recoil and problems with ammunition reliability, an elementary anti-tank weapon with an effective range of about fifty yards.

8   *Go To It! The Illustrated History of the 6th Airborne Division* by Peter Harclerode (Caxton Editions, 1990).

9   *Go To It! The Illustrated History of the 6th Airborne Division* by Peter Harclerode (Caxton Editions, 1990).

Chapter 7

A Matter Of Life and Death

I saw a figure in a long German greatcoat rise to his feet from the centre of a field and walk towards us with his hands up. The man was Volkssturm, about fifty or sixty years of age, a long thin chap. Before we could do anything, three Americans let fly with their carbines and the figure fell. God we were angry! So was Major Wheldon.

Staff Sergeant Cramer, 'C' Company, The 1st Ulster Rifles.

Before volunteering for the airborne forces and joining The Royal Ulster Rifles, 29-year old Major Huw Pyrs Wheldon MC, born in Prestatyn, Wales on 7 May 1916, who on the outbreak of war in 1939 had enlisted in the Buffs and had been commissioned into the Royal Welch Fusiliers in 1940, had earned his award for his actions in Normandy on D+1. Wheldon described his experiences of 'Varsity' in a letter written from the British Military Hospital in Brussels[1] to his father, Sir Wyss Wheldon; a prominent educationalist who fought in the Great War and was awarded the DSO: 'The flight was itself highly unpleasant, my glider pilot being a poor hand at the job and was having difficulties, immeasurably increased by a sky full of slipstreams and air disturbances from aircraft ahead. The whole firmament was spotted and crossed with aircraft. We swung about and long before we reached the Rhine apprehension was crawling into every man's brain. As we approached the Rhine, a pall of smoke from Montgomery's screen became evident. The Rhine could be seen through it, a silver ribbon shining through the uniform grey. Ahead, the other aircraft were still going on and by now we could see bombers who had released their paratrooper loads and gliders dropping downward on our flanks. The smoke underneath grew thicker and I could see very little. Ahead we suddenly saw the silent flak explosions. Knowing we had another four minutes to go and hating the thought like hell, I got into my seat and strapped myself in. A moment later the pilot cast off from the tug.

'I knew quite well he'd cast off too early, but I welcomed the snapping-sound as the tow-rope swung loose. Cowardly, as ever, I was only too pleased to be coming down. For me, strapped in, the descent was blind. We bumped a bit and I recognised this as flak. After some little time I saw the ground through the little window and knew we were within 50 feet of our landing. Simultaneously, there was a methodical, impersonal crackle and machine-gun bullets tore little holes in the fabric overhead, missing everyone. Then we landed in a splintering crash and then sudden quiet. No more wind was passing through the fuselage. The machine gun fired more briskly and everyone unstrapped like mad and made for exits. The crash had buckled my seat and my equipment got stuck between the seat and the side. I was consequently trapped. At the time it seemed ludicrous and I grinned at musical comedy situation, the bullets zipping by my head doing absolutely nothing to disturb my thoughts, which were indescribable, almost insane.

'In the end I grasped my smock and pulled it off and in this way extricated myself. Diving out the door, I found all the boys all unhurt in a ditch alongside the smashed glider; many of them gave that kind of look that said, 'Where the Hell have you been?' and I don't blame them as in situations like this leadership from the front is essential. Beyond the glider, hidden to us, was a farmhouse seventy yards away and in this farm was the machine gun. I decided to leave it to someone else and led off in dead ground to a little wood. The sky was still full of aircraft in astonishing numbers and on the ground all over the place were gliders and parachutes; my own chaps, paratroopers, chaps feverishly unloading guns, hundreds of American, miles from their objective and far away, above the pendant smoke, the quiet sun.

'I found out where we were, and two hours later, after a rum journey, I found the Battalion, all objectives taken, our ebullient Dai [Captain Richard Rees - Regimental Medical Officer and Huw Wheldon's brother-in-law], was still with us thank God, but many have not made it, including my CSM, old McCutcheon, the loyalest and most devoted soldier I ever saw and a very great personal loss. There were hundreds and hundreds of prisoners, all digging away like mad on our positions, while our chaps stood happily by smoking cigars like the Lords of Creation.

'On my way in to the position, moving along the edge of a wood, I suddenly stumbled on three Boche, not five yards away. I was unarmed, the magazine having dropped out of my pistol some time before and all I had in my hand was a ration pack taken from a discarded haversack to make up for my own that was left in the glider. I was naturally petrified with horror. As soon as they saw me, the three Boche dropped to their knees and begged me not to shoot. With superb magnanimity I showed mercy, forbearing to throw my ration pack at them and wheeled them in, now grist to the mill. My own company did magnificently, storming a position, killing many Boche in the process and taking over a hundred prisoners. I was away at the time and did not share this action; possibly fortunately, as under me it might have been a more academic advance and far less deadly. No casualties there thank the Lord, but then he'd already helped cut a big swath through our ranks already.'[2]

By the early afternoon, the fighting had died down and the 1st Battalion, The Royal Ulster Rifles had secured all its objectives. Other elements of it rejoined during the day, having landed some distance away and having fought their way back to the battalion. Lieutenant Colonel Jack Carson was with the other wounded in a house near the railway, awaiting evacuation to 195th Airlanding Field Ambulance's MDS which was later established in the battalion's area. The battalion had suffered heavy casualties which totalled sixteen officers and 243 other ranks. However, it had taken and held all of its objectives and was now in firm control of its area. During the rest of the day there was little enemy activity except for the appearance of three self-propelled guns which were seen off with the assistance of some RAF Typhoon fighter-bombers. However, the enemy were still occupying buildings to the east of the bridge and armoured vehicles were detected moving in the area of Ringenburg and in the wooded areas near it.

Colin J. Goodall, a Battalion Headquarters Dispatch Rider in the Royal Ulster Rifles had set out on his journey in a Horsa with seven other men, one jeep and trailer and his 350cc motorcycle. 'The flight was uneventful except for a few bumps when we were in the slipstream of the plane that towed us. This made us feel rather sick as though the bottom of your stomach had fallen out. As we flew closer to the Rhine, we could see that the flak was coming up thick and fast with airbursts all around us. I looked out and saw one aircraft go down very close to us. Pieces of shrapnel came through the bottom of our glider and most of us received wounds of various degrees. The pilots had trouble finding our landing site owing to the smoke and dust caused by the artillery bombardments. Suddenly, we went into a steep dive. With a mighty bump and seemingly endless skid, we crashed through a fence, which tore off our undercarriage and brought us to a full stop. The impact threw both pilots from the cockpit and tore our harnesses from the side-wall of the glider. We rolled over and over, not knowing what was happening. For the next few moments, I felt sure I was the only survivor of the crash-landing. My Sten gun had snapped at the butt, saving me from a broken arm. I managed to crawl into the rut left by the undercarriage and was then joined by Lance Corporal Gilliland MM. He had flown in the tail end of the glider. This had snapped off as we landed, allowing him to get free. During this time we were under heavy machine gun fire that came from the nearby railway embankment. We lay low until the offending gun had been silenced and then saw that the rest of our lads had taken cover in the hole left by the wing of our glider. The two pilots were lying about twenty yards away, severely injured, where they had been catapulted from the cockpit. When things had quietened down, we started to get the vehicles off-loaded. My motorcycle was bent like a banana. Luckily the anchor points had held fast, stopping the jeep and trailer coming forward into us which could have been a disaster. We managed to get the two pilots and more seriously wounded men onto the jeep and stretchers and made off into open ground to the farmhouse, which was our rendezvous point. The wounded were then taken off to the cowsheds along with a number of other Airborne and German casualties. Our Medical Officer, Captain Rees, was very relieved to see us with field-aid medical supplies and his driver Rifleman Johnson. I spent the rest of the day in charge of around fifty prisoners of war who were later put into a PoW cage.

'By late evening, the wounds I had received during the flight and the back injury I sustained crash-landing were starting to take their toll and I must have passed out. Coming round, I found myself in a cellar alongside other casualties. We were waiting to be evacuated, across the Rhine to a field ambulance station where we were cleaned up and our wounds dressed. We were then transported by ambulance train to Bruges Hospital, Belgium where I spent six weeks recovering before completing my journey back to England for a spell of sick leave. By this time, the war in Europe was over. Unfortunately, my duties as Battalion Headquarters Dispatch Rider ended upon landing on German soil. Luckily though, I am still here to tell the tale for which I thank God and my brave comrades. Some of them were not so lucky, but they will never be forgotten.'[3]

Like all the units of 6th Airlanding Brigade, the 2nd Battalion, The Ox and Bucks had enjoyed a peaceful flight in its Horsas as it moved southwards over the North Sea, then east over Brussels and landed in Hamminkeln area at about 1000 hours. Each company was designated a landing zone in the area of its objective. Lance Corporal Godfrey Yardley related in his memoirs, *A Village Lad Goes to War:* ' I flew in No 2 glider as a member of Bob Preston's 18 Platoon, piloted by Staff Sergeant Bill Rowland and Sergeant Geoff Collins of 'E' Squadron, the Glider Pilot Regiment. Some three hours flying time passed uneventfully as many such flights had in the past, except that once again in less than twelve months this was for real. Darkness turned into a lovely morning, clear sky and the promise of good weather. Now and again the sight of escort fighters gave the feeling of some security against attack by the Luftwaffe.

'At last the Rhine came into view and as we approached it at about 3,000 feet, the order was given to open the doors, one forward on the port side and one rear starboard. As I sat on the starboard side forward, I watched 'Ginger' Belsham pull the forward door upwards and at that precise moment flak burst under the port wing, banking the aircraft over to starboard and almost throwing 'Ginger' out of the door, only to be pulled back by the platoon commander, Lieutenant Bob Preston and our platoon sergeant. This took about two seconds and allowed 'Ginger' to live for another few minutes as he and sixty per cent of the platoon were soon to die.

'The dropping and landing zones were shrouded in smoke and must have made target identification very difficult for the pilots. However, the gentle jerk of the tow-rope being cast off was felt, the nose went down and the landing procedure began, arms linked with each other and a silent prayer. The enemy were waiting for us and had prepared a concentration of ack-ack guns. Being the first in, our regiment took the full weight of the attack.

'Through the heavy barrage of flak we descended, many lives being lost during those first few minutes, including that of one of our pilots, Sergeant Geoff Collins. Our other pilot, Staff Sergeant Bill Rowland, was wounded. One chap by the name of Shrewsbury, who sat opposite me, got a burst of machine gun fire through the back; the bullets passed between the heads of me and Ted Tamplin who sat on my right, through a gap of eight to ten inches. With some of the controls damaged and no compressed air to operate the landing flaps, we flew across the landing zone, over the railway and the River Issel to crash head-on into a wood at ground level. At a speed of over seventy knots a fully loaded wooden glider the size of a heavy bomber becomes a pile of matchwood in one second flat. Whilst all this was going on No. 1 Glider, which was carrying No. 17 Platoon, had been badly hit by flak and was breaking up, spilling out men and equipment before crashing as we had done - except with them, there were no survivors.

'I was one of the lucky ones; having been sat in the centre of five men I was sitting in one piece of seat with my harness on. With the exception of a few cuts and bruises we five were ok. I lay in the wreckage of my glider, amongst my comrades, both dead and alive. The sounds of battle, which had raged since about 1000 hours that morning had begun to recede, but in the distance a faint buzz was heard growing by the second into an enormous crescendo of aircraft engine roar, the ground shook into almost earthquake proportion, the trees shook and whipped about, branches and twigs rained down upon us for a few moments frightening the life out of us. It was so sudden and unexpected that on top of our traumatic experience of the previous few hours to say the least was - what the hell is going on? Battle was what we were trained for and took for granted, but this was totally unexpected and with such violence. It was the supply drop by the Liberators. Despite the planned run-in altitude of 250 feet, I feel this was not adhered to.

'I remember going over to the pilot Staff Sergeant Rowland who had been wounded by the flak and hurt by the crash and asking silly questions like what speed we had been doing and what happened to the break parachutes. Several other chaps were alive but wounded, but most were dead including the platoon commander, sergeant and two corporals, leaving only a corporal, myself and another lance corporal and seven others unhurt. The wounded were attended to by the platoon medic, Lance Corporal Greenwood and Ted Noble who did sterling work during the following few hours during which time a reconnaissance patrol reported a tank at the west end of the next wood and large enemy troop concentrations in the area.'

Rowland saw two ladies dressed in white approach the wreckage. They spoke to him in English and explained that it was dangerous to stay there. 'They did their best to persuade me to go with them but I declined and explained that my comrades would soon be advancing and would pick me up. I also said that I was married and had a baby son back in England and did not want to leave with them. After five to ten minutes they said 'very well we will leave you but you should come with us.' They turned and walked away and disappeared in a cloud of smoke.

'Very shortly after', continues Godfrey Yardley 'the wood and crash site was hit by English artillery shells, some exploding close to Bill, resulting in a leg being severed and an arm almost completely severed. Bill put his one hand down amongst the grass and leaves and found a piece of hessian sacking, dirty with grass, leaves, oil and tar, he shook the loose debris off and wrapped it around his stump. He wrapped a shell dressing round his arm. He was picked up about 48 hours later and taken to a Field Dressing Station (RAMC). He said he told the army surgeon this story who said not to worry about it, that he was lucky, the dirty hessian stemmed the blood flow and luckily was not infected. His arm was finally removed.

'I took compass bearings on artillery fire, assuming that it was our own firing according to plan and established our position on the map. From the information we had on the enemy strength and their position it was agreed that the best plan would be to try and link up with the nearest Allied unit which was the 1st Ulster Rifles at their objective on one of the two bridges over the River Issel. As the shortest distance between two points is a straight line we had to run like hell over 1,000 yards to reach it.

'There were eight of us capable of making the dash. However Ted Tamplin had an injured ankle and offered to stay behind with the wounded knowing that he would probably be taken prisoner or maybe even shot. He was captured but escaped some days later however and managed to rejoin the regiment. Bill Rowland remembers coming round to find himself looking up at a German Officer demanding to know whether he was English or American. Bill was convinced that had they have been American they would have been shot - I wonder why? By the grace of God they were allowed to live and were told that they would be left to their own devices as they would soon be picked up by their own side which they were some 48 hours later.

'The moment of our hasty departure was indicated by the sound of the enemy sweeping the wood from the other end and so with the old saying in mind; 'He who fights and runs away (may) live to fight another day' we ran like bats out of hell. A line of bobbing red berets waving across an open field must have appeared an easy target to the enemy who promptly opened up from all angles, but either we had been trained very well or the Germans were a bad shot as none of us got hit - or maybe we were very lucky?

'Fortunately the Royal Ulster Rifles had taken the bridge and the sound of a rich Irish voice shouting 'Halt, who goes there' was the most welcome of sounds. We crossed the bridge between bursts of machine gun fire and reported to an officer with a request for some stretcher bearers and some help to go back to our wounded. The request was denied and was coupled with an order to stay put. We eventually rejoined our regiment the next day - March 25th - my birthday.'

During the landings, which only lasted ten minutes, 2nd Battalion, The Ox and Bucks lost 400 killed or injured out of the Battalion strength of 800. Many of the battalion's thirty gliders were on fire and casualties included 103 killed during the battle of the landing area. Captain Thomas McMillen carried a jeep, trailer and HQ section of 2nd Ox and Bucks under the command of Captain Henry John Sweeny, predictably nicknamed 'Tod' after the infamous 'Demon barber of Fleet Street who had led the successful coup-de-main party in the taking of Ranville Bridge in Normandy. As his glider approached LZ 'O' north of Hamminkeln a very near burst of ack-ack went off under the starboard wing. The strike had shattered the undercarriage and compressed air for the flap was leaking out. Literally 'flying on a wing and a prayer', McMillen managed to put the glider down in a clearing and used the starboard wing as a brake. In the passenger section, Sweeney was oblivious to all the concern: 'All I knew was that Captain McMillen had suddenly dived down to earth and we landed...With the bullets pinging around us we then realised that we had landed between the autobahn and the River Issel.' Leaving the jeep and trailer, the glider's occupants waded the river to the shelter of its high bank. Making their way towards the railway station, they seemed to be surrounded by gliders crashing into the trees on each side of the river. Before too long there was a good number of casualties from these crashes, but also a formidable force of fit combatants, including a complete platoon from the Ox and Bucks: '...We set off through the woods away from the river towards the railway line. As I called everyone to fall in Sergeant Stevens did not get up from where he had been behind the river bank. I went over to him to find him dead. He had unfortunately been shot through the head.'[4]

Private Harry Pegg's glider crashed disastrously and only three out of 32 men were not wounded; Pegg remained concussed all day. The American medical team reported they had recovered sixteen unattached legs from the crash. Private Harry Clarke of 2nd Ox and Bucks recorded 'At the front of one burning aircraft was its pilot still wearing his headphones, arms outstretched, forming the shape of a crucifix in the flames.' The gliders flew into a barrage of anti-aircraft fire; there were four enemy anti-aircraft gun-pits positioned near the railway station. Gliders made their approaches through thick smoke and heavy anti-aircraft fire, subsequently colliding as they touched down whilst others fell blazing from the sky. Amazingly, the Battalion Ox and Bucks' Quartermaster, Lieutenant Bill Aldworth, seeing both pilots of the glider slump over their joysticks as casualties took over the controls of his glider and, despite having no flying experience, landed the aircraft safely. The Commanding Officer, with tongue firmly in cheek, put him in for a DFC. He did not get it.

The only Conspicuous Gallantry Medal [Air] given to a soldier in World War II was awarded to the veteran Horsa pilot, Warrant Officer2 'Buck' Turnbull. He had cast off for his approach run when a Dakota flew across his front and the tow-rope, which was still attached to the tail of the aircraft, struck the glider's starboard aileron, ripping it off. The rope then wrapped itself around the underside of the Horsa's cockpit, smashing the perspex and ripping out the air-bottles, thereby making both brakes and flaps inoperative and at the same time carrying away half of the control column. The Horsa was turned almost on to its back by the rope, but, displaying remarkable coolness, Turnbull managed to regain control by using what was left of the control column and landed safely in his allotted place, going into action with the troops he had carried. He was introduced to the King as Lawrence 'Buck' Turnbull at his investiture for the Conspicuous Gallantry Medal [Air] after the Rhine crossing.

'Fifteen minutes before landing,' wrote Horsa pilot Staff Sergeant David Brook carrying his small group of Ox and Bucks Light Infantry, 'we were surprised to see the ground partially obscured by slowly drifting smoke. This had not been mentioned at our briefing! It came, I believe, from the great artillery barrage put up by Montgomery, which again was the largest of the whole war including that of El Alamein. Probably adding to this was the smoke from the complete destruction caused to Wesel by Lancasters, which we had been told would 'knock it out' at midnight prior to a Commando crossing of the river. The Rhine showed in silver glimpses below and ahead of us and we began checking off points 'X', 'Y' and 'Z' leading up to our pull-off point. After 'Y' our tug crew, seeing other unfortunate Dakotas beginning to be hit and some going down in flames at a height that no-one could escape from, began asking us whether we had gone far enough.

'Matchbox - are you ready yet?'

'No,' I replied and on we went searching for the landmarks we had memorized whilst searching for our positions on the map.

'The first discomforting thumps of anti-aircraft fire thudded near us and black smears appeared suddenly close to us whilst the rattling of small pieces could be heard as they struck our plywood skin. Suddenly through a gap in the drifting smoke we saw the small town of Hamminkeln with its church spire below us. Or landing zone was the furthest east of all and proved to be the most hotly defended and now with gliders loosing off all around us we pulled the 'tit' having been wished good luck from our tug, which performed the steepest 180° turn to port and for home I had ever seen, whilst we pushed the nose down to increase our flying speed of 110 knots to 140. Others seemed to be climbing in comparison as they pulled up to the usual gliding speed of about eighty knots. But the scene was worrying. It was not where we had expected. Gliders were being shot down all around us by a concentration of flak from the positions which later we were to find in the woods and other places missed by the RAF. Our only chance we felt was to disobey the instructions of Brigadier Chatterton and get down to the ground as quickly as possible. 'Do land those gliders slowly' he had told us as we had gathered around him sitting on the grass at Birch the day before, 'otherwise you will smash your nose wheels and never get your loads out quickly.'

'In different circumstances, this would have been correct, but had we carried out the order and floated around to achieve a spot-on perfect training touch-down on our parking lot, I might well have finished up where many of my friends did. Fifty-two per cent of 'E' Squadron pilots were killed or injured as compared with 25% over the whole operation. Of 416 British gliders which reached the battlefield, only 88 landed intact, but it was calculated afterwards that every glider was hit in the air. It was in the air and on landing that most of the casualties of 'E' Squadron occurred.

'We had shed 1,500 feet off our height in a tense minute or two as we shot earthwards amid the huge black shapes of our friends cart-wheeling and diving in uncontrolled ways never intended as tails, rudders, flaps or whole wings were shot off. We were not aware of the tense troops behind us who could do nothing but pray, or of the fully laden jeep and trailer which would crush us if we dived in helpless as we saw one Horsa do. Luckily, the free flight of a Horsa was heard as a gentle hiss, but as we increased speed to 140 knots it was a roar of wind as we spotted the railway line and seconds later the station. I saw a battery of five Bofors guns frantically training on us as we flashed by too fast for them to score yet another victim. We made our 90° turn dipping the starboard wing down to the earth to bring us north of the station and travelling down on the east side of the track, but already we knew that we were flying too fast to land alongside the station. We sped straight as a die over the fields at about fifty feet and passed the station having got our speed down but still well over that laid down for the application of half flap. We nevertheless applied it and in the culmination of rising tension of the last few minutes of the flight of our lives never even marvelled at the fact that the flaps held. Forward with the stick forcing the six ton machine to hit the ground before it was anywhere near ready to. Bang on the ground and thump went the huge Dunlop wheels and we were in the air again. We knew what we were doing but I would not have been a passenger in the back for twice our flying pay! A leapfrog of 300 yards and the first of several rows of six foot high angle iron stakes and wire fencing crossing our path were smacked down as if they were matches and string. This time she stayed down and rumbled, roared and shook at 60 mph through more fences as a terrified group of German soldiers ran for the cover of a roadside hedge and ditch ahead of us.

'Look,' I said, 'Germans!' I mean allowing for the fact that we had had breakfast only a few hours before in England and also that air travel was virtually unknown who would one expect to see in Germany but Germans? Nevertheless that was my reaction to the sight, in real life, of those ominous steel helmets and unmistakably hostile grey uniforms of respected and brave enemies, who however just at that moment quite sensibly had decided that being in the way of a huge glider with an 88 foot wing span and six tons behind it was to be avoided if at all possible. I remember as if it were yesterday the sight of the slowest rather heavily built soldier as his broad stern disappeared as he clambered desperately up a bank and disappeared behind trees.

'The Horsa came to a halt in soft soil warm with the early spring morning (or was it just that later I found myself laying in it that I was sweating?). Winter corn was showing well through in which our main wheels had ploughed shallow furrows that were to prove a comfort a few minute later.

'There was no more time to admire the view as a rather persistent MG 34 turned its undivided attention on our Horsa. It was a much faster rate of fire than our Bren was unmistakable and I recall the captain of the small group of Ox and Bucks Light Infantry that we were carrying, who had recently won his MC on D-Day, saying as they struggled to open an uncooperative door: This is fucking terrible.'

Frederic Balfour Scott, born at Monifieth, Angus and educated at Fettes College, Edinburgh, was a platoon commander on D-Day, 6 June 1944. He took part in the advance on Hérouvillette and Escoville and was with 2nd Ox and Bucks on Breville ridge until August. On 25 August the 2nd Ox and Bucks were tasked to capture Manneville-la-Raoult which was heavily defended by a German Garrison. Scott's platoon came under attack by machine gun fire and grenades. An extract from the citation for his Military Cross reads: 'During the action this officer's example, leadership and determination were largely responsible for the success of the action and were an inspiration to the men under him.'

David Brook with his small group of Ox and Bucks Light Infantry piled out at last. 'Realising that I was still wearing my flying helmet, I dived back into the cockpit to dress properly for the occasion by fastening on my round pudding basin of an airborne helmet. As I made back for the doorway a steady stream of bullets banged through it and I decided that a slight delay in my departure was necessary and dropped down behind large crates of stew, which were stored under the troop seats. I watched fascinated as the machine gunner slowly raked the glider back and forth from stem to stern. The jeep just in front of my nose became a sort of colander and petrol flowed over the flat wooden flooring. Realising that my feet and legs were sticking up into the cockpit by being draped over the foot high step between the cabin, I strove to pull them down and up into my chest and made myself as small as possible. I remember thinking that this was probably the time in my life when I should say some prayers for it to last a little longer than the 22 years I had so far enjoyed. But then deciding that this would not be acceptable in view of the fact that I had neglected to say them in the ordinary way in which I had been brought up for some considerable time, I consciously made the decision to remain silent.

'The noise of battle outside my plywood coffin (later I was to learn that the three men at the back behind the trailer never got out and were already dead) was overwhelming in its intensity and I barely heard a voice shouting my name and urging me to get out if I was still there as German tanks were coming. There was a pause in the machine gun fire as no doubt the gunner reckoned that no-one else was likely to be in a fit state to get out and I made a headlong dive landing on the soft (warm?) soil 4 feet 6 inches below. It was now that I lay behind the port side main wheel in the furrow it had made and watched the first of several German anti-airborne troops roaring down the road a few yards ahead of us, not on tanks but on the half-tracks which they had designed especially for the opposition of unwelcome visitors like the 6th Airborne of which I was a temporary member by reason of being an Army Air Corps glider pilot. In fact my role when I reached the grounds safely, which I had at last now achieved, was a PIAT man. That is to say I was supposed to use this weapon for its designed purpose of knocking out tanks instead of which it was still with the rest of the gear in the Horsa. All I had on me was my personal 9 mm automatic which I proceeded to fire in earnest at the men seated on the half track and the motor cyclist following them, all of which had the unmistakable mien of hunched shoulders and crouched bodies of people who were no more wishing to find themselves just at that moment where they were than we did. At any rate they did not stop and mop us up in our vulnerable state as they could easily have done, but disappeared down the road in the roar, crack and bang of battle. Some of this noise, although only like the piccolo of the full symphony orchestra, I now discovered was coming from another battery of light anti-aircraft guns which I could see just to my right on the side of the railway track. Evidently they had temporarily tired of knocking our gliders out of the sky which I could see strewn all over the field we were on in every state of destruction. I could see dead men lying everywhere, each a pathetic little heap and only two live ones some distance off firing back from behind the wheel of their glider I then found that the captain and the rest of the men including my co-pilot were sheltering in a small weapon pit recently vacated by the first

Germans I had seen who had thoughtfully made way for us.

'Meanwhile the battery had turned its three guns at a low angle and was proceeding to fire at my Horsa. I felt a blow as if a hammer hit me on the right shoulder. The shells were bursting above me and unknown to me in the heat of the moment I now had a piece of one in my shoulder. I decided that it was time to move. The same idea appeared to occur to all of us that we had landed here to do a job and so far had done nothing very much except keep our heads down. The captain was obviously feeling much better since he had got out of the confines of the Horsa and unrestricted now, proceeded to lean an attack on the gun position. We had to run directly at it and another memory, which is etched in part of me forever, is of turning round as I ran to have what proved to be my last look at the Horsa which had carried us here so well. I was in time to see a shell hit the glazed nose of the machine, which was also the closed cockpit and from a nice shining 'office' it instantly collapsed in drooping pieces. Had I been able to maintain my glance I would have seen her go up in flames, destroying everything in her including the three unfortunate bodies in the back, of which I was told days later by a seasoned veteran that one of the worst he had seen on any battlefield. Apparently, his charred remains struck in the ground upside down with the iron tips on his boots being all that remained of his uniform stuck to his heels.

'We had landed close by a small farmhouse and I and another man ran up to it. A large barnlike door was closed and I fired some bullets through it before bursting it open. We ran in to find a room at the side with a large pile of turnips and hay on the floor. Evidently a cow or two had recently departed together with their owners to a quieter place. Relieved to find that we had captured a building without having to clear anyone out, I realised that I could not move my right arm anymore and that a sharp pain in my shoulder with a stiffening of the arm had developed so I transferred my automatic pistol to my left hand and turned to see the very energetic approach of the Ox and Bucks' captain, his face red and perspiring with the nervous and physical energy he had been under. He ran up pushing a young tough-looking German paratrooper ahead of him. 'Here, glider pilot,' he said, 'you have been wounded; stay here and guard this prisoner until we come back.' At which point he raced off with a small group of men and I pushed my prisoner back into the house and sat him down on the heap of turnips telling him to keep his hands over his head.

'High up there was a small window through which I could still see glimpses of gliders flashing past and I marvelled at the sheer weight of noise which was now turning into a continuous heavy roar. Looking at my watch I remembered our briefing when we had been told that half an hour after landing, 250 Liberators would fly over at only 250 feet to drop resupply in the shape of large airborne containers on small parachutes. This was what was happening now but my small view of what had happened so far led me to suppose that I could be merely part of a bigger disaster even than Arnhem. There after all, the first main landings had taken place without much opposition. Here at Hamminkeln all I knew was that our glider's load had been mainly destroyed and all I had seen was destruction of other gliders and the pinning down of those that had got out by the guns of the heavily defended landing zone.

'The effects of the trauma of landing, the capture of the gun battery and loss of blood from my shoulder wound combined now in the driest of throats and mouth so that I craved a drink that was unavailable. Looking down I saw a nest of hen's eggs on the ground and keeping my eyes on my prisoner I stooped and picked up an egg, broke and swallowed it. This greatly amused the tough looking and potentially dangerous prisoner as it clearly proved that his country's propaganda that the British were starving as a result of the U-boat campaign was true. In fact of course we had all been given a first-class breakfast of eggs and bacon before we had left. For many it had been their last meal on earth but to me that egg was the best thing I had tasted, although it was the first and last I have ever eaten raw.

'I was in a sombre and doubtful mood wondering how all this might end when I heard the captain's voice outside shouting 'Glider pilot; are you still there?' I gave him the all clear and he ran in looking hotter than ever and panting that I should take the prisoner up to join 'the others' at the Hallway station. In some surprise I asked him then if we had captured it. It seemed incredible that those remarkable men of the Ox and Bucks and the Devons had pulled themselves out of their smashed gliders - my own was the only one I saw land almost undamaged albeit for a short time - and successfully challenged defensive positions to achieve our objective. He assured me that the station was ours and I therefore left the house and set off with my charge up the railway line. The chaos here was indescribable. Trucks were overturned and the huge broken remains of a couple of Horsas lay across the tracks. Men were lying alongside the rails as if to shelter from the small arms fire which was still heavy and banging about my ears. The German seemed in no hurry as if he knew they were his own side's bullets and would not harm him but I felt no such inclination to stroll up the line between the open fields on either side as if nothing was happening and I urged him into a trot.

'So we arrived at the station which was more like an ordinary house and where an extraordinary sight met us. The red beret of the 6th Airborne was everywhere. The place was seething with men. Wounded were being carried in by the brave unarmed medical corps who rushed out to the smashed wrecks of gliders to carry the wounded back, completely ignoring the constant small arms fire which criss-crossed the fields from defensive slit positions, yet to be subdued. I handed my prisoner over and went into the station house. Shattered bodies lay everywhere on the floors; their camouflaged smocks torn and mastered by shot, grenade or mortar and stained with the mixture of earth and blood. I recognised a fellow pilot who was in great pain having received a bullet through the bottom of his foot which had continued up into his leg. The elderly stationmaster sat groaning quietly on the only chair. A stray bullet had hit him in the stomach, I think. He looked bewilderedly at the mass of life and death around him which had so suddenly destroyed the former peace and quiet of his small country station.

'The building suddenly came under mortar attack and the walking wounded were told to go below into the cellar. I found myself sitting next to a captain and as a bomb exploded closer to the building I muttered a few soldiers' expletives only to be reprimanded for my language. Peering closer at this officer I perceived in the gloom that he was a padre and apparently wounded. I got up and left him, climbing first to the ground floor again and then upstairs to the bedrooms, the floors of which were covered with seriously wounded men lying on stretchers unable to protect themselves against possible collapse of the ceilings, let alone the roof itself. I gave one a cigarette and sat down with them and waited. Another bomb burst close to the front of the building and as I was waiting for the next one to come through the roof, which with the accuracy of persistent short range mortar fire was inevitable. I heard the heavy thudding of one of our Brens. The mortar fire stopped. Some of our boys had gone out and silenced it.

'I left them lying on their stretchers under the dust, the stink of cordite and a battle still on them, waiting patiently for the time when they could be moved to an advanced Field Hospital. I went downstairs and a medic poured sulphamide powder into my wound and applied a first field dressing. It was to be a week later in England before a piece of shrapnel was removed.'

CSM John Stephenson, meanwhile had been placed in command of a platoon in 'D' Company over the other side of the River Issel, in a house close to the autobahn and Ringenberg. 'Not many men were left, about twelve I think. The others were lying wounded or dead downstairs. Upstairs, I had men firing at the continuous German attacks. I could see the infantry, but only hear the tanks. We managed to break them up but the place was a shambles so I decided to move to another house. We got the wounded out first then we followed; as we withdrew from the house a tank demolished it. My next task was to take a platoon forward. I had about twelve men and three of them were wounded. Anyway, we had to try to capture a farm, but just as we were about to attack, we were stopped. Captain Scott, the company second in command, ordered the raid to be cancelled. It was just as well as we would have had to move over open ground to get to it.

'As the CSM I was sent all over the place to visit different platoons. For a while, at midday, all was quiet for a few minutes. At one point Bernie Walsh, the CQMS and I manned a PIAT to stop any tanks that were approaching. We didn't get any tanks but we did get a half track with a mounted 20 mm cannon on that was creating a bit of havoc.'

CSM John Stevenson was awarded the Distinguished Conduct Medal for defeating several enemy attacks with the platoon he led on the east bank of the Issel.

'On that first day I saw many of our dead hanging in trees by their parachutes where they'd been shot before they could release themselves, yet another problem with parachuting in during daylight hours that you never had at night. Throughout the battle we did not wear our steel helmets - we threw them away in case our own troops thought we were Germans. They simply didn't seem to be able to recognise us and tended to shoot first and ask question later. As for ammunition on that first day, every effort was made to get it and any weapons out of the gliders not totally destroyed. At the time it was pitiful to hear men trapped and being burnt alive, but there was absolutely nothing we could do about it in many cases as you left yourself exposed to machine-gun fire if you went near any of the gliders. An anti-tank gun platoon from 'C' Company disappeared on the night of the 24th/25th. A German patrol must have taken them in the darkness - perhaps their sentries had been knifed. Personally, I kept awake for the first two nights, as did all of 'D' Company. We had been issued with Benzedrine tablets to keep us awake, but in the end it took its toll and after they wore off it was one hell of a job to keep going. How the bomber pilots did it night after night I don't know.'

The 2nd Battalion Ox and Bucks saw very heavy fighting at Hamminkeln, where its objective was to capture the line of the Issel northwest of the town. This included the Hamminkeln-Ringenberg road bridge, the railway bridge, the railway station and the road junction to the west. Lieutenant Hugh Clark led a bayonet charge to take a road bridge for which he was awarded a Military Cross. Despite the severe setbacks the battalion encountered, the Ox and Bucks succeeded in taking all of its objectives by 1100 hours. Up to early on 26 March over 350 men of the Battalion had been wounded. The four rifle companies were severely depleted and non-commissioned officers were frequently required to act as platoon commanders. The medical orderlies and doctors were pushed to keep up with operating on the wounded. There was little help to be had until the main army relieved them in the early hours of the 26th.

Despite the ever-present danger Staff Sergeant Martin Reynolds and his co-pilot, Flying Officer Terry Blackwood, piloting a Hamilcar glider, found time for a spot of humour. 'As we flew in formation toward the Rhine, we could see the first of the anti-aircraft fire we would have to fly through. It was really amazing as the Germans had already been bombed, rocketed, shelled and machine-gunned not an hour previously. We crossed the river and prepared to cast off when Terry casually turned to me and asked, 'Have you booked us a parking space or will it be the usual all-out fight for a spot?'

'I casually answered as he released us from the towing aircraft, 'I tried to book but was told to bugger off, first in first served!'

'He replied, 'I hate that. Some idiots just don't care where they park. I think they should introduce fines for getting it wrong!'

'As some flak exploded right next to us, shaking the hell out of the glider, I remember saying, 'A bloody fat chance of that; especially as the worst offenders are the bloody RAF!'[5]

When we landed, we had no sooner stopped than another glider took the tip off our port wing. We were both badly shaken by it as it could easily have crashed into us. But Terry had the last word when he said, 'The bugger would have to have been an Army driver!'

The 12th Battalion, The Devons landed on LZ 'R' and was tasked with taking and holding Hamminkeln, after first isolating the town by preventing any enemy movement in or out of it west of the main road running north and south. Lieutenant Colonel Paul Gleadell CdeG was flying in Horsa No.

188 flown by Major Maurice Priest. Private Jolly his batman was seated next to him on the forward starboard side of the aircraft. Opposite him sat Lieutenant Ronald Brixey the battalion's Intelligence Officer with Private Bray of the Intelligence Section and Private Tremeer, one of the Regimental Police. As the battalion approached the Reichswald, visibility started to deteriorate. At last, the long winding ribbon of the Rhine appeared but nothing could be seen beyond it. Once over the river, visibility was even worse as the whole of the LZ was covered with a thick pall of smoke, dust and haze. However, the heavy anti-aircraft fire indicated that the glider was over the area of the battle. Major Priest cast off and commenced his descent. At first all was quiet, in marked contrast with the last four hours on tow. Then, as the glider came closer to the ground, the sounds of battle could be distinctly heard. The anti-aircraft and small arms fire was still heavy and the glider shuddered as a shell burst nearby. Priest signalled to his passengers that he was going to try a landing but the restricted view made him level up again with a sudden jerk. A burst and then another, of bullets pierced the glider hull; the first struck the jeep, fortunately missing the petrol tank and the second wounded Private Tremeer in the back. Again Priest tried a landing and again he levelled up, losing height all the while. A few seconds later he turned round and said, 'I can't see a darned thing but I'll do the best I can for you.' There was a crash, the floor boards were torn open and Gleadell and his companions found their feet being dragged along the ground for a few yards; at the same time, Private Tremeer was hurled forward against the cockpit.

The glider came to a halt with a crash and, after the door had been opened, Lieutenant Brixey quickly moved out to take up a covering position with a Bren gun. Gleadell and his men had no idea where they were but they did notice that their glider had stopped inches short of a very large bomb crater. They were under fire from what appeared to be three different directions and a 20 mm gun was also firing at them from the half-completed autobahn about a hundred yards away. Suddenly they heard shouting in English and saw a platoon of the Ox and Bucks who had been firing in their direction.

Lieutenant Colonel Gleadell takes up the story: 'There was no chance of extracting my jeep and so between us we carried our casualty towards our friends. We then realised that they were on the banks of the Issel astride the railway bridge and that we had landed between them and the enemy from Ringenberg. Some Germans came out of a nearby copse and were rounded up. I was naturally anxious to get to Hamminkeln as soon as possible, so we left our casualty with the headquarters of that company of the Ox and Bucks and made our way south along the railway track. The sound of shellfire and machine guns, coming from all sides, was deafening and every now and then we came upon a glider blazing furiously, one or two with their crews trapped within and little one could do to extricate them. One glider, or what was left of it, had wrapped itself around a massive tree. The whole situation seemed chaotic and I wondered if we should ever get it unravelled. Every farmhouse appeared to contain a defended post and isolated battles were being fought all over the LZ and beyond.

'The enemy were in greater confusion than we were. A number managed to concentrate in Hamminkeln, particularly on the north-east side. They consisted mostly of flak gunners, Luftwaffe Regiment, Volkssturm and parachutists. Three self-propelled guns, some tanks, armoured cars and half-tracks were cruising about the LZ and engaging troops who were deplaning. 'I joined up with a platoon of 'D' Company and we concentrated in the area of a road junction. After meeting some resistance, we eventually reached the northern edge of Hamminkeln. Contact was established by wireless with Battalion Headquarters and 'B' Company and so I gave the order for Phase Two to start at 1135 hours. The companies duly assaulted and the objective was taken by midday. Consolidation and mopping up were vigorously carried out in anticipation of the expected counter-attack and to eliminate the remaining flak positions. A German strongpoint of some forty men in a windmill was accounted for by one NCO.'

Meanwhile, the glider containing James N. Corbett of the 12th Battalion, The Devons arrived at LZ 'R'. 'With a collective shock to our system, we felt the glider pilot release the nylon rope that had towed us all the way from England to a point a few thousand feet above the Rhine waterway in the heart of Nazi Germany. The engine noise from our tow-plane, a heavy Stirling bomber, suddenly died away and we were left with the noisy air rushing past the fuselage interspersed with the crack of intense 'flak' from the ground below. From our briefings we knew that we had about four minutes flying time left and all we could do was sit there and endure the rain of fire from the German gunners as they tried to shoot us out of the skies.

'Everyone on board knew that World War II was drawing to its inevitable close and we entered that hellish four minutes with our minds filled with just the one thought; would we survive this last, big battle and, in the fullness of time, be able to go home to our families and friends?

'We banked left and right as the pilot tried to avoid the mass of fire-power streaming up from the ground. Corkscrewing all over the place, he struggled to control the heavy Horsa glider. His twenty-four passengers could only hold their breath and hang on to each other for dear life. My seat was alongside the exit door, which I had opened as soon as we crossed the Rhine. I could see the ribbon of water-way stretched below me. On all sides, the sky was filled with towing-planes and their linked cargoes of tense fighting men; over 4,000 aircraft in total. There were Halifaxes and Stirlings bringing in the 6th Airborne Division and C-47s with the 17th American Division. All, after releasing their load were dodging and weaving to avoid the mayhem. Many were hit and falling in flames.

'The 6th Airborne Division had landed in Normandy in the very early hours of D-Day. Mainly due to bad weather, the landings were not expected and therefore the element of surprise was a huge advantage. But the Rhine operation was different. Not only was this a daylight drop, but seven hours earlier, land-based troops had crossed the Rhine in assault craft and formed a three-mile bridgehead. Thus, the element of surprise was missing from our advantage; for the enemy had anticipated an airborne landing in support of the bridgehead and had plenty of time to bring up multiple air-defence guns from the Ruhr valley. And what a welcome they gave us! I believe there were units who lost 50% casualties. The sky was black with ten thousand parachutes. The German ack-ack gunners couldn't miss! They only had to point their guns skywards and press the trigger.

'We called our gliders, 'flying coffins'. They were built mainly of plywood and had no protection from the accurate German guns. Sitting there with no parachutes, we felt like sitting ducks. One's only hope lay in the skill of the glider pilot, who we prayed would get us down in one piece…then we had a fighting chance.

'Looking out the exit door I saw that more gliders had been hit and set on fire, giving the occupants no chance. As we continued to weave our way down through the crowded skies, I saw two Hamilcar heavy Combat gliders hit. Suddenly, a small half-track vehicle crashed through the front of the first glider with two men hanging on the chains used to secure the load. In the other glider an anti-tank 6-pounder and its gunners made their exit in the same fashion. I shall always remember my whole being becoming suffused with terror. This was simply carnage; the like of which we had never experienced in all the battles across Europe from Normandy to the Rhine. The horrific scenes I was witnessing reminded me of an old film, with giant prehistoric birds-of-prey flying through gunfire and picking off humans on their way.

'Then at ever decreasing speed we had just two more minutes of flying time left. Bullets were whipping through the fuselage like angry bees; I remember thinking that we could never survive this continuous onslaught. I closed my eyes and concentrated on the previous day's briefing, our objective and the job we had to do if we ever reached enemy territory.

'We were now down to 500 feet and out of the trajectory of the 'flak' guns, though small-arms fire was still coming our way from the ground defences. From my position, I could look out the cockpit window and saw a small town, which must be Hamminkeln, straight ahead. Then, the brown earth of the ploughed fields came into sight. Before we knew it, the pilot shouted, 'Stand by' so, holding on to each other and lifting our feet off the deck we braced ourselves for the crash-landing. There was a loud, harsh noise as we hit the ground and the landing gear came up through the floor. As we bounced and slithered along towards the houses ahead, the glider was now virtually out of control. It seemed we would never stop in time, but as the houses took off our wings and brought us to a standstill, we realised that our pilot had timed it magnificently. I had no time to marvel at this tremendous feat of flying. I was first out the door, to be met with a burst of German machine-gun fire. Fortunately, I had hit the ground, but the second man out, my best friend Cyril Eden, (who lived not far from me back in England) was shot through the thigh. I returned fire as best I could to cover the exit for the others. Then something happened which amazed me. I turned back towards the damaged glider to shout something or other, but found I could not utter a single word. Presumably, my vocal chords were paralysed with fear. I spent the next few minutes trying to swallow and get some saliva back into my mouth. Fortunately, this spasm only lasted a few minutes and I soon recovered and crawled away to a safer place.

'The long-range German guns and mortars had now found the range of the LZ and were beginning to saturate surrounding fields. I watched two of our Gliders attempt to land in our area. One tipped up on its nose and the other hit the ground with its starboard wing. They didn't catch fire so, hopefully, most of them got out. I also saw a four-engine bomber on fire with engines screaming as it crashed beyond the town. Meanwhile, one of our Hamilcar gliders, heavily laden, came in very low over the LZ. Desperately, I prayed that he would make it, not only for the lives of the men aboard, but also because I knew it would be carrying heavy equipment, which would have been useful to us at that moment. But he crashed straight into a railway signal-box. I was beginning to realise how lucky we had been to make a safe landing. The next thirty-minutes became even more murderous as small-arms fire and heavy artillery made our position untenable. I crawled further away from the LZ and was surprised to find a five-foot deep foxhole that I dived into with relief.

'I was not there long when I heard someone crawling towards me. Was it friend or foe? With my rifle between my knees, I got ready to blow any enemy's head off. But then a great, black moon-face peered over the parapet. With a deep-southern drawl, he said, *any room down there for me, boss?* He was a parachutist from the US 17th Airborne Division who had also landed on our zone. Facing each other, with our knees drawn up, there was just room for the two of us and I marvelled at the situation. Two soldiers from different countries, meeting up in a foxhole and being shelled to pieces whilst we chatted about the war in general. We also exchanged cigarettes, I smoked his 'Chesterfield' and he took my Players 'Navy Cut'. It was pure heaven, as all around us was death and destruction. I expect 95% of all front-line soldiers smoked when in action: the nicotine drug being a small comfort. Dying later of lung-cancer, in a bed with white sheets, seemed a favourable option for us at the time. Suddenly, the barrage lifted, so we shook hands and left our sanctuary to rejoin our units…never to meet again. I certainly hope he made it back to the States.'

Eddie Horrell in 'D' Company, The Devons was sitting right in the tail of his Horsa glider. As we went into a steep dive I remember being fascinated by little patches of white light appearing in the fuselage; it took me several seconds to realize these were made by pieces of shrapnel coming through the fabric. Then we were down with a terrific crash. We hadn't rolled ten yards and the pilots had put us down right on the button. But at what cost? Both were dead, together with the first six soldiers behind them and there were several injuries. I was slightly hurt as well as Nick, but we scrambled out of the glider to do our job of blowing off its tail. We were coming under heavy fire, with the survivors from the landing trying to give us cover while we fixed our demolition charge. We had just placed it and were getting ready to blow, standing shoulder to shoulder, when Nick gasped and fell. As I caught him I saw he had two bullet holes through the neck, which had killed him instantly. He was another of our original crowd and we had been together since 1940; it was like losing a brother. Our officer told us all to take cover in a nearby ditch, sort ourselves out and proceed to wipe out that damned machine gun, which we did. The scene was indescribable, with Horsas landing, Waco gilders coming in and paratroopers dodging in between. It seems the dense smoke had confused the pilots and in some cases had blotted out the landing areas. I saw a Hamilcar glider hit in mid air about five hundred feet up, when the nose swung open and a 17-pounder gun with its tractor and crew spilled out in mid-air. I saw the gliders of Beethoven Company whose job it was to knock out an identified anti-aircraft battery, landing smack on top of it, the gun barrels poking through the wings of the aircraft.

'When things got a bit quieter I made my way to the centre of Hamminkeln to rendezvous with the rest of my platoon and the first man I saw was my old pal Joe Marks. It's difficult to describe my feelings when I saw him safe and all in one piece, as he had also been flying in a company glider and had experienced a hair-raising landing. After Arnhem we had lost so many trained glider pilots that for the Rhine crossing they had drafted in a number of RAF fighter pilots, one to each experienced man. The RAF man in Joe's glider panicked as the dive began, left the cockpit and ran back through the plane. The glider pilot brought them in alright but it was a nervous moment. The RAF man didn't like the idea of a plane without an engine! By this time the fighting was easing off; Bill Pratt turned up slightly wounded, Wally Briggs and Ron Tarr also. Now we were beginning to find out what had happened to the glider carrying our platoon and all our stores; it turned out that it had been hit in mid-air and caught fire, though they managed to get down and scramble out. 'Babe' Cox, our Canadian officer, emerged only to be knocked down by another glider. Bill Tagg was obviously killed in the aircraft and burned with all our stores, jeeps, trailers and my brand new motor bike - all gone. We had left England that morning with seventeen men and at the end of the day only six answered the roll call, including our officer and me. We settled down in the cellar of a house, hopefully to grab some rations and a little kip and I remember removing my helmet for the first time since taking off that morning to find there in the chinstrap two neat holes made by the bullets that hit poor Nick as he stood beside me demolishing the tail of the glider.

'We lost that day 110 killed and thirty wounded, with over 50% of our transport. At an 'O(fficers')' group called that evening by our CO, which I attended because of the death of my officer, we were told that our battalion would lead the breakout over the River Issel, which was to become the most remarkable pursuit of the war's last stage.'

'The Battalion had taken a number of casualties,' says Jim Corbett; 'not only from shell fire, but from the church tower, where two or three snipers were picking off easy targets. As I was a sniper myself, I tried to use my telescopic sights and nullify this threat, but we were right underneath the tower and I could only see the very top of their helmets. So we remained pinned down, until our colonel brought up a 6-pound-anti-tank gun and blew the tower to pieces. We then rushed the enemy who were occupying the nearby houses and very soon captured the whole town. We took about one hundred prisoners; mostly older men and some Hitler Youth boy soldiers. It was not exactly the cream of the SS, but they were fighting for their Fatherland and had put up a stern resistance. Once captured, they seemed relieved that their war was over, whilst we had another six weeks of fighting before we met up with the Russians in the Baltic and at last called it a day. But for me, at least this Battle of the Rhine was over and amazingly, it had only taken just over the hour since we landed, so I suppose the Generals would be claiming it a resounding success. But at what cost?'

The 53rd (Worcestershire Yeomanry) Airlanding Light Regiment found itself with only about half of its twenty-four pack howitzers in action after landing. The first of the gliders bringing in 211th and 212th Airlanding Light Batteries landed on LZ 'P' at 1050 hours. By 1100 hours eleven pack howitzers were in action, together with one of the two 25-pounders flown in to fire coloured smoke for marking targets to be engaged by the 'cab ranks' of Typhoons on call for support.

Although the visibility was appalling and the anti-aircraft fire heavy, thirty-five gliders managed to land within a thousand yards of the LZ. Fourteen others landed sufficiently near that their gun detachments managed to rejoin the regiment within a few hours. Seven gliders landed to the west of the Rhine and arrived on the following day. However, twenty-two gliders had been lost; fifteen of these had landed some distance away from the landing areas and had been destroyed by enemy action, three had crashed when landing, three had been hit by anti-aircraft fire in mid-air and one had been destroyed on the LZ.

One glider, which crash-landed on LZ 'P', contained a gun detachment under the command of Sergeant Groom who later described what happened when he and his men arrived on the eastern side of the Rhine:

'My detachment consisted of Bombardier Mortibord and Gunners Smith, B. Fenton, J. Fenton, Rogers and Sheppard. Our actual flight was uneventful. Everyone was very impressed by the sight of the destruction and cratering caused by the bombing along the French coast. Then through the haze we caught sight of the Rhine and about then we cast off and started our descent. We flew into smoke and, coming out of it, found ourselves low over a wood. The glider just managed to clear the treetops but its undercarriage hit some power cables and was ripped off, the glider ending up on its nose. The intercom with the pilots had failed and the side door was stuck so we had to get out an axe and cut a hole in the side of the glider. All this took about an hour.

'I dropped out on to the ground and found the pilots emerging from the front. The landing zone was a very vivid sight; there was a glider on fire about fifty yards away and the whole area was filled with drifting smoke in which shells burst continuously. There was also some mortaring going on. After a few minutes I got my detachment together and we tried to pull down the glider tail so that we could get the gun out. We were unsuccessful in this and it looked as if we should have to chop a hole in the glider big enough to get the jeep through. Then I saw Sergeant Thomas of 211th Battery with his gun moving off. I stopped him and we put a tow-rope round the tail of the glider and hooked it to a jeep; that did the trick and we got the gun out without any more trouble. The glider had in fact landed in its correct place on the landing zone and I was easily able to recognise the countryside from my briefing which had been excellent. I then drove to the rendezvous which I found without any difficulty and there discovered Major Russell who showed me to my gun position.'

One of the gliders which had landed wide of the LZ was a Hamilcar carrying much needed ammunition for the pack howitzers. Once it had been located, the problem arose as to how the ammunition could be recovered. An initial attempt in daylight, led by the Commanding Officer, Lieutenant Colonel Robin Eden DSO failed and resulted in one man, Bombardier Bawden being mortally wounded. A second attempt carried out during the night and with an infantry patrol in support, proved successful. A limited amount of ammunition, based on two hundred rounds per howitzer, had been brought in by glider and this was earmarked for use in breaking up any enemy counter-attack. However, there was little risk of such a threat as the ceaseless artillery support from the field and medium regiments west of the Rhine ensured that the enemy was kept off-balance. Whilst the batteries held their fire, however, the crew of the 25-pounder was busy firing red smoke to mark targets for the RAF's Typhoons.[6]

The Worcestershire Yeomanry had suffered heavy casualties amongst its officers. Of its battery commanders, all three had been casualties. Major Charles Knox-Peebles, commanding 212th Battery had been killed as he disembarked from his glider and Major George Culley MC commanding 210th Battery had also been killed in similar circumstances. Major Jim Craigie, commanding 211th Battery was wounded but rejoined the regiment soon afterwards. Of the regiment's six troop commanders only two had survived. One of those who was captured was Captain Keith Thomas, commander of 'B' Troop of 210th Battery. The citation for his subsequent award of the Military Cross described what happened to him and the men who were with him:

'Captain Thomas's glider landed about three miles east of the landing zone well outside the airborne perimeter. He organised his own and two other glider parties into a body which he was leading towards the landing zone when it was engaged at short range by automatic fire. Having twice crawled back to collect wounded and stragglers, he finally established his force in a house and organised its defence. Meanwhile the house had been surrounded by much greater numbers of enemy and from 1200 hours to 1800 hours was subjected to continuous small arms and mortar fire. Nevertheless the little force held out and even broke up an infantry assault on the house with heavy losses to the enemy largely owing to Captain Thomas's courage and leadership. He himself killed seven enemy for certain. It was only when all their ammunition was exhausted that Captain Thomas was compelled to surrender his force.'

By the evening of 24 March the regiment's casualties totalled ninety-two. Two officers and seventeen other ranks had been killed, with one officer and two other ranks mortally wounded. Six officers and forty-four other ranks were wounded, whilst two officers and fifteen men were missing.[7]

The gunners of 2nd Airlanding Anti-Tank Regiment had, like their comrades in the airlanding light regiment, suffered heavy casualties and only about half of the regiment's anti-tank guns were brought into action. Closely followed by 4th Airlanding Anti-Tank Battery under Major Peter Dixon MC, 3rd Airlanding Anti-Tank Battery commanded by Major Joe Woodrow, commenced landing on LZ 'P' at 1030 hours. One of its troop commanders was Lieutenant John Slater who vividly recalls his arrival on the LZ: 'As we crossed the Rhine the phrase fog of war' became a reality as the ground below was almost totally obscured by smoke. Our pilot cast off and the slipstream noise stopped abruptly, leaving us flying in almost complete silence. The peace was soon shattered, however, when we were engaged by German light flak - we discovered later that we had been hit at least twice in the undercarriage and the starboard wing. I remember our pilot saying 'Christ! I'm getting out of this!' and we went into a very steep dive to the accompaniment of rending and tearing sounds from the starboard wing just behind me. Very disconcerting!

'We hit the ground and the undercarriage collapsed immediately. The nose wheel came up through the floor and the glider filled with dust. We attempted to get out but the front port side door had jammed in the crash. The tail could not be dropped because the quick-release bolts had not been properly maintained and had seized up. We couldn't get out at the front because the nose was embedded in a ploughed field. It seemed hard to believe that only three hours earlier we were being given cups of NAAFI tea in England and now here we were in Germany, trapped in a glider in the middle of the enemy gun area!

'After some fairly frantic chopping with an axe, our combined efforts resulted in our managing to open the door and we all got out. My most abiding memory of the first few moments on German soil is of a beautiful spring morning, the smell of newly-turned earth and a lark singing overhead. My battery commander left immediately to try and reach Battery Headquarters and was briefly captured by German paratroops. However, he managed to escape and rejoin the battery.

'We tried to salvage the load from the glider but soon came under mortar fire and moved to a farmhouse nearby. We found this occupied by a couple of German soldiers and two American fighter pilots who had just been shot down - one was badly wounded. Apparently the remainder of the German platoon who had been occupying the farm were in Hamminkeln for a bath parade and had left their heavy weapons behind. We finally reached Battery Headquarters and soon discovered that both our battery and 4th Airlanding Anti-Tank Battery had suffered heavy casualties.'

Subsequently the regiment was joined by 6th Airlanding Anti-Tank Battery which crossed the Rhine together with the rest of the divisional troops.

Forty-eight tugs and their Hamilcars took off from Woodbridge. They carried, among other items of equipment and personnel, eight American-designed M22 Locust airmobile light tanks, so named due to their small size and that they came from the sky in swarms. The tanks were loaded into eight separate Hamilcar gliders during 17-20th March. Divided into two troops of four in the Armoured Reconnaissance Regiment (AAARR), they would land with the 6th Airlanding Brigade, acting as a divisional reserve. The Locusts were to start their engines during the gliders' approach to LZ 'P' east of the Diersfordter Wald to provide initial armoured support in just fifteen seconds after landing. The rest of the regiment would arrive by road after crossing the Rhine with 21st Army Group. Angus McCloud, a tank driver in one of the Hamilcars heading for LZ 'P', says: 'Considering the Locust was built by the Americans, it says a lot about the tank that they refused to use them. Having had what appeared to be every German anti-aircraft gun try and shoot the lumbering giant out of the sky they turned on one of the others and succeeded.'[8]

Over Belgium the Hamilcar carrying the Locust of Sergeant Dawson disintegrated in the air without warning when the tank broke from its moors, crashed through the tail and the glider tow cable breaking apart. Hamilcar pilot Lieutenant Peter Davies was a witness to the disaster. 'Just before we crossed the Rhine, the tank being carried by a Hamilcar flying on our port side shot out through the tail of the aircraft complete with its shackle chains and the crew still sitting on its side. The tank seemed to stand still in mid air then slowly turned over, whilst the rest of the glider began to the break up on the towrope which was eventually released, presumably by the tug aircraft.' Neither glider pilots nor their passengers had parachutes. The Locust was found a few months later in the mud at the edge of Rhine.

Peter Davies' glider made a safe landing despite being holed three times by German flak in the area.

Lieutenant Kenward's glider landed on the LZ but the occupants had to break through the nose of the Hamilcar due to it being broken. Shortly after breaking through the nose of the Glider, Kenward came under fire, most likely from a Panther tank due to the shot being a 75mm. On another glider that crashed, the Locust had only its machine gun damaged. A Locust that flew out of its glider that was crashing landed on a house. Incredibly the crew were unhurt, but the wireless and 37 mm gun were damaged and the problem with the gun was not realized until after it was fired and it sprayed open. Lieutenant Colonel Stewart, the AAARR CO's glider, had one of the landing wheels shot off, probably by flak, which caused it to veer slightly off the LZ but still landed safely. The final glider landed safely by Stewart's glider but then hit a ditch and the tank somersaulted through the air before landing on its turret before being flipped back over again. Trooper K. W. Dowsett, who was one of the men on board, recalled:

'Our ETA at the LZ was 1040 hours and as we approached we secured ourselves into our seats. The 37 mm and .30 coaxial machine guns were loaded the engine started and we were all set. I heard one of the glider pilots say, 'Hang on, chaps. We're going in now.' A very short time later we seemed to be going around and around and then, with an almighty crash, we came to a halt upside down suspended in our safety harnesses. It transpired later that, after casting off, we had glided down very close to a light flak position which took part of the Hamilcar's wing off. In the resulting crash both our pilots were killed and the tank, propelled by its own movement, tore loose from the securing shackles and somersaulted through the air, landing upside down on its turret. We eventually, with great difficulty, released our harnesses and were able to crawl out from under the tank. We were a pretty sore and sorry crew. My personal weapon was a Sten gun which, due to insufficient storage space inside the turret, was strapped to the outside - this was bent and totally unserviceable. A somewhat uninspiring descent into Germany - I didn't even have a weapon! As the three of us laid alongside the wreckage, keeping our heads down and wondering when it would be practical to move on foot towards our RV, we heard the sound of tracks and thought this was the end for us. But, unbelievably, it was our commanding officer's Locust rattling up with the CO himself, bedecked in his brightly coloured cavalry forage cap, sounding his hunting horn as he stood upright in the turret! We climbed on to the back of his tank and set off to the RV where defensive positions in the vicinity of divisional headquarters were being established.'

'A number of Locusts had significant damage and couldn't move,' recalls Angus McCloud. 'Two of these would never reach the RV. One undamaged tank emerged from the front of a Hamilcar, straight into a battle with a Tiger tank; predictably the Tiger came off best. A second tank broke down as it attempted to tow a jeep out of a crashed glider, although the crew did remain with the tank and provided fire support for one of the battalions. Of the six that eventually reached the RV, only four were undamaged and fit for action - mine was one of these. We were immediately deployed to the high ground east of the Diersfordter Wald, while being covered by the two damaged tanks. When we got there we stood out like sore thumbs and were immediately engaged by German troops and required support from an infantry company. Soon every German heavy gun, anti-tank gun and Panzerfaust within range wanted to blow us to kingdom come as four British tanks were prime battlefield targets. We had a lot of near misses, but the infantry company was copping a hell of a bashing, although between us we did a bit of damage to the Germans too. In the end their OC calmly walked up to us and politely asked us to go away as we were attracting too much attention, so we did.[9]

Writing in retrospect Sean Dickson walked around his platoon with a smile on his face and joked with them. 'It was expected of me, a game we all play and they wouldn't have it any other way. It's been like this since we were at Normandy: we all laugh in the face of adversity. Although they appeared happy I noticed the gaps in the ranks where once some of them had been. You learned to live with it, as it is a fact of life in war, but as I looked back on the landing yesterday I remembered how indiscriminate death is. One moment someone is there, the next he is down, dead, never to see the light of day again. If he is lucky he is wounded, although some wounds are so bad maybe it would have been better if they were killed. I remember Private Tanner, the platoon comedian. He had a head wound so bad I expected him to die, but by some miracle he didn't, but he'll never have a normal life - he'll forever sit in a chair with a vacant look on his face, unable to think or speak. Having said that, all of us will be scarred by what we have seen and done - the horror never leaves you. Some cover it up, others can't. Yesterday we must have lost about a quarter of the platoon, either wounded or killed in those first few hours. The Germans put up a stout, spirited fight. I would too if it had been the other way around. I stop for a moment and daydream and I am brought back to life by the platoon sergeant. Under his beret his head is heavily bandaged where a piece of shrapnel tried to scalp him. Anyone else would have gone to hospital - not him. The platoon calls him 'Lucky Lowes' behind his back. At Normandy he charged a machine-gun position over open ground and killed the crew. How he survived without a scratch, God knows. How many has it been since Normandy? I could count on one hand how many are left since those first days. Sergeant Lowes tells me that the OC is having an orders group. I finish off walking around and congratulate Private Arnold on the birth of his daughter. It's the talk of the platoon; they all want to call her 'Pegasus', although I don't think Arnold's wife will agree. I have a large mug of 'compo' tea and a hard biscuit in my hand given to me by my batman, Sykes; he fusses over me like an old washerwoman. He seems to have the knack of knowing what I need and presenting it to me before I can ask. I shall miss him when I leave the regiment and this wretched war is over.'[10]

Endnotes Chapter 7

1   On 29 March in Coesfelt Huw Wheldon was shot by a sniper. His wound was through and through the buttock. Fortunately it had missed bone, artery and sciatic nerve. With Penicillin then available in Military Hospitals he would soon be OK again.

2   In 1952 Wheldon joined the BBC and rose to Managing Director in 1968, a position he held until compulsory retirement in 1975. Sir Huw Pyrs Wheldon OBE MC died on 14 March 1986.

3   'The Journey', a personal account of the Rhine crossing in 1945 by Corporal Colin Goodall.

4   David Brook, from The Eagle - journal of the GPRA.

5   Quoted in Paras: Voices of the British Airborne Forces in the Second World War by Roger Payne OAM (Amberley, 2014 and 2016).

6   Go To It! The Illustrated History of the 6th Airborne Division by Peter Harclerode (Caxton Editions,1990).

7   Go To It! The Illustrated History of the 6th Airborne Division by Peter Harclerode (Caxton Editions,1990).

8   Quoted in Paras: Voices of the British Airborne Forces in the Second World War by Roger Payne OAM (Amberley, 2014 and 2016).

9   Quoted in Paras: Voices of the British Airborne Forces in the Second World War by Roger Payne OAM (Amberley 2014, and 2016).

10   Quoted in Paras: Voices of the British Airborne Forces in the Second World War by Roger Payne OAM (Amberley, 2014 and 2016).

Chapter 8

Low Level Liberators

Although Airborne Army expected its troops to link up with the British ground forces within a few hours, it regarded resupply by air as highly desirable, because Second Army probably could not put more than one bridge in operation on 'D-Day' and at first would need everything that could be brought in by bridge or boat. However, it was in the critical early hours of the operation that the airborne, too, most urgently would need supplies, particularly ammunition. On 'D+1' resupply might be too late or might be prevented by bad weather. Resupply at night might be inaccurate and surely would be hard to recover. On 'D-Day' itself the troop carriers would be fully occupied with the initial missions. The solution was to fly the supplies in by Liberator bombers as had been done during 'Market' when the B-24s hauled 1,900 tons of freight between 29 August and 17 September. Each airborne division was to bring in two M/F beacons and have one in operation on its supply drop zone in time to guide in the B-24 resupply mission.

The use of B-24 bombers for resupply was a valuable supplement to the American troop carrier effort but they had to be withdrawn from their primary mission several days before an operation for modification, loading and other preparations and could only land on good, hard-surfaced bases. It was equally wasteful in that the big aircraft capable of carrying six tons of bombs could deliver less than 2½ tons in a parachute drop.

The field order for Operation 'Varsity' did not arrive at Major General W. E. 'Bill' Kepner's Headquarters, Second Air Division at Ketteringham Hall, the late 15th century mansion standing in 36 acres of woodland and open grassland 7½ miles south-west of Norwich in the usual way. Instead of a message classified 'Secret' on two yards of yellow teleprinter paper, it was delivered by courier; page after page of orders, assignments, orders of battle, routes, times, etc, etc in a fancy folder, all stamped 'Top Secret.' On 9 March Eighth Air Force had told Kepner in general terms to prepare his B-24 Liberators for a resupply mission. On the 14th in collaboration with Eighth Air Force planners the Division had blocked out a tentative plan which called for a run on a south-to-north heading followed by a quick left turn into friendly territory. However, in the big conference at 2nd TAF on the 17th the plan was changed to give the bombers the same route as the troop carriers as far as the drop zones and a right turn after the drop to take advantage of measures to be taken against flak in the Wesel area.

The order began; 'Varsity can be considered the most important combined operation since the invasion of France....' It also said that the Allied armies in the north will have crossed the Rhine at three points at zero hour minus six hours by amphibious assault. The airborne operations, the 1st Allied Airborne

Army, would dispatch 1,593 aircraft towing gliders with troops aboard for release in the landing zone, while paratroops would also be dropped. US Air Forces and the RAF would neutralize defences, interdict road and rail traffic and provide close support. Eighth Air Force bombers would be included. The operation was set for 24 March and most of the 1,700 heavy bombers involved would attack about two dozen airfields in northern Germany within range of the Rhine River. Their task was to crater runways at known jet airfields and to prevent the use of enemy jet aircraft in the areas.

The field order issued by the Second Air Division on the 22nd called for two task groups of 120 Liberators each - one to drop supplies to the American forces and the other to British forces - to take off from Norfolk and Suffolk and pick up the troop carrier route at Hawkinge. The bomber force was to keep in the right-hand lane from Wavre on and was to descend gradually from heights of 3,000 feet over England, 1,500 feet over the Channel and 1,000 feet at Wavre to a drop altitude between 300 and 500 feet. From a cruising speed of 160 mph at Wavre the B-24s were to slow to 155 mph at the IP and to 150 or under for the drop. Any danger that they would overrun the much slower glider formations was to be reported by the escort commander in time for the bombers to regain a proper interval by making a circle or a dogleg. At Wavre the nine groups committed were to fall into trail and at the IP the individual flights would do so. The basic formation would be the nine-plane 'V of V's, loose en route and tightened for the final run. Two weather aircraft twenty minutes ahead were to report on conditions at the destination. First, the Liberators would drop canisters of ammunition and other material to resupply the ground troops during the battle; and second, the drop would be made at 400 feet. 'Probably the greatest danger will come from small-arms fire from enemy troops, although there is little doubt that the majority of these will be otherwise engaged at the time.'

During the resupply mission Allied anti-aircraft batteries were to fire only on aircraft committing hostile acts, except that within 12,000 yards of the Rhine crossings at Xanten and Rees they might fire on aircraft definitely recognized as hostile. This exception destroyed most of the value of the protective clause, for within the 12,000-yard radius around the crossings was the very area where battle-smoke and battle-tension might cause the supply formations to be fired upon. The determination of Second Army to protect its pontoon bridges from German bombers was reasonable enough, but the fact remains that the 'D+1' mission in 'Varsity' was to have no more protection from Allied anti-aircraft fire at the front than the unfortunate follow-up mission to Sicily, which had been smashed by friendly guns.

There was to be no repetition of the heart-rending misplaced drops that occurred in 'Market'. 'Varsity' had been planned well in advance, supplies for the airborne being requisitioned weeks before. Those for the Americans had been packed by the 490th Quartermaster Depot Company and those for the British by the Air Dispatch Group. The packages were then sent to the Third Strategic Air Depot at Neaton and from there between 20 and 23 March they were distributed to the bomber bases, all of which were within thirty miles of the depot. At 1430 on the 23rd loading began. Thanks to careful preparation this unfamiliar task was accomplished without difficulty. The Second Air Division had conducted tests and issued a special letter of instructions; the 490th Quartermaster Company had provided two-instructor-demonstrators and the personnel of the bomb groups had been given special training in loading and dropping procedure. Each plane was to carry about 2½ tons of cargo, wrapped in twenty or 21 bundles, a dozen forward in the bomb racks, five or six in and around the ball turret well (the turret having been removed) and three at the emergency escape hatch in the tail. Because their load was abnormally light, the Liberators tended to be tail-heavy. Consequently ammunition and other heavy articles were concentrated forward. All bundles of gasoline cans were placed at the turret well. Some indestructible items were to be allowed to fall free, but most were to have parachutes, each of the four classes being distinguished by a chute of a different colour.

On 23 March a security clampdown was imposed on the B-24 bases throughout Norfolk and Suffolk and trucks arrived laden with weighted wicker baskets to which parachutes were attached and were loaded into the bomb bays and ball-turret openings of the Liberators. The bulk of the supplies lay in the bomb bay with another eight to nine baskets stowed in the ball-turret and rear fuselage areas. However, this induced a tail-heavy configuration which was rectified by stowing all the ammunition forward.

'It all started for us on the morning of 23 March,' wrote Lieutenant E. Paul Robbins, a navigator in 2nd Lieutenant William 'Ned' Ansell's crew in *Stand By* in the 567th Bomb Squadron, in the 389th 'Sky Scorpions' Bomb Group at Hethel near Norwich. 'The waist and tail gunners of our crew and I were told to report to 'E+' to be shown how to drop supplies from a B-24. This took only half an hour, but it started many wild ideas through our heads. What was up? Evidently something big. A new invasion somewhere? Where? Norway? Denmark? It was anybody's guess. That noon we found out that no one was allowed to leave the post. It must be something really big. What, we still didn't know. The answer came in the evening. At the unusual hour of 8 pm we were called to the main briefing room. Rumours were still running wild. To make things worse the doors were not opened until eight sharp. We were all keyed to a high pitch. When we were all seated, the S-2 Officer mounted the platform and raised the screen from the map. A course line was marked on it. This didn't help much. We could see we were going to go to a spot across the Rhine, just north of the Ruhr Valley. But why? The Intelligence officer said: *This is it men. We're going across the Rhine. Zero hour will be 0400. Starting then, by land, sea and air, we are going over. You will follow the glider and paratroops in, dropping supplies to them.* By now the excited buzz was dying down. The tension was off for the time being and we were ready for the details. We were told where the infantry was going to cross and how. It was the first time I had been given news of this magnitude before the event. We were to go in at 300 to 500 feet with flaps down to slow us up as much as possible. The slow speed was to decrease the danger of the chutes ripping when they opened. As soon as the chutes were out, we were to hit the deck. We must get as low as possible so the enemy fire might not be too accurate. After being cautioned about talking and advised to go to bed, we were released from the briefing room. We went to the barracks but we couldn't help discussing the mission among ourselves.'

Those men who remembered the low-level mission at Arnhem regarded their part in the Rhine crossing with mounting apprehension for they would be flying as low as fifty feet over the dropping zone at Wesel. The supply drop was scheduled to occur at 1300 hours, about twenty minutes after the last gliders landed. So early a drop involved some risk that zones still would be in enemy hands, but it also had great advantages. The same air effort set up to protect the troop carriers from enemy air and ground action would serve to protect the bombers; and the airborne, instead of keeping large numbers of fighting men waiting for hours to guard zones and pick up supplies, could collect their bundles soon after assembling and go about their business. Both troop carrier and resupply missions were to follow the same route. Primarily intended to simplify control of fire from Allied anti-aircraft batteries, this plan also facilitated fighter protection and use of navigational aids.

At Seething Lieutenant Harold Dorfman the lead dead-reckoning navigator for the 448th Bomb Group on Lieutenant William Voight's aircraft, the deputy lead, with the 713th Bomb Squadron commander, Lieutenant Colonel Herbert H. Thompson aboard, recalled: 'The night of the 23rd we were taken in to study the drop area models and maps. Now we knew it was coming off the following day. The route in and out was over friendly territory all the way. We labelled it a 'milk run', another sightseeing trip. Except for about five minutes at the drop area we would never be over enemy territory.'[1] After a 0530 briefing, Voight's Liberator would be one of twenty-six aircraft split in three formations leaving Seething at 0930. Crews passed up the normal heavy flying clothes and donned just 'Class B' uniforms, a light jacket and a back parachute.

When the mission map was revealed during the 44th Flying Eightballs' briefing at Shipdham near East Dereham, it showed a course that crossed Wesel. The bombardier in Leslie Lee's crew in the 67th Bomb Squadron, 1st Lieutenant Donald G. Potter, born 30 November 1921 in Los Animas, Colorado recalled: 'We were to carry cargo only, which would be dropped by parachute, through the ball turret opening when over the target area. Sixty nine tons of supplies were to be dropped. We were to leave all offensive or defensive armament. The thinking was that, if we should get shot down over enemy territory, the enemy would not be as likely to 'chop' any captured prisoner of war they might find since no one invader had fired a shot. This announcement did not make us feel in the least comforted. The official reason was that they felt that we might accidently fire on friendly troops during the operation. Nowhere in the briefing was it mentioned that we might receive fire from tall buildings, actually shooting DOWN at us as we passed by. The situation was doubly exasperating because the only defensive weapons we had on board were our RAF fighting knives, or reasonable facsimiles thereof.

'We were to cross the Channel and Allied country at a height of 50 feet; that was low. Actually, we would fly a little higher over the Channel but descend to about 51 feet when over the coast.'[2]

At Wendling a few miles away, 'Big John' Beder's crew in the 576th Squadron in the 392nd Bomb Group learned at briefing that they would lead a formation of thirteen aircraft as part of the task group resupplying the British.

It was to be their 24th mission. John 'Matt' Matishowski, the navigator, recalled: 'We had by now gotten ourselves into a mind-set where pre-flight preparations were routine, although performed with that feeling of dread in the back of the mind. This day the feeling of routine was gone and was replaced by something I hadn't felt for a while, the fascination of the moth with the flame. The feeling of dread was still there, but there was excitement, too, that the invasion of Germany itself was about to start and the war could end soon after.

'Our part in Operation 'Varsity' would require that we be able to find our way, at very low altitude, across the Channel to the Boulogne area and then across France and Belgium to a drop zone measuring 1,500 by 2,000 yards, just across the Rhine. We would fly very low to ensure surprise and decrease the already high vulnerability we were stuck with. When we found ourselves a few days after the Stettin mission with a small formation tearing across French farmland on a practice mission at only 50 feet, so low that the altimeter pointer sort of sat on zero, I had to admit, war or not, tough mission or milk run, there was nothing as exhilarating as a legal buzz job.'[3]

'At 5 am on the morning of 24 March,' continues Paul Robbins, 'we were awakened for a six o'clock briefing. This was it. Briefing this time was a review of the previous one, only in more detail. One piece of news was given out. That was that the British, under Field Marshal Montgomery, had crossed the Rhine at ten pm last evening. From there, I went to the navigators' briefing. There we were briefed more thoroughly on the course and on the identification of the target. The importance of dropping the stuff in exactly the right place was stressed over and over again. A mistake and it would fall into enemy hands. Everything was complete. With the words of warning ringing in our ears, we dressed and joined our crews at the planes.'

Tech Sergeant Coy H. Lawson, a radio operator in the 389th Bomb Group who in November 1944 upon being assigned a bed in his hut at Hethel, a fellow airman had said, *The Sarg that occupied that bed before you was killed last week.* Now he was well on the way to completing his tour of 31 missions and was of the opinion that, with the war winding down and having survived so far, he was going to get through.

The first bombers rose into the air from their East Anglia bases at 0910. Take-off and group assembly were fast and efficient. The big aircraft rolled away at average intervals of considerably less than a minute apiece.

The first aircraft were to begin dropping supplies for the 17th Airborne at Supply Drop Point 'W' at 1257 hours. This was an oval about 2,000 yards long from east to west and 1,500 yards from north to south, roughly identical with DZ 'W'. The big bend in the river near Xanten, the lake known as the Alter Rhein and the southern edge of the Diersfordter Wald provided convenient landmarks on the way to that zone. Airborne troops on the spot were to mark the zone with a red 'T', white letter 'W' and red smoke and were also to have an M/F beacon in operation. The 120 aircraft in the rear of the column were to deliver their loads to 6th Airborne Division on SDP 'B'. This was a diamond-shaped area about 2,000 yards across located about 4½ miles east of the Rhine and about three-quarters of a mile west of Hamminkeln with the double-track

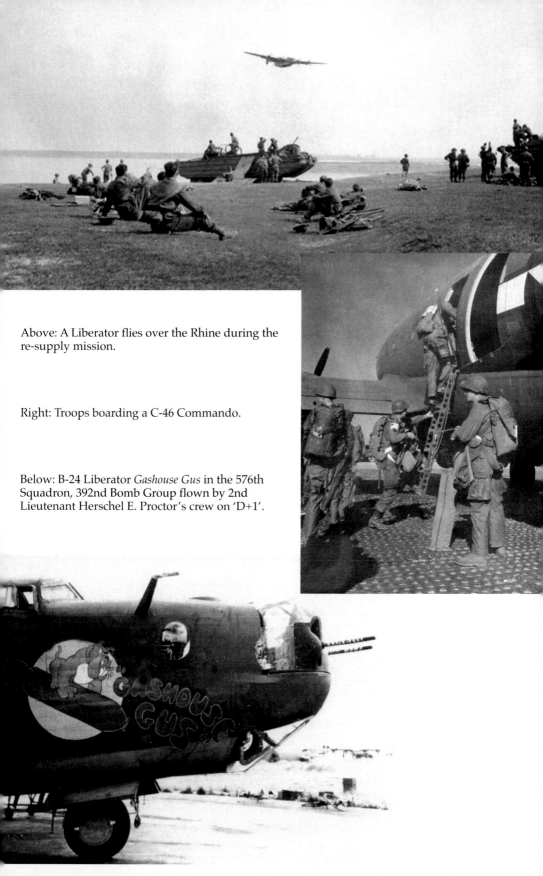

Above: A Liberator flies over the Rhine during the re-supply mission.

Right: Troops boarding a C-46 Commando.

Below: B-24 Liberator *Gashouse Gus* in the 576th Squadron, 392nd Bomb Group flown by 2nd Lieutenant Herschel E. Proctor's crew on 'D+1'.

A B-24 in the 735th Bomb Squadron, 453rd Bomb Group dropping supplies on 'Varsity-Plunder'. Of 240 low-flying Liberators that dropped supplies to Allied troops on 'D+1', fifteen were lost and 104 damaged.

Above: The B-17 that Lieutenant Colonel Benton R. Baldwin crash landed in a field nearby after it was hit by flak in the left wing on 'Varsity' taken from a movie film shot from another observation aircraft.

Below: Richard Curt Hottelet, a Brooklyn-born American broadcast journalist and a Combat Camera motion film unit who flew on a B-17 piloted by Lieutenant Colonel Benton R. Baldwin to witness the airborne operations at first hand, pictured in the CBS wartime office in London, from left: Richard C. Hottelet, Charles Shaw, Larry LeSueur, Edward R. Murrow and seated, Janet Murrow. (CBS)

Left: Colonel (later Brigadier) George Chatterton the commander of the Glider Pilot Regiment.

Below left: Colonel Joel L. Crouch commanding IX Troop Carrier Pathfinder Group.

Right: General der Fallschirmtruppe Wilhelm Schlemm commanding the German 1st Parachute Army.

Below, right: Lieutenant Colonel Jevon Albert 'Jeff' Nicklin OBE, 1st Canadian Battalion who came down right on top of a German machine gun position. As he dangled helplessly from his chute, the Germans riddled him with automatic weapons fire.

Below: Lieutenant Moorehead 'Jay' Phillips (left) and Lieutenant Philip Sarrett of Ada, Oklahoma. Both men were killed on 24 March. (Fenton P. Fleming Collection)

Right: C-47A-70-DL 42-100670 *Arkansas Traveler/Off we go into the Wild Blue Yonder* in the 436th Troop Carrier Group, 79th Troop Carrier Squadron. Assigned to pilot Pete Reed and co-pilot Burwell Buchanan this C-47 took part in the 'D-Day' airborne assault, the invasion of Southern France and 'Market-Garden', moving to Melun-Villaroche (A-55) in France for 'Varsity'. *Arkansas Traveler* soldiered on until at least 1952. (Richard Buchanan)

Left: Captain Hugh J. Nevins, the 50th Troop Carrier Wing's glider officer, in the cockpit of his personal C-47 *War Weary* in the 436th Troop Carrier Group at Bottesford.

Below: C-47A-15-DK 42-92862 in the 32nd Troop Carrier Squadron, 314th Troop Carrier Group taking off from Poix airfield (B-44) on 24 March.

Above: C-47 42-92717 *Stoy Hora* in the 98th Troop Carrier Squadron, 440th Troop Carrier Group, which Col. Frank X. Krebs, CO of the 440th used to lead the Group into battle on all operations he flew except 'Market-Garden', the invasion of Holland.

Left: Lieutenant Colonel Frank X. Krebs, CO, 440th Troop Carrier Group (left) and Lieutenant Colonel Howard W. Cannon.

Above: Low level B-24 Liberators over a RAF Typhoon fighter-bomber airfield during the supply drop on 'D+1'.

Right: B-24 *Piccadilly Lilly* in the 448th Bomb Group (which was flying its 106th mission on 'D+1') flown by 2nd Lieutenant Hugh McFarland had their control lines shot out and crashed into a hill. Eight of the crew were killed; only two crew survived. (USAF)

Below: B-24 *Kay Bar* in the 67th Bomb Squadron, 44th Bomb Group at Shipdham, Norfolk flown by 1st Lieutenant Leonard J. Crandell's crew, all of whom were lost on 'D+1'.

Left and inset: Flight Officer Rosemary Britten, a WAAF intelligence officer who flew to Wesel from Earls Colne on Halifax NA698 'D for Dog', piloted by Flying Officer Ron Lamshed. This airfield in 38 Group RAF operated Halifaxes of 296 and 297 Squadrons and was used as a glider towing unit.

Below, left: Staff Sergeant Arthur 'Shack' Shackleton.

Below. right: Major Ian Jodrell Toler DFC, Officer Commanding, 'B' Squadron, 1 Wing Glider Pilot Regiment.

C-47 going down on fire.

Above: Stirlings over the
Rhine during 'Varsity'

.
Right: British Paratroopers
prepare to board C-47
Skytrain *Virginia Ann* of
the 59th Troop Carrier
Squadron, 61st Troop
Carrier Group at Chipping
Ongar.

Above: C-46 Commandos making a practice drop.

Below: Paratroopers of the 513th Parachute Infantry Regiment ready to load on the C-46s of the 48th Troop Carrier Squadron, 313th Troop Carrier Group at Achiet-le-Grand (B-54). (National Archives).

Left: Alan McCrae Moorehead, the Australian born war correspondent, one of several who covered the 'Varsity' operation.

Below: German prisoners, believed to be on LZ 'U', guarded by the seated man to the right, probably a glider pilot.

Below: Chaplain Captain Jesse W. Wood of Bogalusa, La., 437th Troop Carrier Group, posts confession notice for troops of the 1st Allied Airborne Army who are ready to take off for the Rhine Crossing and landing at Wesel.

Above: General Montgomery with (back row, 1st and 2nd left) Lieutenant Colonels Napier Crookenden, 9th Battalion and Paul Gleadell, 12th Devons and (middle row, from left); Lieutenant Colonels Kenneth Thomas Darling, 12th Battalion; Geoffrey Pine-Coffin DSO MC, 7th Battalion; Jeff Nicklin, 1st Canadian Battalion; Peter Luard, 13th Battalion. Front Row, 2nd from left, Major General Eric Louis Bols CB DSO, Commander, 6th Airborne Division; Brigadier Stanley James Ledger 'Speedy' Hill, 3rd Parachute Brigade; Montgomery and Brigadier Joseph Howard Nigel Poett, 5th Parachute Brigade.
Right: Chaplain Captain Jesse W. Wood of Bogalusa, La., 437th Troop Carrier Group, posts confession notice for troops of the 1st Allied Airborne Army who are ready to take off for the Rhine Crossing and landing at Wesel.

Above: Richard Dimbleby recording his commentary on the Rhine crossing on the morning of 24 March with Stanley Maxted on one of the tug and glider combinations.

Below: Winston Churchill stands on a demolished Rhine rail bridge on 25 March. When US officers demanded that he return to a safer position, the prime minister 'put both his arms round one of the twisted girders of the bridge and looked over his shoulder…with pouting mouth and angry eyes.' (US Army Military History Institute)

Above: Using a Remington Model 2 portable typewriter to write his story in a ditch astride the Utrechtseweg after the 1st Airborne Division's landing near Oosterbeek, Australian-born war correspondent Alliott Alan Whitfeld Wood had the distinction of being the only newspaperman to send dispatches from Arnhem. Unluckily Wood was wounded in the leg during 'Varsity' and lost the limb.

Below: A sign proclaiming 'Rhine Railroad Bridge across the Rhine courtesy of the 1056 Engineer Group'.

C-47s overhead the ruins at Wesel.

railway on its southwest edge. It was to be marked with a yellow 'T', green smoke and a white letter 'B', supplemented by an M/F beacon. In addition a VHF landing beacon (SCS-51) was to be set up at the IP and aimed at SDP B so that the bombers could ride along its beam to their objective. After completing the drop the bombers were to turn to the right, climb to 2,500 feet and return along the troop carrier route to Wavre. From there they would make almost a bee-line return to their bases by way of Ostend.

'At the plane,' continues Paul Robbins, 'our whole crew got together and went over the details once more to make sure everything was understood. The gunners were checked on how to kick out the supplies that would be carried in the waist position. I showed them my target photographs and reminded them again to keep their eyes open all the time - not that a reminder was necessary. Not on this day. I checked the toggle switch and the bomb racks to make sure everything would go all right. We carried no bombardier. I would toggle the bundles out. 'Ned' and 'Jim' (co-pilot) checked their instruments and controls. Everything was checked and rechecked.

'We took off at 0925. There wasn't a cloud in the sky. We couldn't have asked for better weather. The group was formed by 1030 and we were on our way. We crossed the Channel and hit the French coast at 2,000 feet instead of the usual 20,000 feet. Then we began letting down. Soon we were at 500 feet. This was different than four miles up. I could see the people stopping to look up at us. Cattle in the fields were running aimlessly, frightened by the roar of the engines. I saw a GI snap a photo of us as we passed over his head.'[4]

As far as Coy Lawson was concerned the forming of the 389th Bomb Group 'took forever and the route in was evasive and long. You were down low at cruising speed and counting every house, dead cow, wrecked vehicle and the few trees left standing in northeast France. As you approached the combat zone you saw miles of tanks, half-tracks, trucks and ambulances close parked on the roads pointing north-east. You were down on the deck where the action was for what seemed like hours. After a while you realized these turkeys are just sitting waiting for you to go in first.'

At Wendling Lieutenant John 'Jack' R. Hummel's crew in the 392nd had been on a mission on 23 March and they were due a three day pass, as Tech Sergeant Hollis C. Powell the tail gunner recalls: 'I usually went to London where I enjoyed visiting. But upon checking the bulletin board we saw we were up for a mission the next day. We were unhappy about losing our pass privilege. After breakfast and at briefing we were told that we were to drop supplies to the gliders and airborne who had jumped the Rhine and had taken a good foothold near Wesel. It was believed that it would be a milk run as to fighters and flak. They didn't mention ground fire! We were to go in at tree top level and drop or kick out the supplies out of there. Ellis H. Morse, nose gunner and James A. Deaton, radio operator were to kick the bundles out the bomb bay doors.'[5]

'Eddy' White was a last minute replacement for a captain who refused to fly and lead the mission. The captain had 'crapped out' the day before and Colonel Myron Keilman, the 579th Squadron commander, had acted quickly, as he recalls: 'I didn't have much time to 'dawdle'. Eddy White and crew was my choice. Back in my jeep I jumped and headed for the Squadron combat crew Nissen hut area with the dreaded thought that Eddy and crew may have gone 'pubbing', as they usually did if they weren't on alert. I was in luck. 'Eddy' was about to leave for the movies. I told him that I needed him and his crew. He sensed that it was something important - or I wouldn't be doing the asking. Eddy was given a real quick idea of what the mission entailed. With only a moment's thought, he looked me in the eye and said, 'I will if you will.' That seemed really impertinent and as squadron commander, I felt like 'dressing him down' but he had a point. I wouldn't ask him to do anything I wouldn't do. This would be his thirtieth and last mission of his combat tour. He and I hoped it would be a 'milk-run'. Having got approval from Colonel Loren Johnson to fly with Eddy as command pilot I crowded Eddy, his navigator and bombardier into my jeep and headed for the group intelligence building. We were given a thorough, but hasty briefing: studied the route into the target, turning points, land marks on the Rhine, the dropping area coloured smoke signals, 500 foot altitude approach, slow to 130 mph air speed for bundles release at 1,000 feet and then 'get the hell out of there' tactic. Rest assured that I didn't sleep much that night - the mission would be my 43rd - more than anyone had flown in the 392nd.'

John 'Matt' Matishowski, the navigator in 'Big John' Beder's crew also took off at 0930 before climbing to 3,000 feet to form up, which took a whole hour, then let down to 1,000 feet and headed out. 'Our point of departure was near Folkestone and we got a good view of Dover's white cliffs as we headed across the Channel. As we approached landfall on the French side, the leaders up ahead turned left and flew directly over Boulogne, about eight miles south of our course. To have a large formation of Liberators pass overhead at 1,000 feet must have been quite a sight to the citizens of that city, but I thought, hell, we can show off some other time.

'We were still heading southwest when we left Boulogne and held that course until we reached a point twenty miles southwest of Lille and then altered course due east. I noted that we had gotten nine minutes late, which was not worrisome, since it made us less likely to interfere with the glider landings. If we had gotten early, we would need to kill time somehow before going into the drop zone.

'The whole world certainly looked different on this mission. 'Big John' was keeping a 1,000-foot reading on the pressure altimeter as the ground rose up to meet us south of Brussels. The terrain was not flat like the countryside we had practiced over and we were clearing it by 500 or 600 feet. The navigation was a lot easier than I had anticipated, because the 'Gee box' was working well and I was never in doubt as to our position and our progress. The 'Gee' signals appeared to come in okay at low altitude, but I knew better than to depend on a gadget that could easily be jammed or crap out, so I concentrated on navigating by reading the landmarks. I felt confident enough so that if the other formations took off on a weird heading, I would tell 'Big John' to wave goodbye to them and take off on our own.

'Imagine yourself in an upper level of a double-decker bus screaming along at our speed and that's the kind of navigation job I was faced with. The check points blew by us so fast I was only half-sure I had the right road or rail intersections, bends in small rivers, small towns with church steeples tall enough to make us turn aside.

'The flight-level wind was surprisingly high, at about 25 knots gusting into us from the east and I wondered what problems it would pose for the glider pilots and paratroops.

'We blasted across the farmlands, sometimes so low that it appeared we could drop the gear and wheel along some road that ran along with us, then 'Big John' would ease back on the yoke to slide over a row of trees or a set of wires, then drop back down again, skimming across the furrowed sea like 150-knot dolphins. We crossed into Belgium and came upon a hard-working farmer ploughing his field with a pair of draft horses. 'Big John' tried to give him some distance, but the horses reared up and he let them go. Then the farmer furiously picked up a rock or clod of dirt and flung it at us as we cruised by.

'On we raced until we found our target, a town about the size of Wesel. We reached the final turning point about fifteen miles southeast of Brussels and headed northeast on a 60-degree heading with ninety miles to go. I was free to move around as we had no need to use oxygen, so I went into the nose section to get a better view of the terrain. The tempo picked up as we slowly let down and the ground sped by more quickly. The gunners in the rear were getting ready to dump the bundles of supplies, which were rigged with parachutes and would be dropped through a hatch in the floor of the waist section. The biggest load however, was hung on shackles in the bomb bay and would be toggled out by Jack Murray. The whole drop totalled 2½ tons in each airplane. The sooner we got the stuff out, the sooner we could turn out of there and we expected the whole drop to be made very quickly.

'Now we were coming up to the Initial Point, with the Maas River flashing by, with ten miles to the Rhine and then five more to the drop zone. 'Big John' was getting us down on the deck and we wondered again, as we shot forward, whether the drop zone would be in our hands or theirs. The Rhine was coming up fast when suddenly someone yelled and a flight of Royal Air Force Typhoon fighters came dead at us and then scattered in all directions, barely missing us. They had been on close support and were heading back.

'The Rhine flashed by and we came into the fantastic panorama of a big battle in progress, with first-row seats suspended a hundred feet above the battleground, heading for the main action at 160 knots. Gliders were everywhere on the ground, some intact, some broken. Tow planes were splattered here and there, still burning. We passed flaming farm buildings on our left, their roofs blown off and columns of bluish smoke rising from them into the haze. There were troops all over the place, some crouching down; some scurrying around.

'Here's the drop zone!' I yelled, about the same time Jack Hummel did and 'Big John' pulled the Lib' up to 400 feet and slowed her down to 150 knots, the drop speed. The bomb bay load went out cleanly and the gunners were scrambling to get their bundles out. Then they were all gone. We had done our job. As the parachute-borne canister went down I looked forward and could see great flashes pretty close by and columns of smoke rising through the haze left by the smoke-screen of the early morning amphibious crossing.

'Big John' made his turn and got the formation around to the right and got back down and we realized with a shock that we were now directly over the battle line on the German side. We could see the enemy up very close for the first time, firing at us and moving around. We came up on a self-propelled gun, a monstrous thing marked with a black cross, its barrel swivelling around, tracking us. As we passed overhead, there was a big thump as it fired too late and missed us.

'E for Easy' is going down!' came a shout from the back end, but it was flying on the wing of the slot man directly behind us and I couldn't see it from where I was. There were calls of distress as Liberators were being hit behind us, big-calibre bullets smashing through the thin aluminium into fuel tanks, engines, hydraulic lines, living bone and flesh. The scene on the ground was very confused, with firing everywhere and tracers flying around and tanks moving off to our left in the haze and smoke. The noise of our engines seemed amplified, the noise bouncing off the ground just beneath us as we raced on, holding our breath; hearts' pumping a mile a minute.'

2nd Lieutenant James E. Reynolds, 'Jack' Hummel's co-pilot in 'E for Easy' wrote:[6] 'It was truly a low level mission all the way as I'm sure we never got over 200 to 300 feet at any time across England and France. I could see buildings and people as never before. We were flying formation and our lead airplane was to drop down to around 250 feet when we entered the drop zone. As we approached the drop area we found that there was considerable smoke or haze covering the area. We began getting a little small arms fire during the supply drop, for we could hear it hitting the plane. Our radio operator, James Deaton, stood at the entrance of the bomb bay, waiting for the drop, so he could enter and pull the static lines. The supplies we were carrying were enclosed in pods and hung on racks in the bomb bay of the airplane just like bombs. Each pod had a parachute attached to it and a static line was attached to the airplane that would pull the static lines attached to the bomb racks. When the pods were dropped, the static line attached to the airplane would pull the parachute open and break the 'free fall' of the pod. After the pods were dropped someone from the crew would go into the bomb bay and pull the static lines attached to the bomb rack back into the airplane so the bomb bay doors could be closed. Since there is little space in walking the 'catwalk', the person pulling the static lines back into the bomb bay could not wear a parachute.

'We made our drop and we started receiving intense ground fire from what we later learned to be 20 mm and 30 mm shells. Jack was flying the plane at the time and I kept glancing at the instrument panel for any signs of engine trouble. Shells kept hitting the aircraft and suddenly I noticed fire coming from No.3 engine. I hollered at Jack and told him engine No.3 was on fire and I was going to shut it down. All of the switches were on my side of the cockpit. I feathered the engine, cut off the gasoline supply to that engine, closed the cowling flaps and cut the electrical switches. The fire continued to burn. Jack hollered that No.2 engine had been hit and oil pressure was dropping. At the time of our drop we had slowed our air speed and with two engines out at this speed we could not gain altitude. Jack used what air speed we had to pull the airplane up to around 500 feet and hit the alarm bell button for everyone to 'bail out'. He and I both knew there was no way we could get out before the plane crashed. I remember saying a short prayer, 'Lord, it is all up to you now.'

'Jack picked out the first field he could find, which also contained the remains of some gliders, so we could make a controlled crash. No.3 engine continued to burn and just before we crashed Jack hollered for me to get on the rudders with him so I never saw the fire in number 3 engine go out... I had no recollection of the crash after the airplane touched down, so I must have been knocked out for a few seconds. The first thing I remember was 'Jack' asking me if I was hurt. I replied, 'I didn't get a scratch' and he replied, 'Oh, yes you did.' I then realized blood was running down in my face and the front of my flight suit was bloody.

'The crash had torn a large hole in the plane on my side of the cockpit. I crawled out through it and Jack followed. We stood about twenty feet from the plane and examined each other's wounds. Jack had a bad cut on the back of his head that was bleeding and I had a cut on my forehead that was still bleeding. As we stood there, we noticed the ground kicking up about us and heard gunfire, but we did not realize we were being shot at... As we stood examining our wounds, we heard voices coming from behind and we saw Hollis Powell, waist gunner Paul E. Keagle and engineer, Herb Finney standing beside what remained of the plane. Elmer Milchak was leaning out the waist window. They had all been in the back of the plane. Usually Herb Finney would have been on the flight deck with Jack and me since he was the flight engineer, but for some reason he was in the back and fortunate for him, for it is doubtful he would have survived the crash, since the top turret fell just where he would have been standing.

'We were getting rifle fire from soldiers that were shooting and walking toward us. There was also a German Tiger tank about fifty yards from us. The firing stopped after one of the crew opened a parachute and waved it at the Germans who were shooting at us.

Hollis Powell saw Elmer Milchak look out the waist window and then pull back, look at him and ask, 'Powell, are you alright?' Powell said, 'Yes.' He looked out the window again after he had turned to Finney and said, 'Powell's okay.' Those were his last words as a sniper (about 150 yards away in a wood thicket) shot him through the head and he slumped over the window edge.

Reynolds said, 'German soldiers arrived and Elmer's body was removed from the plane before it caught fire. Before the soldiers led us away I said the 23rd Psalm over Elmer Milchak's body. Our concern then was about Barney Knudson and Ellis Morse, who were in the nose of the aircraft and James Deaton for we knew there was no way they could have survived the crash.'

Deaton either fell or was hit by rifle fire over enemy territory. Knudson and Morse had bailed out of the nose position at only about 300 feet. The day after the crash, at a US aid station, Morse 'a sight for sore eyes', turned up wearing one flight boot and carrying the other. He said Knudson had opened the nose turret doors and pointed to the escape hatch as a signal to bail out. As Morse came out of the turret Knudson put on his chute and left the ship. He saw his 'chute come out of the pack but did not see it open.

The remaining crewmembers were taken to a farmhouse occupied by German soldiers, some of whom were shooting at B-24s as they flew overhead. In just a short time, the airmen were rescued by US soldiers from the 513th Paratroop Infantry Regiment. 'Afterwards we went outside and the airborne and glider troops were talking around, smoking and joking while a sniper was taking pot shots at us,' Hollis Powell said. 'Me? I'm under a German half-track or something, praying to be gotten out of this mess. Flak, high altitude, fighters whatever, I'll take, but this is not my kind of activity yet these airborne seem like it's just a walk through the woods.'

Within a day or two the survivors were flown back to Wendling where they were debriefed and given a ten-day 'R and R' in Southport. Then back to the base where they took a flight in the Black Widow under supervision to see if they still had the nerve to fly. They passed and went back to flying missions.

'We reached and crossed that critical, imaginary, political line separating allies from the enemy,' continues Donald G. Potter. 'We passed over, flying at an altitude where a well-thrown rock by a 118lb weakling presented a danger to planes and crews. At our height farms, houses, towns and people passed rapidly, about 150 mph, underneath. You could actually see the whites of their eyes as they raised whatever weapons they had handy to fire on those lumbering, huge targets, skimming by above. Many of the small calibre rounds struck the wings and fuselage. Some of the rounds went right through. However, many of the bullets entered at such an angle that they ricocheted randomly throughout the plane. The sounds the rounds made as they were skimming off interior multiple surfaces made you want to shrink at a rapid rate. Most of us, all through the mission, were sitting on our flak suits. The logic behind this decision was, almost all of the fire we would receive would probably come from the ground and who wanted to risk the very real possibility that one might hit you in the butt - a very un-heroic place to get your Purple Heart. What could you say when people asked you how and where you got wounded?

'As we flew over the town of Wesel at about 50 feet a tower that had to be at least one hundred feet high had a machine gun positioned at the very top 'hosing down' every plane flying by; we were no exception. We took a few rounds there and then we were over the river and past the town.

'We began to see gliders on the ground, hundreds of them. Some seemed to be relatively intact, while others looked like piles of junk. These represented the transportation that was used to drop a large number of troops and armaments behind the German lines. I presume, clear the right-of-way and secure the bridges for the movement of Allied forces. The story of the 'boondoggles' and the 'successes' of that command decision has filled volumes.'

In the 576th Squadron, 392nd Bomb Group, 2nd Lieutenant Carroll E. Russell, co-pilot on 2nd Lieutenant Herschel E. Proctor's crew in *Gashouse Gus* recalled: 'Our B-24 had been altered by removing the floor panel where the belly gun turret would have been. This left a gaping hole just back of the bomb bay section of the plane. Around this hole were the crates of supplies. Corporal George [Kouzes] and his partner, Corporal Jessie Gill from Texas were to push them out over the target area. When our group was assembled after takeoff, we made a low level flight over the North Sea to the drop zone. I remember the scene clearly because we were so low. It was much like a scene in the movies with much smoke and the ground littered with parachutes and gliders askew. Some gliders were upside down, others were missing wings. With our load out, we turned back immediately, but one doesn't turn a B-24 around quickly. The beachhead was small and we necessarily flew over German held territory as we turned. At our low altitude we were an easy mark for German ground fire and we were hit immediately. One engine quit and as soon as I could feather the propeller we were hit again back in George's area of the plane.

'I called back for a damage report but received no answer. I feared everyone was dead. I tried several times before Jessie answered and reported that they had been fighting fires - too busy to answer. There were no injuries. The fires were likely burning hydraulic fluid from lines pierced by the shots. Meanwhile Proctor had asked the navigator, Stanley Plagenhoef for a heading to the nearest airstrip. Stan found one twenty minutes away. Just then a second engine died from fuel starvation due to the ruptured lines from the shots. We could not gain altitude with one engine gone and with two out we were not able to maintain what we had. Proctor called for more power and I shoved the throttles through the safety wire into and past the red line. It didn't help.

'Obviously, we were not going to reach the airstrip, so we both began searching the ground for any clearing in the woods. Mind you we were just a hundred metres or so above the trees. I notified the crew to assume their crash positions. None of them, other than the flight engineer on the deck with us had any idea of our situation. Corporal Denver Kerfoot on the flight deck directly behind me was on his radio and had not heard my order to prepare for a crash. I ordered him to his station but by then it was too late. Proctor spotted a field just ahead and ordered the wheels down. I said a belly landing might be safer but he repeated his order and down went the landing gear and then the flaps. In this entire low-level ride, perhaps thirty minutes in all, I don't remember seeing a town or even a house. But then we were pretty busy and not sightseeing.

'As we came to a clearing I spotted a rock wall we had to clear before reaching the field. I used that wall as my benchmark to pass over before I threw the crash bar (a switch to kill all circuits to lessen the chance of fire.)

'Once over the wall we touched down with as nice a landing as Proctor ever made. The ground was soft which slowed and shortened our roll. A brick house at the far end of the field loomed larger by the second. Then the nose wheel broke back and we stopped abruptly, some good distance from the house. We gathered away from the plane and ministered to Kerfoot who suffered a broken leg when he was thrown out through the cargo hole. He didn't quite make it to his position in time.

'George Kouzes recalled that they did manage to get out and two of our crew was hurt badly and as best as we could we got them out because we were sure the plane was going to explode or start on fire. But we were saved of that possible problem. Many people gathered by their homes and our plane. One was within 75 to one hundred yards of going into the houses if we hadn't come to a stop! Then many gathered out around the plane; among them, a 3 to 4 year-old boy and his mother. The boy was crying and his mother, who could not speak English, managed to tell us the boy was crying for our crewmember that was hurt so bad.'

Gashouse Gus had got them as far as Hechtel-Eksel, a village in Allied-controlled northeast Belgium. The Liberator was one of two aircraft flying alongside Hummel that had to quit the formation due to damage and wounded crew members and land on the Continent.[7]

Suddenly, after 'E for Easy' had gone down 'Big John Beder's crew were again flying over the broken gliders and spilled parachutes, the pockmarked ground, all shrouded in the smoke of war. 'Matt' Matishowski picks up the story: 'British paratroops stood around in small groups, unpacking their gear, looking up and waving as we passed, ignoring a small group of German prisoners being marched off somewhere. 'Big John' got a little altitude and we could see the Rhine again, no longer a formidable barrier to be assaulted and, for this mission at least, the boundary of the promised land where we could sit back and see if we were still in one piece.

'I clambered back up to the flight deck and stood between 'Big John' and Sam for a while, all three of us talking at the same time about the Germans and the crashed airplanes and gliders, feeling a relief so profound that it drained us and then we were silent, back at 1,000 feet indicated, bumping along the countryside like a school of tired whales.

'Twenty airplanes? Twenty goddamn airplanes?' some disbelieving, rising voice said at breakfast two days later, as we read the write-up of our mission in *Stars and Stripes*. That was the initial report of the toll. Fourteen Liberators out of 240 had gone down in the target area, in all the different ways a mortally-wounded bomber can finish its life - and the lives of the crew dogs within. The rest comprised a trail of wrecked airplanes and wounded crewmen at emergency airfields on the route home. We had been directly over the enemy, or within range of his guns, or a matter of a few minutes and that was the price we paid.

'All of us on 'Big John's crew had a tough time digesting all of this. We had come through without a scratch, perhaps because the German gunners aiming at us didn't lead us enough and hit people behind us instead. The expectation that most of us had before the mission that the drop zone would be completely in Allied hands had not panned out. A low bluff we had passed over on the way out was expected to be full of British, but the Germans had not been dislodged. Well, everything else had been right on; the timing, the right drop area and altitude, the track in and out. And the drop itself couldn't have been much better, with the percentage in the drop zone up in the high 90s. And we hadn't seen one enemy fighter. But Jesus - twenty airplanes?'[8]

There was one final casualty in the 392nd Bomb Group this day, aboard *Ruptured Duck*. This ship had received heavy ground fire and two of the crew were wounded. The pilot, 2nd Lieutenant Lester Frazier landed at an airfield at Sint-Truiden, Belgium so that his men could get medical attention. He later said the bottom of the B-24 looked like a sieve from all the gunfire. The injured airmen were treated at the 40th Field Hospital. Radio operator Staff Sergeant Hervy V. Latour had been wounded in the arm and back while waist gunner Staff Sergeant Raymond Hamment's arm was badly shot up. Hamment died of his injuries later that day at 298th General Hospital in Liège.

Navigation was very good and unintentional deviations from course were few and generally unimportant. Two flights of the 389th Bomb Group did find themselves heading to the south of SDP 'W' and had to circle for a second pass. Coy Lawson recalled: 'The action quickened, when we saw the Rhine below. All hell broke loose - small arms, machine gun fire, a burst rattled off the fuselage. You quickly recall the time the Briefing Officer promised you over enemy territory. Finally, the load was pushed out the back hatch; we thrilled when you felt the thrust of full throttle. Flaps up and we accelerated from 160 to 190 as you turned tail and prayed. The pilot pulled up violently as we cleared the high lines atop the levee on the Rhine's east bank. We looked up from the radio position and saw the perspiration streaming down the pilot's right side of his face. I closed my mike and screamed, shouted, cursed, or did whatever was necessary to relieve the pent-up emotions. All four engines were still roaring and we were headed home. The entire mission was only five hours and twenty minutes long, but it seemed like ten hours waiting to see if you would be shot down by a rifle or machine gun.

'I hoped no frontline soldier would ever hear of or read this brief story, because I would not want him to know that I had an egg omelette at the Norwich Anglo-American Club that night and reserve Royal Circle seats at the Hippodrome!'

As the 389th Bomb Group neared the Rhine the 'Sky Scorpions' ran into a great deal of smoke from smoke screens and fires on the east bank of the river. 'This cut the visibility considerably' wrote Paul Robbins. 'We crossed the river at less than 200 feet. I remember calling Ned and warning him of a church steeple directly ahead of us. As we neared the target, we pulled up and lowered the flaps to slow us down as much as possible. And then; 'Bombs Away!' We immediately let down with full power on. I could see tracer bullets passing just in front of the nose. All I can remember is my wondering if the sandbags, which we had placed in the nose to counterbalance the extra weight in the waist, would stop the bullets. I could see flashes of guns on the ground everywhere and could hear the chatter of machine guns. I saw bursts of flak off to the side. On the way out we went over a town neutralized by the RAF the night before. It just wasn't there. You could still feel the heat from the fires. Nothing could have been more welcome than the Rhine as we came out and pulled up to 2,000 feet again. Men in PT boats, crossing the river, waved to us. I realized how glad I was to be up where I was rather than down in that living hell we had just left.

'Five miles beyond the Rhine to the west, it was hard to believe what we had just seen. Farmers were ploughing, women were hanging out washing and children were playing. Could it be possible that I had dreamed it up? I didn't want to go back to find out.'

At 1000 hours Gunner John White of the 25th Field Regiment Royal Artillery who, despite the hazy conditions prevailing, had witnessed 'a marvellous and inspiring sight' when the first troop-carrying Dakotas arrived from all directions, streaming across the sky in their hundreds with fighter escorts, to be later followed by gliders, 'one plane trailing two gliders'. Then, at 1300 hours he saw the Liberators, 'which went roaring overhead just skimming the treetops, with supplies for the troops. The bomb doors were already open and the cylinders containing supplies could be clearly seen all ready to be released.'

Dave Beadham of the 13th Parachute Battalion recalled: 'Full use was made of the German prisoners in the digging of weapon slits but it was easy soil to dig and the work was soon completed. Before it was we were to witness yet another display of Allied air superiority, this time by American Liberators. In its own way, it was every bit as spectacular as the mass gliders on the evening of 'D-Day' and the heavy daylight bombing raid on Caen. This show only lasted a minute from the first whisper of the fast approaching aircraft to the dropping of the Division's resupply. In a mighty crescendo of over one hundred engines the heavy bombers swept overhead only a few hundred feet up. No sooner had they passed, when the sky in front was filled with blossoming parachutes of all colours, drifting slowly to earth. The noise of the planes drowned the sound of the still active flak. One of the left hand planes reared almost vertically skywards, turned and dived steeply, exploding in a vast ball of flames as it hit the ground. Then all that could be seen of the resupply was the huge cloud of ugly grey smoke drifting up into the heavens.' Pfc Jack Trovato in the 155th Anti-aircraft Artillery Battalion wrote: A B-24 was one hundred feet up, directly over my head, with its wings aflame and a guy pushing cargo out the door. Seconds later, we witnessed a thunderous explosion as the plane hit the tree line.

The 446th 'Bungay Buckeroos' Bomb Group from Flixton, two miles south of the little Suffolk town, with Lieutenant Colonel William A. Schmidt, the Air Executive, flying as 20th Wing Commander, led the Wing with twenty-seven aircraft. Behind them came the 93rd 'Travelling Circus' at Hardwick and twenty-six B-24s in the 448th Bomb Group at Seething. Five out of the twenty officers at 20th Wing Headquarters flew on the mission, including General 'Ted' Timberlake, who flew in an escort aircraft.

Grey-white smoke shrouded the battlefields and engulfed the city of Wesel. Smoke canisters which had blacked out over sixty miles of the front for over two days were still burning. The Liberators passed the German city a mile to the south and continued to the dropping zone, pock-marked with wrecked and abandoned gliders, smouldering haystacks and dead livestock. The tremendous artillery barrage preceding the attack had devastated the countryside.

Flying as low as fifty feet, eight out of the nine 20th Wing Squadrons droned over the dropping zone at 145 mph using ten to fifteen degrees of flap to aid accuracy in the drop and loosed their wicker loads with attached multi-coloured parachutes. The blossoms transformed the zone into a Texas-size flower garden.

In the 448th Bomb Group, headed for SDP 'B', Sergeant Donald Zeldin, flying on *Old Glory* gazed out at the ravages of war. Brightly coloured chutes littered the ground and dead animals were strewn around the area. An accidental drop west of the Rhine by one B-24 in the lead element caused four more to drop all or most of their loads west of the river. Two other pilots in that group reported dropping at random in the American sector. The first formation made its drop at 1310 and the last about 1330.There seem to have been no major errors, but minor ones were sufficient to spread supplies all over the Diersfordt area. Fortunately, few pilots overshot the mark by so much as to put them beyond the territory held by the airborne, so almost all the bundles were recoverable.

The Liberators met with some spasmodic and highly accurate small-arms fire. Twenty millimetre fire pierced armour-plating and struck the formation stick of one of the 93rd Liberators but the pilot and co-pilot escaped injury in the subsequent explosion. The crew of *Wee Willy* in the 'Travelling Circus' had some close calls and watched the Hamminkeln church steeple go past at about the same height as the wing before the pilot turned around and regained altitude. Lieutenant William Voight's B-24 was one of those in the 448th Bomb Group that experienced the lethal fire put up by the German gunners, as navigator, Lieutenant Harold Dorfman recalled: 'A large bullet hole the size of a handball appeared in the skin (of the plane) along side of me, probably a 20 mm shell. I dropped to the armoured floor between the ammunition cans and landed on Lieutenant 'Shabby' Shabsis the bombardier. Our faces were about eighteen inches apart from the nose window and we watched more holes appear in the glass from machine gun fire. We covered ourselves with our flak jackets. I expected a bullet in the face at any moment. I could hear and feel the machine gun bullets raking the bottom of our armour plate that we were laying on. Suddenly there was a loud whine of high pressure being released behind us. We looked back. The nose wheel had been hit, just about a foot from my rear end. Still the machine guns raked the nose. The hydraulic lines in the wheel housing were hit; red fluid came out over everything, including my chute, which was soaked. A shell exploded between the pilot's legs, but mercifully the direction was away from him. However, the pilot's control cables were shot out. Voight lost control of the rudder; his controls were crippled. The thing that saved us was their snapping-on the autopilot which continued to work. We were at fifty feet all this time and still to clear one hundred foot high electric wires as we came out of the turn to re-cross the Rhine. By the grace of God did we get over that line of wires and out across to the friendly side of the Rhine.'[9]

Piccadilly Lilly (which was flying its 106th mission) flown by 2nd Lieutenant Hugh McFarland had their control lines shot out and crashed into a hill. Eight of the crew were killed; only Sergeants Fred Yule and Girthel Morrison survived. Lieutenant Francis Piliere landed *Miss Minookie* on the continent after two men suffered life-threatening injuries. Medics carried Sergeant William Garrett and Private Ronald Burke to the 40th Field Hospital for medical care. *Miss Muff*, the 448th lead ship piloted by Captain William Wilhelmi with Colonel Charles B. Westover, the Commanding Officer aboard, suffered serious damage by ground fire as they crossed the target. Wilhelmi suffered a gunshot wound to the leg and a waist gunner was shot in the shoulder. The tremendous barrage of small arms fire also damaged the landing gear. Miss Muff made it back to England and because of the damaged landing gear, Wilhelmi and Westover chose to crash land at the emergency airfield at Manston. No one was injured in the landing.

Arriving over Manston, Lieutenant William Voight's crew circled for thirty minutes assessing the damage of their plane. Its hydraulic lines were pierced, its tyres blown out, its wheels would not retract or extend and manual control cables were out and the only control the pilots had over the Liberator was the elevator. The autopilot kept the B-24 level but could only make left turns. Finally, Voight ordered the crew to abandon the Liberator. Harold Dorfman, with his parachute soaked with hydraulic fluid, was the second man out. The radio operator snagged his parachute and Lieutenant Fred Risinger gave him his and attempted to repack the damaged chute. At 6,000 feet he jumped with some of the parachute still flapping about. He pulled the ripcord with great anticipation and it opened. One man was injured while jumping out of the doomed aircraft. Everyone else, including Lieutenant Colonel Thompson, landed without injury. The badly damaged Liberator valiantly continued flying before eventually crashing into the sea.

In the 446th Bomb Group 1st Lieutenant Wright, 1st Lieutenant Laurence R. Lofgren and 2nd Lieutenant Dale D. Beasley had their aircraft knocked out of the sky. Wright's co-pilot, 1st Lieutenant William T. O'Connor left the aircraft with his parachute under his jacket and the chute failed to open. The rest of the crew returned to Bungay three days' later. *Queen of Angels*, piloted by Lofgren, who died on his 26th birthday, had its No.3 engine on fire in the drop zone and only two crew members were seen to bail out. One chute failed to open. The tail gunner Staff Sergeant Alan W. Keenen was the only survivor. The Liberator burst into flames after crashing from 300 feet. Beasley's B-24, 'F for Freddie' was hit by small arms fire. Two engines on the left side of the ship were out and the aircraft was burning while still in the air and blew up as it crashed. Beasley fought to keep the B-24 in the air rather than bail out and rode the ship down to his death. Navigator, Flight Officer James H. Anderson, who jumped through the open bomb bay after failing to get the nose-wheel doors open, was killed. Nose turret gunner, Sergeant John R. Heslin, bailed out and was picked up by a patrol of infantrymen from the 30th Division. Sergeants Thaddeus D. Nannam, top turret gunner and radio operator, Richard C. Brown also survived; Brown after parachuting into the Rhine.

A nose turret gunner, Staff Sergeant Floyd M. Bieniek saw one of the B-24s go down. 'He was too low and made a sharp bank. His wing hit the ground and he rolled in a ball of fire. We carried no guns and came in at an altitude of 500 feet. It was a sight to see, landed gliders, crashed gliders, some burning and some torn to hell. It was like a seat on the fifty yard line. Amazingly in the middle of all the fighting I saw this farmer with his ox ploughing a field. I guess it was time to plough. We received 102 small arms holes in our plane.' Sergeant Myron B. Bickel, one of the other gunners, was killed instantly by a .30 calibre bullet through the head.

Seventeen of the Bungay 'Buckeroos' sustained battle damage. In one of the Group's B-24s was Chaplain Captain John E. Gannon who recalled: 'They couldn't take any extras on this trip, so I went as a member of the crew. My job was to pull the rip cord on a pannier of ammo so it would drop through the ball turret opening. We were flying about 200 feet above ground and it was bumpy. Every bush had an airstream of its own and there were many bushes. Everything was ups and downs except my stomach which was always up. I lay down with my mouth over the opening and I gave Belgium everything I had eaten during the past several weeks. When I had nothing more to give I was still trying. We lost three planes on the Wesel mission. Two shot down; the other pin-wheeled while turning. An early returnee said that they thought the Chaplain was on that plane. The Operations Officer was up-a-tree, in-a-hole, down-a-well trying to figure out how to explain a missing Chaplain on a combat mission. When he saw me he heaved a sigh of relief and said: 'Chaplain, if you want to go on a training mission - OK - but don't you ever go on a combat mission again.' And so I didn't.'[10]

Myron Keilman in the 392nd Bomb Group had taken off with Eddy White and crew at 0930. 'Our assembly of 26 airplanes and the route to the drop zone near Wesel were bright and clear except for the tremendous smoke screen the Allies had laid down to hide their intentions and movements along the Rhine. As we flew across Holland at 500 foot altitude, I remember the windmills, the neat green fields of the countryside; and as we neared the Rhine, the scattered gliders and crashed transport planes. The navigator and bombardier kept us right on course and we spotted the coloured smoke signal at the drop zone just across the Rhine. Eddy throttled back, climbed to 1,000 feet slowing the airspeed for the release of the bundles. The bombardier released them in a salvo and Eddy turned the formation for home. The last airplanes in the formation swung wide after their bundles released and they were shot up very badly with 20 and 37 millimetre ground weapons. Three B-24s were shot up so badly they had to crash-land. Several men were killed. Some were taken prisoner by the Germans - but they were soon overtaken by American forces and freed. I vividly remember the 'scary' exit. As we rolled out of our 1800 outbound turn in the dense smoke, we were confronted with being on near collision course and altitude of an inbound group of B-24s. Talk about brushing wing tips! It didn't take long to ram the throttles to climb power setting and 'get the hell out of there!'

'As we zoomed across France and hadn't taken our positions as yet,' continues Hollis Powell, 'Jack' Hummel called back to Sergeant Paul Keagle's left waist gun position and wanted to talk with me. I hooked up to Keagle's intercom line and 'Jack' said to look out the left waist window. 'Jack' said, 'See that smoke stack up ahead?' I replied, 'I see it.' He said, 'Watch this' and he headed with his left wing right at the smoke stack which was about 75 feet high and I could see our wing was at least ten feet below the top of the stack, yet Jack kept course at the stack and just as it looked like he was going to take the top of the stack off, he deftly raised the left wing and cleared it by inches. Then in a pleased voice said, 'Powell; how's that for flying?'

'You don't express your true opinions to your commanding officer.

'As we neared the Rhine near our drop zone we took our positions. Sergeant Elmer Milchak the right waist gunner came up to me on the way over and said, 'Powell, you know what the first thing I'm going to do when I get out?'

'I answered that I didn't.

'He said, 'I'm going to punch you right in the nose.'

'As all these fellows were five to seven years younger than me, Jack had asked me to kind of keep a hold on things and at times I had to be a little bossy but never was there a better crew of buddies to fly with. Anyway I told him, 'Don't wait too long.' He walked away. About five minutes later he came back and said, 'Powell, I was just talking, forget it.'

'We were now in our positions and I saw we were up about 300 feet and all of a sudden my turret glass became fogged over as I understood later Jack had used the relief tube just before the run and I couldn't see anything. I do remember seeing vaguely, moments before the crash, it looked like two parachutes. I believe they were Lieutenant Bernard Knudson the navigator and Ellis Morse the nose gunner bailing out of the nose position. I couldn't see, yet it sounded like hail hitting our plane and a small explosion hit my right gun and my ear piece connection at the left side of my head was knocked out.

'Someone tapped me on the right shoulder and I turned. Staff Sergeant Herbert Finney the top turret gunner said, 'Jack said to jump.' I slid out of the turret. I always sat on my flak suit. I put my chest chute on. Wrong again. I always put the darn thing so that the rip cord handle was on the left side. I looked at the right waist window and saw that #3 engine was on fire and I could see the wing was melting and at a glance, I could see that only one engine was working. We were descending fast. I opened the escape hatch and immediately saw we were too low to jump. So we went into ditch or crash position. Up near the bulkhead we sat down with our backs to each other. I remember Milchak was looking for a place and I cursed him (sorrowfully) and pulled him down between someone and me. Milchak, Keagle, Finney and I were in crash position. We had only a second or two to wait and then we had our first bump, which I remember thinking wasn't all that bad and then the next bump settled us in and we got separated from our position. All I can remember is tossing and turning in all directions. At the very last I could feel my throat mike dragging the ground and then the top of my helmet kind of bumping along. I can still remember saying, 'God, help me' and no sooner I uttered the last syllable when we came to an abrupt stop. I found myself sticking from the waist out of a hole at ground level on the right side (the direction the plane was sliding). As I lay there for a second or two I saw Milchak look out the waist window and then pulled back and looked at me and asked, 'Powell, are you all right?' I said, 'Yes!' I felt no pain or lack of movement. He looked out the window again after he had turned to Finney and said, 'Powell's okay.' Those were his last words as a sniper (about fifty yards away in a wood thicket) shot him through the head and he slumped over the window edge. I did not see this part about Milchak but was told later.

'I was so dazed when I crawled out that I started to walk away, passed the tail section of the plane toward another little gulley with little bushes and small trees around it. I heard a lot of firing but I thought it was the ammunition in the plane going off. Then I thought 'why am I out here'. I'd got to see if anyone is hurt and turned and started back to the plane. As I got near, Finney said, 'Get down, they are shooting at us.' We lay with our feet in opposite directions and our foreheads together. We could hear the bullets hitting the plane. Finney said that he would look up and all of a sudden about fifteen holes would appear. They were using a burp gun. While we were laying there with our foreheads together a bullet kicked up dirt between our noses. I hadn't seen Jack or Jim Reynolds the co-pilot as yet. I had no weapons and I could now see the Germans in the gulley that I had been walking toward. I had an eight inch knife strapped under my pant leg. (It was useless).

'I remember looking around for something white to wave. Then I thought of that upside down chute and pulled the cord and it opened. I moved out about ten feet along the right wing and I could see Reynolds had a cut on his forehead and Hummel was hurt (later diagnosed as a broken collar bone). The crash was such that when it ended they only had to step from their seat to the ground. Everything had been stripped clean in front of them. As they stood there I heard Hummel say 'Let's fight them' but Jim said 'With what? You'll get us all killed.' All this time the Germans were still firing. 'Jack', his being an officer could perhaps have more effect so I said, 'Jack', they won't stop shooting; maybe you can get them to.' He (I know) reluctantly came under the wing and took the end of the chute and began to wave it. Almost immediately a man with an automatic rifle (burp gun) and a rifleman came out of the thicket about twenty feet and hollered and motioned for us to come to them. As the firing had stopped the others began to look for Milchak and Deaton.

'When they began to look for Deaton, I began to walk with my hands up toward those two Germans. As I got halfway there I came upon an American aid man with the white cross on his arm moaning and groaning upon the ground, wounded. I hesitated for just a second and said, 'Hold on, fellow, someone will get you in a few minutes.' Just as I hesitated to speak to the aid man the sniper who I believe got Milchak took his crack at me as I felt the air and concussion of the bullet as it went past my left ear. It sounded like someone clapping two boards together in my ear. I reached the two Germans and the one with the automatic rifle came up and directed me toward a farm house a hundred yards away. He spoke perfect English and I found out he had been educated in England. As we passed the gulley and thicket some German called out *Americana*? I said, 'Yes.' They replied, *Das is good, das is good*. The English speaking German said: *If you were English it would not be good*. He said something else about their dislike for the English. Just about that time a little short fat German coming from the direction of the farm came up and with visible hate in his eyes, stuck his bayonet against my belly and was really talking to the other one. I could see the gun was cocked and his finger was heavy on the trigger. I'm certainly no hero but somehow I believed this English speaking German was more human than soldier at that time and for some reason I remember no fear. I turned my head to the English speaking one and in an impatient way said, 'Make him leave me alone!' (Sounds foolish and I thought so on reflection.) He said something to the little fat one and he mumbled and moved on.

'We arrived at the farm house after passing a short smoking cannon. Other Germans were milling around, shooting at B-24s as they flew over. They looked me over and took a curious look at my throat mike and took my knife. Then we were put down into the basement where there were more Germans and two or three were wounded. Later the rest of the crew was brought in and sometime later Jack came out of the unit commander's office and said that in five to fifteen minutes the Germans were going to break out and they couldn't take us with them. They were going to have to shoot us. Then I was worried. The soldiers were friendly for the most part and I tried to convey my rights to be taken to a prisoner of war camp etc.

'The English speaking German took us into another room. Finney and I were questioned and things were getting more active but it didn't last long. All of a sudden he turned a heavy wooden table on its side and told us to get down behind it. We asked 'Why?' He said that the Americans might run by and toss a grenade in the window. We got down and shortly after he left we heard an American yelling, 'Anyone in there?' Finney and I jumped up. Finney went to the window, looked out and yelled back, 'Yes, we're in here, come in and get us.' To me at this time a stickler for details, it didn't sound exactly right so I got up and yelled, 'We are Americans; we are in here.' I can still remember that airborne man, tall, loose and gangly, rifle at the ready, coming down the basement steps kind of glancing over to a room on the left. I said, 'We are over here.' Then he asked, 'Did they hurt you?' I said, 'No.' Afterwards we went outside and the airborne and glider troops were walking around smoking and joking while a sniper was taking pot shots at us. Me, I was under a German half track or something, praying to be gotten out of this mess. Flak, high altitude, fighters whatever, I'd take, but this was not my kind of activity. Yet those airborne seemed like it was just a walk through the woods.

'While we were in the Germans' hands in the house I saw a soldier run up the stairs and at the window on the landing at the turn of the stairs take his position. He had no more than knelt down when you could hear the splat as a bullet hit him in the head and he tumbled down the stairs and a couple of his buddies just looked down at him as they passed, showing no emotion.

'When outside a sniper was being irritating. Someone gave the order to get that SOB and two soldiers walked around behind the shed or barn and pretty soon I heard a shot and no more sniper. I hope it was the one that got Milchak. It was from that direction.

'We crashed at 1310 England time and were at the aid station where we stayed the night about 1800 or a little later. As the firing was too close for comfort, we dug a good sized fox hole and lined it with grenades and weapons we didn't know how to use. As night came on we could see the fire fight less than a mile away, probably 500 yards and those tracers made the most beautiful sight. Yet we knew how deadly was the battle going on. We could hear the big guns all night, across the Rhine River sending their shells overhead and the whistling noise they made. For a long time I thought it was thunder and a storm was coming up. Many, many times we could hear a call out,

'Comrade, comrade,' as a German tried to infiltrate and often an English voice say, 'Get that SOB' and a burst of automatic - no more comrade.

'The next day we walked back to the plane and through the battlefield and young fellows were lying all over the place, some of them looking like they were just sleeping there, yet I turned such a one over to look at his back to see where he had been hit and he had no back, it had been blown away. I saw three glider men in crawling positions burned to a crisp, Germans by the score in their fox holes burned or shot. Finney and I took a walk with a soldier into a German farm home where a middle aged couple were eating, but I believe the man had shed his uniform because a belt, canteen and bayonet were in the middle of the floor. I started to pick it up but the soldier said no and made the woman pick it up and hand it to me. He said it might be booby trapped.

'The next day we were taken to the farmhouse or somewhere in that area and it seemed the Germans were columned up for miles and we were to help march them out. I believe it was just so we wouldn't get lost. But I saw the English speaking German as we passed or he passed us and our eyes met because I truly believe he saved our lives and let us surrender and kept us from being shot.

'On our way marching the Germans, we had a five minute rest, smoke, whatever, break and I remember sitting with my hand in touching reach of a young blond headed German who had that day or night before been killed and thought of searching but I felt it would be ghoulish; therefore I did not.

'Things began to be a little hazy to me after our rescue from the farmhouse but I know the events in this order because you don't forget such an experience. In fact at the aid station that evening we were wondering what had happened to Deaton, Knudson and Morse; the latter two had jumped we knew but no one had seen Deaton jump. Then all of a sudden coming across the field with one flight boot on and carrying the other, came Morse and he was a sight for sore eyes. He said Knudson had been killed on the ground.

'I remember the second night being cold at the front of a flight commander's tent at some fighter base in Holland. The rest had gone to some building to sleep in beds but I don't know why I stayed there. It may have been shock setting in. I refused to go in and lay there all night and about froze listening to the fighters landing and taking off. The next day we crossed the Rhine in a boat operated by about a dozen or more or less of British Commandoes with their blackened faces and grenades, knives, etc. You could just smell death around them; friendly but not talkative. They had jumped behind the lines before the invasion. I'll never forget them or the feeling they left with me, a special breed of men. I slept in one of their barracks that night and the next day we were flown back to our base in a transport plane. We were debriefed and given a ten day 'R and R' in Southport. Then back to the base where we took a flight in the *Black Widow* under supervision to see if we still had the nerve to fly - we passed - and were back to flying missions.'[11]

Briefing errors had caused some groups to take wrong positions in the line and though attempts were made to correct this situation, the confusion thus created seems to have caused recurrent overrunning and stringing out. Most inconvenienced by this was the 491st Bomb Group at North Pickenham, which led the drop at SDP 'B'. It had to make several 'S's' and doglegs to keep behind the 44th 'Flying Eightballs' and had to swerve again to avoid them as they reached the Rhine. At least one group went down on the deck to avoid the prop wash of its predecessor.

Donald G. Potter recalled: 'Our drop zone was coming up, so we did a pop-up to two hundred feet. On command, we started to manhandle the supply pallets and shove them through the ball turret opening. There was a lot of stuff and it took some time to get it all out. One of the troops [Sergeant Anibal C. Diaz] in a sister ship [Joplin Jalopy in the 506th Bomb Squadron] flying just ahead of us, had put his chest 'chute on during the unloading process. Probably thinking that if he was going to fall out of the turret opening, he would save himself by using his parachute. Now, a parachute at one hundred feet altitude is probably one of the most useless things a guy could own. Somehow his 'rip cord' got caught on one of the pallets and his chute opened in the plane. The chute was sucked down through the opening and opened with great force, pulling him to and through, the hole. No one in the crew had time to pull a knife and cut the parachute risers, it happened so fast. He had time to swing once before he struck the ground. His body was almost parallel to the surface when he hit. He did not survive.

'We descended to 50 feet again and started our 180 degree turn to take a reciprocal heading to 'get the hell out of Dodge.' As we steadied on course, Dick, the tail gunner was resting in the waist of the ship, after dumping supplies. Someone down below with an automatic weapon got a good sight on us and riddled the tail section. Lynch just happened to be in the right place at the right time. Dame Fortune was smiling. He would keep one of the slugs of that incident as a memento.

'We started to receive light 20 mm flak in addition to massive small arms fire from the ground. Shell was sitting in the waist just beneath on oxygen bottle. A round came through and punctured the flask. It entered at just the right angle so that the bullet spent the rest of its energy circling within the bottle, making spiral grooves on the outside that made it look like a mashed screw. The shrieking noise it made and the fire it caused scared the hell out of Bud. No casualties on board as yet. The fire was promptly killed with a handy fire extinguisher.

'We were flying in an element of three, V-formation, on the left. We flew over a gun position which possessed an '88', the most accurate and deadly gun the Germans had and he was firing... at us. The slow, lumbering shapes of the Liberators were made to order targets. The B-24 on our right received a hit on what appeared to be the number one engine, at an altitude of about thirty feet. The wing dropped and the pilot lost altitude. With a beautiful piece of handling, he managed to bring the wings level. His bomb bay hit the ground and the craft seemed to give a little bounce and was flying again. The pilot would have made it, but immediately ahead was a string of telephone or power poles and wire. (As I recall) he had to bank left in order to lift his right wing over a pole. In doing this his left wing dug into the ground and the plane started cart wheeling and exploded. In a great black and crimson flash, the crew and plane were gone. Nothing left but scorched earth and debris. I felt empty.'

It was *Southern Comfort III* in the 506th Bomb Squadron. In mythology the phoenix is 'a bird that can only be reborn by dying in flames'. So it was with *Southern Comfort*. Second Lieutenant Max E. Chandler and his crew, on their fourth mission, flew the 'phoenix' on the supply mission. *Southern Comfort's* gunners strafed the German gun emplacements in an effort to help the troops who were wading across the river with their guns held above their heads. The Liberators had to drop the supplies on the opposite bank. *Southern Comfort* was less than a hundred feet above ground-level when, hit by German small-arms fire, it lost an engine. The 'phoenix' rolled over and her belly struck the ground. She raised a cloud of dust and bounced into the air again to perhaps fifty feet and then exploded. Only two men, the 21-year-old tail gunner, Sergeant Robert D. Vance from Empire, Ohio and one of the waist gunners, Sergeant Louis J. DeBlasio survived. Robert Vance recalled: 'Our waist guns and ammo were removed in order to carry around nine supply bundles in the waist and aft section. This created a weight and balance problem. The bomb bay and number three engine were on fire when we hit the ground (belly and verticals), became airborne again for about ninety seconds, then hit the ground again the right wing hitting first, spinning us around and tearing the ship apart and then exploding after a few seconds. My right arm was put in a sling due to a cracked collarbone and my head was bandaged because of a severe laceration to my left scalp. We were hospitalized in Ahlen, the third German hospital, when we were liberated by American troops.'

'Lee', continues Donald Potter, 'was flying as low as he could possibly get. We were over a mature forest of pine trees that seemed to stretch forever. It seemed as if we were brushing the tops of some of the taller trees on our bomb bay. We could hear the scrapes. The other plane was also flying on our right. He was, perhaps, twenty feet higher. Hardly a minute had passed when he was hit also. It appeared to be the left wing area. He tried to control it as his nose went up and he stalled. Turned into his left wing and slowly, ponderously, majestically dove straight into the ground; it seemed to take forever. Time seemed to kick into ultra slow motion. There was another explosion, another crew and plane lost; another sooty scar on the land.

Kay Bar flown by 1st Lieutenant Leonard J. Crandell of Peoria, Illinois in the 67th Bomb Squadron had gone down seconds after *Southern Comfort* at 1314 hours, after the supplies were dropped. *Kay Bar* took a sudden climbing attitude nose high and at the same time the number one engine was observed smoking. The aircraft then stalled out and nosed directly into the ground from around 300 feet and exploded immediately a short distance from *Southern Comfort*. Crandell's entire crew, including 2nd Lieutenant William M. Hummer, navigator, of Mine Hill, New Jersey, a last-minute addition, were killed. Born 3 November 1923 in Dover, New Jersey. Hummer was a keen sportsman who, in 1939 broke his right clavicle playing football; in 1940 he broke his left leg playing baseball and in 1941 he broke his jaw wrestling.

At the point when *Kay Bar* was hit, Lee's crew assumed that they were still in range as Donald Potter recalled. 'Lee found a road that was cutting through the forest and in order to make our target smaller, set the fuselage down as far as he could over the road bed. All of our engines were running normally. All it would take would be one of those beautiful fourteen piston engines to falter and we would be history. The propellers were making kindling of the tops of the trees on each side of the road. This may have caused the adrenaline high of a lifetime. We were still receiving flak, but it was apparent the gun could not depress enough to make a hit.

'On our way out we lost our tail skid when we hit the top wire of a 'high tension' wire. Since I had returned to the nose, I had the best seat in the house when I spied two horsemen up the road riding like Valkyries. As the plane passed over them, both the sound and air compression sent them both tumbling and rolling in the roadbed, giving all of us a little comic relief.

'Finally we reached Allied territory and were able to climb to a more comfortable altitude. We had no problems getting back to home base and all kissed good old Mother Earth when we deplaned. I have forgotten how many bullet holes we counted on the plane. It seemed there must have been a hundred and no injuries, unbelievable.

'The Wing lost eleven ships on the mission; expensive. I had always wanted to go on a low level mission; now that I had I never wanted to go on another. The main thing that saved our hides was the judgment and execution of pilot, Leslie Lee and co-pilot, Don Wells and to a superb ground crew. We give credit when it is due.'[12]

The murderous ground-fire probably accounted for all fourteen B-24s that failed to return from the Wesel mission.[13] Apart from those in the 44th and 392nd Bomb Groups already mentioned, the 20th Wing lost three B-24s from the 27 dispatched by the 491st Bomb Group. *Hot Rock* captained by Lieutenant Paul Fox, 42-50749 O+ piloted by Lieutenant James W. Brown of Albuquerque, New Mexico and *The Green Hornet* piloted by Lieutenant Andy T. Wilson were the ones that failed to return. An eye-witness recalled: 'I was flying next to Brown and noticed his #3 engine was on fire. I called him and told him about the fire. Brown answered 'Roger' and seemed completely cool as if he had the situation under control. Then a second or two later his ship blew up with a sickening explosion. He wasn't more than 50 feet off the ground at the time.' There were just two survivors.

Hot Rock was seen to pull up into a steep climb with its bomb bay on fire. Paul Fox was evidently trying to reach a safe bail out altitude, but the B-24 went out of control, rolled over on its back and crashed hopelessly in an ugly burst of black smoke and orange flame. Andy Wilson reported his *Green Hornet* was severely damaged by ground fire and he was going to crash land approximately ten miles west of the Rhine. No one escaped from any of the three crashes. On a second mission the same day, 2nd Lieutenant Richard P. Rice returned over England with *The Flying Jackass* badly shot up and the hydraulic system out. He landed at Manston without incident, but the next day a Lancaster came down on top of the parked B-24, putting it out of the running for good.

The 445th Bomb Group lost two Liberators. The Group's 27-year old Deputy Commanding Officer, Lieutenant Colonel Carl Fleming of Henrico County Virginia, was killed on this mission when his B-24 was hit by small arms fire at 300 feet three miles southeast of Wesel and caught fire. No chutes were observed. The 22-year old co-pilot, 1st Lieutenant Jennis Morell 'Jack' Strickland was originally from Rocky Mount, North Carolina. Many of his letters to his wife Kitty at home in Prince Georges County, Maryland with their newborn son, Jennis III, dealt on his dreams for the future and were filled with different combinations of girl's names as they planned for the birth of their second child. Although he promised he 'would be home in a couple of months or so' his luck ran out. The B-24 was observed crashing in flames and exploding. Jack's brother Harold, an infantryman in the same battle, witnessed the crash but did not know that his brother was on the Liberator.

Also, *Ten Gun Dottie* piloted by Lieutenant Raymond P. Schultz which was flying off the port side of *Ole King Cole* flown by First Lieutenant Thomas A. Shafer and his crew on his 17th mission, just two weeks before his twenty-first birthday was lost with all nine crew. After dropping their bundles, Shafer took *Ole King Cole* down to fifty feet to avoid as much of the small arms fire as possible. In some cases he flew lower, having to pull up to avoid a row of trees engulfed in flames from the ground fighting. His Liberator was one of twenty-five Liberators that returned to Tibenham with varying degrees of battle damage.[14]

At Hethel *Stand By* in the 567th Bomb Squadron was the first B-24 in the 'Sky Scorpions' to land and the questioning began immediately, as Paul Robbins' recalled: 'Had everything gone all right? Did we hit the right spot? Did any planes go down? How did it look below? Was our plane damaged? From there we went to the lounge for coffee and sandwiches and then on to the interrogation. By now, the others were streaming in. Exciting talk was filling the air. Seven ships hadn't reported in as yet. Who were they? We filled out our reports and answered more questions. Yes, all the bundles had gone away on time. Our engineer had seen one ship crash and explode. I had seen a P-47 burning on the ground. No, our plane was not damaged (the next day we found that a 20 mm shell had hit our number three engine). Nothing was forgotten in their questions.

'Before returning to our barracks, we checked and found that six planes were still out. Our part was finished. Those on the ground were still fighting and other bombers were out bombing. But our small part was over. The mission was 'successful.' Three ships never came back.'[15]

One of these was the B-24J flown by Lieutenant Robert B. Bloore in the 565th Bomb Squadron. The nose turret gunner, Staff Sergeant John Young, who was on his 20th mission, recalled:

'We started across the field at about 150 feet. Suddenly, over the noise of the engines, I heard what sounded like banging of pots and pans. Puzzled by the racket, I began looking about and was surprised to see holes appearing in our engine nacelles and wings. It was shockingly clear that troops were in the area, but far from welcoming the bombers, were at pains to halt their progress. The woods were full of German troops, who were shooting and couldn't miss even with a hand gun. Their first shots struck the aircraft on our right and blew the No. 2 engine completely off; it banked to the left in an almost vertical attitude and disappeared. Then the lead aircraft absorbed hits that blew off the entire left fin and rudder, whereupon the bomber staggered off to the right.

Then it was our turn.

'My mind only began to function several seconds after the enemy began to open up. I knew we had definite orders not to shoot at anything on the ground for fear we might hit our own troops. As it was, I flipped on my gun switches and was traversing the turret in the direction of the gunfire when I observed two tracer shells coming slowly like Roman Candles. These slashed into the turret and reduced the interior to bent and torn metal, as well as entering the bombardier's compartment. Now Lieutenant Bloore shouted into the intercom

'We're crashing!'

'I experienced problems in opening the turret doors, but forced enough of a gap to drop back and down into the nose, where I and the bombardier, who was unhurt, briefly grinned at each other. Then, we moved towards the flight deck, which was interesting, since the supplies in the bomb bay were on fire. We got a little singed, but managed to take up our crash position, which in my case was behind the co-pilot. From here I could see the perilous state of our engines - No.1 feathered, No.2 on fire, No.3 running wild and No.4 windmilling.

'A large field with a row of trees appeared in front, but one wing smashed into them after the aircraft rolled. My next conscious image was of explosions, bullets going off, English and German voices and someone cutting off my jacket. I could not see a thing and promptly passed out again. (My eyes were swollen up and cutting off all vision, while my eyelashes, eyebrows and hair were reduced to burnt stubble.) On recovering consciousness again, my head was completely bandaged with just a slit for my mouth and my hands were also bandaged up to my wrists. My overall injuries were later confirmed as a semi-fracture of the skull, a collapsed lung and deep gashes across one eyebrow and the back of my head. I also suffered a severe concussion and my back was very painful.'[16]

Lieutenant Colonel Arthur Arend, Captain Jim Flynn and Tech Sergeant George Rollo of the 131st AAA unit, seeing the B-24 crash, immediately jumped into a Jeep, raced to the crash site and pulled out seven of the crew. Incredibly, the B-24 had crashed on an ammunition dump, in between rows of TNT! The wings and the tail section were torn off and the bulk of the fuselage was split open but had not exploded, but the soldiers had barely made one hundred yards when the blast of seventy-four tons of explosives knocked them over. Several people among the rescuers, which included German civilians, were killed in the blast, while the complete roof of a farmhouse was blown off. The explosion crater was one hundred yards long, twenty-five yards wide and fifteen feet deep. John Young said that he 'could never thank the fellows enough. They received the Soldier's Medal, but it should have been the Congressional Medal of Honor!'

Skerby and most of Lieutenant Richard J. Bennett's crew were killed when the Liberator nosed up to the right before sagging down from 300 feet, striking the ground. The bomb doors were closed, which indicated the supplies had been released but the supplies were still on board, though several crewmembers had already departed, including both pilots. Bennett later recalled that ground fire had made its presence felt early on when he was struck in one leg, followed soon after by a second hit on one hand. Then what he felt were 40 mm calibre shells that inflicted at least three blows, the last of which impacted with the nose turret; the resultant fracture of hydraulic lines set the fluid on fire, with the flames sweeping back over the cockpit. Now co-pilot 2nd Lieutenant Victor Surico called for a general bail out, to which no response was heard, after which he moved back through the fuselage to jump. Bennett put the crippled bomber on auto-pilot and followed Surico, although the prospects of getting out, let alone deploying a parachute at the current low height, seemed very poor. Great good fortune was on Bennett's side, since he got out just ahead of a ravine, whose extra depth worked in his parachute's favour, allowing it to expand and take its human load down to a safe landing. As he gathered up his canopy, the pilot could see his aircraft burning three miles distant. He could not know that just one other crewmember, radio operator Tech Sergeant Frank Wallace had shared his pilot's luck; the other seven either failed to survive their bail out attempts, or were killed inside the aircraft.

The third crew lost was captained by Lieutenant Harvey R. Mosher piloting *The Old Veteran*, which had flown no less than 113 missions with just three aborts. The supply drop had just been completed when the B-24 was hit by ground fire at 300 feet altitude and exploded on impact with the ground that left nobody alive.

The Liberators had met no opposition until after the supplies were dropped, but after that they ran into light flak and small-arms fire which in the opinion of some participants surpassed anything they had encountered on bombing missions. Astonishing to relate, the bombers' loss ratio was seven times that of the C-47s which had flown to LZ 'N' only a few minutes earlier. The losses and damage were so distributed that no single battery could have caused more than a small fraction of them. Some aircraft were hit very near their zones, others near Wesel after turning homeward. It seems possible that in some cases the momentum of the relatively fast and heavy Liberators carried them beyond the Issel before they could complete their turns, thus giving German gunners who had never had a shot at the C-47s nor revealed themselves to the flak eradicators of 83 Group an opportunity to spray the bombers at close range.

Wayne E. DeCou, a pilot in the 458th Bomb Group at Horesham St. Faith near Norwich, considered his was one of the lucky crews. 'We flew 34 combat missions over Germany and never had any serious battle damage or any crew member injured but after dropping our supplies it was every plane on its own, so I poured on the coal and headed for the deck but got trapped behind several other B-24s whose pilots weren't nearly as scared as I was, judging by their slow speed. There was no room to go under them, so I banked to the right to get around them. The plane I got behind evidently had a supply container hung up and it came tumbling out when we were right behind and below it. What a place to be! It was another lucky day for us as the chute was tangled up on the plane and the box was held up just long enough for us to get out of the way.

'It wasn't but a few seconds later that we ran into our first actual unusual battle damage. It was caused by machine gun fire from about forty or fifty yards away. I didn't enjoy looking down the barrel of a machine gun and having those bullets exploding only inches away on the flight deck. At least it didn't last long and there was only light damage to the plane as far as flying is concerned, but plenty of extra work for the ground crew to repair.

'Our next unusual damage lasted a little longer even though it was only a few seconds from start to finish. We were stuck in what was called the 'coffin corner,' which was the low plane on the left and rear of the Group. It was almost always the plane that German jets selected as a victim to work over with their four 30 mm cannons. First there was a short burst from our tail gunner and real quick a steady pounding from his twin fifties. It seemed like several minutes of this (probably only a few seconds) and then several loud explosions somewhere in the rear of our plane and almost at the same time a Me 262 jet went flashing by us, only a few feet from our right wing. Again, not much serious damage as far as flying the plane, but a lot of repair work for the ground crew.

'The next unusual damage involved a direct hit by an anti-aircraft projectile. It must have been an 88 mm as it was going pretty slow when it made a direct hit about two-thirds of the way back from the front of our left wing and only about four feet from the fuselage. Of course, it was a dud or I probably wouldn't be telling about it, but what makes it so unusual is that it made a gouge in the wing and then slammed into our left vertical stabilizer. If it exploded it was far enough away that it didn't bother us. In fact, we didn't even know that we had received two direct hits from one anti-aircraft projectile until we were back on the ground in England. So again, no big problem for us but more work for the ground crew. If this isn't a record for unusual enemy battle damage, I bet it is pretty close.'[17]

'Eddy' White landed back at Wendling five hours and fifty minutes after take-off - 'tired but satisfied with a job well done,' recalls Myron Keilman. 'Eddy, his crew and his close friend, Charlie Neundorf went pubbing that night on their bicycles to celebrate. The results of 'that mission' were more harrowing than actual combat. Can you imagine riding hell bent from a pub on narrow English country roads on a dark night? But that's another story.'[18]

Waiting to meet the crews were members of the Press who had sensed a big story. The audacious mission had gone well and that night Brig-General 'Ted' Timberlake, 20th Combat Wing received word through regular channels that Troop Carrier Command had expressed gratitude for the supply drop and had disclosed that 'immediate objectives had been successfully taken'. However, fifteen Liberators were missing and 104 B-24s returned to their bases with some degree of damage. At Seething, damaged aircraft filled the hardstands after the mission. *Wag's Wagon* flown by Lieutenant Neil McCluhan suffered numerous hits and serious damage. 'We lost the 'Gee Box', VHF, radio compass, remote compasses, vacuum and inverters and engine instruments for No.1 and No.2. Engines one and four were shot up so that we could only get about twenty inches of mercury on each of them. We climbed to up to 5,000 feet and came back to the enemy coastline. We then decided to come on across the Channel. Just as we got over England, our No.1 and No.4 engines went out. The hydraulic fluid was gone and only one good pump on the brakes. Just as we sighted the field, we lost No.3 engine and so we came in with only No.2 engine operating. We cranked the gear down. We landed at 150 mph and then we went off to the right side of the runway.'

Captain James Shafter taxied a damaged *Joker's Wild* around the perimeter track toward its designated hardstand after returning from their 24th combat mission. As they taxied on the perimeter track, Shafter experienced difficulties with the nose wheel and stopped to check if it was flat. As he stopped, Lieutenant McCluhan landed his battle-damaged aircraft. After veering off the runway, they continued across the grass toward the perimeter track directly toward *Joker's Wild*. Seeing the out of control Liberator heading their way, the co-pilot of *Joker's Wild*, Lieutenant John Paxson, gunned the engines in a vain attempt to avoid a collision but despite their efforts, the two aircraft collided, right wing tip to right wing tip, shearing the horizontal stabilizer off of *Joker's Wild*. Fortunately, only Sergeant Donald Clark was slightly injured. McCluhan received the DFC for his gallant efforts bringing his crew and badly damaged Liberator home. Other aircraft, including *Mother Of Ten* and *BTO*, landed at Seething with wounded on board.

The fifty-two tons of supplies dropped by the 448th at Seething were quickly utilized by the ground troops in exploiting the new bridgehead. The 17th Division G-4 was unable to collect more than about fifty percent of 306 tons of supplies dropped for that division. However, it was known that many bundles had been picked up and used on the battlefield without any report.

The British airborne reported that about 85 percent of their 292-ton consignment landed in the divisional area and ten percent to the north of it. On 7 April they reported having recovered about eighty percent, a very high ratio for parachute resupply. Probably the actual recovery ratio for the 17th Division was equally good.

The bomber men blamed the dispersion of the supplies on haze and smoke so thick that a formation half a mile ahead was invisible. Because the bombers were making their run at speeds 20-30 percent faster than those of the troop carriers and were engaged in an unfamiliar type of operation, this short field of vision was a particularly serious handicap for them. They also complained that reception of the M/F beacons had been poor. However, their 'Gee' sets had functioned perfectly, the VHF beacon beamed at SDP 'B' had worked very well and the columns of coloured smoke at the drop points had been plainly seen by many pilots.

Probably the biggest source of error was approach from too low an altitude. Many flights came in at altitudes between one hundred and three hundred feet and some pilots had to zoom to clear the high tension line. This sort of hedge-hopping was not conducive to accurate navigation, nor could pilots coming in on the deck have a right to expect much assistance from either radio beacons or visual aids. Another factor contributing to dispersion was the time taken to eject the bundles. Bundles in the bomb bay could be released by turning a switch and those in the rear of the B-24 could, if all went well, be shoved out in six seconds after the men there were notified by the alarm bell, but a bulky bundle or a fouled line could easily cause enough delay for a plane moving at

150 mph to go a mile or two. There was also an element of risk inhibiting hasty movement around an open hole. One man was whisked through the turret well along with the bundles he was pitching out.

Before the last bomber dropped its load of supplies, the airborne troops had made contact with advance elements of Second Army. As the afternoon advanced other contacts were made and German resistance disintegrated at an accelerating tempo. Accordingly, although 6th Airborne Division requested that the resupply mission for 'D+1' be sent as scheduled, Second Army cancelled it about 1600 on the 24th on the grounds that it was not needed.

Endnotes Chapter 8

1   Quoted in *The 448th Bomb Group (H): Liberators over Germany in WWII* by Jeffrey E. Brett (Schiffer Publishing, 2002).

2   *Mission Most Memorable* by Donald G. Potter, quoted in *44th Bomb Group: The Flying Eightballs* (Turner Publishing Company, 1997).

3   Quoted in *392nd Bomb Group; Twentieth Century Crusaders* (Turner Publishing Co, 1997).

4   *24 March 1945, A Small Part In The War* by E. Paul Robbins, quoted in *Stories of the Eighth: An Anthology of the 8th Air Force in WW2.*1983.

5   *Not A Good Day* by Hollis C. Powell Sr., writing in the *2nd AD Journal*.

6   *The Liberators Who Never Returned*.

7.   *The Liberators Who Never Returned, 24 March 1945* by Peter Loncke.

8   Quoted in *392nd Bomb Group; Twentieth Century Crusaders* (Turner Publishing Co, 1997).

9   Quoted in *The 448th Bomb Group (H): Liberators over Germany in WWII* by Jeffrey E. Brett (Schiffer Publishing, 2002).

10   Quoted in *The History of the 446th Bomb Group (H)* compiled by Harold E. Jansen.

11   *Not A Good Day* by Hollis C. Powell Senior, writing in the *2nd AD Journal*.

12   *Mission Most Memorable* by Donald G. Potter, quoted in *44th Bomb Group: The Flying Eightballs* (Turner Publishing Company, 1997). Don flew a total of 33 combat missions.

13   Total casualties were five men KIA, 116 MIA and thirty WIA.

14   *Red Rose and Silver Wings; a WWII Memoir* by Kitty Strickland Shore (Bill Adler Books Inc, 2002).

15   On 14 April Lieutenant Ned Ansell's crew had a lucky escape when *Stand By* was one of two B-24s crippled by fragmentation bombs dropped from above by B-17s on the daylight raid on Royan just after Robbins had closed the bomb bay doors. Two crewmembers who died were probably killed instantly but the remaining men on board parachuted to safety before the Liberator crashed. Quoted in *The Sky Scorpions: The Story of the 389th Bomb Group in WWII* by Paul Wilson and Ron Mackay (Schiffer Publishing, 2006).

16   Of the two other survivors, co-pilot Lieutenant Donald Smith and bomb aimer Donald Huelsman, the latter later died of his injuries. Quoted in *The Sky Scorpions: The Story of the 389th Bomb Group in WWII* by Paul Wilson and Ron Mackay (Schiffer Publishing, 2006).

17   Wayne E. DeCou writing in the *2nd AD Journal*.

18   *I Remember:Eddy White* by Colonel Myron Keilman, writing in the *2nd AD Journal*.

Chapter 9

A Bankrupt Estate

The Rhine lies left and right across our path below us, shining in the sunlight - wide and with sweeping curves; and the whole of this mighty airborne army is now crossing and filling the whole sky. We haven't come as far as this without some loss; on our right-hand side a Dakota has just gone down in flames. We watched it go to the ground and I've just seen the parachutes of it blossoming and floating down towards the river. Above us and below us, collecting close round us now, are the tugs as they take their gliders in. Down there is the smoke of battle. There is the smoke-screen laid by the army lying right across the far bank of the river; dense clouds of brown and grey smoke coming up. And now our skipper's talking to the glider pilot and warning him that we're nearly there, preparing to cast him off. Ahead of us, another pillar of black smoke marks the spot where an aircraft has gone down and - yet another one, it's a Stirling; it's going down with flames coming out from under its belly - four parachutes have come out of the Stirling; it goes on its way to the ground. We haven't got time to watch it further because we're coming up now to the exact chosen landing-ground where our airborne forces have to be put down; and no matter what the opposition may be, we have got to keep straight on, dead on the exact position. There's only a minute or two to go, we cross the Rhine - we're on the east bank of the river. We're passing now over the smoke-cloud. 'Stand by and I'll tell you when to jump off.' The pilot is calling - warning us - in just one moment we shall have let go. All over the sky ahead of us - here comes the voice - Now! - The glider has gone: we've cast off our glider. We've let her go. There she goes down behind us. We've turned hard away, hard away in a tight circle to port to get out of this area. I'm sorry if I'm shouting - this is a very tremendous sight.

32-year old BBC radio broadcaster Richard Dimbleby flying with 6th Airborne.

In that same glider (a Hamilcar) there was another BBC correspondent, Stanley Maxted, the Canadian Broadcasting correspondent who had landed with First Airborne at Arnhem during 'Market-Garden'. Maxted wrote later: 'There was just a minute or two of quiet as the great Hamilcar ran in with the sound of the rushing wind in her wings. Then when just a few feet off the ground, pandemonium broke loose - the wicked snap of Spandau machine-guns, mixed with the slower bang of 20 mm incendiaries for just a fraction of a second before they started pricking out their trademark in the thin skin of the glider. Things seemed to happen too quickly for me to take them all in at once. There was an explosion that appeared to be inside my head, the smell of burnt cordite. I went down on one knee. Something hot and sickly was dripping over my right eye and off my chin and all over my clothes. There was a doom-like lurch and a great rending as smoke, dust and daylight came from nowhere. I saw the Bren carrier go inexorably out of the nose of the glider, carrying the whole works ahead of it and wiping two signallers off the top of it like flies. Even then the bullets kept crashing through the wreckage. It didn't seem fair; but then there is no 'fair' or 'unfair' in airborne fighting.

'At the moment of impact a jeep trailer that was chained just behind me came forward about six inches and caught me in the small of the back. Mercifully the chains held on. Somehow Captain Peter Cattle and I hurled ourselves off the mess into a shallow ditch by a hedge. Looking up and clearing my eyes with the back of my hand, I saw a man pinned across the chest by wreckage. One of the glider pilots was getting him out. How those glider pilots and the two signallers on top of the carrier escaped the mass of that hurtling iron carrier I'll never know, but they did. A doctor came along and dressed Peter and me and helped us to a dressing station. On the way I saw burning gliders, crashed gliders and the great courage of men going in to fight almost before they had finished touching down. It was the old story of the men with the maroon berets who never worry about odds. The ground was covered with a mist of smoke from our artillery bombardment and that was what had made it nearly impossible for the men to find their landing zones and spots. We spent the next four hours with that regiment; we had to. When contact was made with the men on our left, we made our painful way through them to Divisional HQ. Here, that remarkable young firebrand, their general, told us that all objectives had been reached and that when the Second Army linked up he would hand them over in good shape and his job would be done. That has now taken place.'

Stanley Maxted was one of three war correspondents that went in by glider. The other two were Leonard Marsland Gander and Geoffrey Bocca. Three other war correspondents elected to parachute; Reuters correspondent, Seaghan Joseph Maynes, Australian-born Alliott Alan Whitfeld Wood and American Bob Vermillion. Using a Remington Model 2 portable typewriter to write his story in a ditch astride the Utrechtseweg after the 1st Airborne Division's landing near Oosterbeek, Wood had the distinction of being the only newspaperman to send dispatches from Arnhem. Unluckily Wood, 'the bravest war reporter I ever met' according to Gander, was wounded in the leg during 'Varsity' and lost the limb. Bocca was later captured, but was released after a few days none the worse.

Watching the drop from a church tower, war correspondent R. W. Thompson was prompted to write: 'It was a heroic, a glorious and terrible sight. I saw one Dakota in flames fail to land by inches. He was coming in perfectly when his wheels touched the telegraph wires and over he went in flames. An inch, a split second and all would have been well. They had survived the worst. They were almost home.' Choked with grief, the correspondent added: 'The burning bodies of those young men are one of the images that can never be washed out. We did not speak for a long time and never of that.' Thompson would add later, 'the screeching of panic-stricken beasts beneath the harsh wheezing stutter of the machine guns and the bursting squawk of the Bofors and the thunder and cracks of every kind of artillery... The wet smack of Spandau bullets on the earth wall on which we lay and the whang of bullets hitting the telegraph wires... And I shall never forget the tragic sight of Dakotas in flames and the price paid in human life for victory. And overhead, above the flaming wreckage of aircraft and men, a lark trilled its spring song.'

Australian born war correspondent, Alan McCrae Moorehead wrote: 'Indeed it was a wonderful sight. They passed only two or three hundred feet above our heads, the tow planes drawing sometimes one or sometimes two gliders and flying in tight formation. Then single planes with the parachutists waiting intensely inside for the moment to plunge out of the open hatches. Here and there among all these hundreds of planes one would be hit by ack-ack fire and it was an agonizing thing to see it break formation and start questing vainly back and forth in search of any sort of landing field and then at last plunge headlong to the ground. Within a few minutes nothing would be left but the black pillar of petrol smoke and the unidentifiable scraps of wings, propellers and human beings... The Germans were waiting for. '

Ground resistance in many parts of the landing area was at first vigorous and effective. Artillery and incendiary bullets destroyed 32 gliders and the occupants of 38 others were so pinned down by German gunners that they could not unload. That unloading went as well as it did was attributed to the fact that most of the gliders were Mark II Horsas which had hinged noses as well as detachable tails.

At 1021, as soon as the British paratroops had finished jumping, 6th Airlanding Brigade commanded by Brigadier Robert Hugh Bellamy DSO was to arrive. Two hostile aircraft were sighted en route, but none attacked and the high-flying British column suffered little from flak. It lost only seven aircraft and had 32 damaged. At least 402 of the gliders were successfully released in the combat area. Haze, smoke and dust from the artillery and air bombardments reduced visibility to between 1,000 and 3,000 yards but helped to some extent to shield the fliers. Releases began about ten minutes early and ranged from the planned height of 2,500 feet to 3,500 feet. So accurate were the releases that about 90 percent of the gliders landed on or very near their zones, many of them within one hundred yards of their objectives. Only half a dozen missed the landing area by more than a mile and those landed to the south in the territory of the American airborne. The Horsas and Hamilcars fared much worse than their tugs. About ten of them were shot down and 284 were damaged by flak. The high releases gave German gunners plenty of time to get their sights on the gliders and they made the most of it. About half of the gliders were damaged in landing, which is not surprising considering the brittle nature of the Horsa, the inexperience of many of the pilots and the difficulties of landing through smoke and under severe fire.

Staff Sergeant John Free who served with 'B' Squadron, 1 Wing the Glider Pilot Regiment had trained as a parachutist in 1942 and served in North Africa and Italy. Reveille was at 0400 that morning and after an early breakfast and a great deal of preparation, 'B' Squadron took off at 0730. On board his glider, Staff Sergeant Free carried a jeep and trailer, a heavy motorcycle, miscellaneous wireless equipment and seven personnel from the

Royal Corps of Signals. The trip took two and a half hours and the glider landed at Hamminkeln at almost exactly 10 o'clock. There was a good deal of enemy opposition as they landed, consisting of ack-ack guns and small arms fire. Nevertheless, the glider landed intact and personnel and equipment were evacuated safely, finding themselves in the thick of fighting that went on for the rest of the morning. Initial opposition was dealt with fairly swiftly and troops rendezvoused at Hamminkeln and dug in expecting some form of counter attack. However, the remnants of the German troops in the area withdrew past the task force during the night. They could be heard talking as they retreated. At this point, the operational involvement of the Glider Pilot Regiment was officially finished and Staff Sergeant Free and his colleagues were transported to Eindhoven airfield in Holland from where they flew home with RAF Transport Command. Their gliders were of course left on the Rhine Plain. Only 88 gliders, less than a quarter of those reaching the battle area came through unscathed. In total, 98 Army and RAF glider pilots were killed on this operation and Staff Sergeant Free counts himself a very lucky man to have survived.

There was extraordinary air pollution above the landing zones, a stratum of murk described by a reporter in a Halifax as 'a gigantic curtain over the battlefield, hiding all that was going on underneath'. Sergeant Vic Miller, flying a Horsa towed by a Stirling from Great Dunmow, remembers the green light signalling him to release from his Stirling tug and being unable to pick out anything on the ground. 'I hung on hoping for a gap, a glimpse of something. It was a total blank.' Howard Cowan, a reporter, was aboard the Horsa and as it cast off Miller told him, 'Now is when you pray.' Turning to his RAF co-pilot, Miller shouted 'For God's sake, if you see a space with a glider on it, we'll have a go.' As they broke through the bottom of the cloud, Miller was shocked to find himself down in the very field he had been searching for.

Thirty-two year old Lieutenant Sydney St. John, who piloted a Horsa carrying a jeep, a motor cycle and a dozen men, was, like most pilots, nonplussed by the great cloud. No warning had been given of the phenomenon and he pondered its proportions with trepidation. Some fliers, remembering Merville, attributed it to shelling or bomb attacks. 'Visibility was perfect and everywhere you looked there were tugs and gliders. It was extraordinary.' Earlier, at one of the many briefings and pep-talks the men had endured, a brigadier had exclaimed excitedly, 'won't those blighters be amazed when we cross the Rhine!' Looking around, St. John could not help but feel that 'anyone would be amazed to find 1,300 gliders suddenly heading towards him.'

A description of the approach and glider landing was given by Brigadier Geoffrey Kemp Bourne in *By Air to Battle*, the official account of the British Airborne Divisions, published in 1945, shortly after the operation.'[1]

'From the Meuse I could see the Rhine, a silver streak and beyond it a thick, black haze, for the world like Manchester or Birmingham from the air. For the moment, I wondered whether the bombing of Wesel, which had preceded the attack upon that town by Commando troops, had been mistimed. If this was so, then the whole landing zone would be obscured by the clouds of dust which would be blowing from the rubble created by the attack. In accordance with orders, but against my will, for I wanted to see what was happening, I had strapped myself in. We began to go down in a steep glide and I listened with strained interest to the excited converse of our two pilots, neither of whom had been on operation before... Presently, I heard the first pilot say to the second, 'I can see the railway'. Then I felt much relieved and soon I saw the landscape flying past the windows. We landed very fast, went through a couple of fences and stopped with a jerk. All of us, consisting of the Defence Platoon of Divisional Headquarters, nipped out and took cover under a low bank on top of which was a post and rail fence. There was a lot of shooting about a mile away. We had arrived only about 600 yards from the pre-ordained spot.'[2]

The Glider Pilot Regiment's task to land Brigadier Bourne's 6th Air Landing Brigade[3] at Hamminkeln and elements of 3rd and 5th Parachute Brigades within their DZs and Divisional Headquarters east of the Diersfordter Wald went almost as planned. 6th Air Landing Brigade arrived at its landing zone with only one mishap. A light tank in one of the huge Hamilcars broke free from its lashings en route and fell through the floor. Tank, glider and all personnel on board went down like a rock. The large Horsa and Hamilcar gliders were towed singly, but their size necessitated a longer landing run, making landings even more perilous. The 440 British gliders came in from 2,500 feet, dropping through the smoke and into heavy fire. The 6th Airborne came under heavy fire as the troopers began to land. With their heavy loads and long landing runs, the British gliders quite often plowed into other gliders, trees or buildings before their pilots could brake to stop. Although 416 made it into the landing zone and delivered their loads safely, the other 24 crashed, raked by enemy fire.

Although wounded in the glider landing, Stanley Maxted had covered the action: 'The clock in the station was still going, the ticket racks were full of tickets and the booking clerk's peaked cap was lying just inside the wicket on a table. Out beyond the platform was a line of box-cars. Men were standing between the box-cars and firing. Others were lying at the bases of some of the trees beyond with Bren guns and automatic rifles. Smack in the middle of the booking hall on the floor was a wireless set with its fishing-rod aerial. A signaller sitting beside it was listening. Coming through those headphones just then were sounds of some of Germany's best remaining troops in a terrible state of nerves calling through to their command posts that they were surrounded - or under fire - or being attacked and please send up guns or tanks - send up anything. This struck me as being the shape of things to come. A major with a lisp who had discarded his helmet and put his red beret back on was kneeling by a window looking through binoculars at some farm buildings behind us. Out by the box cars a man was setting up a mortar. There was a crack from the buildings the major was looking at and he yelled, 'I've got the so-an-so! Mortar, left one degree - Three rounds gunfire.' I watched while the loading number put out three, dropped three fan-tailed demons in the muzzle of the mortar. They banged out high into the air and the second one obliterated a sort of dovecot in the end of a low barn among the buildings. The major called, 'That's it - that's got him - give him three more.' There was no more from those farm buildings. Down toward the river beyond the trees a company of men were deployed. The glider-borne troops involved in this part of the action wear the badges of three very famous old county regiments - the Royal Ulster Rifles, the Ox and Bucks and the Devons. In some other setting their actions might have reminded you of some nursery game. One section would rise up and go forward like Indian bush fighters. They'd be covered by fire from the rest. Then another section went forward in the same way until all the platoons had worked their way in a converging movement on to the bridge that was one of their objectives. It really is an occasion, to watch these airborne troops fight. When they first come out of their gliders, with magazines blazing, to fight for their landing zone it's more or less of a scramble, but from then on their operations are cold - deadly methodical.'

At the railway station meanwhile, Staff Sergeant David Brook and the troops had now dug themselves in and were preparing for a night counter attack. 'The walking wounded were told to get themselves to a large country house about half a mile away known as 'Gut Vogelsang'. We walked through trees, some with great difficulty, the seriously wounded being carried on stretchers. It was nightfall when we saw the tall imposing building among the trees. Exhausted, I lay down on the floorboards of a large downstairs room. I dozed fitfully and later was aware of a trooper in an adjoining small room which I had the door open, gasping in a terrible way at about 120 to the minute. He had fearful chest injuries and had been injected with morphine by the small toothpaste like tubes with a needle which we all carried. They had turned him over on what remained of his chest and left him.

'For some time now the heavy background rumble of Monty's artillery on the other side of the Rhine had been growing in intensity and the house was beginning to vibrate. I noticed that at about half hourly intervals as if at a stroke the noise increased in volume as the barrage lifted and crept nearer. The whole earth seemed to be shaking now and one could not identify individual explosions. It was just one vast eternal explosion that never varied, or dropped for a second only to get closer and closer to where we were. 'A creeping barrage,' I thought. 'I wonder whether they know exactly where we are and whether they will stop in time?'

'Outside the machine guns started up again as the promised counter-attack developed. Close fighting was taking place in the orchard round the house and the woods beyond. Our Ox and Bucks, Devons and Royal Ulster Rifles were defending our position whilst the barrage lifted again so that it must only be half a mile away, or so it seemed. The noise increased until it filled everything. The building was now shaking and I could not believe that we were going to live through it. I could not conceive of a noise any greater than this. It seemed to fill my whole being and when suddenly it stopped, it was as instantaneous as if the conductor of a symphony orchestra had waved his baton for the final chord. The silence that followed for a minute or so was uncanny and I realised that something was missing. As the barrage had stopped so had the struggle for life of the wounded trooper. After the terribly fast gasping for air the silence was uncanny.

'In the morning some tea was prepared in buckets and I chewed a few more of the concentrated biscuit-like food from my 24-hour ration pack which was all any of us had to eat since leaving England. Later we learned that the tanks from the Panzer Division were approaching down the half-completed autobahn. A little AOP Auster appeared, circled and dipped only to be fired at. It climbed up again and continued circling lower when again it danced away from some light ack-ack. The dodging and circling by the brave army pilot continued until the first of the 'Taxi Rank' rocket-firing Typhoons arrived. One by one, they dived over our heads and the swooshing of their rockets hissed off to find their mark until the threatened tank attack was no more.

'At 10 am the linkup between the airborne forces and the 2nd Army was forged. The operation had been an unqualified success, opening up as it did the way to the Ruhr and the heartland of Germany. But of the 8,000 British Airborne troops, over 1,000 were casualties and of these by far the greatest percentage of killed and wounded was sustained by the Ox and Bucks and the glider pilots who carried them to the easternmost landing zone round the railway station.[4]

Medic John Cooper in one of thirteen gliders from Earls Colne carrying the 195th (Air Landing) Field Ambulance to LZ 'R' had an uneventful flight until nearing the Rhine, where a smokescreen covered the countryside. 'This made it extremely difficult for the pilots to determine where our LZ was. The LZ comprised a circle approximately twenty miles in diameter with the nearest point to the Rhine ten miles east of the river. We would occupy half while the Yanks occupied the other half. Not only was there flak, it was accurate and targeted specific gliders and aircraft. Creating further problems, our own fighter escort weaved in and out of the gliders and dived to attack specific flak guns. Although, as promised, there was little heavy artillery fire, it has to be remembered that the gliders were made out of plywood and therefore were very susceptible to light AA or anti-aircraft fire and even to small-arms fire.

'We were cast off at 3,000 feet and came down to ground level in three swoops and below 2,000 feet machine guns targeted us. Despite the warnings received at the briefing, the undercarriage of our glider did catch the power lines and we nose-dived into a ploughed field. The skid, in addition to the tricycle wheels, was forced through the floor of our glider, later leading to difficulties in getting the jeep out. All of us inside thought it was the end when we crashed so heavily into the ground, so half hanging in and half hanging out of our seat straps, we clumsily released ourselves. My instructions were that I was to be first out of the rear section. I would then receive the packs of the remaining occupants. This I did. My first sight on disembarking was an 88 mm self-propelled gun. Fortunately, it was pointing away from us. While fortunate for us, it was not fortunate for a Hamilcar glider. Larger than our Horsa, the Hamilcar landed and proceeded to unload its cargo of two armoured cars laden with ammunition. The first of these had just reached the foot of the ramp when the 88 mm gun scored a direct hit, sending the whole assembly into the air in a terrible explosion. I don't think anyone on the Hamilcar could have survived. I prayed they wouldn't look in our direction, but they had plenty of targets to choose from. There was nothing left for it but to get on with my job and when I'd finally put all our packs on the ground, I noticed a hole 24 inches in diameter through the tail of the glider. It wasn't far from the place that I had just recently been occupying. It sent a cold chill down my spine. In Normandy, fighting had taken place over a period of two or three weeks over the landing zone and a great deal of damage had occurred to the gliders.

'We set about disconnecting the glider's tail section and according to the drill that we had performed on many occasions this was accomplished by unscrewing eight quick-release bolts. We had to take care to release the last two simultaneously, at which point the tail would fall away from the fuselage. This was done most meticulously, but nothing happened. In an effort to dislodge the tail, we swung on it. It was all to no avail, because all that happened was that the glider rocked on to its belly! It seemed ridiculous that in the middle of a battle we were swinging on a glider's tail like a bunch of naughty children. Then someone realised the pilots weren't anywhere to be seen. So off we went to look for them. They were trapped in the smashed cockpit and couldn't get out. So in the end we said 'Bugger it' and we decided that the only course of action was to chop away the glider's nose. This we did and the pilots were eventually released.

'We now had a nose-less glider with the hole large enough for the jeep to be driven out. The driver started up the engine and released the clutch. However, due to the damage to the floor the jeep's wheels were resting on the ploughed earth and simply spun around. A solution was quickly found as German machine guns were firing in every direction. Bits of the glider were pushed under the wheels. Consequently, when the driver engaged the clutch again, the jeep shot out like a champagne cork from a bottle. It travelled one hundred yards before he could stop and return to us. He was still shaken when he did as a sniper took a shot at him and hit the steering wheel. I've never seen a jeep reverse so fast. We loaded the equipment on to the jeep but after a discussion to determine the direction of the assembly point machine-gun fire persuaded us to take refuge in a nearby farmhouse. We found a glider party of eight from brigade headquarters had already occupied the house. Not a minute before we arrived, two of them that had been outside behind a wall had got shot. Four of our party dashed out and brought them in and tended to them. Unfortunately one died a minute or so later; the other one had a serious wound through his shoulder. Luckily we had the medical ability and stores to help him and we took him with us when we left.

'The officer in charge, seeing that I had a revolver, detailed me to guard one side of the house. So there I was at an open window, protected only by a mattress, armed with a pistol with which I doubted I could hit a barn door at six paces. Fortunately, I was not called upon to prove it. At approximately

15.00, we saw the brigade major, a very tall Scot wearing a kilt, stroll across the landing zone as if he was out for a leisurely walk in Hyde Park. How he was never killed I don't know as he stood out like a red lamp post in the middle of Dartmoor. We were advised that our route to the main dressing station was clear and so with the wounded man on the jeep we headed in its direction. When we got there we were immediately put to work. The initial casualties had been fairly heavy. A first count revealed a loss of 40 per cent of the brigade. A number had been taken prisoner, only to be released after a brief period and were therefore able to rejoin their units.

'Of the thirteen gliders carrying 195th Field Ambulance personnel, one came down in Holland. Another, with fifteen personnel, was captured as it landed, although the Americans released them a few hours later. A third, carrying twenty-five personnel, was also captured and they remained prisoners of war till the end of the hostilities. Because of the number of casualties, I was put on stretcher duties. At midnight, half the unit was stood down and I was able to get some sleep till 0600, at which time I had to complete a report for divisional headquarters. Finally, we ate some breakfast. It was the first meal we'd had since leaving England over twenty-four hours earlier, although we'd been sustained during that time by cigarettes. During the afternoon the 15th Scottish Division, spearheading the land troops, reached us after crossing the river. Some of them seemed to have a problem with distinguishing our men from the Germans and there were a few angry confrontations because of it. The Field Ambulance moved on 26 March. Travelling 30-40 miles a day, on the way we passed numerous unarmed and unguarded Germans soldiers, twenty to thirty in number. Some were Fallschirmjäger Luftwaffe paratroopers and if they were giving up then the war was near its end, thank God.'[5]

Landing on 24 March the 225th (Parachute) Field Ambulance established their MDS in some farm buildings at the edge of the woods and were soon treating the casualties from the landings. The German infantry pulling back from the Rhine actually marched through the farm buildings without discovering the MDS. On the afternoon of 25 March the leading units of the 15th (Scottish) Division, linked up with the airborne division.

Major General Bols and his HQ party were piloted by county cricketer Major Hugh Bartlett, who delivered them to within one hundred yards of the projected command post at Kopenhof Farm.

Sergeant 'Tug' Wilson and Sergeant Tony Wadley's journey took three and a half hours and the only incident Wadley recalled was the sight of a Horsa 'a little to our right breaking its tow over the North Sea; the Air Sea Rescue boys no doubt speedily picked them up.'

'When we reached the Rhine we could see smoke rising from the ruins of Wesel and as we passed over the river a bit of flak started to come up. The release point came and we cast off and headed towards the field. Our touchdown was smooth enough but slightly too far into the LZ as we realised when we rapidly approached the end of the field and a low embankment. It was obvious that even with the 'barn door' flaps down and brakes hard on, we had no hope of stopping in time. With an almighty crash the undercarriage was wiped off by the embankment and the nose ended up in the ditch on the other side with the rest of the aircraft pointing towards the sky behind us. Everyone climbed out somewhat dazed but unhurt and we took stock of the situation. Normally we would have swung the nose section open, laid down our two portable ramps and driven the load out of the glider - that is how it had been done on exercise! 'Tug' Wilson offered to place some plastic explosive round the hinges of the nose section and we all retired behind the embankment to await results. Nothing happened so 'Tug', with a show of commendable courage went back and fitted some new detonators and this did the trick. After a good deal of effort on all our parts we got the jeep and trailer out, the troops on board and off they went down the road. Our Horsa, or what was left of it, was forming an effective road block which required the assistance of a passing Bren carrier before the road was made passable. In the process large pieces - the whole tail unit for example - came adrift and anyone passing later must have thought we had made a singularly bad landing.

'Our group of glider pilots were allotted the task of providing defence for Division HQ and each crew dug themselves into foxholes in the small orchard by the farmhouse and awaited developments. As it turned out, we didn't need to do any 'defending' as it was fairly peaceful in our area. The weather was fine and sunny and we spent the time watching the 2nd TAF Typhoons peeling off above us and diving down to fire their rockets at an unseen enemy to the east of us. We spent three nights by the farmhouse before being ordered to return. On 29 March we were flown back to England and landed at Down Ampney in Gloucestershire.'[6]

Twenty-nine Stirlings had reached the DZ and several were hit by flak. LK137 on 570 Squadron piloted by Warrant Officer Symmons never returned. Symmons gallantly held the Stirling steady while his crew bailed out and left it too late to make a successful escape himself, being killed by striking the tow hook. The aircraft was seen to crash in flames. Two of his crew reported back to Rivenhall a few days later. At their return to Rivenhall in time for lunch after a five-hour flight several crews on 570 Squadron reported having seen the launching of a V2 from North-West Germany. 'A bouquet' was also given to the ground crews for one hundred per cent serviceability of the aircraft. The following day all crews were briefed for possible re-supply dropping to the Allied troops on the Rhine but in the event no sorties were flown and all the crews were eventually stood down.

196 Squadron at Shepherd's Grove, which supplied thirty Stirlings carrying a total of 89 troops plus many vehicles lost only one aircraft, flown by Flight Lieutenant Van Rennan, to flak. This aircraft made a safe crash-landing in Holland. A member of the crew was badly wounded but happily he survived. 299 Squadron at Shepherd's Grove supplied 29 aircraft (103 troops carried plus many vehicles) without loss. Nos. 190 and 620 Squadrons at Great Dunmow each supplied thirty Stirlings and 24 Hamilcars and six Horsas.

As Halifax 'N-Nan' on 297 Squadron approached the coast they were joined by more and more squadrons of tug aircraft, more Halifaxes, Stirlings and some Albemarles. By the time they had crossed the coast, south of Harwich' David Vickery, from his vantage point in the nose, could see the whole sky in front of him: 'Ahead were the formations of C-46 Commandos and C-47s and Dakotas carrying the paratroops. Aircraft, tightly packed, aircraft above, aircraft below and to port and starboard, each with its attendant Horsa or Hamilcar. Over the sea, I went up to have a look out of the astrodome and looking aft, could see hundreds and hundreds of 'kites' in a huge phalanx, stretching back about forty miles. It really was indescribably impressive. Returning to the nose, I observed squadrons of fighters overtaking our formation at about angels five, whilst other members of the crew who could see switched on their mikes and excitedly remarked on the hundreds of our bombers. Lancs, Mitchells and Bostons returning from their task of softening up targets on the east bank of the Rhine. Somewhere between Rotterdam and Antwerp we were joined by a huge formation of Dakotas towing Waco gliders flying beneath us at 500 feet.

'The landing zone selected for our gliders was east of a wooded area about six miles north of Wesel and the release point over an elongated lake three miles before the LZ. We made a 10° starboard turn south of Goch and I got a pinpoint over Udem. Then I saw the Rhine ahead. I was struck by its width; truly, a big river! Five minutes to the RP. A Stirling down on our starboard bow about seventy yards away received a direct hit, probably from an 88. It disintegrated (apparently slowly) and its glider disengaged smartly. I vividly remember watching the air bomber come out through the shattered nose, doubled up and turning over and over in the air and thinking, 'My God! He hasn't got his chute on'.

'Then the big river was below us. There was masses of activity on the ground; flashes of gunfire; lots of smoke. I counted many burned and broken Messerschmitts. I learned later that the 51st Highland Division and Guards' Armoured had crossed earlier in the day at Xanten and were then engaged on the east bank of the Rhine, I called to 'Pinky' in the tail, 'Stand by' and then 'Release' and he flashed the signal to our glider pilot. We all felt the effect of the glider's release and 'Baldy' put the Horsa into a steep dive - a lesson learned on 'D-Day'! The Skipper came on the intercom and asked for a course for the rope dropping area. The flak was lighter on the starboard side so, without hesitation, I said 'Diving turn starboard and we'll drop the ruddy thing in the river'. Jack Tipper, the wireless op, remarked that there was enough nylon in the towrope to make two thousand pairs of nylon stockings. He would! You could hear which way his mind worked. Then we emerged from the chaos and set course for base.[7]

Tom Staniforth continues: By the time we arrived with the rest of the enormous gaggle of gliders and tugs at about 1030 hours, the defences were fully alert and as we trundled along at 500 feet, they shot at us with everything including rifles. We released our glider and made a wide sweep over the dense wood which must have hidden a large number of enemy troops so we let go the heavy glider towrope in the hope that one of the massive fittings on the end would lay a German low.'

Over Holland Rosemary Britten saw the shattered towns and villages below and the vast smoke-screen over the Rhine and wished their glider luck as it cast off towards the dust and smoke. Immediately, Langtry began evasive manoeuvres to dodge the flak now directed at them. A shell hit the Halifax, almost severing the control column and peppering the fuselage but miraculously missed the fuel tanks and the crew. As 'D for Dog' limped back across the Rhine it was clear they were out of immediate danger from the battle below but it seemed certain they would be forced to bail out soon. 'By that time, I knew I was going to be either killed or court- martialled and was amazed to find I didn't really mind either. I remember thinking that now I wouldn't have to live to a dreary old age, which was a good thing. But I could do with a year or two, now it had come to the point... George went back to the turret to get his hat, so I got mine too, just in case we survived, in which event, one might as well put up as good a show as possible.' Fortunately, 'D for Dog' made a safe landing at an American base at Merville, near Lille and Rosemary was flown home later to find that four crews had reported 'D-Dog' shot down. 'I felt rather bad about turning up after all and decided to acquire an operational twitch at least!' Of course as an Intelligence Officer she should not have been on the operation and she kept it secret for forty years!

Rosemary Britten's uncle, Major Ian Toler, found himself surrounded on his LZ by misplaced American troops but without hearing a shot for the first few minutes. He had landed short of an area raked by 88 mm fire but soon small arms rounds began to hit the glider. With a Bren gunner covering them from behind the wheels, Toler and George Telman struggled to unload their Horsa, sawing through the joints to get it open. Once clear, he made his way to a nearby farmhouse where the German farmer's wife began to scream at him in German. Angrily, Toler shouted back: *Das is deine Kreig - this is your bloody war. You started it. If we want to use your house we jolly well will.* Realizing that there were pigeons in the loft that might be used for messages, he ordered them killed but relented when he found they were the pets of the farmer's young son, his anger suddenly gone as he saw the tears in the child's eyes and realized that these people were not his enemy. 'Within a short time,' said Toler, 'we heard the unmistakeable noise of tanks. Surely we weren't going to be attacked by Panzers? Then they appeared. The Sherman tanks of the Guards Armoured Division. What a wonderful sight. It brought a lump to my throat to see them as they roared past and to realise that they were now advancing into Germany.' It was then that he was informed of the death of one of his fellow officers.

However, his erstwhile pilot, Staff Sergeant Arthur Shackleton, came through unscathed. After release and on final approach, anti-aircraft gunners blew away a large part of his Horsa's starboard main plane and shredded his rudder but he managed to land with his members of the six-pounder anti-tank gun. However, the quick release mechanism used to secure the gun and jeep towing vehicle had become fused after being struck by anti-aircraft fire and rendered inoperable. A nearby REME unit came to the rescue, remedied the damage and off went the gun and crew. While the gunners were salvaging their six-pounder, 'Shack' and 'Willy' Williamson joined up with Arnold Baldwin, Joe Mitchie and Jock Glover who had taken up defensive positions with Canadian paratroopers. During this time they enjoyed the services of Luigi Marco Antonio, a young Italian who had been conscripted into the Wehrmacht. The Canadians had taken him prisoner and left the glider pilots to guard him. Because his life had been spared Antonio showed his appreciation by brewing up and performing similar domestic duties for his guards. Arthur and his pals had taken a liking to the young Italian and were sorry to say their goodbyes when the time came to depart Hamminkeln and return to England.

Weather conditions were favourable and all combinations of 1,500 aircraft and 1,300 gliders. German fighters were conspicuous by their absence. Two tugs of the Woodbridge force returned early with engine trouble and one glider broke loose soon after take-off. With the Channel safely behind them, a further two Hamilcars parted company with their tugs because of broken tow-ropes, one over France, the other near Brussels, while near Goch a Hamilcar lost its tail unit, went out of control and crashed. Despite the laid-out aids, a smokescreen along the Rhine's east bank made it difficult for the glider pilots to pick out their correct landing zones. Five Halifaxes were lost to flak and three others were damaged, but the trailing tow-ropes and the risk of collision were a greater peril. Apart from one glider of the Woodbridge force, which landed prematurely on the west bank of the river, the remainder released correctly.[8]

Captain Richard Smith in the Ox and Bucks recalled that when he had taken off it was a lovely morning. 'We had a perfect flight up to the Rhine itself. Our purpose was to attack the gun emplacements about eleven miles the other side of the Rhine to prevent them shelling the Rhine crossing. We met the most incredible flak which was supposed to have been neutralised beforehand by the RAF.' Smith's glider landed near the dropping zone close to Hamminkeln railway station. The front of the glider was hit by a shell and the glider caught fire. He and the signals sergeant hauled their door open and tumbled into a German slit trench. The two pilots scrambled out and ran for cover to a farmhouse, but the signallers in the glider were burned to death. The glider was burning furiously and the ammunition inside was exploding. After some nasty adventures the survivors found some champagne in the farmhouse cellar. What was left of the regiment was placed in defensive positions. Altogether a rather unpleasant 24 hours.'[9]

Glider pilot Alan Spicer whose Horsa was towed by a Dakota picks up the story: 'Our company was supposed to be dropped at Hamminkeln, on the far side of the Rhine, not far, someone said, from the town of Hamelin of Pied Piper fame. We didn't need to be told when we were near our Dropping Zone. Those innocent-looking little black and white puffs were familiar enough from all the war films I'd seen - what wasn't so entertaining was the crump, crump of their explosions above the hissing of the glider as we were released from our rope to start our long descent and now we could also hear the very realistic sound effects of rifles, machine guns, bigger guns and see those puffs getting bigger and closer - and the realisation came to me that this was not just a bit dangerous, it could be suicidal, especially as some of those machine-gun rounds came straight through the side of the glider and wounded four of the lads and killed one of them. But it was all happening too fast to have time to worry properly and seemed quite unreal. Then, as we could see the flaming and broken gliders on the ground below and other gliders milling around, apparently aimlessly, I had the not very comforting thought that the only way out of this thing was to land on that hostile ground and then begin to fight our way to our first objective, whatever that was to be.

'While I was telling myself that one problem at a time was plenty, our pilot was more usefully engaged in wrestling with his rather limited controls and losing height far too quickly and too steeply I thought, quite prepared now to risk the landing, as long as it was a landing. They say fear is relative, well I'd got enough for ten men going around in my stomach. Then, in what seemed one continuous manoeuvre, we suddenly flattened out of our dive and seconds later there was an almighty thump and a lot more bumping and grating than I thought you should get in the air, until I realised that we were juddering along on the ground. We had landed. Knowing that the longer we remained in our Horsa, a prime target, the greater the danger of being trapped, we set about leaving it with the minimum possible delay, dragging the wounded with us. Get out first and worry about what's outside once we're there - that was our immediate philosophy. And then I found I had one less cause for concern. Along with more pressing problems, the prospect of the eight-foot drop to the ground with all my battle gear and among unfriendly people had been exercising my mind on and off since take-off. But fortunately our undercarriage had smashed off on landing, not to mention half a wing and the exit was now at ground level. All I had to do was step out and run for it, but where to?

'I recall a scene of utter confusion like nothing we had done in training. Figures were running, shouting, running, shooting; jeeps were revving and skittering off on urgent missions; guns and trailers were being hauled out of gliders and parts of gliders scattered about the landscape at crazy, impossible angles with dead men hanging from them. And more gliders were coming in to land, or crash, from all directions. And our faithful transport, our home for the past three or four hours, was now abandoned and skewed across the field with one wing snapped off and its back broken, its job done, our safe arrival a testimony to the skill and cool bravery of our pilots, for the moment unappreciated, unthought of. I certainly thought of them and their passive charges as one of the larger, jeep carrying, gliders, ablaze from about halfway along its fuselage hissed by low over our heads like a flaming torch before hitting the ground and skidding along on its belly to come to rest in a blazing pyre of broken wings and fuselage. There was no sign of life as it blazed from one end to the other like a Viking ship set ablaze for a funeral pyre. There but for the grace of God... And, through it all, a haze of writhing smoke and mist pierced by the sun, still shining as if the world was still normal.

'The apparent chaos evolved into some semblance of order and we moved off to take our first objective, the town of Hamminkeln, about a mile or so down the road. Not too far unless you are being sniped at for most of the way, but we eventually got there and proceeded to move through the town, virtually house by house. Every house is a potential nest of Germans. Some fight to the bitter end, others give up after a short fight. Our casualties are building one at a time. By the time we get to the last houses, we clear them with grenades. Each room gets one as we are fed up with Germans popping up from nowhere. Two of us stand either side of the door, in goes the grenade, when it detonates we follow it in, firing our Sten guns. If there is anyone in here they know what they can expect. We do the same upstairs. At the top of the stairs I throw the first grenade down the landing corridor. After it detonates, I hear the words 'Kamerad!', 'Kamerad!' I signal the lads following me and we cautiously work our way down the short corridor at the top of the landing, checking each room as we go, ready to fire at anything that moves. We find an old dead German in one of them, one of Hitler's last-ditch, makeshift army made up of boys and old men, the Volkssturm. They are everywhere in the town. All they have as a uniform is a coal scuttle helmet and an armband. But they all have weapons of one sort or another, so they are extremely dangerous and can expect no mercy if they fire on us. Then I hear the word Kamerad again and it's coming from the room at the end of the corridor. We edge our way toward it and I kick the door open and wait to throw the grenade while the others cover me.

'There are four bodies in there, all dead, all in contorted positions. Two of them couldn't have been more than fifteen years of age. The other two are old men at least sixty years of age. They have an assortment of weapons including an MG34 and stick grenades. Half the outer wall has been blown away and bricks and cement dust lie on top of them. It looks like a PIAT was used against them. And there in the far corner was the origin of the moaning. An old man with a chest wound. He was lucky in some ways as he'd been away from the main blast. We walk over to him and he looks up at us as if he expects us to shoot him. Instead we tend to his wound, give him water, inject him with morphine and I wait with him until the overworked medical orderlies come and pick him up. I even share a block of chocolate with him and a cigarette while we wait. We now have Hamminkeln firmly in our hands. The rest of those first days are a series of disjointed scenes, a sort of screen montage.'

Sniper John 'Snowy' Wiley recalls: 'We were now down to 450 feet and underneath the trajectory of the 88 mm guns, although the machine guns and multiple 20 mm cannon were still having a field day. I was looking out of the cockpit window, over the shoulder of one of the pilots, when I saw a Hamilcar glider ahead of us bracketed by 20 mm cannon fire break in two as it was hit. The tail slowly came off, as did one wing and then it gently turned on to its back and spiralled earthward; black smoke followed it downwards. Below and slightly in front of us was a small town, which must be Hamminkeln, our objective. The pilot suddenly shouted 'Stand By!' and we all interlocked arms and lifted our feet, bracing ourselves for the crash-landing, for that's exactly what it was, like all landings; once you hit the ground, the only thing the pilots could do was use the huge wing flaps to slow the glider down. There was a loud, harsh noise as we collided with the ground and the landing gear came up through the floor. We literally bounced into the air three times and finally slithered along the ground towards the houses ahead. It seemed we would never stop before colliding with them. As it was, two houses took off our wings and a large shed in between acted as our final brake. It smashed the nose of the glider to a pulp and killed both pilots, but by a miracle, although it threw us around, it stopped short of seriously injuring any of us.

'There was no time to worry about the pilots so the platoon commander was up and screaming 'Go! Go! Go!' and was their first out the door, followed by Corporal Trubshaw. I was next. Both of them never made it - they were knocked back into nil by a machine gun that opened fire from about 200 yards away. Behind me there was a mad rush and I was pushed forward and by sheer luck escaped getting shot as the two bodies absorbed the impact of the rounds and then just fell to the ground. I just scrambled over the bodies and threw myself on to the ground. The machine gun killed another couple of the lads as they emerged. In all, we lost five men getting out of the glider and had six wounded. Those of us that got out poured fire into the building where the machine gun was and it stopped firing. But now we had another problem. German artillery and mortar had now begun to pound the LZ and surrounding fields. In one way we were lucky as we were actually on the outskirts of Hamminkeln and the guns weren't registered on the town.

'Before I moved I was totally mesmerised as I watched two Horsa gliders attempt to land nearby. One tipped up on its nose and fell over on to its back; the other hit the ground with its starboard wing and cart wheeled before becoming upright, saw a couple of men scrambling out of the second one; nobody got out of the other one. I also watched a Dakota trailing flames with men still trying to get out of it; it crashed just beyond the town. Meanwhile, one of our heavily laden Hamilcar gliders came in very low over the LZ. You could see the tracer round hitting it, some going right through. I prayed that they would make it, but it smashed into a railway signal box and broke up like a child's glider when it nose-dived into the ground. By now, all around us there was organised chaos as units pushed forward to their objectives regardless of their casualties. As we entered Hamminkeln there was a church tower that cost us a few men as it had snipers in it that were picking off easy targets. As I was a sniper myself, I tried to fire on them, but I was so close to the church all I could see was the very top of their helmets. The CO organised a 6-pound anti-tank gun to sort the problem out. It blew the tower to pieces and we were in no mood to take one of them who survived as a prisoner when he came out of the church door with half a grin on his face. The Germans had also fortified a number of houses and we had to use PIATs on them before we rushed them. At one point we were getting fired upon from somewhere down the end of a street. The CSM yelled at me to sort the problem out before we lost any more men so I carefully looked at where he could possibly be firing from through my telescopic sight. The obvious place was a large house and a slight movement in the back of a darkened room caught my eye. Once I looked closer, I saw it was a boy of no more than sixteen or seventeen years of age. He was resting his rifle on a couple of sandbags set on a table in the middle of the room, typical of someone trained as a sniper. I didn't hesitate. I shot him in the head and clearly saw the impact of the round knock his head back and send him backwards. I never felt any emotion as I had seen too many of my mates killed the same way. Sometime later, two of us went to confirm the kill and sure enough he was there, dead. He was no more than seventeen years of age, one of Herr Hitler's SS Hitler Jugend judging by his collar tags.

'The battalion took about 120 prisoners, mostly older men and some Hitler Youth. Unlike the one I shot, these weren't fanatics. They were not exactly the cream of the SS that we'd expected, but they were fighting for their Fatherland and had put up stern resistance. Once captured, they seemed relieved that their war was over, while we had another six weeks of fighting before we met up with the Russians in the Baltic and called it a day. But for me, at least, the battle of the Rhine was over and, amazingly, it had only taken just over two hours since we landed, so I suppose the generals would be claiming it a resounding success, but the cost - was it worth it in the end?'

Ken Giles recalled: 'Inside the Horsa there was absolute chaos. We had come through the intense anti-aircraft barrage and the machine-gun fire, only to hit the ground like an out-of-control roller coaster. We'd rebounded off one crashed glider, hit another and taken off a wing, finally coming to rest against a bank. Inside there were several dead and injured. Five minutes later, those on their feet were running, shouting, cursing and shooting. Guns, jeeps and trailers were being hauled out of other gliders and parts of gliders were scattered about the landscape at crazy, impossible angles. From all directions, more gliders kept coming in to land. Our faithful transport, home for the past few hours, was now abandoned, skewed across the field with one wing snapped off and its back broken, its job done and our relatively safe arrival a testimony to the skill and cool bravery of the pilots.

'Through it all, a haze of thick smoke and mist was pierced by the sun, still shining as if the world was completely normal and not a holocaust of death and fire. For an eternity nobody seemed to know what to do, where to go, at least from where I was lying. Eventually someone, it could have been our platoon commander, took charge, ordering us to run like hell for some nearby cover, where we joined up with more of our scattered company. From there we took stock while the lieutenant decided where we were in relation to where we should have been. We could see that there had been five casualties from our platoon; four were still in the glider dead and one was lying one hundred yards away, between the broken glider and us. From the unnatural position of his body and by its stillness, I was sure he was dead too, but while I was rehearsing in my mind the many reasons why I couldn't go and check that this was true, someone else had rushed out to him and came back with his rifle, which they then used. Only then did I realise how scared I was. I'd been chewing gum since the last stages of the flight and it had literally turned to powder in my mouth, a phenomenon that I would not have believed possible had not experienced it.

'I was supposed to stand by an open window and watch for the flash of gunfire and return fire, keeping the German's head down while part of the company advanced to the next objective and cleared the church from the ground up. It occurred to me that if I can see a German's rifle flash then the German can also see mine. Sure enough there were Germans there. So I let off a few shots in their general direction, ducked down until they returned fire, then bobbed up very briefly for a quick shot to keep them quiet. I didn't know about their heads but I kept mine down most of the time. I yelled out that there were definitely Germans in the church tower, two windows down from the top and the lads fired a PIAT rocket into it not long afterwards and I was able to come down.

'As we slowly advanced the Germans were forced back, but they put up a good fight. When we got to the outskirts, there was yet another building reportedly holding more snipers and three of us were ordered to flush out its occupants. There was no cover anywhere so we rushed the place and made it to the front door. I threw in a grenade and we followed it. There was a lot of smoke coming from the top floor, where one of the others had lobbed two more grenades and then two of us raked the ceiling with Sten gun fire. There was a dull thud as if someone had fallen over and then silence. The other lad rushed upstairs, firing his Sten gun as he went. He came back down and told us there were five dead Germans up there; all of them were Volkssturm, old men in odd bits of uniform - they weren't even proper fighting soldiers. As far as we were concerned, the town of Hamminkeln was now ours.'[10]

When Flight Sergeant Leslie Kershaw landed his glider it went in nose first. Les had been trained as a pilot in Canada and returned to the UK in late 1943. On parade one day volunteers were required for the Fleet Air Arm and the Glider Pilot Regiment. Les shouted out *Fleet Air Arm*. Back came the reply: *Glider Pilot Regiment* and that was it! Unable to open the nose of his glider, a Company Sergeant threw some det cord around the tail section and blew it off. That was dragged away and they were able to drag out the jeep and the gun. The equipment was taken off before the glider was completely engulfed in flames after tracer rounds hit the wings and upper fuselage. Germans had them pinned down behind a bank with heavy machine gun and sniper fire. A few soldiers had already been shot. An officer approached Les and said *You there, crawl up there and see if there is a tank in that farm courtyard!* Les looked at him and said, *What me? Yes you!* Off he crawled very slowly with his rifle across his forearms and then he noticed out of the corner of his eye, a German also crawling coming the other way. They both paused and looked at each other then the German waved at Les and Les waved back then they both continued! Modestly, Les said later that *all I bloody did was fly a glider over the Rhine and crash land it!*

Altogether 4,844 troops, 342 jeeps, 348 trailers, three gun-trailers, seven Locust tanks, fourteen lorries, two bulldozers, eleven carriers, nineteen x 5cwt cars, 59 light motorcycles, 127 heavy motorcycles, 68 bicycles, twenty field cycles, 378 panniers, 53 handcarts, ten 4.2-inch mortars, two 75 mm guns, fifty 6-pounder anti-tank guns, twelve 17-pounder guns and two x 25-pounder guns were delivered to the battlefield by the British gliders. The entire force involved in 'Varsity' was landed in a space of sixty-three minutes.

Sergeant pilot Stan Jarvis recalls: 'When we reached the Rhine, the strength of the flak became apparent. A few of the tug aircraft flew past us on our way home; some of them were on fire and others were bullet-ridden - not a welcome sight to us who were going in to stay. As we flew across the Rhine, to our dismay we found that the whole area was covered with gun smoke and other smoke artificially created to conceal the ground troops who were going across the Rhine by boat and amphibious tanks etc.' Jarvis cast off from Alex Blythe's Dakota tug aircraft while in the dense smoke, with no sight of the ground whatsoever.

Private Denis Edwards on Sergeant Stan Jarvis' glider picks up the story. 'While Jarvis and Geddes were looking desperately for clues as to our exact whereabouts, pieces of our glider were literally being shot away. As they identified a stretch of autobahn to the east of Hamminkeln, they steered towards where they would expect the railway station to be, while four feet of the starboard wing, together with most of the aileron, were blown off by a flak burst... Regrettably, the Germans knew only too well that we were on our way and they were ready and waiting. Following the British glider-borne landings in Normandy and Arnhem, the Germans had certainly realized that the most effective way to deal with the British troop-carrying Horsa and the equally large and flimsy Hamilcar gliders was to hit them with incendiary bullets. Perhaps even tracer bullets were sufficient to set these large and slow gliders aflame long before they reached the ground. Bullets zipped through one side of the flimsy plywood fuselage and out of the other as we approached our landing zone and as we came in to land part of one wing, an aileron and the tail section were shot to pieces by shellfire. Listening to the bullets ripping through woodwork around us was none too pleasant, but amazingly none of us was hit by them. Even more miraculously, unlike most of our comrades in other gliders and those paratroops who jumped, we suffered no casualties at all during the actual landing.

'Stan Jarvis and Peter Geddes had landed as close as possible to the station to avoid being exposed running over open ground. Many years later Stan recounted how, after we had all fled the wrecked glider, taking cover wherever we could amid a hail of incoming missiles and bullets, one of the lads said to him, 'I know that before you left the airfield we asked you to get us as close as possible to the railway station, but if you had landed any closer we would have been in the ruddy booking office!' Jarvis said it was compliments of the RAF and they had a little laugh in the seriousness of war.

'The gliders had to land in open ground and the well-positioned German forces equipped with their tanks, artillery, mortars, heavy, medium and light machine guns, accompanied by well-positioned snipers, picked us off at will as we sought what little cover was available. The casualty figures testify to the advantage enjoyed by the defenders as we delivered our cargoes of thirty men at a time, gift-wrapped in plywood Horsas.'[11]

Seated in the tail-end of the glider Private Harry 'Nobby' Clark recalled that the area at the time of landing was covered by a dense cloud of smoke. 'As we took up our positions, two Horsa gliders appeared out of the cloud passing low overhead and within a few seconds there came a fearful noise as they crashed. One of them hit the railway station and disintegrated. There were no survivors. The second passed over and crashed between the railway and the road.

Denis Edwards saw them too. 'I recall a glider coming in just above us. It was aflame end to end and while still some way above, men with their clothing alight were jumping from the stricken craft. Although they were individually not recognizable, we knew that they were our mates, men we knew well and with whom we had shared barrack rooms. It was a truly terrible sight. My own twenty-six-man platoon was relatively lucky and every one of us got clear of our glider and reached the station yard where we took refuge from the murderous German fire. The yard covered a considerable area, part of it being stacked with neat piles of timber, each approximately the size of a two-storey house.

'Unfortunately it turned out that the Germans were using the stacks of timber to cover their approach as they advanced towards us. We spent the first few hours playing hide-and-seek among the wood-piles, dodging the German Mk.IV tanks which trundled up and down the rows of stacked timber seeking us out. We were not equipped to deal with German heavy tanks. Indeed, the anti-tank guns that we did possess, six-pounders which could dispose of even a Tiger at close range, were almost certainly still within the Hamilcar gliders used to transport our heavier equipment. The concentration of enemy fire over the landing zones would have made it virtually impossible for such weapons to be removed. Most men were just thankful if they were able to crawl away from their gliders and find some sort of shelter from the incoming German fire.

'If German tanks dared to roam about in daylight they were quickly neutralized by RAF Tempest and Typhoon rocket-firing aircraft. The Luftwaffe was virtually out of action by this time, out of fuel if not quite out of aircraft and these Allied aerial tank destroyers were unopposed. They could afford to loiter close by until called in whenever tanks posed a threat. It was a very one-sided match and in the open and in daylight the tank stood little chance. When moving about in close cover, however, such as the timber yard at Hamminkeln, or with smoke cover, or at night or in semi-darkness, then the German tanks became a problem - quite terrifying and lethally dangerous to lightly equipped infantry.

'After our nerve-racking game of hide and seek with the German tanks, we were finally forced to vacate the yard. We withdrew to 'D' Company's arranged rendezvous point on the other side of the glider landing zone. We then moved up to take over the river bridge, defending it against repeated enemy attacks and probes with tanks and infantry. It was some time later - I am unsure of the exact time for reasons that will become clear, but probably in the late afternoon or evening - that my section was sheltering below a high railway or river embankment when the enemy began a powerful bombardment of the area. A lot of heavy stuff was crashing in all around the place and, without well-dug trenches such as we had in Normandy, it was impossible to find anywhere that offered good protection. There were several of us crouched in the lee of the embankment when apparently a large shell exploded on the top of the bank just above my head, killing many of those in the immediate area, as well as some others who were further away. I neither remember the shell burst nor anything more for a period of thirty-six hours or so.[12]

The resistance encountered by the other glider troops varied tremendously from place to place. However, by nightfall all organized resistance in the British sector from the western edge of the woods to the Issel had been broken, six bridges across the river had been seized intact and over 600 prisoners had been taken. The cost to 6th Airborne was 347 dead, 731 wounded and 319 missing, but many of those missing soon rejoined their units.

Anti-aircraft fire over the landing zones was particularly heavy, several of the Battalion's gliders were shot out of the air and a considerable toll was taken on the troops as they came in to land. To make matters worse, the preliminary bombardment by the ground forces had obscured the battlefield with dense smoke and glider pilots experienced difficulty in identifying their zones, as a consequence of which many gliders landed some distance from where they should have been.

Those in the 6th Airlanding Brigade landed its battalions on separate drop zones around Hamminkeln. The 12th Battalion Devons who reached 'LZ R' south-west of the town disembarked to find themselves under attack from small pockets of resistance in almost every direction. As a result of this, the scene was very confusing for several hours as small, isolated parties of troops attacked and overwhelmed these positions. 'C' Company were tasked with clearing the neighbouring 'LZ P' of enemy resistance before the Division's support units began to land on it, however they arrived to discover that elements of the 17th US Airborne Division had been mistakenly dropped there and had already accomplished this. 'D' Company, in spite of heavy opposition, were able to secure the road junction to the west of Hamminkeln and when radio contact was established with the remainder of the Battalion at 1135, the order was given to advance into the town. 'A' and 'B' Companies put in a determined attack and after half an hour of sharp actions against enemy infantry and armoured vehicles, Hamminkeln was declared secure. During the afternoon the scene became much more peaceful and, in spite of sporadic shelling of their positions, the Battalion encountered little opposition throughout the remainder of the day. In all, the landings on this first day had cost the Battalion one hundred and ten dead and thirty wounded.

German anti-aircraft guns in the dropping and landing zones had been softened up by the previous air strikes and by the overnight artillery barrage. Now, fighter-bombers escorting the armada were given the task of spotting and attacking the many guns still active as the airborne troops were landing. Fire from the ground was indeed intense, forty-six transport aircraft being lost; of the 242 aircraft carrying the 6th Airborne paratroops alone, eighteen were shot down and 125 damaged by anti-aircraft fire. Of the 416 6th Airborne Hamilcar and Horsa gliders, only twenty-four were later salvaged in serviceable condition. During the action, one C-47 transport, on fire and streaming flame and smoke, headed westward and rapidly lost height.

Immediately over the flood bank the pilot managed to make his exit, his parachute opening just in time and landed a few yards from a group of gunners resting after their long night's labour. The pilot turned out to be American and seemed less concerned by the narrow escape from death and the loss of the aircraft, which had by then crashed a few hundred yards away, than he was by the fact that he would miss a heavy date he had lined up in London that evening.

The battlefield haze resulting from the nightlong shelling and dust that had drifted from the blasted town of Wesel, made matters difficult for the airborne men. Paratroops could not see the ground below them - they simply had to go down through the haze and hope they were not landing in trees or on German bayonets. For the pilots of the CG-4, Horsa and Hamilcar gliders there was great difficulty in finding their allotted Landing Zones and many crashed, cartwheeling as a wingtip touched the unseen ground, or shot out of the air by the German gunners. Matters were made worse by the smoke from many of the gliders themselves set ablaze by German incendiary bullets. It is a tribute to the remarkable skill of the glider pilots that so many landed accurately in the Landing Zones.

Alan Lloyd, in his book *The Gliders*, tells of one glider pilot's experience: Apprehensively, Lieutenant Sydney St. John approached a farmhouse. He was confronted there by an imperturbable German matron, the first enemy he had met face to face. 'She put a plate of steak and chips in front of me... I certainly hadn't expected a cooked meal. We were lads and she fussed like anybody's mum might'.'

The Germans may not have been all that thick on the ground and there was a lack of armour to counter the airborne troops. What defenders there were, however, were some of the best the Wehrmacht had at this stage of the war: the 7th Parachute Division to the north of the area and the 84th Infantry Division to the south, both reinforced with some hastily formed units. The German commander was well aware of the probability of an airborne assault and had small combat groups of his best-trained efficient soldiers posted at all places where a landing might reasonably be expected; their brief was to attack the invaders when they were most vulnerable - before they had time to muster themselves into a combatant force. They put up a formidable resistance in countryside tailor-made for defence; fields and plantations criss-crossed by ditches and narrow roads. The 8th Parachute Battalion cleared DZ 'A' within an hour of its drop and by 1400 hours had occupied all objectives in its sector, which was on the northwest side of the Diersfordter Wald. Heavily engaged in this terrain it was isolated until the following day. At about 1500 hours a battalion of the 15th Division pushed up the hill and entered the paratroop positions. East of the Wald the troops on DZ 'B' suffered about 300 casualties in hard fighting around their drop zone and were not able to take their assigned place on the north flank of the division until about 1530. Not all the airborne men found their movements so restricted and there was a gradual infiltration of the Diersfordter Wald to meet the surface assault forces. Four Locust light tanks proved their worth when, with a company of the Devons and a group of glider pilots, they were able to contain some German tanks and a considerable force of infantry through the night until they could be mopped up the following day. Also during the night the Germans made a counter-attack on the River Issel with infantry supported by Tiger tanks.

It was a night of mixed fortunes at individual level but the main plan was working well. In the night, most of the German 84th Division, with its gunners who had been causing delays to the surface assault, passed through the Airborne lines. Many Germans surrendered but, as neither side was in any state to make battle, large numbers plodded their way eastwards, weary and shattered by the experiences of the past two days. 'Varsity' was over.

Jim Corbett of the 12th Devons wrote: 'From my lowly position, I couldn't help but wonder why the two Airborne Divisions didn't land as dawn was breaking; long before the land forces went in and advertised the attack. Because in Germany we landed on flat plains; there was no need to blast away at any concrete fortifications with bombers and heavy artillery like we did at the Atlantic Wall in Normandy. By this strategy we may have effected complete surprise and got away with very few casualties. I suppose, at the back of his mind, Monty had the memory of Arnhem where it all went wrong for us. This final battle he certainly didn't want to lose.

'Apparently, Monty took over a large chateau just a few kilometres from the assault point for his Headquarters and invited Winston and all the American Generals. They sat down to enjoy a sumptuous champagne breakfast under the chandeliers. As 10 am approached, they went out on the balcony to witness this great armada of planes flying over their heads. I hope they were suitably impressed. I would gladly have exchanged places with any one of them!'

On the night of 24/25 March Major General Ridgway accompanied by Major General Miley visited Major General Bols main divisional headquarters in a farm at Kopenhof. In his orders to General Bols, Ridgway stated that 6th Airborne Division would remain in the positions it was occupying, with the exception of 6th Airlanding Brigade which would be relieved by 157th Infantry Brigade of 52nd (Lowland) Division during the night of 25/26 March. 6th Airborne Division was to be ready to advance towards the east at dawn on 26 March.[13] Ridgway was wounded in the shoulder by German grenade fragments on 24 March. Quickly recovering, he was promoted to lieutenant general in June 1945 and dispatched to the Pacific to serve under General Douglas MacArthur.

At 0900 hours on 26 March the 12th Devonshires, supported by a squadron of Churchill tanks of the 3rd Battalion, The Grenadier Guards and a troop of self-propelled anti-tank guns under command, led the 6th Airborne Division's push out of the Rhine bridgehead. Two miles into the advance, the Battalion was halted by two companies of enemy infantry supported by self-propelled guns, but following a softening up bombardment, the Devons attacked this position and took sixty prisoners at no loss to themselves. The Battalion's main objective for the day was the capture of an area of high ground overlooking Brunen and it was here that they were met by a determined enemy. 'B' Company were faced with the daunting prospect of an assault across open ground, but fortunately their advance got under way so quickly that they were able to surprise most of the defenders and at the cost of several casualties had the position under their control by mid-afternoon.

Tom Staniforth concluded: 'The Rhine crossing was a great success and several planned resupply trips were cancelled. In due course the occupants of our glider returned to Earls Colne and told us their story. When they landed they were promptly surrounded and made prisoner and put to digging foxholes. Then another Horsa landed, the Germans surrendered - and they finished digging the foxholes for our lads. That night we had a hell of a party and the wing commander was seen swinging from the rafters at one point. He was later awarded the DFC for his part in the operation and thoroughly deserved it.'[14]

Wing Commander Musgrave, leading his squadron on his fourth airborne attack, praised the glider pilots who, without swerving, went straight into the flak to reach their target points. 'Although the show was so successful, there is no doubt that the glider boys had a tough time going in.' His personal recollection of the flight was the discomfiture of his navigator, Warrant Officer G. A. 'Gerry' Foster who, when flak broke the point from his pencil, had to calculate the return trip navigation in his head.'

David Vickery remembered thinking to himself triumphantly, 'Well, we've as good as won now - it's all over, bar the shouting'. It felt good to be alive. Six weeks later a newspaper placard appeared outside the mess bearing the legend: *Latest war result - Allies 1: Germany nil'*.

General Brereton described 'Varsity' as a 'tremendous success' and rated it the most successful airborne operation hitherto attempted. Through the use of multiple traffic lanes, the C-46 aircraft and 300 double-tow glider sorties, nearly 17,000 well-equipped airborne troops using 540 planeloads of paratroopers and 1,348 gliders had been poured into an area of less than 25 square miles within four hours. (In 'Market' Brereton had restricted glider missions to 'single-tows' and the shorter hours of daylight in September caused him to refuse authorization for two lifts per day and as a result of the limited number of troop carrier aircraft, the air movement of the Army required three consecutive days to complete). Of 908 American gliders, about two-thirds of which were in double-tow, all but 23, or 2.5 percent, reached the Rhine despite windy, turbulent weather. Of the British gliders 36 or 8.2 percent of their quota of 440 failed to get there. The over-all cost of 'Varsity' was seven British troop carrier aircraft destroyed, 46 American aircraft destroyed (plus nine salvaged) and fifteen of the Liberators in the resupply mission destroyed. Damaged were 32 British aircraft, 339 from IX TCC and 104 of the bombers.

With the fighting over, the *Schlachtenbummler* or 'battle tourists' like Alan McCrae Moorehead, the Australian born war correspondent began to cross the conquered Rhine to view the scene of death and destruction. Moorehead was more interested in the German civilians he encountered in the 'strange numbness, a kind of vacuum' behind the fighting troops. 'Odd incongruities spring up in this unusual atmosphere. The bargee's wife continues to hang out the washing... she clings to this routine as one sane thing in a world gone mad. The house beyond has collapsed like a house of cards... but a man still digs a vegetable patch in the garden.'

Major Huw Wheldon of the Royal Ulster Rifles saw 'stick-thin children of five, born to an unspeakable world, playing King of the Castle on a heap of naked and rotting dead women'... Pleasant faced women walk the streets of rubble, with a Lutheran church untouched in an open square and a Prisoner of War camp full of unutterable emaciation behind the railway. Emaciation of the mind. Single men, daft after five years of utter emptiness squat down by themselves and crooning, cook billycans of rubbishy tea. They are helplessly mad and starved of everything. This, of course, is pleasant and normal compared with the Concentration Camps which honestly are beyond all imaginable horror.'

Gerard Mansell, at twenty-four years old the senior intelligence officer with 9th Corps, now pushing out from the bridgehead, strolled through the ruins which he later described as 'apocalyptic'. 'Destroyed towns, deserted countryside, hostility in the air. Dejected prisoners - often old men or boys - drifting back past us in crowds, with refugees and displaced persons. Chaos and a feeling of disintegration and putrescence everywhere.'

Mansell had fought at El Alamein and had taken part in the assault landing in Sicily and Normandy. But as the long column of vehicles rolled through the shattered village of Weldar, he did not yet know that his own younger brother had been murdered here the previous night. Bob Mansell was one of the glider pilots who had brought in the 6th Airborne on 24 March. During the confused fighting he had fallen into German hands, but somehow he had escaped and for three days had been trying to make his way back to Allied lines. He had not succeeded. On the night before, he had been cornered by a band of fanatical Hitler Youth teenagers. They had slaughtered him savagely among the ruins through which an unsuspecting Major Mansell now drove.[15]

Alan Moorehead wrote this tribute to the paratrooper battalions: 'Nobody has yet succeeded in explaining satisfactorily how these men, recovering from their dreadful tragedies on the Rhine, picked themselves up and without any military transport to speak of, projected themselves for three hundred miles across Germany to arrive on the Baltic ahead of the tanks and armour, indeed ahead of everyone else. Having no vehicles at the outset, they simply seized from the Germans anything they could get hold of, bakers' vans and butchers' van and post office trucks. They did not bother to repaint them. One man was seen driving a steam roller, anything to get forward. I commandeered the village fire engine, a beautiful, almost brand new Mercedes, painted white. I was quite pleased with my capture until the CO said, 'You can't possibly use that; they'll see you coming from Berlin.' So reluctantly I had to let it go, though we used anything else we could get our hands on.'

'Varsity' was destined to be the last ever action by glider-carried troops. Ninety-eight members of the Glider Pilot Regiment lost their lives, fifty-eight of whom were ex-RAF pilots; a casualty rate of 28 percent. Many others had been wounded. The gliders in 'Varsity' had fared much worse than their occupants. An American 'caretaker detachment' sent in on 'D+2' found them in bad shape with most of their clocks and compasses gone. Six hundred repairmen arrived on 4 April and repaired 148 Wacos enough so they could be snatched and flown to Grimberghen for complete overhaul. In the case of the big British gliders, pick-up tactics were not considered feasible. Of those conveniently located and in good condition, 24 were disassembled and hauled away by road to a base where they could be repaired, reassembled and flown back. The rest of the American and British gliders were salvaged. Salvaged materiel from the Wacos alone filled 47 trucks and thirty trailers. Nevertheless, the fact remains that less than seventeen percent of the American gliders and six percent of the British gliders which had landed east of the Rhine were recovered in usable condition.

The Glider Pilot Regiment was awarded the Battle Honour 'Rhine' for its part in the operation. After 'Varsity' Brigadier Chatterton immediately began planning the next operation. Even larger than 'Varsity', Operation 'Arena' would have landed troops near Kassel to seize the airfields there and use them to fly in infantry deep inside Germany. The Allied advance soon made the plan redundant. Operation 'Eclipse', the attack on Berlin itself had barely reached the end of the planning stage when the Russians reached the German capital. As it was it had become abundantly obvious that the cost in lives and equipment was unavoidably and unjustifiably high. A higher proportion of British glider pilots were killed in 'Varsity' than during 'Neptune' or even 'Market'. After the war it was revealed that the estimated life expectancy for bomber crews was about one hour 46 minutes; for fighter pilots it was nineteen minutes and for glider pilots it was seventeen seconds.

Gathering together as many glider pilots as he could find, Major Ian Toler DFC led them back towards the Rhine, passing a large group of prisoners being herded along by an American trooper stripped to the waist and riding bareback on a horse. Amphibious trucks took the pilots back to the west bank where a camp called 'The Rhine Hotel' - (*Glider Pilots a Speciality*) had been set up offering hot food, showers, kitchens and stores of fresh clothing. Arriving back at Down Ampney, the pilots found a customs official demanding to know if they had anything to declare. He quickly got the message. The Custom Officials had been asked and had agreed to let glider pilots through customs on the signature of the senior officers. This was not adhered to and some delay was caused by each glider pilot having to complete forms. Luckily after 300 had done so, they ran out of forms.

The Chief of the Imperial General Staff, General Sir Alan Brooke, wrote: *'My heartiest congratulations on their* (the Glider Pilots') *wonderful performance in operations connected with the crossing of the Rhine. The skill and bravery displayed by them in this magnificent action of airborne forces will pass down to history as one of the highlights amongst the deeds of valour of this war.*

By nightfall of the 24th, the British 15th Infantry Division had joined up with elements of the 6th Airborne Division and by midnight the first light bridge was across the Rhine. By the 27th, twelve bridges suitable for heavy armour had been installed over the Rhine and the Allies had fourteen divisions on the east bank of the river which had penetrated up to ten miles.

The war was not over with the crossing of the Rhine. There were to be more battles, some difficult and memorable for the participants and there were times when some of the victors were to show signs of battle weariness for the first time in the face of remarkably brave resistance encountered along the way. The end seemed to be an intolerably long time in coming, with battles for each village and city suburb. Before he went across the Rhine, Churchill delivered a simple and accurate analysis of the situation to Eisenhower. Watching the offensive go forward, Churchill repeated to Eisenhower, 'My dear general, the German is whipped. We have got him. He is all through.'

Endnotes Chapter 9

1   Quoted in *The Gliders: An Action Packed Story of the Wooden Chariots of World War II* by Alan Lloyd (Leo Cooper, 1982).

2   In 1948 Brigadier Geoffrey Kemp Bourne's heroism was recognition by the award of the US Silver Star.

3   Comprising 2nd Battalion, the Ox and Bucks Light Infantry; 1st Battalion, the Royal Ulster Rifles; 12th Battalion, the Devonshire Regiment; 53rd Light Regiment Royal Artillery; 3rd and 4th Air Landing Anti-tank Batteries Royal Artillery; the Airborne Armoured Reconnaissance Regiment; Royal Engineers and Field Ambulance Units.

4   By Wendy George. Staff Sergeant Brook was flown back to England in a C-47, spending some weeks in Ronkswood Hospital, Worcester.

5   Quoted in *Paras: Voices of the British Airborne Forces in the Second World War* by Roger Payne OAM (Amberley, 2014 and 2016).

6   *Rivenhall: The History of an Essex Airfield* by Bruce Stait (Amberley, 2015).

7   *Intercom* magazine, winter 1986.

8   *Handley Page Halifax: From Hell to Victory and Beyond* by K. A. Merrick (Chevron Publishing Ltd, 2009).

9   See *Onslaught On Hitler's Rhine: Operations Plunder and Varsity March 1945* by Patrick Delaforce (Fonthill, 2015).

10   Quoted in *Paras: Voices of the British Airborne Forces in the Second World War* by Roger Payne OAM (Amberley, 2014 and 2016).

11   Denis Edwards: *Devils Own Luck: Pegasus Bridge To The Baltic 1944-45*. (Pen & Sword, 1999, 2001, 2009).

12   See *Devils Own Luck: Pegasus Bridge To The Baltic 1944-45* by Denis Edwards. (Pen & Sword, 1999, 2001, 2009).

13   For his actions on the Rhine Crossing, Major General Bols CB DSO was awarded a Bar to the DSO. On the recommendation of Major General Ridgway, the Commander 18th US Airborne Corps under whom the Division was operating, he was also awarded the US Silver Star.

14   Quoted in *Halifax At War* by Brian J. Rapier (Ian Allan, 1987).

15   Quoted in *Bounce the Rhine* by Charles Whiting .

Appendix

Timeline Operations 'Plunder' and 'Varsity'

Objectives

XVIII Airborne Corps: Commanded by General Matthew B. Ridgway of the US Army and his British deputy, Major General Richard Nelson 'Windy' Gale it was made up of divisions that had recently seen action in Belgium and Luxembourg in support of the winter operations in the Ardennes. The Corps is carried by an armada of 1,572 transport aircraft and over 900 gliders, escorted by 889 fighters. They are to be put down around the Hamminkeln area, about seven miles from the east bank of the Rhine. This area, like most of the battlefield, is shrouded in the smoke of the action that had been raging through the night and in the suspended rubble dust resulting from the destruction of Wesel twelve hours earlier, obscuring the low ground, the most prominent feature of which was a wooded ridge, the Diersfordter Wald, rising 60 feet above the level of the river. Along this ridge ran the road linking the towns of Emmerich, Rees and Wesel. It overlooked the river crossing places being used by the British XII Corps and it was vital to relieve the Germans of this advantage as early as possible.

Another task for the airborne men was to take intact some of the bridges over the River Ijssel, which flows parallel to the Rhine between Wesel and Emmerich and lying to the east of the Diersfordter Wald. Between the river and the ridge lay level open farmland, providing ideal dropping and landing zones.

The final important objective was the small town of Hamminkeln, astride the River Ijssel.

British 6th Airborne Division Tasks: Led by Major General Eric Louis Bols CB DSO they are to take the northern part of the Diersfordter Wald, the town of Hamminkeln and one railway and two road bridges over the Ijssel. Of the transports and glider tugs, 416 are British, from 38 and 46 Groups of the RAF: 38 Group, under the command of Air Vice-Marshal James Rowland Scarlett-Streatfield takes the Air Landing Brigade of the 6th Airborne Division into action, while 46 Group, under Air Commodore L. Darvell carries the paratroops. The 3rd Parachute Brigade under Brigadier Stanley James Ledger 'Speedy' Hill and the 5th under Brigadier Joseph Howard Nigel Poett are to land first, to be closely followed by the gliders of the 6th Air Landing Brigade under Brigadier R. M. Bellamy. With the paratroops are officers of the Forward Observer Unit whose task it is to control, by radio, artillery fire from the surface forces. Airborne artillery and other divisional troops are to be landed in the centre of the area.

US 17th Airborne Division with Major General William E. Miley commanding are given similar responsibility to the south and were to link up with the British 1st Commando Brigade in Wesel.

'D-Day-2' (22 March) In the German village of Walbeck Montgomery calls an 'O Group' to give his final orders to his British and Canadian Army Commanders, Corps and Divisional Commanders and Chiefs-of-Staff.

1,284 B-17s and B-24s bomb targets east of Frankfurt and ten military encampments in the Ruhr, in preparation for the Allied amphibious crossing of the lower Rhine. Nine fighter groups strafe airfields.

'D-Day-1' (23 March) By the night of 23 March Montgomery has the equivalent of more than 30 divisions under his command, while the Germans field around ten divisions, all weakened from constant fighting. The best German formation the Allied airborne troops would face is the 1st Parachute Army, although even this formation had been weakened from the losses it had sustained in earlier fighting, particularly when it had engaged Allied forces in the Reichswald Forest in February. The seven divisions that form the 1st Parachute Army are short of manpower and munitions and although farms and villages are well prepared for defensive purposes, there are few mobile reserves, ensuring that the defenders have little way to concentrate their forces against the Allied bridgehead when the assault begins. The mobile reserves that the Germans possess consist of 150 armoured fighting vehicles under the command of 1st Parachute Army, the majority of which belong to XLVII Panzer Corps. Allied intelligence believes that of the two divisions that formed XLVII Panzer Corps, 116th Panzer Division have up to seventy tanks and 15th Panzergrenadier Division fifteen tanks and between 20-30 assault guns. Intelligence also points to the possibility of a heavy anti-tank battalion being stationed in the area. However, the Germans possess a great number of anti-aircraft weapons; on 17 March Allied intelligence estimated that the Germans had 103 heavy and 153 light anti-aircraft guns, a number which was drastically revised a week later to 114 heavy and 712 light anti-aircraft guns. The situation of the German defenders and their ability to counter any assault effectively is worsened when the Allies launch a large-scale air attack one week prior to 'Varsity'. The air attack involves more than 10,000 Allied aircraft and are concentrated primarily on Luftwaffe airfields and the German transportation system. The German defenders are also hampered by the fact that they have no reliable intelligence as to where the actual assault would be launched; although German forces along the Rhine have been alerted as to the general possibility of an Allied airborne attack, it is only when British engineers begin to set up smoke generators opposite Emmerich and begin laying a 60-mile long smokescreen that the Germans know where the assault will come. 1st Parachute Army have three corps stationed along the river; 2nd Parachute Corps to the north, 86th Corps in the centre and 63rd Corps in the south. 2nd Parachute Corps and 86th Corps have a shared boundary that runs through the proposed landing zones for the Allied airborne divisions, meaning that the leading formation of each corps (7th Parachute Division and 84th Infantry Division) will face the airborne assault. After their retreat to the Rhine both divisions are under-strength and do not number more than 4,000 men each, with 84th Infantry Division supported by only fifty or so medium artillery pieces.

Operation 'Plunder' begins at 2100 and by the early hours of the morning of 24 March Allied ground units have secured a number of crossings on the eastern bank of the Rhine. In the first few hours of the day, the transport aircraft carrying the two airborne divisions begin to take off from air bases in England and France and begin to rendezvous over Brussels, before turning northeast for the Rhine dropping zones. The airlift consists of 541 transport aircraft containing airborne troops and a further 1,050 troop-carriers towing 1,350 gliders. The 17th Airborne Division consists of 9,387 personnel, who are transported in 836 C-47 Skytrain transports, 72 C-46 Commando transports and more than 900 Waco CG-4A gliders. The 6th Airborne Division consists of 7,220 personnel transported by 42 C-54 and 752 C-47 transport aircraft, as well as 420 Horsa and Hamilcar gliders. This immense armada stretches more than 200 miles in the sky and takes two hours and 37 minutes to pass any given point and is protected by 2,153 Allied fighters of the US Ninth Air Force and the RAF. The combination of the two divisions in one lift makes this the largest single day airborne drop in history. At 10 am British and American airborne troops of the 6th Airborne Division and 17th Airborne Division begin landing on German soil, thirteen hours after the Allied ground assault began.

2100 hours is 'H-Hour' for the 51st (Highland) Division and a brigade of Canadian infantry on the British XXX Corps' front in the northern sector of the Second Army. The 153rd Brigade crosses either side of the town of Rees to capture the village of Esserden and then block and defend the approach to Rees. The crossing starts with The 7th Black Watch, who lose one 'Buffalo' (troop Carrier amphibious) on a Teller mine and some leading troops on Schu Mines. This information was sent back and the following 7th Argyle's called up two 'wasps' to assist their landing and meet their objectives and set up a platoon of Middlesex Machine Gunners, the 1st Gordons cross without a single casualty and take their objectives.

Major General Thomas Rennie is able to get four of his battalions across the river in seven minutes using 150 Buffalo tracked amphibious vehicles trundling down to the water and swimming their way across. Some make dry land without trouble but others become bogged down in the mud, forcing men to wade the last few yards to the shore on foot. Waiting to meet the Highlanders and Canadians are the 15th Panzer Grenadier Division together with the elite 6th and 7th Parachute Divisions. In a difficult and hard-fought battle around the riverside town of Rees some of the Highlanders are cut off for a while by the paratroops at the village of Speldorp. Major General Rennie is among those killed.

Night of 23-24 March Under a 66-mile-long smoke screen and aided by 1,747 bombers of the 8th Air Force, Field Marshal Bernard Montgomery's 2nd Army cross the Rhine at Wesel. General Patton's 3rd Army makes simultaneous crossings further south. On the right of XII Corps sector the 1st Commando Brigade under the command of Brigadier Derek Mills-Roberts cross the Rhine at 2200 hours. The northern sector proves the most difficult and most costly action of the entire surface operation with the Highlanders finding that the Germans are fighting more fiercely than at any time since the campaign in Normandy.

'D-Day' (24 March) Dawn breaks over the Rhine with battle engaged on a front twenty miles wide. At 'H-Hour' (0200 hours) at Rheinberg ('Flashpoint') to the south of Wesel, the 30th and 79th Divisions of XVI Corps, Ninth American Army, cross the Rhine on both sides of the town, suffering 31 fatal casualties against minimal opposition. The task of the 30th Division is to strike eastward on an axis parallel with the River Lippe, which joins the Rhine at Wesel, while the 70th Division head for the small but important town of Dinslaken, three miles inland. All American objectives are achieved without major problems and by dusk US Corps Engineers have bridged the Rhine with a 1,150-foot 'treadway'.

By 0700 the 1st Gordons has regrouped and has started to advance to Rees. Snipers become a big problem in this area but Captain McNair of the 454 Mountain Battery comes up with the idea to carry the 3.7 howitzers and use them in the street to street fighting pulling the round corners or assembling them in houses to surprise the enemy who are only expecting small arms fire. By the end of the day Captain McNair has reached legend status and within 48 Hours the Division has captured all their objectives under continuous fighting not seen since 'D' Day.

Approximately 6,000 aircraft, including Liberators, gliders, transports and fighters take part in the Wesel operation. Covering the US operations and the building of the British Second Army's pontoon bridge at Wesel, the 2nd TAF and the US 29th Tactical Air Command fly almost 8,000 sorties at the cost of 56 aircraft. Fifty-two German aircraft are destroyed in the air. Also, in two days, ten German airfields receive no less than 2,700 tons of bombs and a total of 168 enemy aircraft are destroyed by the RAF and USAAF.

By 1345 hours the village of Schappenberg is in British hands and by the middle of the afternoon nearly all the main objectives have been achieved. The airborne men were in action at once, Hamminkeln being taken by the glider troops by midday. Fresh waves of surface forces pass through those who had initiated the assault. The 1st Battalion The Cheshire Regiment cross the river to support the 1st Commando Brigade in Wesel on the afternoon of the 24th and 152nd Brigade of the 51st (Highland) Division advance north of the Diersfordter Wald.

As night falls 21 Army Group has established a bridgehead of nearly thirty miles wide, the depth in the XII Corps sector being nearly eight miles. 15th (Scottish) Infantry Division has joined up with elements of 6th Airborne and by midnight the first light bridge is across the Rhine. The Germans of the First Parachute Army are still resisting but Allied Engineers are able to set about bridging the Rhine without hindrance from German artillery.

By nightfall 6th Airborne Division has suffered around 1,400 personnel killed, WIA or MIA out of the 7,220 personnel who were landed. The division also claims to have secured around 1,500 PoWs. The 17th Airborne Division reports around 1,300 casualties out of 9,650 personnel who took part in the operation, while the division claims to have taken 2,000 PoWs. Between 24 March and 29 March, 17th Airborne has taken a total of 1,346 casualties. The air forces involved have lost 56 aircraft in total during the 24th, 21 out of the

144 transport aircraft transporting the 17th Airborne shot down and 59 damaged by anti-aircraft fire. Sixteen bombers of the Eighth Air Force were also shot down during supply drops.

'D-Day+1' (25 March) By dawn on Palm Sunday news of increasing surrenders improves the mood and morale of the men of the 6th Airborne Division. By 1000 hours advanced armour and infantry of the Second British Army and Ninth US Army reach the airborne forces and by afternoon the links are strong. In the British sector the 6th Guards Armoured Brigade and men of the King's Own Scottish Borderers come around the north side of the Diersfordter Wald and clear the route for the evacuation of the 6th Airborne Division. On the west bank they find camps with showers, kitchens and stores of fresh clothing. One of these camps is given the name 'Rhine Hotel' and displays a sign proclaiming 'Glider Pilots a Speciality'.

It was not the end of the road for the British 6th Airborne division which was reorganised to join the 2nd Army and ended the war meeting Russian troops at Wismar on the Baltic, 350 miles beyond the Rhine.

'D-Day+2' (26 March) Twelve bridges are in service across the Rhine by evening, the bridges at Wesel being built at a remarkable speed despite the activities of snipers from among the ruins of the town. A battalion of German paratroops which has been holding out at Rees finally ends during the morning when troops from the Canadian 3rd Division clear the village. A further four days would elapse before the Canadians are finally able to remove all the Germans from Emmerich.

By 27 March the Allies have fourteen divisions on the east bank of the river, penetrating up to ten miles. According to Major General Martin Fiebig, commanding officer of one of the defending German formations, 84 Infantry Division, the German forces defending the area had been greatly surprised by the speed with which the two airborne divisions had landed their troops, explaining that their sudden appearance had had a 'shattering effect' on the greatly outnumbered defenders. He reveals during his interrogation that his division had been badly depleted and could muster barely 4,000 soldiers.[1]

Endnotes Appendix

1   Fiebig was executed in Belgrade for war crimes.

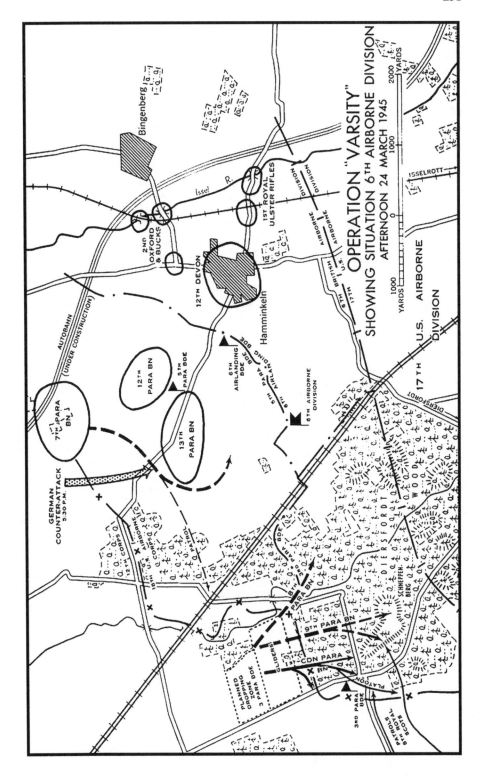

OPERATION "VARSITY"

SHOWING SITUATION 6TH AIRBORNE DIVISION

AFTERNOON 24 MARCH 1945

Acknowledgements

Much information has been gleaned from 'Airborne Operations in World War II, European Theater; USAF Historical Studies No.97, produced by the USAF Historical Division, Research Studies Institute, Air University by Dr. John C. Warren, published at Maxwell Air Force Base, Alabama in September 1956.

I am indebted to all the contributors for their words and photographs. My thanks go to Mike Bailey; Paul Wilson; Nigel McTeer; The Pegasus Archive; Silver Wings Museum. Thanks also go to my fellow author, friend and colleague, Graham Simons, for getting the book to press ready standard and for his detailed work on the photographs; to Pen & Sword and in particular, Laura Hirst; and Jon Wilkinson, for his unique jacket design once again.

Below: B-24 Liberators of the 93rd Bomb Group in the Second Air Division 8th Air Force at Hardwick, returning from a low level drop over Holland in 1945. On 23 March two task groups of 120 Liberators dropped supplies to the American and British forces at Wesel.

Index

256